An Introduction
to Human
Communication

Understanding and Sharing

eighth edition

An Introduction to Human Communication

Understanding and Sharing

Judy C. Pearson

Virginia Polytechnic Institute and State University

Paul E. Nelson

Ohio University, Athens

Boston   Burr Ridge, IL   Dubuque, IA   Madison, WI   New York   San Francisco   St. Louis   Bangkok   Bogotá   Caracas   Lisbon   London   Madrid   Mexico City   Milan   New Delhi   Seoul   Singapore   Sydney   Taipei   Toronto

McGraw-Hill Higher Education

A Division of The **McGraw-Hill** Companies

AN INTRODUCTION TO HUMAN COMMUNICATION: UNDERSTANDING AND SHARING

This book is printed on acid-free paper.

4 5 6 7 8 9 0 VNH/VNH 9 0 9 8 7 6 5 4 3 2 1

ISBN 0-07-233693-5 (student ed.)
ISBN 0-07-233694-3 (annotated instructor's ed.)

Editorial director: *Phillip A. Butcher*
Sponsoring editor: *Marjorie Byers*
Developmental editor: *Jennie Katsaros*
Marketing manager: *Kelly M. May*
Project manager: *Kimberly Moranda*
Production supervisor: *Michael R. McCormick*
Designer: *Kiera Cunningham*
Interior design: *Cynthia Crampton*
Cover illustration: *© Dave La Fleur, 1999*
Photo research coordinator: *Sharon Miller*
Photo researcher: *Marty Levick*
Supplement coordinator: *Mark Sienicki*
Compositor: *Shepherd Incorporated*
Typeface: *10.5/12 New Aster*
Printer: *Von Hoffmann Press, Inc.*

Library of Congress Cataloging-in-Publication Data

Pearson, Judy C.
  An introduction to human communication: understanding and sharing
/ Judy C. Pearson, Paul E. Nelson. -- 8th ed.
    p. cm.
  Includes bibliographical references and index.
  ISBN 0-07-233693-5 (student : alk. paper). -- ISBN 0-07-233694-3
(annotated instructor's : alk. paper)
  1. Communication.   I. Nelson, Paul E. (Paul Edward), 1941- .
II. Title.
P90.P372 2000
302.2--dc21

                        99-30979
                          CIP

http://www.mhhe.com

dedicated

to Harry B. and Ferne G. Nelson

to the student

This book is about you. It is about how you communicate with yourself, with another person, within teams and groups, and with large audiences. The book is about you as the creator and sender of messages and about you as the listener and receiver of messages. You can apply immediately the ideas learned in the introductory course, and you can practice them for a lifetime.

This book is intended for beginning students of any age. The text does not require prior knowledge of communication studies. Written in a conversational, easy-to-read style, the book is practical and applicable. You may never dissect another frog or do another physics experiment, but you will spend the remainder of your life communicating. The purpose of this book is to increase your competence as a communicator.

about the authors

Judy C. Pearson and Paul E. Nelson are the primary authors of this textbook. Both of them have considerable experience with the basic courses in speech communication. Both have served as basic course directors, both have served as primary lecturers in the introductory courses, and both have earned teaching awards for outstanding instruction from a number of universities and professional organizations.

Judy Pearson earned her bachelors at St. Cloud State University in Minnesota and both her master's and doctorate at Indiana University. She taught for Purdue University, for Bradley University, for Iowa State University, for Michigan State University, and for Ohio University before becoming Director of the Northern Virginia Center, Virginia Tech's Washington, DC, area campus.

Paul Nelson earned his B.S., B.A., M.A., and Ph.D. from the University of Minnesota. He served as basic course director and Director of the Honors College at the University of Missouri; as Departmental Executive Officer (chair) at Iowa State University; and as Dean of the College of Communication at Ohio University. Judy Pearson and Paul Nelson are a married couple who have six children and live in Northern Virginia.

Other authors contributed to the text by writing chapters which appeared first in the seventh edition. They are Gloria J. Galanes of Southwest Missouri State University, who wrote Chapters 8 and 9 on small-group communication and leadership; and Margaret A. King of Purdue University, who wrote a chapter for the seventh edition which now appears as an appendix on interviewing for information and employment. The remaining chapters were co-authored by Judy Pearson and Paul Nelson, whose dedication to the basic communication courses was apparent from the very beginning of their relationship: they first met at a basic course conference at Northern Illinois University.

The authors enjoy hearing from students and would welcome your feedback. Judy Pearson can be contacted on e-mail at jcp@vt.edu and Paul Nelson can be contacted on e-mail at nelsonp@ouvaxa.cats.ohiou.edu. Judy's phone number is 703-538-8310; Paul's is 703-534-5071.

contents

contents

part **4**   FUNDAMENTALS OF PUBLIC SPEAKING: PREPARATION AND DELIVERY   265

chapter **11**   Topic Selection and Audience Analysis   267

Fundamentals of Communication Studies

HAVE YOU EVER WONDERED how communication works, why it often fails, and why it is important to study it? Chapter 1, The Nature of Communication, provides some answers to those questions by introducing you to the terms, the models, and the contexts of communication.

Chapter 2, Perception, Self-Awareness, and Self-Concept, reveals how perception functions in communication, how the way you see yourself affects how you communicate with others, and how the messages you receive from others affect the way you see yourself.

Chapter 3, Verbal Communication, addresses the role language plays in communication, how language relates to meaning, and how people reach shared meaning through language.

In Chapter 4, Nonverbal Communication, you will learn about the major nonverbal codes that people use to communicate, such as body movement, vocal cues, and clothing.

When you have read and thought about this chapter, you will be able to:

1. State reasons why you should study communication.

2. Define *communication*.

3. Explain how communication begins with the self and involves others.

4. Name the components of communication.

5. Differentiate between the action, interaction, transaction, and constructivist models.

6. Explain the ways in which intrapersonal, interpersonal, public, and mass communication differ from each other.

1

The Nature of Communication

> "Speech is civilization itself. The word, even the most contradictory word, preserves contact—it is silence which isolates."
>
> **THOMAS MANN**

> "Effective loving calls for knowledge of the object. . . . How can I love a person whom I do not know? How can the other person love me if she does not know me?"
>
> **SIDNEY M. JOURARD**

In this chapter you will be introduced to communication, including some of the fundamental concepts and terms you will need to know for the remainder of this text. You will learn why it is important to study communication, and how communication is defined. This chapter will show you how communication begins with you and extends to other people, and it will identify the components of communication. Finally, you will learn about four communication models and the characteristics of the various communication contexts.

> "Americans report that their greatest fear is the fear of speaking in front of a group."
>
> **BRUSKIN REPORT**

Jan Johnson was delighted when her executive manager chose her to be the team leader for the Phoenix project. After all, Phoenix, Inc., was one of the firm's most important customers, and heading this project would give Jan an opportunity to prove her leadership abilities so that she could advance in the company. Although Jan looked forward to the challenge of her new assignment, she was also a little nervous. It was a big project, and she had never been a team leader before. She wondered if the others in the group would take her seriously. She also worried about the presentation she would have to give to her executive manager and to Phoenix's upper management.

Rudolpho Alvarez, a senior at Miami Dade Community College, was nervous about an employment interview for his first professional job. He had interviewed successfully for his jobs during high school and college, but this was his first interview for a position in his major field. He had high hopes that this interview would lead to his first job in what would be a long career in business. Rudolpho was worried about the questions the interviewer might ask. "What if he asks about my so-so grades or my marginal computer skills?" Rudolpho wondered. He was afraid he'd be so nervous on the day of the interview that the interviewer would be able to see the sweat beads on his face. Rudolpho didn't get much sleep the night before the interview. He lay awake fretting about the various questions that might be asked and how he'd respond to them.

Jan and Rudolpho are both dealing with different communication contexts. This chapter will introduce you to valuable terminology, including communication contexts, which you will need to know as you study communication.

Why Study Communication?

Communication plays a major role in nearly every aspect of life. Effective communication not only can help us solve problems but can also improve lives. Communication experts believe that poor communication is at the root of many problems and that effective communication is one solution to these problems. Understanding the theory and principles of good communication, and putting them into practice, can resolve disputes between friends, countries, management and labor, teachers and students, and husbands and wives, to name only a few. Effective communication may not solve all the world's problems, but it probably can solve or avoid many of them.

Communication also plays a role in improving lives. Think of all the situations in which you use verbal and nonverbal communication in your life—for instance, going to school, meeting friends, and courting someone you love. And how would you celebrate major milestones such as graduations, birthdays, weddings, anniversaries, christenings, and bar or bas mitzvahs without communication?

Clearly, communication plays a vital role in our lives. Thus, regardless of your interests and goals, the ability to communicate effectively will enhance and enrich your life. But learning *how* to communicate is just as important as learning *about* communication. Studying communication comprehensively offers a number of advantages:

1. *It can improve the way you see yourself.* Knowing how to communicate effectively in a variety of situations—from interpersonal relationships to public speeches—will increase your self-confidence.
2. *It can improve the way others see you.* People like communicating with others who can communicate well.
3. *It can increase what you know about human relationships.* The field of communication studies includes learning about how people relate to each other and about what type of communication is appropriate for a given situation.
4. *It can teach you important life skills.* Studying communication involves learning important skills that everyone will use at some point in his or her life, such as problem solving, decision making, conflict resolution, team building, and public speaking.
5. *It can help you exercise your constitutionally guaranteed freedom of speech.* Few nations have a bill of rights that invites people to convey their opinions and ideas, yet freedom of speech is essential to a democratic form of government. Being a practicing citizen in a democratic society involves knowing about current issues and being able to speak about them in conversations, in speeches, and through the mass media; it also involves being able to critically examine messages from others.
6. *It can help you succeed professionally.* A look at the job postings in any newspaper will give you an immediate understanding of the importance of improving your knowledge and practice of communication. The employment section of *The Washington Post* provides some examples (Today's Employment, 1998):

   ◆ "We need a results-oriented, seasoned professional who is a good communicator and innovator" reads one ad for a marketing manager.
   ◆ Another ad, this one for a marketing analyst, reads, "You should be creative, inquisitive, and a good communicator both in writing and orally."
   ◆ An ad for a training specialist calls for "excellent presentation, verbal, and written communication skills, with ability to interact with all levels within organization."

What Is Communication?

Now that you have considered why learning about communication is important, you need to know exactly what the term means.

Human communication involves understanding and sharing among people.

Over the years, scholars have created hundreds of definitions of communication. How they define the term can limit or expand the study of the subject. In this text, the definition is simple and broad—simple enough to allow understanding and broad enough to include many contexts of communication.

Communication: The Process of Understanding and Sharing Meaning

Communication comes from the Latin word *communicare,* which means "to make common" or "to share." The root definition is consistent with our definition of communication. In this text, **communication** is defined as *the process of understanding and sharing meaning.* Communication is considered a **process** because it is *an activity, an exchange, or a set of behaviors*—not an unchanging product. Communication is not an object you can hold in your hands—it is an activity in which you participate. David Berlo (1960), a pioneer in the field of communication, probably provided the clearest statement about communication as a process:

> If we accept the concept of process, we view events and relationships as dynamic, ongoing, ever changing, continuous. When we label something as a process, we also mean that it does not have a beginning, an end, a fixed sequence of events. It is not static, at rest. It is moving. The ingredients within a process interact; each affects all the others.

What is an example of how process works in everyday communication? Picture three students meeting on the sidewalk between classes and exchanging a few sentences. This "snapshot" does not begin and end with the stu-

communication

The process of understanding and sharing meaning.

process

An activity, exchange, or set of behaviors that occur over time.

dents' first word and last sentence. Since they all stopped to chat with each other, you might assume that their relationship began before this encounter. Since they all seem to have a common understanding of what is being said, you might assume that they share experiences that similarly shape their perceptions. You also might assume that this brief encounter does not end when the students leave each other but, rather, that they think about their conversation later in the day or that it leads to another meeting later in the week. In other words, a snapshot cannot capture all that occurs during communication because it is a process that starts before the words begin and can end long after the last words end.

Our definition says that communication is a process that requires **understanding**—*perceiving, interpreting, and comprehending the meaning of the verbal and nonverbal behavior of others.* Suppose your professor asks, "What is the ontogeny of your misogyny?" Although you hear the words, you may not understand what the professor is asking if you don't know the meaning of *ontogeny* or *misogyny*. (The professor is asking, "What is the origin of your hatred of women?") Understanding the meaning of another person's message does not occur unless the two communicators can elicit common meanings for words, phrases, and nonverbal codes.

In addition to understanding, our definition tells us that communication involves **sharing,** which is *an interaction between people to exchange meaning.* Consider the popular use of the word *sharing:* We share a meal, we share an event, and we share a sunset. Sharing is a gift that people exchange. We can also share with ourselves when we allow ourselves time to relax and daydream—time to consider who we are and what our goals are. We share with others when we talk to them alone or in larger groups. Regardless of the context, communication involves sharing.

The last key word in the definition of communication is **meaning,** which is *the shared understanding of the message.* When you use language, meaning facilitates an appropriate response that indicates that the message was understood. For example, you ask a friend for a sheet of paper. She says nothing, and gives you one sheet of paper. You and your friend share the same meaning of the message exchanged. But a message can be interpreted in more than one way especially if the people involved have little shared experience. In such a case, a more accurate understanding of the intended meaning can be discerned by *negotiating,* that is, by asking questions.

understanding

Perceiving, interpreting, and comprehending the meaning of the verbal and nonverbal behavior of others.

sharing

An interaction between people in order to exchange meaning.

meaning

The shared understanding of the message constructed in the minds of the communicators.

While animals have their own ways of communicating with each other, this discussion is limited to human communication: communication that occurs within, between, and among people. First, let's explore human communication that begins with the self.

How Does Communication Work?

Instant Recall

Communication Begins with the Self

Communication starts with the self. How you see yourself can make a great difference in how you communicate. Carl Rogers (1951) wrote, "Every individual exists in a continually changing world of experience of which he [or she] is the center" (p. 483). For instance, when people are treated as though they are inferior, intelligent, gifted, or attractive, they will often begin acting accordingly. Many communication scholars and social scientists believe that people are products of how others treat them and of the messages others send them.

The theory behind this point of view was developed about 30 years ago by Dean Barnlund, a communication theorist. He introduced the idea that individuals "construct" themselves through the relationships they have, wish to have, or perceive themselves as having. Barnlund (1970) also developed the idea that "six persons" are involved in every two-person communication situation. By looking at Figure 1.1, you can see that these six persons emerge in the following ways:

1. How you view yourself
2. How you view the other person
3. How you believe the other person views you
4. How the other person views himself or herself
5. How the other person views you
6. How the other person believes you view him or her

An example may clarify Barnlund's six-person concept. Suppose you see yourself as an enthusiastic, highly motivated student (person 1). You perceive

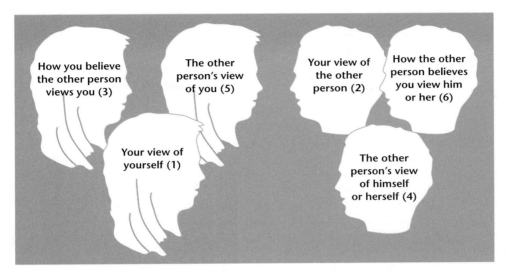

How you believe the other person views you (3)

The other person's view of you (5)

Your view of the other person (2)

How the other person believes you view him or her (6)

Your view of yourself (1)

The other person's view of himself or herself (4)

Figure 1.1 Barnlund's "six people" involved in every two-person communication.

your best friend as very intelligent, yet judgmental (2). She sees you as fun-loving and achievement-oriented, yet somewhat rigid (5); she views herself as moderately intelligent and a good conversationalist (4). Your tendency may be to downplay your goals and accomplishments and to emphasize your sense of humor (3) when you are with your friend. You frequently turn to your friend for advice on academic matters, yet discount any negative messages in other areas. She, in turn, frequently offers advice but fails to share her opinions (6). Barnlund encourages us to consider the various perspectives involved in communication and to recognize the centrality of the self in communication.

As a participant in communication, you are limited by your own view of the situation. A student, for instance, may describe a conflict with an instructor as unfair treatment: "I know my instructor doesn't like the fact that I don't agree with his opinions, and that's why he gave me such a poor grade in that class." Conversely, the instructor might think, "That student doesn't understand all the factors that go into a final grade."

Communication Involves Others

George Herbert Mead (quoted in DeFlueur et al., 1977) said that the self originates in communication. Through verbal and nonverbal symbols, a child learns to accept roles in response to the expectations of others. For example, Dominique Moceneau, a successful Olympic gymnast, was influenced quite early in life by what others wanted her to be. Apparently her father was a gymnast and told her for years that her destiny was to be a world-class gymnast (Hamilton, 1998). Most likely she had an inherent ability to be a good one, but she may not have become an accomplished, medal-winning gymnast

Cultural Note

Americans name their children after relatives, entertainers, famous people, and biblical figures. Many Spanish-speaking males are named after Jesus, and thousands of Muslim males are named after Mohammed. In China, too, names have meaning that can influence how a person feels about himself or herself. Wen Shu Lee (1998), a professor originally from Taiwan, published an article about the names of women in China. She claims that naming practices often reflect gender- and class-based oppression. The name *Zhao Di,* for example, "commands a daughter to bring to the family a younger brother, while 'expelling' more younger sisters." The name reflects a higher value on male children. Does your name influence what you think of yourself? Does your name affect how, when, and with whom you communicate? What's in a name?

without the early messages she received from her parents and trainers. Like Dominique, you establish self-image, the sort of person you believe you are, by the ways others categorize you. Positive, negative, and neutral messages that you receive from others all play a role in determining who you are.

Communication also involves others in the sense that a competent communicator considers the other person's needs and expectations when selecting messages to share. The competent communicator understands that a large number of messages can be shared at any time, but sensitivity and responsiveness to the other communicators are essential. Thus, we observe that communication begins with the self, as defined largely by others, and involves others, as defined largely by the self. Now that you understand how the self originates and develops through communication, turn to the communication process itself and communication models.

What Are the Components of Communication?

In this section you will learn how communication in action really works. The components of communication are people, messages, codes, channels, feedback, encoding and decoding, and noise.

People

People are involved in the human communication process in two roles. They serve as both the sources and the receivers of messages. A **source** *initiates a* *message,* and a **receiver** is *the intended target of the message.* Individuals do not perform these two roles independently. Instead, they are the sources and the receivers of messages simultaneously and continually.

People do not respond uniformly to all messages, nor do they always provide the same messages in exactly the same way. Individual characteristics of people, including race, gender, age, culture, values, and attitudes, affect the way they send and receive messages. (Throughout this text, you will find discussions about the ways in which culture and gender affect communication.)

The Message

The **message** is *the verbal and nonverbal form of the idea, thought, or feeling that one person (the source) wishes to communicate to another person or group of people (the receivers).* The message is the content of the interaction. The message includes the symbols (words and phrases) you use to communicate your ideas, as well as your facial expressions, bodily movements, gestures, touch, tone of voice, and other nonverbal codes. The message may be relatively brief and easy to understand or long and complex. Some experts believe that real communication stems only from messages that are intentional, or have a purpose. However, since intent is sometimes difficult to prove in a communication situation, the authors of this text believe that real communication can occur through either intentional or unintentional messages.

The Channel

The **channel** is *the means by which a message moves from the source to the receiver of the message.* A message moves from one place to another, from one person to another, by traveling through a medium, or channel. Airwaves, sound waves, twisted copper wires, glass fibers, and cable are all communication channels. Airwaves and cable are two of the various channels through which you receive television messages. Radio messages move through sound waves. Computer images (and sound, if there is any) travel through light waves, and sometimes both light and sound waves. In person-to-person communication, you send your messages through a channel of sound waves and light waves that enable receivers to see and hear you.

Feedback

Feedback is *the receiver's verbal and nonverbal response to the source's message.* Ideally, you respond to another person's messages by providing feedback so that the source knows the message was received as intended. Feedback is part of any communication situation. Even no response, or silence, is feedback, as are restless behavior and quizzical looks from students in a lecture hall. Say you're in a building you've never been in before, looking for a restroom. You ask a person quickly passing by, "Excuse me, can you tell

source

A message initiator.

receiver

A message target.

message

The verbal or nonverbal form of the idea, thought, or feeling that one person (the source) wishes to communicate to another person or group of people (the receivers).

channel

The means by which a message moves from the source to the receiver of the message.

feedback

The receiver's verbal and nonverbal response to the source's message.

me . . . ," but the person keeps on going without acknowledging you. In this case, the intended receiver did not respond, yet even the lack of a response provides you with some feedback. You may surmise that perhaps the receiver didn't hear you or was in too much of a hurry to stop.

Code

code

A systematic arrangement of symbols used to create meanings in the mind of another person or persons.

syntax

The rules of arrangement in language.

grammar

The rules of function in language.

verbal codes

Symbols and their grammatical arrangement, such as languages.

nonverbal codes

All symbols that are not words, including bodily movements, use of space and time, clothing and adornments, and sounds other than words.

encoding

Converting an idea or thought into a code.

decoding

Assigning meaning to the idea or thought in a code.

A computer carries messages via binary code on cable, wire, or fiber; similarly, you converse with others by using a code called language. A **code** is a *systematic arrangement of symbols used to create meanings in the mind of another person or persons.* Language rules of **syntax** and **grammar** result in the "systematic arrangement" that becomes a code. Words, phrases, and sentences become "symbols" that are used to evoke images, thoughts, and ideas in the mind of others. If someone yells "Stop" as you approach the street, the word *stop* has become a symbol that you are likely to interpret as a warning of danger.

Verbal and nonverbal codes are the two types of codes used in communication. **Verbal codes** consist of *symbols and their grammatical arrangement.* All languages are codes. **Nonverbal codes** consist of *all symbols that are not words, including bodily movements, your use of space and time, your clothing and other adornments, and sounds other than words.* Nonverbal codes should not be confused with non-oral codes. All non-oral codes, such as bodily movement, are nonverbal codes. However, nonverbal codes also include *oral* codes, such as pitch, duration, rate of speech, and sounds like *eh* and *ah.*

Encoding and Decoding

If communication involves the use of codes, the process of communicating can be viewed as one of encoding and decoding. **Encoding** is defined as *the act of putting an idea or a thought into a code.* **Decoding** is *assigning meaning to that idea or thought.* For instance, suppose you are interested in purchasing a new car. You are trying to describe a compact model to your father, who wants to help you with your purchase. You might be visualizing the car with the black interior, sporty design, and red exterior that belongs to your best friend. Putting this vision into words, you tell your father you are interested in a car that is "small and well designed." You encode your perceptions of a particular car into words that describe the model. Your father, on hearing this, decodes your words and develops his own picture. His love of larger cars affects this process. As a result of your definition, he envisions a sedan. As you can see, misunderstanding often occurs because of the limitations of language and the inadequacy of descriptions. Nonetheless, encoding and decoding are essential in sharing your thoughts, ideas, and feelings with others.

1.2 COMPONENTS OF COMMUNICATION

For each statement, write T *for true or* F *for false in the blank on the left:*

_____ 1. The German language consists of verbal codes.

_____ 2. Nonverbal and non-oral codes are the same thing.

_____ 3. Even no response is considered feedback.

_____ 4. Decoding is assigning meaning to symbols.

_____ 5. Noise is always a loud sound.

Answers: 1. T   2. F   3. T   4. T   5. F

Noise

In the communication process, **noise** is *any interference in the encoding and decoding processes that reduces the clarity of a message.* Noise can be physical noise, such as loud sounds; distracting sights, such as a piece of food between someone's front teeth; or an unusual behavior, such as someone's standing too close for comfort. Noise can be mental, psychological, or semantic, such as daydreams about a loved one, worry about the bills, pain from a tooth, or uncertainty about what the other person's words are supposed to mean. Noise can be anything that interferes with receiving, interpreting, or providing feedback about a message.

noise

Any interference in the encoding and decoding processes that reduces message clarity.

TRY ◀▶ THIS

Think of as many examples as you can of noise that interferes with communication.

How Does Communication Occur?

Barnlund's six-person theory of communication is a model, a pictorial depiction of how communication would look if you drew it. While a model is a simplification, it serves as a predictor

Communication as interaction.

Communication as action.

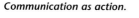

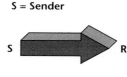

R = Receiver

Figure 1.2 Communication
as action.

S = Sender

R = Receiver

Figure 1.3 Communication as
interaction.

Communication as transaction.

S/R = Sender and Receiver

Figure 1.4 Communication as
transaction.

of how communication might occur. Earlier models—the action model, the interaction model, and the transaction model—reveal how communication models have evolved over time.

The Action Model

action model

A depiction of communication as one person sending a message and another person or group of persons receiving it.

In the past, people believed communication could be viewed as action; thus, in the **action model,** *one person sends a message and another person (or persons) receives it.* Experts in communication derided this simple model (Figure 1.2) by calling it the "inoculation model" because it seemed to depict a speaker injecting an audience with a message. The model is linear, with movement in only one direction, and it was faulted for not revealing anything about how audiences influence speakers. The action model seems to depict a public-speaking situation, but even in that context audiences affect speakers through nonverbal and verbal feedback, which is not reflected in the action model.

The Interaction Model

interaction model

A depiction of communication as one person sending a message and a second person receiving the message and then responding with a return message.

The interaction model of communication adds another dimension to the action model. In the **interaction model,** *one person sends a message to a second person, who receives it and responds with another message.* This model (Figure 1.3) seems to depict a conversation between two people in which the communicators take turns sending and receiving messages. Communication of this type can be compared to a basketball game. Just as a basketball cannot be thrown back until it is caught, in the interaction model, the receiver cannot return a message until the speaker's message is received.

The Transaction Model

transaction model

A depiction of communication as communicators simultaneously sending and receiving messages.

Rather than act exclusively as senders or receivers, in the **transaction model** of communication, *communicators simultaneously send and receive messages* (Figure 1.4). Thus, sending and receiving are no longer separate activities, nor do they occur one at a time. According to the transactional view, people are continually sending and receiving messages; they cannot avoid communication. With this model, communication becomes a confusing ball game in which a person catches and throws an unlimited number of balls at any time, in any direction, and to any person. Whether or not an individual throws a ball is not dependent on his or her ability to catch one first. Individuals do not have to take turns in this game. The game has some rules and predictability, but from time to time balls fly through the air without preparation. Similarly, in the transaction model messages are everywhere. So the person talking to you on the sidewalk can also be nodding to a passerby. How you look, what you say, how receptive you are, and what is happening around you all are part of the transactional model.

The Constructivist Model

The first three models—action, interaction, and transaction—are mechanistic models that are limited in that they simply show the direction of communication movement: source to receiver, source to receiver to source, or source and receiver simultaneously. In the constructivist model, the focus shifts from sources, messages, receivers, and feedback to what occurs in the minds of the communicators: interpreting meaning.

The **constructivist model** (Figure 1.5) posits that *receivers create their own reality in their minds*. The sender's words are symbols to be interpreted, and the receiver constructs his or her own meaning. However, the receiver's interpretation of the sender's message may or may not be the same as what the sender intended it to be. The only way to reach agreement about the message is by discussing what the sender intended and what the receiver interpreted. This is called *negotiating meaning*.

The constructivist model significantly reframes the communication process. The message is no longer something that is simply sent one way to a passive audience that receives it like an injection; it is no longer passed back

constructivist model

A theory of communication which posits that receivers create their own reality in their minds.

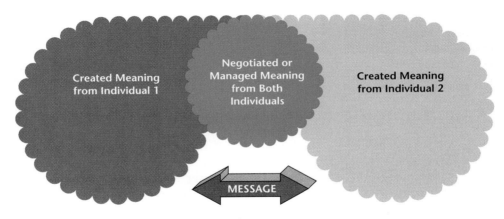

Figure 1.5 Constructivists believe people create meaning.

Instant Recall

Intrapersonal communication is the process of understanding and sharing meaning within the self.

and forth like a basketball; and it is no longer tossed about in a confusing game whose participants might be bombarded with multiple balls. In this model, the ball (or the message) may be something else by the time it is received and interpreted. Communication becomes more confusing under this model. But in reality, communication isn't as easy as the earlier models described it as being. Under the best of communication circumstances the two people involved learn to manage meaning by negotiating what each believes the message to be.

What Are Communication Contexts?

Communication occurs in a **context,** *a set of circumstances or a situation*. It occurs between two friends, among five business acquaintances in a small-group setting, and between a lecturer and an audience that fills an auditorium. At many colleges and universities, the communication courses are arranged by context: interpersonal communication, interviewing,

16

Individually, or in groups, provide answers to these questions about technology and communication models:

1. How has the Internet—with its e-mail, chat rooms, and web sites—altered the way individuals communicate with each other?
2. What is lost and what is gained when a human transaction is mediated by a computer?

small-group communication, public speaking, and mass communication. The number of people involved in communication affects the kind of communication that occurs. You may communicate with yourself, with another person, or with many others. The differences among these situations affect your choices of the most appropriate verbal and nonverbal codes.

context

A set of circumstances or a situation.

Intrapersonal Communication

Intrapersonal communication is *the process of understanding and sharing meaning within the self.* It is the communication that occurs within your own mind. For example, suppose you and the person you've been dating for 2 years share the same attitude toward education and a future career. After the two of you finish your undergraduate degrees, you both plan to attend graduate school together and later to operate your own business. One day, your partner informs you that he or she has decided to work in the family's business immediately after graduating. In your opinion, this action changes everything, including you and your partner's future together. When you begin to share your feelings with your partner, he or she becomes angry and says your attitude is just another example of your inflexibility. You tell your partner that you can't discuss the issue with him or her now and that you need to think things over for a while. You leave, thinking about what has just happened and what the future holds for you and your partner. You are engaged in intrapersonal communication.

intrapersonal communication

The process of understanding and sharing meaning within the self.

Intrapersonal communication occurs, as this example suggests, when you evaluate or examine the interaction that occurs between yourself and others, but it is not limited to such situations. This form of communication occurs before and during other forms of communication as well. For instance, you might argue with yourself during a conversation in which someone asks you to do something you don't really want to do: Before you accept or decline, you mull over the alternatives in your mind.

17

Intrapersonal communication also includes such activities as solving problems internally, resolving internal conflict, planning for the future, and evaluating yourself and your relationships with others. Intrapersonal communication—the basis for all other communication—involves only the self.

Each one of us is continually engaged in intrapersonal communication. While you might become more easily absorbed in talking to yourself when you are alone (while walking to class, driving to work, or taking a shower, for instance), you are also likely to be involved in this form of communication in crowded circumstances as well (such as during a lecture, at a party, or when visiting friends). Think about the last time you looked at yourself in a mirror. What were your thoughts? Although intrapersonal communication is almost continuous, people seldom focus on this form of communication.

Indeed, not all communication experts believe intrapersonal communication should be examined within communication studies. In their opinion, communication requires two or more receivers of a message, and since there are no receivers in intrapersonal communication, no communication actually occurs. They reason that intrapersonal communication should be studied in a discipline such as psychology or neurology—some field in which experts study the mind or the brain. Nonetheless, intrapersonal communication is recognized by most scholars within the discipline as one context of communication.

Interpersonal Communication

interpersonal communication

The personal process of coordinating meaning between at least two people in a situation that allows mutual opportunities for both speaking and listening.

When you move from intrapersonal communication to interpersonal communication, you move from communication that occurs within your own mind to communication that involves one or more other persons. **Interpersonal communication** is *the personal process of coordinating meaning between at least two people in a situation that allows mutual opportunities for both speaking and listening.* Like intrapersonal communication, interpersonal communication occurs for a variety of reasons: to solve problems, to resolve conflicts, to share information, to improve your perception of yourself, or to fulfill social needs, such as the need to belong or to be loved. Through our interpersonal communication, people are able to establish relationships with others that include friendships and romantic relationships.

dyadic communication

Two-person communication.

small-group communication

The interaction of a small group of people to achieve an interdependent goal.

Dyadic and small-group communication are two subsets of interpersonal communication. **Dyadic communication** is *two-person communication,* and it includes interviews with an employer or a teacher; talks with a parent, spouse, or child; and interactions among strangers, acquaintances, and friends. **Small-group communication** is *the interaction of a small group of people to achieve an interdependent goal* (Brilhart & Galanes, 1998). Small-group communication occurs in families, work groups, support groups, religious groups, and study groups. Communication experts agree that two people are a dyad and more than two people are a small group if they have a common purpose, goal, or mission. However, disagreement emerges about

COMMUNICATION CHALLENGE

The Case of Sharon Black

Sharon Black, a sophomore at an extension university, worked 30 hours a week at a local department store—a very busy schedule. Sharon wanted to spend more time with her coworkers, but her college work interfered. The other workers usually ate lunch together, but Sharon had a class that started at 12:30 P.M. 4 days a week. She usually couldn't attend parties because she had homework to do.

Sharon became increasingly quiet at work and felt more alienated as time passed. Her coworkers began to suspect that "the college girl" was avoiding them because she felt superior. They began to plan activities that excluded Sharon.

Sharon's work was exemplary, and she became eligible for promotion to supervisor. Her boss told her that a lot depended on whether the other workers would accept her leadership and cooperate with her. Sharon's coworkers were resentful of the possible promotion of a person who had so little experience at the store. They also felt she was being "pushed ahead" because she was a college student. At lunch that day, they decided that Sharon would not get the promotion if they had anything to say about it. One of the employees offered to tell the boss how they felt.

Sharon was called into the office 2 days later. Her boss explained that she wasn't going to be promoted because she didn't seem to be getting along well with the others, and it did not look as if they would cooperate with her.

1. What made Sharon's coworkers feel that Sharon thought she was superior to them?
2. Explain the intrapersonal communication that may have occurred for Sharon. What kinds of internal conflicts was she likely to have been experiencing?
3. Why did the misunderstanding between Sharon and the others grow to this level? Why did they not discuss their differences?
4. Is Sharon's situation realistic? Identify a similar experience in which you had a misunderstanding with another person or with other people. How did you resolve it?

the maximum number of participants in a small group. Technology also poses questions for communication scholars to debate: Does a small group have to meet face-to-face? That teleconferences can be small-group communication is uncontroversial, but what about discussions in chat rooms on the Internet? Small-group communication is discussed in greater detail later in this text.

Public Communication

Public communication is *the process of generating meanings in a situation where a single source transmits a message to a number of receivers who give nonverbal and, sometimes, question-and-answer feedback.* In public communication the source adapts the message to the audience in an attempt to achieve maximum understanding. Sometimes, virtually everyone in the audience understands the speaker's message; other times, many people fail to understand it.

Public communication, or public speaking, is recognized by its formality, structure, and planning. You probably are frequently a receiver of public communication in lecture classes, at convocations, and at religious services. Occasionally, you also may be a source: when you speak in a group, when you try to convince other voters of the merits of a particular candidate for office, or when you introduce a guest speaker to a large audience. Public communication most often informs or persuades, but it can also entertain, introduce, announce, welcome, or pay tribute.

Mass Communication

Mass communication, or *communication mediated between a source and a large number of unseen receivers,* always has some transmission system (mediator) between the sender and the receiver. When you watch your favorite TV show, the signals are going from a broadcast studio to a satellite or cable system and then from that system to your TV set: the mediator is the channel, the method of distribution. This type of communication is called "mass" because the message goes to newspaper and magazine readers, TV watchers, and radio listeners. Mass communication is often taught in a college's or university's department of mass communication, radio and television, or journalism.

The various communication contexts can be determined by several factors: the number of people involved, the degree of the setting's formality or intimacy, the opportunities for feedback, the need for restructuring messages, and the degree of stability of the roles of speaker and listener. Table 1.1 compares the contexts on the basis of these factors.

Summary

This chapter has introduced you to the world of communication studies. In this chapter, you explored the basic terminology and some of the essential concepts of the discipline. You learned several important reasons to study communication, such as for personal development, for professional opportunity, and for participation in the democratic process.

You learned that communication is the process of understanding and sharing meaning. In this book, the discussion is limited to human communication, which begins with the self and involves others. The components of

TABLE 1.1 DIFFERENCES AMONG COMMUNICATION CONTEXTS

| | INTRAPERSONAL COMMUNICATION | INTERPERSONAL COMMUNICATION | | PUBLIC COMMUNICATION | MASS COMMUNICATION |
		DYADIC COMMUNICATION	SMALL-GROUP COMMUNICATION		
Number of people	1	2	Usually 3 to 10; maybe more	Usually more than 10	Usually thousands
Degree of formality or intimacy	Most intimate	Generally intimate; interview is formal	Intimate or formal	Generally formal	Generally formal
Opportunities for feedback	Complete feedback	A great deal of feedback	Less than in intrapersonal communication but more than in public communication	Less than in small-group communication but more than in mass communication	Usually none
Need for prestructuring messages	None	Some	Some	A great deal	Almost totally scripted
Degree of stability of the roles of speaker and listener	Highly unstable; the individual as both speaker and listener	Unstable; speaker and listener alternate	Unstable; speakers and listeners alternate	Highly stable; one speaker with many listeners	Highly stable; on-air speakers, invisible listeners

communication are people, messages, channels, feedback, codes, encoding and decoding, and noise. This chapter discussed four communication models: action, interaction, transaction, and the constructivist model.

Communication occurs in intrapersonal, interpersonal, public, and mass contexts. The number of people involved, the degree of formality or intimacy, the opportunities for feedback, the need for prestructuring messages, and the degree of stability of the roles of speaker and listener all vary with the communication context. This text is organized on a contextual basis, with a consideration of self and others in each context.

Although you may spend a great deal of your time engaged in communication, you may find that you do not communicate as effectively as you wish. This text will assist you in improving your ability to communicate with other people.

Issues in Communication

This Issues in Communication narrative is designed to provoke individual thought or discussion about key concepts raised in the chapter.

Kyle Gorton was one of the founders of a successful company, KyMo, which created virtual-reality software. Before the company was sold, Kyle often worked 18-hour days. He sold products, wrote business plans, handled the company's finances, oversaw production, and was familiar with all aspects of the operation. While Kyle did most of the behind-the-scenes work, his cofounder, Morton Giamani, made presentations to trade shows and venture capitalists. Morton recruited potential employees, but Kyle interviewed them, and if they were hired, he often took them under his wing and became their mentor. Because he thought all his employees had valuable skills and ideas to contribute to the company, he frequently employed work teams. As a result, the employees of KyMo thought highly of him. However, because Morton was the one who was out meeting all the movers and shakers in the industry, the industry leaders believed that Morton was primarily responsible for the company's success.

Now that the company has been sold, Kyle is faced with what to do with his future. Although Kyle and Morton's company was successful, Kyle doesn't have the contacts in the industry that Morton has, so very few would associate his name with the company. Although Kyle knows he's intelligent and hardworking, he finds himself comparing himself to Morton and doubting his own abilities. Kyle thinks, "Why couldn't I have been more of a charismatic people-person like Morton? I should have spent more time writing articles, giving speeches, and rubbing shoulders with venture capitalists. But then again, I just don't think I'm as good as Morton at that sort of thing. I have my strengths, and he has his. We were a great team. I don't know why, but we really haven't talked about starting up another company together. I think I'm going to take the initiative and talk to him about it."

The next day Kyle and Morton begin discussing what kind of company they'd like to start next.

Apply what you have learned about communication as you ponder and discuss the following questions: Which communication context(s) do you think Kyle was most comfortable in as the head of KyMo? Which one(s) do you think Morton was the most comfortable in? How does intrapersonal communication help Kyle?

Additional Resources

Rolls, J. (1998, June). Facing the fears associated with public speaking. *Business Communication Quarterly, 61* (2), 103–104. An article for the nonexpert that discusses fear of public speaking as being normal.

Severin, W., & Tankard, J., Jr. (1997). *Communication theories: Origins, methods, and uses in the mass media* (4th ed.). New York: Longman. A text that provides more information on communication models and mass communication.

Wood, J. (1997). *Communication theories in action.* Belmont, CA: Wadsworth. An excellent introduction to theory that provides more detail about rules theory and coordinated management of meaning.

References

Barnlund, D. (1970). A transactional model of communication. In K. K. Sereno & C. D. Mortensen (Eds.), *Foundations of communication theory* (pp. 98–101). New York: Harper & Row.

Berlo, D. (1960). *The process of communication.* New York: Holt, Rinehart and Winston.

Brilhart, J. K., & Galanes, G. J. (1998). *Effective group discussion* (9th ed.). New York: McGraw-Hill.

DeFlueur, M., et al. (1977). *Sociology: Human society* (p. 138). Glenview, IL: Scott, Foresman.

Hamilton, K. (1998, November 2). A very ugly gym suit. *Newsweek,* p. 52.

Lee, W. S. (1998). In the names of Chinese women. *Quarterly Journal of Speech, 84,* 283–302.

Rogers, C. (1951). *Client-centered therapy.* Boston: Houghton-Mifflin.

Today's employment section (1998, October 18). *The Washington Post,* pp. K33, K49.

When you have read and thought about this chapter, you will be able to:

1. Explain some of the reasons why differences in perception occur.

2. Describe how selection, organization, and interpretation occur during perception.

3. Differentiate figure and ground, proximity, closure, and similarity.

4. Understand how self-awareness is related to communication.

5. Differentiate self-awareness, self-fulfilling prophesies, self-concept, self-image, and self-esteem.

6. Provide examples of confirmation, rejection, and disconfirmation.

7. List steps you can take to improve your self-concept.

2

Perception, Self-Awareness, and Self-Concept

> "Everyone has his [her] own set of goggles."
>
> MARSHALL MCLUHAN

> "Know thyself."
>
> THALES

> "To love oneself is the beginning of a life-long romance."
>
> OSCAR WILDE

This chapter introduces you to perception and self-awareness and the role they play in communication. The chapter opens by explaining what perception is; then it describes why differences in perception occur and what occurs during perception. Next, the chapter moves to a discussion of self-awareness and self-concept, and it provides some ways to improve your self-concept. After reading this chapter, you will have a better understanding of why each person sees the world a little differently and how this affects people's communication. You will also have a better understanding of the importance of knowing yourself, as well as of how what you know and think about yourself affects communication.

Myron, a reporter for the campus newspaper, is trying to get the scoop on an accident that occurred this morning on campus. He's having difficulty determining what actually happened because he's getting conflicting stories from his sources. The police report said, "A late-model blue sedan was involved in a collision with a red 10-speed bicycle. The bicyclist took the blame for the accident, saying he failed to stop for a red light. A warning was issued, and the driver, who was not injured, did not press charges. The bicyclist suffered superficial wounds, and refused medical assistance. The driver was not injured."

However, the only eyewitness said, "It was clearly the driver's fault. He accelerated when he saw the light ahead turning yellow, and he actually ended up going through it when it was red."

How will Myron determine whose story is correct? Neither individual experiences nor perceptions are identical—even regarding the same event.

Amy has decided to attend an assertiveness training workshop because she feels she is often unable to talk with her husband, Bob, about things that are bothering her. One example of a "problem topic" is their personal finances. During their 10-year marriage, Bob has always taken care of the finances, but after several financial mishaps, Amy understood that he simply wasn't very good with money. Every time a problem occurred, Amy tried to talk with Bob, but he always acted sullen and withdrawn. As a result, Amy kept her thoughts and ideas to herself, even though she thought she could do a better job. Amy needed to become better at confronting Bob and at talking to him in a way that would get him to open up.

When Amy and her husband finally talked openly about the situation, she discovered that he didn't really like handling the money because he knew he wasn't very good at it. Bob said he kept doing it for all these years because he thought she thought it was the man's responsibility to handle the finances. He had been sullen and withdrawn before because he was embarrassed by his incompetence in this area. Once Amy started managing their finances, she discovered she was quite good at it.

Amy's and Bob's self-concepts and their perceptions of each other played a crucial role in their ability to communicate with each other.

What Is Perception?

The way you sense the world—the way you see, hear, smell, touch and taste—is subjective, uniquely your own. Nobody else sees the world the way you do, and nobody experiences events exactly as you do. The uniqueness of human experience is based largely on differences in **perception,** *"the process of becoming aware of objects and events from the senses"* (DeVito, 1986).

At one time, experts tended to see perception as passive. **Passive perception** means that, like video recorders, *people are simply recorders of stimuli.*

perception

The process of becoming aware of objects and events from the senses.

Today perception is considered to be more active. **Active perception** means that *your mind selects, organizes, and interprets that which you sense.* So each person is a different video camera, and each person aims the camera at different things; each person's lens is different; each person sees different colors; and each person's audio picks up different sounds. Perception is subjective in that you interpret what you sense; you make it your own, and you add to and subtract from what you see, hear, smell, and touch. **Subjective perception** is *your uniquely constructed meaning attributed to sensed stimuli.* As depicted in Figure 2.1, your perception of an apple is not the same as anyone else's perception of an apple.

passive perception

Perception in which people are simply recorders of stimuli.

active perception

Perception in which our minds select, organize, and interpret that which we sense.

subjective perception

Your uniquely constructed meaning attributed to sensed stimuli.

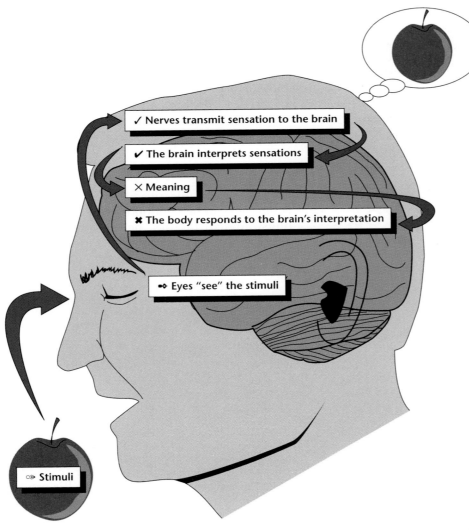

✓ Nerves transmit sensation to the brain

✔ The brain interprets sensations

✕ Meaning

✖ The body responds to the brain's interpretation

↦ Eyes "see" the stimuli

↦ Stimuli

Figure 2.1 Perception is far more complex than merely sensing stimuli. For example, this color-blind individual "sees" a different apple than you do.

Consider how much your inner state affects your perceptions. If you have a bad headache, the pain probably will affect the way you treat your children, the way you respond to your instructor's giving a pop quiz, and even the way you see yourself in the mirror. Consider also how complicated communication becomes when you know that everyone has his or her own view, uniquely developed and varying by what is happening both outside and inside the mind. Finally, consider what happens to Barnlund's six-person model when you add to the equation all the variations that occur with perception. Perception is just one of the many factors that complicate communication.

How do you see the world around you? Perhaps to compare the way your mind works to the way a computer works would help. Think of your conscious experiences as the images that appear on your computer monitor. Think of what you sense with your eyes, nose, tongue, ears, and fingertips as that which is read off your computer disk. The picture you see on the screen is not the same as the bits on the disk; instead, an image is generated from the bits to create something you can see. "What we perceive in the world around us is not a direct and faithful representation of that world itself, but, rather, a 'computer-enhanced' version based upon very limited data from that world" (Wright, 1994), according to one scholar.

Why Do Differences in Perception Occur?

Perception is subjective, active, and creative. Differences in perception may be the result of physiological factors, people's past experiences and roles, their cultures and co-cultures, and their present feelings and circumstances.

TRY ◀▶ THIS

Think of an event that recently occurred in your life in which your perception of what happened might be quite different from the perceptions of others.

Physiological Factors

You are not physiologically identical to anyone else. People differ from each other in height, weight, body type, sex, and senses. You may be tall or short, have poor eyesight, or have impaired hearing; you may be particularly sensitive to smells; or your body temperature may be colder than the rest of your family's body temperatures.

Gender is another physiological factor that may lead to perceptual differences. Some authors have suggested that hemispheric differences in the cerebral cortex of the brain are sex-linked. One study showed that these differences account for females' language facility and fine hand control and males' spatial and mathematical abilities, as well as their increased likelihood of dyslexia, stuttering, delayed speech, autism, and hyperactivity (Restak, 1984). Regardless of these findings, conclusive evidence has not been established for an anatomic difference between the brain structures of human females and males.

Differences in perception also may arise from temporary conditions. A headache, fatigue, or a pulled muscle can cause you to perceive a critical comment when a friendly one is being offered. You may not see a stop sign if your thoughts are elsewhere. Similarly, if you are tired, you may perceive stimuli differently than you do when you are well rested. Other physiological needs, such as hunger and thirst, may also affect your perceptive skills.

Past Experiences and Roles

Just as your size, gender, and physical needs can affect your perceptions, so can your past experiences and your various roles.

The concept that best explains the influence of your past experiences on your perceptions is **perceptual constancy:** the idea that *your past experiences lead you to see the world in a way that is difficult to change; your initial perceptions persist.* What happened to you in the past influences your perception of the present and the future. A bad experience in a given situation may cause you to avoid that situation in the future. Your experiences affect how you respond to professors, police, politicians, and lawyers.

Roles also influence perceptions. A **role** is *"the part an individual plays in a group; an individual's function or expected behavior"* (DeVito, 1986, p. 269). You may be a student, a single mother or father, a political leader, or a business major. Your roles affect your communication: whom you talk to, how you talk to people, the language you use, and the way you respond to feedback. A good example of how perceptual constancy and role are related is how parents treat their children. Even after some people become adults, their parents still treat them like they did when they were growing up. Roles also tend to change with context: In your parents' home you are a son or daughter; in your own home you may be a roommate or a mother or father; in the classroom you are a student; and at work you may be an editor or a manager.

Culture and Co-culture

The ways people greet each other, position themselves when they talk, and even eat and sleep are all influenced by culture. **Culture** can be defined as *a system of shared beliefs, values, customs, behaviors, and artifacts that the members of a society use to cope with one another and with their world.* Marshall R.

perceptual constancy

The idea that our past experiences lead us to see the world in a way that is difficult to change; that is, our initial perceptions persist.

role

The part an individual plays in a group; an individual's function or expected behavior.

culture

A system of shared beliefs, values, customs, behaviors, and artifacts that the members of a society use to cope with one another and with their world.

Differences in perception can be overcome in our interaction with others.

Singer (1985), an intercultural communication researcher, maintains that what people see, hear, taste, touch, and smell is conditioned by their culture. He says that people's perceptions are largely learned; the greater the experiential differences among people, the greater the disparity in their perceptions. Conversely, the more similar their backgrounds, the more similarly they perceive the world.

To complicate matters further, your co-culture also affects your perceptions of the world. A **co-culture** is *"a group whose beliefs or behaviors distinguish it from the larger culture of which it is a part and with which it shares numerous similarities"* (DeVito, 1986). Four of the more common co-cultures in the United States today are Latinos, African Americans, women, and gays and lesbians (Samovar, Porter, & Stefani, 1998). Women and men, for example, tend to see the world differently, communicate about it differently, and even practice and perceive communication itself differently. Women tend to see talk as relational, as a way to share and understand feelings, and men tend to see talk as instrumental, as a way to achieve a task (Pearson, 1995). Culture and co-culture are discussed in greater detail in Chapter 11.

co-culture

A group whose beliefs or behaviors distinguish it from the larger culture of which it is a part and with which it shares numerous similarities.

TRY ◄►THIS

Think of ways your cultural or co-cultural affiliation affects the way you perceive the world.

Present Feelings and Circumstances

Your daily, monthly, or yearly cycle may affect how you perceive stimuli. If you are an "evening person," you might not be able to discriminate among

COMMUNICATION CHALLENGE

Differences in Perception

Jack can see he sees
what he can see Jill can't see,
and he can see
that Jill can't see that she can't see,
but he can't see WHY
Jill can't see that Jill can't see. . . .
Jill can see Jack can't see
and can't see he can't see.
Jill can see WHY
Jack can't see,
but Jill cannot see WHY
Jack can't see he can't see. . . .
Jack can't see he can't see
and can't see
Jill can't see Jill can't see it,
and vice versa.*

Differences in perception can be overcome in our interaction with others.

The poem captures the complexity of perception and the difficulty of establishing common perceptions.

    Discuss an experience in which you and another person attempted to reach an agreement but could not. Identify the differences in perception, suggest reasons for those differences, and list the methods you used to validate your perceptions.

*"Differences in Perception," from *Knots* by R. D. Laing. Copyright © 1970 by R. D. Laing. Reprinted by permission of Pantheon Books, a division of Random House, Inc. and Tavistock Publications.

multiple-choice answers on an exam at 8 A.M. as well as you could later in the day. If you are having a bad week, you might be offended by the humor of one of your friends; later in the month, you might find the same remark very funny. You might perceive stimuli more acutely in the cooler months of winter than you do in the warmer summer months.

    If you have ever spent a night alone in a large house, a deserted dormitory, or an unfamiliar residence, you probably understand that perceptions are altered by circumstances. Most people experience a remarkable change in their hearing at night when they are alone. They hear creaking, whining, scraping, cracking sounds at night but not during the day. The lack of other stimuli—including light, other sounds, and other people with whom to talk—coupled with a slight feeling of anxiety provides circumstances that result in more acute hearing.

What Occurs in Perception?

You engage in three separate activities during perception: selection, organization, and interpretation. No one is aware of these separate processes because they occur quickly and almost simultaneously. Nonetheless, each activity is involved in perception.

Selection

selection

The process of neglecting some stimuli in the environment to focus on other stimuli.

No one perceives all the stimuli in his or her environment. Through **selection,** *you neglect some stimuli in your environment to focus on other stimuli.* For example, when you drive or walk to your classes, you are probably bombarded with sights, sounds, smells, and other sensations. At the time, you elect to perceive some of the stimuli and to disregard others. Afterward, it's likely you will recall the stimuli you perceived but will have forgotten the other stimuli.

Four types of selectivity are selective exposure, selective attention, selective perception, and selective retention. In **selective exposure,** *you expose yourself to information that reinforces, rather than contradicts, your beliefs or opinions* (Wilson & Wilson, 1998). In other words, conservative Republicans are more likely than liberal Democrats to listen to Rush Limbaugh and Oliver North on the radio, and to read editorials by George Will. Liberal Democrats, on the other hand, are more likely to avoid these sources of information and listen to sources that support their beliefs.

selective exposure

The tendency to expose ourselves to information that reinforces rather than contradicts our beliefs or opinions.

selective attention

The tendency, when we expose ourselves to information and ideas, to focus on certain cues and ignore others.

In **selective attention,** even when you do expose yourself to information and ideas, *you focus on certain cues and ignore others.* In class, you might notice the new outfit your friend is wearing but not the earring worn by the man three seats in front of you. At a buffet table, you might be drawn to the smells and the foods that you recognize and select only those. In an elevator, you may notice the conversation between the two other people in the elevator with you but not the music that's being piped in overhead.

selective perception

The tendency to see, hear, and believe only what we want to see, hear, and believe.

After you expose yourself to a message and then select it for further attention, you see that message through your own special lens. **Selective perception** is *the tendency to see, hear, and believe only what you want to see, hear, and believe* (Wilson & Wilson, 1998). If someone accused your trustworthy, law-abiding friend of 20 years of stealing, would you believe that person? You may not listen to the accusations, or even look at the evidence, because you believe it simply is not possible that your friend would ever do such a thing.

selective retention

The tendency to remember better the things that reinforce our beliefs than those that oppose them.

Finally, you select the stimuli you will recall or remember. **Selective retention** is *the tendency to remember better the things that reinforce your beliefs than those that oppose them* (Wilson & Wilson, 1998). For example, make a list of some of the bad qualities of someone you dislike and a list of some of the bad qualities of someone you admire. Compare your lists. Usually, people can easily think of the negative qualities of someone they dislike, but they often find it difficult to think of an admirable person's negative qualities (Wilson & Wilson, 1998).

So selection is the first process that occurs during perception; the next is organization.

2.1 THE SELECTIVITIES OF PERCEPTION

For each statement, identify the underlying process by writing the correct letter from the options below in the blank on the left:

A. **Selection**   D. **Selective perception**
B. **Selective exposure**   E. **Selective retention**
C. **Selective attention**

_____ 1. "While I enjoy listening to 'talk radio,' I will tune in to only those hosts who support my viewpoint."

_____ 2. "President Clinton's impeachment trial was the result of a Republican 'witch hunt.' "

_____ 3. "I remember the nose ring she was wearing, but I really can't remember what she looked like."

_____ 4. "The hustle and bustle of Chicago's O'Hare Airport can be overwhelming. So I just concentrate on getting to my gate on time and reading my book if I have time to spare when I get there."

_____ 5. "The book I'm reading has a wealth of historical information, but I'm really most interested in the Native American experience."

Answers: 1. B   2. D or E   3. C or E   4. A   5. C

Organization

Each person organizes the stimuli in his or her environment. **Organization** is *the grouping of stimuli into meaningful units or wholes.* You organize stimuli in a number of ways, through figure and ground, closure, proximity, and similarity.

Figure and Ground

One organization method is to distinguish between figure and ground. **Figure** is *the focal point of your attention,* and **ground** is *the background against which your focused attention occurs.* When looking at Figure 2.2, some people might perceive a vase or a candlestick, whereas others perceive twins facing each other. People who see a vase identify the center of the drawing as the figure and the area on the right and left as the ground, or background. Conversely, people who see twins facing each other see the center as the background and the area on the right and left as the figure.

organization

The grouping of stimuli into meaningful units or wholes.

33

Figure 2.2 An example of figure and ground: a vase or twins?

Figure 2.3 An example of figure and ground: ink blobs or a bearded man?

figure

The focal point of a person's attention.

ground

The background against which a person's focused attention occurs.

Figure 2.3 is another illustration of the principle of figure and ground. As you first glance at the drawing, you probably perceive only ink blobs—nothing is clearly distinguishable as either figure or ground. However, if you continue to look at the drawing, you perceive the face of a bearded man at the center of the picture. When you see the face, it becomes the figure; the rest of the drawing becomes the ground.

How does figure and ground work in communication encounters? In your verbal and nonverbal exchanges you perform a similar feat of focusing on some parts (figure) and distancing yourself from others (ground). When you hear your name in a noisy room, your name becomes figure and the rest becomes ground; on a posted grade list, your student identification number becomes figure and the other numbers become ground. Here's another example: During a job evaluation, your employer may talk about your weaknesses and strengths, but the so-called weaknesses may make you so angry that you don't even remember the strengths. The messages about weaknesses were figure, and the ones about strengths were ground. Because of who and what you are, and because of your own unique perceptual processes, your attention focuses and fades, and you choose the figure or ground of what you see, hear, smell, touch, and taste.

Closure

closure

The tendency to fill in missing information in order to complete an otherwise incomplete figure or statement.

Another way of organizing stimuli is **closure,** *the tendency to fill in missing information in order to provide the appearance of a complete unit.* If someone were to show you Figure 2.4 and ask you what you see, you might say it is a picture of a cat. But as you can see, the figure is incomplete. You see a cat only if you are willing to fill in the blank areas. Additional examples of closure appear in Figures 2.5 and 2.6. Most people would identify Figure 2.5 as a triangle and Figure 2.6 as a circle, rather than seeing both as simply a number of short lines.

Figure 2.4 An example of closure: ink blobs or a cat?

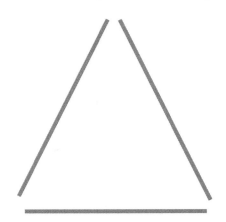

Figure 2.5 An example of closure: triangle or straight lines?

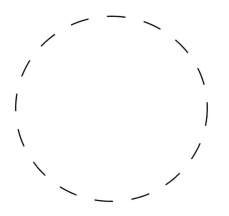

Figure 2.6 An example of closure: a circle or straight lines?

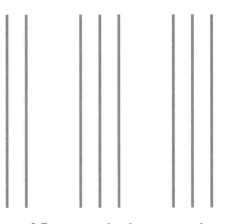

Figure 2.7 An example of proximity: three groups of lines or nine separate lines?

Closure also functions in your communication interactions. You see two people standing face-to-face and looking deeply into each other's eyes, and you "fill in" your inference that they are lovers. A public speaker says, "We need to preserve our neighborhoods," and you assume she is against the proposed low-income housing. Visual closure might be completing the circle or seeing the cat, but mental closure means filling in the meaning of what you hear and observe.

Proximity

You also organize stimuli on the basis of their proximity. According to the principle of **proximity,** *objects physically close to each other will be perceived as a unit or group* (DeVito, 1986). This principle is at work in Figure 2.7. You

proximity

The principle that objects which are physically close to each other will be perceived as a unit or group.

are most likely to perceive three groups of three lines, rather than nine separate lines.

Proximity works verbally and nonverbally in communication. Some nonverbal examples include thinking that the person standing next to the cash register is the cashier or assuming that the two people entering the room at the same time are a couple. And here is a verbal example: Suppose your boss announces that due to an economic downturn he is forced to lay off 25 employees, and 1 hour later he calls you into his office—the proximity of the messages leads you to believe that you will be laid off.

Similarity

similarity

The principle that elements are grouped together because they share attributes such as size, color, or belief.

Similarity is probably one of the simplest means of organizing stimuli. On the basis of **similarity,** *elements are grouped together because they resemble each other in size, color, shape, or other attributes.* The saying "Birds of a feather flock together" can hold true for human groups as well, who often organize by ethnicity, religion, political leaning, or interest. In Figure 2.8, you probably perceive circles and squares, rather than a group of geometric shapes, because of the principle of similarity.

To understand the relationship between the organization of stimuli and communication, think about a classroom setting. When you enter the room, your tendency is to organize the stimuli, or people there, into specific groups. Your primary focus is on acquaintances and friends—the *figure*—rather than on the strangers, who function as the *ground*. You talk to friends sitting near the doorway as you enter, due to their *proximity*. You then seat yourself near a group of students you perceive as having interests identical to yours, thus illustrating *similarity*. Lastly, you notice your instructor arrive with another professor of communication. They are laughing, smiling, and conversing enthusiastically. *Closure* is a result of your assumption that they have a social relationship outside the classroom.

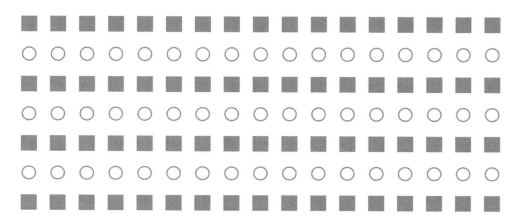

Figure 2.8 An example of similarity: squares and circles or a group of geometric shapes?

Interpretation

The third activity you engage in during perception is **interpretation,** *the assignment of meaning to stimuli.* **Interpretive perception,** then, is *a blend of internal states and external stimuli.* The more ambiguous the stimuli, the more room for interpretation. The basis for the well-known inkblot test lies in the principle of interpretation of stimuli. Figure 2.9 shows three inkblots that a psychologist might ask you to interpret. The ambiguity of the figures is typical.

When interpreting stimuli, people frequently rely on the context in which the stimuli are perceived or they compare the stimuli to other stimuli (Figure 2.10). Sometimes context helps, but other times it can create confusion

interpretation

The process of assigning meaning to stimuli.

interpretive perception

Perception that involves a blend of internal states and external stimuli.

Figure 2.9 An example of interpretation: the inkblot.

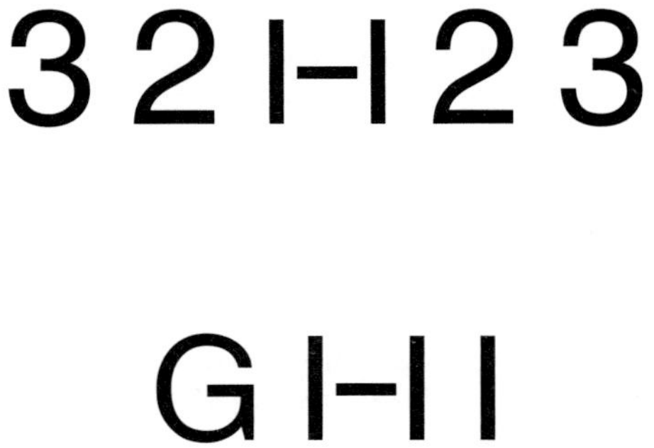

3 2 I-I 2 3

G I-I I

Figure 2.10 An example of the usefulness of context in the interpretation of stimuli.

Instant Recall

Fill in each blank with the word from the choices below that seems most appropriate in the context:

similarity   proximity   closure   figure   ground

1. "Ivan and Svetlana were together in class, during every work break, and during every vacation, so their _____ means they must really like each other."

2. "Ryoko's clothing was so stunning that nobody remembered what she looked like, which means her clothing was _____."

3. "Because all 20 of the young men wore blue blazers with the same coat of arms, I assumed from their _____ that they were in the same fraternity."

4. "Alicia was 4 hours late from work, so when the police appeared at our front door, I achieved _____; I knew what they were going to say before they said it."

5. "As the Mack truck started cutting across the center line, I could focus on nothing else; everything else became _____."

Answers: 1. proximity   2. figure   3. similarity   4. closure   5. ground

in interpretation. You have probably seen Figures 2.11 and 2.12 before. When looking at these figures, you probably perceive differences in the length of the lines in Figure 2.10 and in the height and width of the candle-holder in Figure 2.11. However, no differences exist.

You can become so accustomed to seeing people, places, and situations in a certain way that your senses do not pick up on the obvious. Many people who read the following sentence will overlook the problem with it:

The cop saw the man standing on the the street corner.

We achieve closure on the sentence and interpret its meaning without consciousness of the details, so the repeated *the* is overlooked. Context provides cues for how an action, an object, or a situation is to be interpreted or perceived. Not seeing the double *the* in the sentence would be no problem for a reader trying to comprehend meaning, but a proofreader's job would be in jeopardy if such an error were missed often.

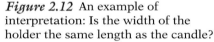

Figure 2.11 An example of interpretation: Which line is longer?

Figure 2.12 An example of interpretation: Is the width of the holder the same length as the candle?

A discussion of perception naturally leads to a look at self-perception or self-awareness.

What Is Self-Awareness?

How you perceive yourself plays a central role in communication, regardless of whether the communication is in a daydream, in a journal, in a small group, or at a podium. An early step in considering yourself a communicator is to contemplate your **self-awareness,** *an understanding of the self, including your attitudes, values, beliefs, strengths, and weaknesses* (DeVito, 1986, p. 274). Self-awareness is linked to your past, present, and future. Your past goes all the way back to how you were reared, or the way your family taught you to think, believe, and behave. You began as a spontaneous creature that cried when hungry or frustrated, lashed out at others when angry, and giggled and beamed when happy. Over time, adults took away some of your spontaneity until you behaved like an adult—until you ate at mealtimes, held your anger in check with your teachers, laughed when appropriate, and cried little if at all. Your emotions, as well as your physical responses, were altered to make you responsible for your own behavior.

Once you mastered language, symbolic interactionism shaped you in ways that made you what you are today. The term **symbolic interactionism** refers to *the development of the self through the messages and feedback received from others* (Mead, 1934). You may have been punished for acting up in class, rewarded for athletic skill, or ignored for saying too little. The result is the person you see in the mirror today.

self-awareness

An understanding of and insight into one's self, including one's attitudes, values, beliefs, strengths, and weaknesses.

symbolic interactionism

The process in which the self develops through the messages and feedback received from others.

self-fulfilling prophecy

The idea that we behave and see ourselves in ways that are consistent with how others see us.

An aspect of symbolic interactionism is the **self-fulfilling prophecy,** the idea that *you behave and see yourself in ways that are consistent with how others see you* (Wood, 1997, p. 383). Through a number of studies on academic performance, Rosenthal and Jacobson (1968) found that students who were expected to do well actually performed better than students who were not expected to perform well. In other words, "We learn to see ourselves in terms of the labels others apply to us. Those labels shape our self-concepts and behaviors" (Wood, 1997, p. 128).

Indeed, your concept of yourself originated in the responses you received when you were young, and, to some extent, self-fulfilling prophecies help maintain your self-concept. In many ways, individuals attempt to behave in ways consistent with other people's expectations, regardless of whether those expectations are positive or negative. But the self-fulfilling prophecy is not a simple, straightforward concept: Individuals do not simply and routinely behave in the ways other people expect. For you, it may be that other people's expectations play a more important role than your own or, conversely, that you see your own expectations as more relevant. In either case, however, others' observations about who and what you are can have a powerful influence on the self.

Perhaps you now understand why the ancients said, "Know thyself." They, like people today, believed that self-awareness is a discovery worth making. It tells you which choices are open to you and which ones are not. If you are bad at math, you will not have a future as an accountant. If you hate chemistry, you should not become a physician or pharmacist. If you like to write and are good at it, you may have a future as a writer. If you are skillful at athletics, perhaps you can exploit that talent with scholarships, varsity sports, and professional teams. What you have learned about yourself in the past, and what you learn about yourself today, will affect your future.

In the here-and-now you should be aware of what kind of person you are. Are you timid, shy, unassertive? Are you healthy, vigorous, energetic? Do you welcome change, adventure, and risk? Do you see yourself as capable, unstoppable, and hard-driving? The answers to these and many other questions are the key to your self-awareness. Will Schutz (1982) wrote, "Given a complete knowledge of myself, I can determine my life; lacking that mastery, I am controlled in ways that are often undesirable, unproductive, worrisome, and confusing" (p. 1).

Joseph O'Connor was a high school junior when he spent 2 weeks in the Sierra Mountains of northeastern California—a challenge that changed his level of self-awareness. Rain poured, hail pelted, and the beauty of dawn at 13,000 feet entranced him. Writing about his self-awareness in an article entitled "A View from Mount Ritter: Two Weeks in the Sierras Changed My Attitude toward Life and What It Takes to Succeed," O'Connor (1998) stated:

> The Wonder of all I'd experienced made me think seriously about what comes next. "Life after high school," I said to myself. "Uh-oh." What had I been doing the last three years? I was so caught up in defying the advice of my parents and teachers to study and play by the rules that I hadn't considered the effects my actions would have on me. (p. 17)

COMMUNICATION CHALLENGE

Increasing Your Self-Awareness

Joseph DeVito, in *The Communication Handbook* (1986, p. 274), suggests some ways of increasing self-awareness. They include the following:

1. Answer the question "Who am I?" by writing 10 to 20 times "I am . . ." Complete the sentence with what comes to mind first.
2. Take a sheet of paper and divide it into two columns: "Strengths" and "Weaknesses." Fill the two columns as quickly as possible with strengths and weaknesses you see in yourself.
3. Take another sheet of paper and, under the heading "Self-Improvement Goals," complete the statement "I want to improve my . . ." as many times as you can in 5 minutes.

These three exercises are the beginning of a dialogue with and about yourself, but remember that you change, so update the exercise occasionally.

From *The Communication Handbook* by Joseph DeVito. Reprinted by permission of the author.

O'Connor's experience changed his self-awareness, and he went from being a D student to one who made the honor roll.

You don't have to go to the mountains to come to a new awareness of yourself. You can challenge yourself and alter your self-awareness by taking a public-speaking course, acting in a community play, finishing your undergraduate degree after years away from school, accepting your employer's invitation to lead a work team, or deciding to quit your paying job to care for your children. The more you can learn about yourself, the easier it will be to learn how and why you communicate with others. Your self-awareness also concerns your potential, your future prospects. Abraham Maslow (1970) called this concept **self-actualization**—*the fulfillment of one's potential as a person*—and saw it as the highest level in the hierarchy of human needs. Carl Rogers labeled the self-actualized person as the "fully functioning person"; Sidney Jourard called it the "disclosed self"; and Charles Morris identified it as the "open self." All these writers recognized that self-awareness leads to self-actualization.

self-actualization

According to Maslow, the fulfillment of one's potential as a person.

What Is Self-Concept?

Self-concept is *each person's evaluation of himself or herself, that is, self-appraisal* (DeVito, 1986, p. 275). Your self-concept develops from words and actions (symbolic interactionism); from what others say to you and do with you (self-fulfilling prophecies); and from the way you perceive yourself (self-concept). The self is socially constructed through communication; that is,

self-concept

An individual's evaluation of himself or herself, that is, an individual's self-appraisal.

your self is a result of how others speak to you and treat you and how you see yourself. Self-concept is composed of two parts: self-image and self-esteem.

Self-Image

Self-image is *the picture you have of yourself, the sort of person you believe you are.* Included in your self-image are the categories in which you place yourself, the roles you play, and other similar descriptors you use to identify yourself. If you tell an acquaintance you are a grandfather who recently lost his wife and who does volunteer work on weekends, several elements of your self-image are brought to light—the roles of grandparent, widower, and conscientious citizen.

But self-image is more than how you picture yourself; it also involves how others see you. Michael Argyle (1969) noted that self-image is originally based on characterizations by others and that others characterize us most often by family roles, followed by occupation, marital status, and religious affiliation.

Three types of feedback from others are indicative of how they see us: confirmation, rejection, and disconfirmation (Watzlawick, Beavin, & Jackson, 1967). **Confirmation** occurs when *others treat you in a manner consistent with who you believe you are.* You see yourself as intelligent, and your parents praise you for your excellent grades in school; you believe you have leadership abilities, and your boss puts you in charge of a new work team. On the other hand, **rejection** occurs when *others treat you in a manner that is inconsistent with your self-definition.* Pierre Salinger was appointed senator from California but subsequently lost his first election. He thought he was a good public official, but the voters obviously thought otherwise—their vote was inconsistent with his self-concept. The third type of feedback is **disconfirmation,** which occurs when *others fail to respond to your notion of self by responding neutrally.* A small child repeatedly tries to get a parent to look at something he has drawn, but the parent gives it only a cursory glance and buries her head back in her newspaper. A student writes what he thinks is an excellent composition, but the teacher writes no encouraging remarks. Rather than relying on how others classify you, consider how you identify yourself. The way in which you identify yourself is the best reflection of your self-image.

self-image

The picture an individual has of himself or herself; the sort of person an individual believes he or she is.

confirmation

Feedback in which others treat us in a manner consistent with who we believe we are.

rejection

Feedback in which others treat us in a manner that is inconsistent with our self-definition.

disconfirmation

Feedback in which others fail to respond to our notion of self by responding neutrally.

TRY ◀ THIS

When meeting people for the first time, observe how they identify themselves. What does their self-description tell you about their self-concept? How do you identify yourself when meeting people for the first time? What does your self-description tell you about your own self-concept?

Self-Esteem

The second part of self-concept is **self-esteem**—*how you feel about yourself, how well you like and value yourself.* Self-esteem is usually based on perceptions of your successes or failures. Think of self-esteem as the plus or minus you place on your self-perception. If you have an unfavorable perception of yourself, you are said to have low self-esteem; if you have a favorable perception of yourself, you have high self-esteem.

But perception and communication are affected regardless of whether self-esteem is high or low. For example, Baumgardner and Levy (1988) found that people with high self-esteem tend to view others who are motivated as bright people and those who are not motivated as less bright. In other words, they think people who put forth effort also have great ability. People with low self-esteem do not make this distinction. This lack of discrimination may prevent people with low self-esteem from understanding the behaviors necessary for succeeding.

Although self-esteem is important, some critics believe educators have spent too much time and effort trying to get young people to feel good about themselves and too little time and effort trying to get them to earn the right to those good feelings. For example, Shaw (1994) showed that although self-esteem had risen among young people to all-time highs, test scores had plummeted to new lows.

You communicate in a variety of ways whether or not you value yourself. At the same time, what other people say about you can affect your self-esteem.

self-esteem

The feeling an individual has about his or her self-concept, that is, how well the individual likes and values himself or herself.

those jeans make you look fat.

Gender Differences

Previous sections have discussed people's tendency to behave in ways that others encourage and avoid behavior that others discourage. From the time you were born, you may have been treated according to your biological gender. Many parents dress male and female babies in different kinds of clothing and respond differently to male and female infants (Bell & Carver, 1980). Male and female babies are described using different adjectives: Boys are strong, solid, and independent, whereas girls are loving, cute, and sweet. Preschool children observe commercials and cartoons on television, are read books, and play with toys in which "appropriate" gender roles are depicted. In many ways, people are treated differently because of their biological gender.

Since the messages about gender roles are abundant, children develop specific gender-role conceptions early in life. Before the age of 3, children have little notion of their gender roles, but between the ages of 3 and 5, gender roles develop (Seegmiller, 1980). Between the ages of 5 and 7, **gender constancy,** or *the tendency to see oneself consistently as male or female,* develops in most children (Tibbits, 1975). Role models, educational institutions, games and toys, and children's literature all reinforce different male and female roles.

gender constancy

The tendency to see oneself consistently as male or female.

In the United States the dominant culture tends to be "masculinist"—that is, the so-called masculine attitudes, predispositions, and characteristics are generally more highly valued than are those associated with femininity. For example, men and women are more likely to be rewarded for typically "masculine" characteristics—such as independence, assertiveness, confidence, dominance, inventiveness, and shrewdness—than for more "feminine" characteristics—such as sensitivity, sincerity, cooperation, timidity, and modesty. Since men are more likely to possess masculine characteristics and women are more likely to possess feminine characteristics, men are more likely to rise to leadership positions.

The tendency of women to act in a more feminine manner within the American culture, which is biased toward men, often causes women to report lower self-esteem than men do. But self-concept is changeable. In the next section, you will learn ideas for changing your self-concept that apply to both men and women.

Improving Self-Concept

Numerous people have made dramatic changes in their lifestyle, their behavior, and, in turn, their self-concept. The news is filled with stories of ex-convicts who become responsible members of the community, alcoholics who are able to abstain from drinking, and highly paid television, movie, and rock stars who are able to overcome their fame and have fairly normal family lives. Dramatic changes occur in people. Although you might not choose to follow the paths of those in the news, their stories do provide evidence that people can change.

Usually people want to change their self-concept when it is inhibiting their development as an individual, as an upwardly mobile employee, or as a member of a family. Perhaps you have never been comfortable in conversations with strangers; as a result, you often feel inadequate at receptions, parties, and business social events. Maybe you have never worked well in groups and thus have a hard time picturing yourself as part of a work team. Your inability to work with others can be regarded as a detriment to professional advancement. Or perhaps you bicker often with your spouse or partner, and you worry about how your argumentative style affects your relationship not only with that person but with others as well. A sensed need to change is what inspires people to improve their self-concept.

If you wish to change your self-concept in order to improve your ability to communicate with others, at least two steps are essential. First, you need to become aware of yourself; second, you need to establish a positive attitude toward yourself and toward others. The first step is not an automatic, natural process. People are conditioned to be out of touch with themselves.

To acknowledge all of your feelings is essential. People are usually more familiar with certain aspects of themselves than with others. If you have low self-esteem, you probably focus on aspects of yourself that you see as problems or deficiencies. If you have high self-esteem, you probably ignore your

2.3 COMMUNICATION AND THE SELF

Fill in the blanks:

1. One of the first steps in considering yourself as a communicator is
   _____, which is an understanding of the _____, including your
   attitudes, values, beliefs, strengths, and weaknesses.

2. The fulfillment of one's potential is ___2. self-act.___

3. Self-image is the _____ you have of yourself.

4. _____ is your evaluation of yourself.

5. If you have an unfavorable perception of yourself you have _low self-esteem_.

*Answers: 1. self-awareness/self   2. self-actualization   3. picture   4. Self-concept   5. low
self-esteem*

liabilities and focus on your assets. Each person has negative and positive
characteristics, and to recognize both aspects is important.

To become more aware of yourself, you need to focus on yourself, rather
than on others. Instead of using your parents' perception of you, try to establish your own viewpoint. Rather than deciding who you are on the basis of
cultural standards and norms, try to assess yourself on the basis of your own
standards.

Establishing a positive attitude toward yourself and others—the second
step in changing your self-concept—is more difficult than increasing self-
awareness. If you are to alter your self-concept, you must strive to believe
that you, and others, are worthy of being liked and accepted. You need to reject highly critical attitudes about yourself and others. You need to develop
the belief that you, and others, have potentialities worthy of respect. You
need to rid yourself of anxiety, insecurity, cynicism, defensiveness, and the
tendency to be highly evaluative. Your goal should be to free yourself so that
you can establish meaningful relationships with yourself and others.

Barriers to Improving Self-Concept

Altering your self-concept is not a simple matter. One of the factors that
makes change difficult is that people who know you expect you to behave in a
certain way. In fact, they helped create and maintain your self-concept. These

people may continue to insist that you maintain a particular self-concept, even when you are attempting to change.

Sometimes, people work against themselves when they try to change their self-concept. For example, you might label yourself "passive;" that is, even when others voice opinions contrary to yours or attack values you hold, you say nothing in defense. This passivity may be consistent with other aspects of your self-concept such as "open-minded" and "nonargumentative." You can alter one aspect of your self-concept only to the extent that it does not contradict other aspects. If your passivity fits with your self-concept of being warm and supportive of others, you may find that becoming more assertive is difficult unless you are also willing to be less supportive on some occasions.

Summary

This chapter examined perception and self-awareness. In the past, people were considered passive receivers of information. Today, perception is viewed as active, subjective, and creative.

Differences in perception are due to physiological factors, past experiences, culture and co-culture, and present feelings and circumstances.

During perception, three separate activities are occurring: selection, organization, and interpretation. These processes occur quickly and nearly simultaneously, so you are not aware they are occurring. You do not perceive all the stimuli in your environment. Through selection, you neglect some stimuli in your environment and focus on others. Four types of selectivity are selective exposure, selective attention, selective perception, and selective retention. The stimuli that you focus on are organized in a number of ways—through figure and ground, closure, proximity, and similarity.

How you perceive yourself plays a central role in communication. Self-awareness is an understanding of the self—your attitudes, values, beliefs, strengths, and weaknesses. Self-awareness involves the important concepts of symbolic interactionism, self-fulfilling prophesy, and self-actualization.

Self-concept, defined as each person's evaluation of himself or herself, consists of self-image and self-esteem. Self-image is the picture you have of yourself. Your self-image also involves how others see you. Three types of feedback from others indicate how they see you: confirmation, rejection, and disconfirmation. Self-esteem, the second part of self-concept, is how you feel about yourself.

You can improve your self-concept. The two essential steps are becoming aware of yourself and establishing a positive attitude toward yourself and others. Although altering self-concept is challenging and you may be confronted with barriers along the way, self-concepts can be changed.

Issues in Communication

This Issues in Communication narrative is designed to provoke individual thought or discussion about concepts raised in the chapter.

During the last part of the nineteenth century, a prestigious Ohio banker raised his daughter Florence, as if she were the son he would never have. He trained her in the ways of business, and instilled in her a sense of independence and a spirit of self-reliance. This upbringing proved effective when she gravitated toward male-dominated courses in school such as math, surveying, and science. A talented musician as well, she enrolled in the Cincinnati Conservatory at 17 to study piano.

Her ambitious plans for a career in the arts ended abruptly when her mother's illness forced her to return home. Embittered, disdainful of housework, and plagued by quarrels with her dominating father, Florence didn't remain home long. At 19, she was rebellious, pregnant, and unmarried. It was not until she was thirty that this single mom found her ideal husband. The good-looking editor of the local paper, and five years her junior, he shared her many interests.

Florence, always an independent soul, refused to wear a wedding band (she would never "belong" to anyone) and at the wedding reception announced her goal to make her husband President of the United States. Appropriately he gave her the nicknames "Boss" and "Duchess." Florence's opinionated father could not help but broadcast his view that his new son-in-law,

Warren, would not amount to much. Warren's well-known reputation as a salacious lady's man was reconfirmed throughout his marriage by his highly publicized philandering, and rumors of several illegitimate children. The prophecy of his failure might have come true but for Florence's persistence.

Overlooking his indiscretions, she used her position as his wife to advance the cause of women, keep racists out of appointed offices, and to reform prisons. When Warren G. Harding died in office, Florence was at his side not just as his wife but as the First Lady who reopened the White House to the public, became a master of presidential public relations, and who was the architect of her husband's short-lived presidency.*

Apply what you have learned about self-awareness and self-concept as you ponder and discuss the following questions: How did the feedback Florence received from her father appear to affect her self-concept? What type of feedback did he give her? How do you think Florence would describe her self-concept? How has your family influenced your self-concept?

*Based on Sylvia Jukes Morris, "Standing by Her Man" (a review of Carl S. Anthony's *Florence Harding: The First Lady, the Jazz Age, and the Death of America's Most Scandalous President*, New York: Morrow), *The Washington Post* Book World, July 5, 1998, pp. 3, 11.

Additional Resources

Barnett, H. (1998). *Maintaining the self in communication: Concept and guidebook.* Novato, CA: Alpha and Omega. A book on self-awareness.

Corey, G. (1997). *I never knew I had a choice.* Pacific Grove, CA: Brooks/Cole. A book on self-awareness.

Pogrebin, L. C. (1987). The same and different: Crossing boundaries of color, culture, sexual preference, disability, and age. In J. Stewart (Ed.), *Bridges not walls* (7th ed. pp. 500–517), New York: McGraw-Hill. An article about co-cultures.

References

Argyle, M. (1969). *Social interaction.* New York: Atherton.

Baumgardner, A. H., & Levy, P. E. (1988). Role of self-esteem in perceptions of ability and effort: Illogic or insight? *Personality and Social Psychology Bulletin, 14,* 429–438.

Bell, N. J., & Carver, W. (1980). A reevaluation of gender label effects: Expectant mothers' responses to infants. *Child Development, 51,* 925–927.

DeVito, J. A. (1986). *The communication handbook: A dictionary.* New York: Harper & Row.

Maslow, A. H. (1970). *Motivation and personality* (2nd ed., pp. 35–72). New York: Harper & Row.

Mead, G. H. (1934). *Mind, self, and society.* Chicago: University of Chicago Press.

O'Connor, J. T. (1998, May 25). A view from Mount Ritter: Two weeks in the Sierras changed my attitude toward life and what it takes to succeed. *Newsweek,* p. 17.

Pearson, J. C. (1995). *Gender and communication* (3rd ed.). Madison, WI: Brown & Benchmark.

Restak, R. (1984). *The brain.* New York: Bantam Books.

Rosenthal, R., & Jacobson, L. (1968). *Pygmalion in the classroom.* New York: Holt, Rinehart and Winston.

Samovar, L. A., Porter, R. E., & Stefani, L. (1998). *Communication between cultures.* Belmont, CA: Wadsworth.

Schutz, W. (1982). *Here comes everyone* (2nd ed.). New York: Irvington.

Seegmiller, B. R. (1980). Sex typed behavior in pre-schoolers: Sex, age, and social class effects. *Journal of Psychology, 104,* 31–33.

Shaw, P. (1994, Summer). Self-esteem rises to all-time high; Test scores hit new lows. *Antioch Review,* pp. 467–474.

Singer, M. R. (1985). Culture: A perceptual approach. In L. A. Samovar & R. E. Porter (Eds.), *Intercultural communication: A reader* (4th ed.). Belmont, CA: Wadsworth.

Tibbits, S. (1975). Sex role stereotyping in the lower grades: Part of a solution. *Journal of Vocational Behavior, 6,* 255–261.

Watzlawick, P., Beavin, J. H., & Jackson, D. D. (1967). *Pragmatics of human communication: A study of interactional patterns, pathologies, and paradoxes.* New York: Norton.

Wilson, J., & Wilson, S. (Eds.). (1998). *Mass media/mass culture.* New York: McGraw-Hill.

Wood, J. T. (1997). *Communication theories in action.* Belmont, CA: Wadsworth.

Wright, R. (1994, July–August). That never really happened. *The Humanist,* pp. 30–31.

When you have read and thought about this chapter, you will be able to:

1. Define *language* and state several of its characteristics.

2. Define relevant terminology like *syntax, semantics, denotative,* and *connotative.*

3. Understand the various forms of unconventional language and how they can present a barrier to communication.

4. Use specific techniques, like paraphrasing and dating, to improve your verbal communication skills.

3

Verbal Communication

"Kind words can be short and easy to speak, but their echoes are truly endless."

MOTHER TERESA

"Tell me how much a nation knows about its own language, and I will tell you how much that nation cares about its own identity."

JOHN CIARDI

"The world of silence may be a cold and bitter one; like the deep wastes of the Arctic regions, it is fit for neither man nor beast. Holding one's tongue may be prudent, but it is an act of rejection; silence builds walls— and walls are the symbols of failure."

DON FABUN

This chapter is about the importance of language and how language functions in communication. In this chapter, you will learn about the world of language, including the definition of language and its many characteristics. Perhaps ironically, language can be an obstacle to communication. You will explore how unconventional language usage presents a barrier to communication. Finally, specific suggestions are provided for improving your verbal skills.

Nathan had his first big job interview for a sales representative position with a national computer-software company. He wanted to be certain he looked professional, so he bought a new suit and a new briefcase for the interview. He arrived for the interview early and then waited patiently in the reception area for the interviewer to come for him. When Mr. Baughman arrived, Nathan rose, shook his hand with a firm grip, and looked him directly in the eye as he said, "Nice to meet you Mr. Baughman." They sat down in Mr. Baughman's office, and the interview began.

"So, Nathan. Tell me why you're interested in a job with our company," said Mr. Baughman.

"Well, I, ah, umm . . . Like, you know Mr. Baughman. I just think it would be awesome to work for a company like this. I mean, who wouldn't want a job with this company?"

"Awesome, huh?" Mr. Baughman, surprised by Nathan's response, paused for a few moments before he posed his next question: "It says here that you'll be graduating with a business degree in May. Explain how your experiences as an undergraduate make you qualified to work as a sales representative for our company."

"Well, geez man. I mean, I've had to work on computers nearly every day for 4 years. Every paper I've done has been on a computer, and I've even used your software. I also sell some of your software at the electronics store I work at now. We sell some other stuff too, of course."

Not surprisingly, Nathan did not get the job. When one of his friends asked him what he thought went wrong, he said, "I don't know man. I just don't think we spoke the same language." While Nathan recognized the importance of looking professional, he had failed to recognize the effect his verbal communication skills would have on the interview.

What Is Language?

language

A code consisting of symbols, letters, or words with arbitrary meanings that are arranged according to the rules of syntax.

Language is *a code, a collection of symbols, letters, or words with arbitrary meanings that are arranged according to the rules of syntax and are used to communicate.* Language consists of words or symbols that represent things without being those things. The word *automobile* is a symbol for a vehicle that runs on gasoline, but it is not the vehicle itself. **Syntax** is *the way in which words are arranged to form phrases and sentences.* For example, in the English language the subject is usually placed before the verb and the object after the verb. Other languages have different rules of syntax, including reading from right to left. You **encode** by *translating your thoughts into words.* When you listen to others' verbal communication, you **decode** (*assign meaning to*) their words in order to translate them into thoughts of your own. Because language is an imperfect means of transmission, the thoughts encoded by one person never exactly match the thoughts decoded by another.

The definition above tells you that language consists of words or symbols, has rules, and is arbitrary, but the definition does not reveal some of the other important characteristics of language. Language is also representational and presentational, it is abstract, it organizes and classifies reality, and it shapes perceptions. The following is a closer look at each of these characteristics.

Language Has Rules

Language also has rules of **semantics,** *the study of the way humans use language to evoke meaning in others.* Semanticists—people who study semantics—are interested in how language and its meaning change over time. Together, syntax and semantics create meaning. For example, the declarative statement "I am going tomorrow" uses syntax to signal that someone is leaving the next day. If you change the word arrangement to "Am I going tomorrow?" the statement becomes a question and acquires a different meaning.

Language Is Arbitrary

To understand language, you need to understand how words come to have meaning. Words are *arbitrary:* They have no inherent meanings; they have only the meanings people give them. For example, in the English language one type of furry, four-legged, domesticated mammal is called a "dog." This concept is illustrated by Ogden and Richards' (1923) semantic triangle,

syntax

A set of rules about language that determines how words are arranged to form phrases and sentences.

encode

The process of translating your thoughts into words.

decode

The process of assigning meaning to others' words in order to translate them into thoughts of your own.

semantics

The branch of language study that is concerned with meaning.

53

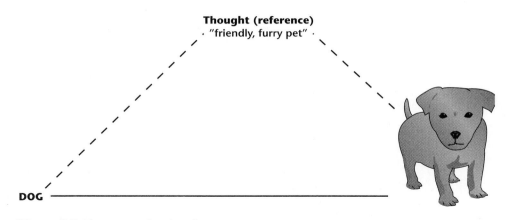

Thought (reference)
· "friendly, furry pet" ·

DOG

Figure 3.1 The semantic triangle.
SOURCE: Concept adapted from Ogden and Richards (1923).

adapted in Figure 3.1. This figure illustrates the connection between people's concept of a dog, the word *dog*, and an actual dog. When many people use a word to represent an object or idea, the word is included in the dictionary. *The agreed-upon meaning or dictionary meaning* is called the **denotative meaning.** Including a word in the dictionary, however, does not keep its meaning from changing, nor does it tell you the **connotative meaning**—*an individualized or personalized meaning that may be emotionally laden.* Connotative meanings are meanings others have come to hold because of a personal or individual experience with a word. For example, the word *love* holds vastly different meanings for people because of their unique experiences with that concept.

Language and its meaning are personal. Each person talks, listens, and thinks in a unique language (and sometimes several) that contains slight variations of its agreed-upon meanings and that may change each minute. Your personal language varies slightly from the agreed-upon meanings. It is shaped by your culture, country, neighborhood, job, personality, education, family, friends, recreation, gender, experiences, age, and other factors. The uniqueness of each individual's language provides valuable information as people attempt to achieve common meaning with each other. But because language is so personal, it can also present some difficulties in communication.

The meanings of words also vary when someone uses the same words in different contexts and situations. For example, *glasses* might mean "drinking glasses" if you are in a houseware store but most likely would mean "eyeglasses" if you are at the optometrist's. Semanticists say that meaning emerges from context. But in the case of language, context is more than just the situation in which the communication occurred: context includes the communicators' histories, relationships, thoughts, and feelings.

Language Is Representational and Presentational

Communication scholars also say that language is representational and presentational. Language is *representational* in that it represents a concrete and

denotative meaning

The agreed-upon meaning or dictionary meaning of a word.

connotative meaning

An individualized or personalized meaning of a word, which may be emotionally laden.

Think of an instance when another person's word arrangement or intended meaning created misunderstanding. What could have been done to avoid the misunderstanding?

objective reality of objects and things. For example, the word *dog* represents a concrete object. Language is also *presentational* in that it presents images, ideas, and perspectives (Stewart, 1991; Wood & Duck, 1995). For instance, if you call Tina the dog a "fat-bellied beagle," the words conjure up a certain image for someone who wants to know more about Tina the dog.

Language Is Abstract

Words are **abstractions,** or *simplifications of what they stand for.* Words stand for ideas and things, but they are not the same as those ideas and things. People who study meaning say, "The word is not the thing." Semanticist S. I. Hayakawa (1978) introduced the "ladder of abstraction," which illustrates that words fall somewhere on a continuum from concrete to abstract. Figure 3.2 shows an example of a ladder of abstraction for a dog named Tina. The words used to describe her become increasingly abstract as you go up the ladder.

abstractions

Simplifications of what words stand for.

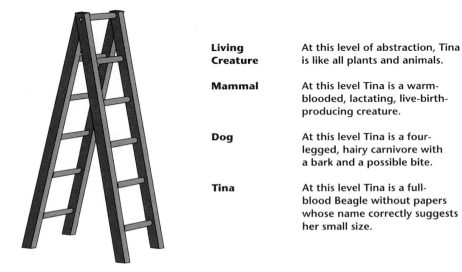

Living Creature At this level of abstraction, Tina is like all plants and animals.

Mammal At this level Tina is a warm-blooded, lactating, live-birth-producing creature.

Dog At this level Tina is a four-legged, hairy carnivore with a bark and a possible bite.

Tina At this level Tina is a full-blood Beagle without papers whose name correctly suggests her small size.

Figure 3.2 The ladder of abstraction.
SOURCE: Concept adapted from Hayakawa (1978).

Cultural Note

White people in coastal South Carolina thought the black people in their area spoke a very strange kind of English until a linguist unlocked a 200-year-old mystery. The linguist discovered, through ancient records of slave dealers, that the Gullahs—the black people of lowland, coastal Carolina—originally came from Sierra Leone in West Africa.

The reason the Gullahs' language persisted for so long when other tribal languages disappeared in America was that the Gullahs proved highly resistant to malaria, a disease that drove white slave owners inland and left the Gullahs in relative isolation.

SOURCE: *Family across the Sea,* a public television documentary produced by Educational Television of South Carolina.

Language Organizes and Classifies Reality

Because you cannot account for all the individual things in the world when you speak, you lump them into groups; thus, all four-legged pieces of furniture with seats and backs are called "chairs." Following is an example of how you might use classification when trying to identify someone in a crowd:

> "See that guy over there?"
> "Which one?"
> "The tall one."
> "The one with short brown hair?"
> "No, the heavy one with shoulder-length hair and glasses."

In this case, language is used to classify by gender, height, weight, hair color, and adornment.

Language Shapes Perceptions

Sapir-Whorf hypothesis

A theory which holds that our perception of reality is determined by our thought processes and our thought processes are limited by our language and, therefore, that language shapes our reality.

Edward Sapir and Benjamin Lee Whorf were among the first to discuss the relationship between language and perception. The **Sapir-Whorf hypothesis,** as their theory has become known, states that *our perception of reality is determined by our thought processes and our thought processes are limited by*

3.1 DEFINING LANGUAGE

Fill in the blanks:

1. _____ are interested in how language changes over time.

2. _____ meaning comes from someone's personal experience with a word.

3. The _____ _____ _____ says that our perception of reality is determined by our thought processes.

4. The way words are arranged to form phrases and sentences is called _____ .

5. The dictionary meaning is the _____ meaning.

Answers: 1. Semanticists   2. Connotative   3. Sapir-Whorf hypothesis   4. syntax   5. denotative

our language and, therefore, language shapes our reality (Whorf, 1956). Similarly, European scholars like Derrida (1974), Foucault (1980), Habermas (1984), and Lucan (1981) assume that language creates reality: that "our knowledge of the world, ourselves, and others is determined by language" (Wood, 1997, p. 366). You cannot think of your own identity without words because you are symbolically created through language. Your existence emerges through language, yet language is an inadequate means of describing you. You can describe yourself as "an Italian Roman Catholic," but those words do not describe your height, weight, age, gender, personality, IQ, ambitions, or dreams. So language creates us, but it is an inadequate means of capturing our complexities.

How Can Language Be an Obstacle to Communication?

People sometimes use language in unusual ways, and clear communication can be difficult when individuals do not follow certain language conventions. For example, people sometimes break the semantic and syntactical rules that others agree upon, replacing cultural language rules with those from a particular co-culture. At other times, more personal decisions dictate the choice of words and the structuring of them.

A co-culture can create its own language.

Unconventional Language

People in your culture and co-culture may sometimes be able to make sense of unconventional language usage; other times, language used in an unconventional way can be an obstacle to communication. Unconventional language includes grammatical errors and the use of colloquialisms, metatalk, clichés, euphemisms, slang, profanity, doublespeak, jargon, regionalisms, street language, and sexist or racist language.

Grammatical Errors

Most people do not speak as grammatically correctly as they write. For example, to hear people say, "Can I go with?" or "We're not sure which restaurant we're going to" is common, but neither of these sentences is grammatically correct. "Can I go?" "Can I go with you?" or "We're not sure to which restaurant we're going" is correct. While you may be corrected for making such mistakes in your writing, it's unlikely that you will be corrected for speaking that way. On the other hand, some grammatical errors are more obvious than others—for example, "I told him I ain't going to do it," or "Could you pass them there peanuts?" Making such errors allows people to form negative opinions about you, and grammatically incorrect speaking will be a problem when you're trying to impress someone or get a job or when you are giving a speech. Figure 3.3, on page 59, provides a brief list of some common grammatical errors.

Colloquialisms

colloquialisms

Words and phrases that are used informally.

Colloquialisms are *words and phrases used informally.* Sometimes colloquial words and phrases are unclear, particularly to someone who is a stranger to your region. International people may be particularly confused by colloquialisms. Similarly, people from other co-cultures may not understand your intended meaning. Typical examples of colloquialisms are "Have a good day," "Good to see you," "Take care now," and "See you."

Metatalk

metatalk

Talk in which meaning is not literal.

Metatalk is *talk in which meaning is not literal.* For instance, everyday phrases like "Call me," "How are you?" "Let's have lunch," and "We must get together" do not derive meaning from the words. "Call me" generally means you are too busy to talk right now, and the other person should call if he or she really needs to talk. "How are you?" is a greeting that acknowledges the

Incorrect	Correct
He (or she) don't	He (or she) doesn't
You was	You were
I done it	I did it
Between you and I	Between you and me
I been thinking	I've been thinking
I've already took algebra	I've already taken algebra
We seen it	We saw it
Him and me went	He and I went
Give me them apples	Give me those apples

Figure 3.3 Common grammatical errors.

SOURCE: Adapted from H. Gregory, *Public Speaking for College and Career,* 4th ed. New York: McGraw-Hill. Reprinted by permission of the McGraw-Hill Companies.

other person's presence; the speaker is not usually inquiring about the other person's physical or psychological health. "Let's have lunch" is typically a positive comment suggesting that the two people might get together, but only if they are both without other plans. "We must get together" is similarly positive, but the likelihood that the speaker will actively attempt to arrange a social occasion is very low. Metatalk is confusing to anyone who is not familiar with American customs.

Clichés

A **cliché** is *an expression that has lost originality and force through overuse.* Common clichés include "No pain, no gain," "Beauty is only skin deep," "One for all and all for one," and "No use crying over spilled milk." So many clichés exist that avoiding them would be impossible in your day-to-day conversations, nor is it necessary to do so. But clichés may be unclear to individuals who are unfamiliar with the underlying idea, and they are usually ineffective ways to express ideas.

cliché

An expression that has lost originality and force through overuse.

Euphemisms

Like clichés, euphemisms can confuse people who are unfamiliar with their meaning. A **euphemism** is *a more polite, pleasant expression used in place of a socially unacceptable form* (DeVito, 1986). Rothwell (1982) says euphemisms enter the language to "camouflage the naked truth" (p. 93). Most people use euphemisms in their everyday language. Euphemisms are frequently substituted for short, abrupt words, the names of physical functions, or the terms for some unpleasant social situations. Although euphemisms are frequently considered more polite than the words for which they are substituted, they distort reality. For example, you might hear people say "go to the bathroom" instead of "urinate."

euphemism

A polite, more pleasant expression used instead of a socially unacceptable form.

Slang

slang

A specialized language of a group of people who share a common interest or belong to a similar co-culture.

Slang is *a specialized language of a group of people who share a common interest or belong to a similar co-culture.* Although many people understand slang, they avoid using it in formal oral or formal written communication. Slang is temporary in nature. For example, in the 1950s, common terms used by young women and men were *scuzz* and *zilch*. In the 1960s, young people used the words *pic, groovy,* and *uptight*. In the 1970s, young people said *turkey, gross,* and *queer*. You probably know better than the authors of this book which slang terms are popular today.

Profanity

profanity

Language that is disrespectful of things sacred, commonly known as "swearing."

The word *profane* comes from a Latin word meaning "outside the temple." Thus, **profanity** is language that is disrespectful of things sacred. Certainly, some people participate in groups where profanity is normative. But when you are speaking to people outside your "group"—especially in professional interviews, work teams, or public-speaking situations—the use of profanity is an unwise choice.

Doublespeak

doublespeak

Language used to mask a reality by portraying something ugly as neutral or positive.

Doublespeak is *language that masks a reality by portraying something ugly as neutral or positive.* For example, saying a company is "downsizing" or "restructuring" masks the reality that people will be losing their jobs. Communication based on delusion allows people to ignore real human problems and avoid unpleasant situations.

Jargon

jargon

The technical language developed by a professional group.

Jargon is *the technical language developed by a professional group,* such as physicians, educators, electricians, economists, and computer operators. Some examples of jargon include *CPR, InCo, brief,* and *storyboard*. Jargon can be an efficient and effective aid in communicating with those who share an understanding of the terms. However, like slang, jargon can lead to confusion when individuals who understand such terms attempt communication with those who do not.

TRY ◄►THIS

Make a list of the jargon used in your area of study or in a job you have or have had in the past. Ask a friend to do the same. Do you know what the words on your friend's list mean? Can he or she determine what the words on your list mean?

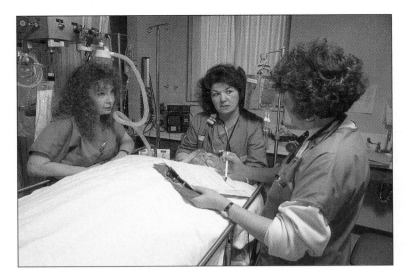

Nurses use technical language as part of their in-group communication systems.

Regionalisms

Regionalisms are *words and phrases specific to a particular region or part of the country*. The word *coke* in Texas has the same meaning as *soda* in New York and *pop* in Indiana. When people from different parts of the country try to talk with each other, clarity can break down.

Street Language

Street language consists of *highly informal words or phrases, often specific to one area, that are used to demonstrate unity*. "Boys in the hood" is street language for the gang in the neighborhood. Students refer to "the quad," "the green," and "the square" for parts of the campus. This kind of language unifies a group with terms that are unique to it and difficult for outsiders to interpret.

Sexist and Racist Language

Sexist language is *language that excludes individuals on the basis of gender*, and **racist language** is *language that insults a group because of its color or ethnicity*. Avoid generalizations and **stereotypes,** *beliefs, based on previously formed opinions and attitudes, that all members of a group are more or less alike.* For example, not all nurses are women, and not all doctors and lawyers are men. So rather than saying, "All attorneys and their wives are invited to the reception," you could say, "All attorneys and their spouses are invited to the reception." Try to avoid pronouns that exclude either sex. Rather than "A professor needs to read incessantly to keep up with his field," say "Professors need to read incessantly to keep up with their field." Also, avoid gender-specific compound words, like *salesman,* and gender-specific occupational

regionalisms

Words and phrases that are specific to a particular region or part of the country.

street language

Language that consists of highly informal words or phrases, often specific to one area, that are used to demonstrate unity.

sexist language

Language that excludes individuals on the basis of gender.

racist language

Language that insults a group because of its color or ethnicity.

stereotypes

Beliefs, based on previously formed opinions and attitudes, that all members of a group are more or less alike.

titles when the gender is irrelevant. For example, instead of "Our clergyman is a great fisherman," say "Our pastor is a great angler."

Most people have a good idea of what racist language is. Rather than using racist language, call people what they want to be called. White people should not decide what black people should be called, and straight people should not decide what gay and lesbian individuals should be called.

To note that the names for different kinds of language are not mutually exclusive is important; that is, a particular expression could fit in more than one category. Can you see how this brief sentence could be a colloquialism, a cliché, metatalk, and perhaps even a regionalism—"How's it going?" Nonetheless, these categories provide a vocabulary you can use to describe the language you hear every day.

TRY◀▶THIS

Think of words you could use in place of those that are gender-specific, such as anchorman, chairman, congressman, forefathers, freshman, housewife, handyman, *and* mankind.

How Can Language Skills Be Improved?

Words need not be obstacles to communication. You can make specific changes in your language usage that will help you become a more effective communicator. Three suggestions are to be descriptive, to be concrete, and to differentiate between observation and inference. Before examining those changes, two notes of caution are in order.

First, you are limited in your language changes by factors you do not always understand or control. Before reading this chapter, you may have been unaware of all the influences—such as your culture, co-culture, religion, gender, and neighborhood—on language. Even now, you may be influenced by factors of which you are unaware. For example, earlier in the chapter you learned that language shapes perception. But the intimate relationship between language and perception also creates difficulties for people in changing their language and, simultaneously, in changing their perceptions.

Second, when experimenting with new language behavior, you should consider the purpose of your former behavior and the purpose of your new verbal patterns. Sometimes ambiguous, colloquial, or distorted language serves an important purpose for an individual. You may use such terminology to protect yourself—to establish a healthy self-concept or to maintain a distorted self-concept; to deny self-awareness or to gain time to develop self-

3.2 LANGUAGE BARRIERS

Write T *for true or* F *for false in each blank on the left:*

_____1. Most people do not speak grammatically correctly all the time.

_____2. Metatalk is language in which the meaning is literal.

_____3. Calling the same object a "bubbler" in one part of the United States and a "water fountain" in another part of the country is an example of street language.

_____4. "I don't got none of that" is grammatically correct.

_____5. Euphemisms are polite words used as substitutes for socially unacceptable words.

Answers: 1. T   2. F   3. F   4. F   5. T

awareness. You may also use such forms to protect others—to help them maintain a selective view of reality, to help them distort their world, or to help them acknowledge successes or deny difficulties. A "gifted child" may feel pressure to succeed. The term *sanitation specialist* changes our perception of a "garbage man." The cliché "No pain, no gain" is verbalized to justify overstrenuous exercise.

Your choice of language provides information to others about how you see yourself, how you see others, and what relationships you believe exist between yourself and others. You may relax around friends and use language deemed "inappropriate" by your parents or coworkers. If you are being interviewed for a job, you may use language that is particular to your profession and may be careful to use correct grammar. With an intimate lover, you may use words that have special meaning. Changes in your verbal behavior must occur within the context of the situation in which you find yourself. You must consider what you wish to share with others through your language, and how clearly you wish to be known. Your prior relationships with others and your current goals in the interactions are important considerations. Understanding and sharing are the ultimate benefits of verbal clarity; you must decide the extent to which goals are important to you and which ones are possible. With these points in mind, you are ready to consider how you can improve your verbal skills.

Avoid Intentional Confusion

Some people's verbal patterns have become so habitual that the people using them no longer realize such patterns are intentionally confusing. They begin to believe that "everyone" speaks the way they do. They take comfort in their clichés. You should strive to become increasingly sensitive to your own use of empty language, ambiguities, clichés, and euphemisms. To have someone else monitor your statements and point out problem areas is often helpful. After someone else has sensitized you to your confusing phraseology, you can "take the reins in your own hands," that is, do the job yourself.

Use Descriptiveness

descriptiveness

The practice of describing observed behavior or phenomena instead of offering personal reactions or judgments.

Descriptiveness is *the practice of describing observed behavior or phenomena instead of offering personal reactions or judgments.* You can be descriptive in different ways: by checking on your perceptions, paraphrasing, using operational definitions, and defining terms.

Check Your Perceptions

One of the most common ways you can be descriptive is through simple checks on your perception. To communicate effectively with another person, you and the other person need to have a common understanding of an event that has occurred or a common definition of a particular phenomenon. You can check with another person to determine if his or her perception is the same as yours. For example, if a room feels too hot to you, you would ask, "Isn't it hot in here?" After a particularly difficult week for you, you might ask, "It's been a long week, hasn't it?" Or after an exam, you might ask, "Wasn't that test difficult?" Many disagreements occur because people do not stop to make these simple checks on their perception.

Paraphrase

paraphrasing

Restating another person's message by rephrasing the content or intent of the message.

operational definitions

Definitions that identify something by revealing how it works, how it is made, or what it consists of.

Paraphrasing can also help you improve your use of language. **Paraphrasing** is *restating the other person's message by rephrasing the content or intent of the message.* Paraphrasing is not simply repeating exactly what you heard in the same words. Paraphrasing allows the other person—the original speaker—to make corrections in case you misinterpreted what he or she said. The original speaker must actively listen to your paraphrase to determine whether you understood both the *content* and the *intent* of what he or she said.

Use Operational Definitions

Another kind of descriptiveness is using **operational definitions,** that is, *definitions that identify something by revealing how it works, how it is made, or what it consists of.* Suppose a professor's syllabus states that students will be allowed an excused absence for illness. A student spends a sleepless night studying for an exam in another course, misses class, and claims an excused absence because of illness. The student explains that she was too tired to come to class, and the professor explains that illness is surgery, injury, vomiting, diarrhea, or a very bad headache. This operational definition of illness does not please the student, but it does clarify the meaning of the term by saying what the professor defines as illness. In other examples, a cake can be operationally defined by a recipe, and a job by its description. Even abstractions become understandable when they are operationalized. Saying that someone is "romantic" does not reveal much compared with saying someone prepared a four-course dinner for you and then slow-danced with you in your living room.

Define Your Terms

Confusion can also arise when you use unusual terms or use words in a special way. If you suspect someone might misunderstand your terminology, you must define the term. In such an instance, you need to be careful not to offend the other person; simply offer a definition that is clearer than the term itself. Similarly, you need to ask others for definitions when they use words in new or unusual ways.

Be Concrete

A person whose language is **concrete** uses *statements that are specific*, rather than abstract or vague. "You have interrupted me three times when I have begun to talk. I feel as though you do not consider my point of view as important as yours" is specific. On the other hand, "You should consider my viewpoint, too," is vague.

Earlier in the chapter, semanticists were briefly mentioned. Count Alfred Korzybski started the field of *general semantics* with the noble purpose of improving human behavior through the careful use of language. The general semanticists' contribution includes the use of more precise, concrete language to facilitate the transmission and reception of symbols as accurately as possible. They encouraged practices that make language more certain to engender shared meanings. Two such concepts are dating and indexing.

concrete language
Words and statements that are specific rather than abstract or vague.

Dating

Dating is *specifying when you made an observation, which is necessary because everything changes over time.* Often, you view objects, people, or situations as remaining the same. You form a judgment or point of view about a person, an idea, or a phenomenon, and you maintain that view even though the person, idea, or phenomenon may have changed. Dating is the opposite of *frozen evaluation*, in which you do not allow your assessment to change over time. When using dating, instead of saying something is always or

dating
Specifying when you made an observation, since everything changes over time.

COMMUNICATION CHALLENGE

Practicing Concreteness

To gain some practice in being concrete, rewrite each statement below to make it more specific, to date the statement, or to index it. (For instance, if you were given the statement "I don't like algebra," you would date it by stating, "I don't like the algebra course I have this semester." If you were asked to index the statement, you might write, "I don't like the algebra course taught by Professor Smith." If you were asked to make the statement more specific, you might write either of the previous alternatives or something such as "I don't like the algebra course required at this university.")

1. I love the *Today* show.

Dated alteration: _____

2. My mom is my friend.

Indexed alteration: _____

3. My roommate never listens to me.

More specific alteration: _____

4. My boyfriend is hard to get along with.

Dated alteration: _____

5. Where's my book?

More specific alteration: _____

universally a certain way, you state *when* you made your judgment and clarify that your perception was based on that experience.

For example, if you took a course with a particular instructor 2 years ago, any judgment you make about the course and the instructor must be qualified as to time. You may tell someone, "English 101 with Professor Jones is a breeze," but that judgment may no longer be true. Or suppose you went out with someone a year ago, and now your friend is thinking about going out with him. You might say he is quiet and withdrawn, but that may no longer be accurate: Time has passed, the situation is different, and the person you knew may have changed. You can prevent communication problems by saying "English 101 with Professor Jones was a breeze for me when I took it in 1998," or "Joe seemed quiet and withdrawn when I dated him last year, but I haven't seen him since."

3.3 IMPROVING LANGUAGE SKILLS

Fill in the blanks:

1. The practice of describing observed behavior is _____.

2. Rephrasing the content or intent of a message is _____.

3. _____ means specifying when an observation was made.

4. _____ are conclusions drawn from observations.

5. _____ is identifying the uniqueness of objects, events, and people.

Answers: 1. descriptiveness 2. paraphrasing 3. Dating 4. Inferences 5. Indexing

Indexing

Indexing is *identifying the uniqueness of objects, events, and people.* It is simply recognizing the differences among the various members of a group. Stereotyping, which was defined earlier in the chapter, is the opposite of indexing. For people to assume that the characteristics of one member of a group apply to all members of a group is common. For example, you might assume that because you have a good communication instructor, all instructors in the department are exceptional, but that may not be the case. Indexing can help you avoid such generalizations. You could say, "I have a great communication instructor. What is yours like?" Instead of a statement such as "Hyundais get good gas mileage—I know, I own one," which is a generalization about all Hyundais based on only one, try "I have a Hyundai that uses very little gas. How does your Hyundai do on gas mileage?" Rather than "Firstborn children are more responsible than their younger brothers or sisters," try using indexing: "My older brother is far more responsible than I. Is the same true of your older brother?"

indexing

Identifying the uniqueness of objects, events, and people.

Differentiate between Observations and Inferences

Another way to improve language practice is to discern between observations and inferences. **Observations** are *descriptions of what is sensed;* **inferences** are *conclusions drawn from observations.* For example, during the day you make observations as to where objects in a room are placed. However, during the night when you walk through the room, although you cannot see where

observations

Descriptions of what is sensed.

inferences

Conclusions drawn from observations.

the objects are placed, you conclude that they are still where they were during the day and you are able to walk through the room without running into anything. You have no problem with this kind of simple exchange of an inference for an observation—unless someone has moved the furniture or placed a new object in the room or unless your memory is inaccurate. Even simple inferences can be wrong. Many shins have been bruised because someone relied on inference rather than observation.

Summary

This chapter explores the world of language use in communication. Language is a code, a collection of symbols, letters, or words with arbitrary meanings that are arranged according to the rules of syntax and are used to communicate. Language consists of words or symbols that represent something without being that thing. Language also has rules of semantics, is arbitrary, is representational and presentational, organizes and classifies reality, is abstract, and shapes perceptions.

People sometimes use language in unconventional ways, which can present a barrier to communication. Examples of unconventional language described in the chapter are grammatical errors, clichés, euphemisms, slang, profanity, doublespeak, jargon, colloquialisms, metatalk, regionalisms, street language, and sexist and racist language.

People sometimes have limited success in improving verbal skills because they are unaware of the factors that affect language or they cannot control those factors. Nonetheless, you can change and improve your use of language. The first way you can use language to communicate more effectively is by avoiding intentional confusion. Second, be more descriptive; this includes checking your perceptions, paraphrasing, using operational definitions, and defining your terms. Third, try to be more concrete by using methods such as dating and indexing. The fourth way you can use language to improve your verbal skills is by differentiating between observations and inferences.

Issues in Communication

This Issues in Communication narrative is designed to provoke individual thought or discussion about concepts raised in the chapter.

If you have not read Mark Twain's *The Adventures of Huckleberry Finn,* you have certainly heard of it. According to the American Library Association, no book has been censored by more school systems than *Huckleberry Finn.* One of the main reasons for the censorship is the 215 times that Twain uses the word *nigger* in the novel.

Of course, Twain was writing about a time in America's history when that word, now forbidden, was more commonly used, and when black and white people were separate and unequal. In case you haven't read the book, you should know that the theme of the novel is positive: Young Huck learns that Jim, a runaway slave, is the only person he can trust. Jim is portrayed as a fine human being; Huck's father is negatively portrayed. Nonetheless, the schools that have censored the book have done so because of the use of the forbidden word.

A lawsuit that emerged from this controversy is *Kathy Monteiro* v. *The Tempe Union High School District.* Kathy Monteiro is an African-American mother of a 14-year-old girl (Huck Finn's age in the book), a ninth-grader who, with her classmates, was assigned to read Twain's book. Monteiro argued that her daughter suffered psychological damage because the book created a hostile environment. Apparently, after students read the book, racial hostility toward Monteiro's daughter and other black children increased, as did the use of the racial slur. The school district was notified of the problem, but it did nothing. So Monteiro filed suit.

Judge Stephen Reinhardt of the 9th Circuit Court of Appeals wrote the decision for the three-judge panel that heard the case. The decision came to two conclusions. The first was that "it is simply not the role of the courts to serve as literary censors or to make judgments as to whether reading particular books does students more harm than good." Therefore, courts cannot "ban books or other literary works from school curricula on the basis of their content . . . even when the words are accused of being racist." So the school district's decision to keep the book in the classroom was upheld, but that decision is not the end of the story.

The second conclusion of the opinion ruled—for the first time in a federal court—that the parent, Kathy Monteiro, did have a case against the school system for the students' racial harassment, which the school system failed to stop. The claim falls under Title VII of the Civil Rights Act of 1964, which states: "No person in the United States shall, on the ground of race, color, or national origin . . . be subject to discrimination under any program or activity receiving federal financial assistance." In other words, the three-judge panel did not find Twain's book at fault, but it did find the school system at fault for ignoring the plight of black students subjected to harassment because of their race.

Judge Reinhardt wrote, "It goes without saying that being called a 'nigger' by your white peers (or hearing that term applied to your black classmates) exposes black children to a 'risk of discrimination' that is so substantial and obvious that a failure to act can only be the result of deliberate indifference." Finally, the judge ruled, "We reject the notion that putting books on trial is the proper way to determine the appropriateness of their use in the classroom."*

Apply what you have learned about language as you ponder and discuss the following questions: How can people with entirely different experiences create different meanings for the same word? Can you think of an instance in which your experiences have created a meaning that was different from the intended meaning? Who should be the judge of whether or not words inflict psychological damage? Do you agree with the judge's decision? Why or why not?

*Based on Nat Hentoff, "Huck's Narrow Escape," *The Washington Post*, Nov. 28, 1998, p. A23. The quotes from the judges' decision and the Civil Rights Act are from the same article.

Additional Resources

Cragan, J. F., & Shields, D. C. (Eds.). (1995). *Symbolic theories in applied communication research:* Bormann, Burke and Fisher.

Cresskill, NJ: Hampton Press.

Hecht, M. L. (Ed.). (1998). *Communicating prejudice.* Thousand Oaks, CA: Sage.

Taylor, A., Hardman, M. J. (Eds.) (1998). *Hearing muted voices.* Cresskill, NJ: Hampton Press.

References

Derrida, J. (1974). *Of grammatology* (G. Spivak, Trans.). Baltimore: Johns Hopkins Press.

DeVito, J. A. (1986). *The communication handbook: A dictionary.* New York: Harper & Row.

Foucault, M. (1980). *Power/knowledge: Selected interviews and other writings:*

1972–1977 (C. Gordon, Ed.). Brighton, UK: Harvester.

Habermas, J. (1984). *The theory of communicative action. Vol. 1: Reason and the rationalization of society* (T. McCarthy, Trans.). Boston: Beacon.

Hayakawa, S. I. (1978). *Language in thought and action.* Orlando, FL: Harcourt Brace Jovanovich.

Lucan, J. (1981). *The four fundamental concepts of psychoanalysis.* London: Penguin.

Ogden, C. K., & Richards, I. A. (1923). *The meaning of meaning: A study of the influence of language upon thought and of the science of symbolism.* New York: Harcourt Brace and World.

Rothwell, J. D. (1982). *Telling it like it isn't: Language misuse and malpractice/What we can do about it.* Englewood Cliffs, NJ: Prentice Hall.

Stewart, J. (1991). A postmodern look at traditional communication postulates. *Western*

Journal of Speech Communication, 55, 354–379.

Whorf, B. L. (1956). Science and linguistics. In J. B. Carroll (Ed.), *Language, thought and reality* (pp. 207–219). Cambridge, MA: M. I. T. Press.

Wood, J. T., (1997). *Communication theories in action.* Belmont, CA: Wadsworth.

Wood, J. T. & Duck, S. (1995). Off the beaten track: New shores for relationship research. In J. T. Wood & S. Duck (Eds.), *Understanding relationship processes: Vol. 6. Understudied relationships: Off the beaten track* (pp. 1–21). Thousand Oaks, CA: Sage.

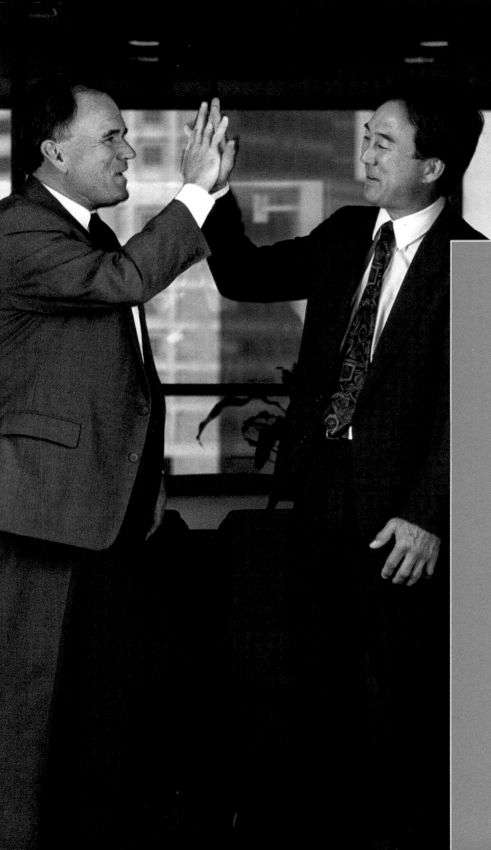

When you have read and thought about this chapter, you will be able to:

1. Identify three problems people have in interpreting nonverbal codes.

2. Define and identify nonverbal codes.

3. Recognize the types of bodily movement in nonverbal communication.

4. State the factors that determine the amount of personal space you use.

5. State the factors that influence the meaning and use of touch.

6. Understand how objects are used in nonverbal communication.

7. Utilize strategies for improving your nonverbal communication.

4

Nonverbal Communication

> **"A smile is the shortest distance between two people."**
>
> VICTOR BORGE

> **"You cannot shake hands with a clenched fist."**
>
> INDIRA GANDHI

> **"When one is pretending, the entire body revolts."**
>
> ANAIS NIN

This chapter focuses on the role of nonverbal codes in communication. The chapter first looks at the problems that can occur in interpreting nonverbal codes. Next, some of the major nonverbal codes are identified and defined, including kinesics, proxemics, tactile communication, paralinguistic features, and objectics. If these terms are not familiar to you now, by the time you finish this chapter they will be both familiar and useful. The chapter concludes with a discussion of some solutions to the problems you might encounter in interpreting nonverbal codes.

On any given weekday, most high school students gather together to talk to each other between classes. Marla and her friends are no exception. Their discussions are often animated, and they touch each other occasionally when one person is speaking to another. You can tell when they're talking about something serious or personal because their voices drop, they gather more closely together, and their eyes occasionally dart suspiciously at others outside of their group. Marla and her friends dress alike (they often borrow each other's clothing), and even their hairstyles are similar.

As they stand together talking to each other, someone occasionally approaches the group. Today, Sam, a boy Marla has been seeing, approaches the group. Marla immediately stops talking and moves away from the group and towards Sam. Marla and Sam begin conversing with each other. Sam keeps his baseball-cap-covered head down, they speak in quiet tones, and they do not touch each other. Marla looks at the top of his head intently as he speaks, apparently trying to establish some sort of eye contact. Twice, she moves closer to him, but she maintains enough distance that they never physically touch each other. After Sam leaves, Marla's friends gather around her, asking her what she and Sam will be doing this weekend. "I have no idea," she replies. "I don't know if he even wants to go out with me again. I just can't read him."

Nonverbal communication often says much more than people realize. This chapter will help you make sense of the most common nonverbal codes, as well as provide you with some suggestions for improving your nonverbal communication.

Why Are Nonverbal Codes Difficult to Interpret?

Nonverbal communication is responsible for much of the misunderstanding that occurs during communication. Just as people have difficulty interpreting verbal symbols, so do they struggle to interpret nonverbal codes. Three reasons for this difficulty are: often people use the same code to communicate a variety of meanings, they use a variety of codes to communicate the same meaning, and people have different interpretations of the purpose of nonverbal codes.

One Code Communicates a Variety of Meanings

Examples of situations in which one code communicates a variety of different meanings will clarify this problem. The nonverbal code of raising your right hand may mean that you are taking an oath, you are demonstrating for a cause, you are indicating to an instructor that you would like to answer a question, a physician is examining your right side, or you want a taxi to stop for you. You may stand close to someone because of a feeling of affection, because the room is crowded, or because you have difficulty hearing. You may speak softly because you were taught that softly is the "correct" way for you to speak, because you are suffering from a sore throat, or because you are sharing a secret. You may wear khaki pants because they are an acceptable mode of dress, because they symbolize your rebellion against higher-priced clothing, or because they are the only clothes you have that are clean that day.

A Variety of Codes Communicate the Same Meaning

One example of different nonverbal codes that communicate the same meaning is the many nonverbal ways by which adults communicate love or affection. You may sit or stand more closely to someone you love. You might speak more softly, use a certain vocal intonation, or alter how quickly you speak when you communicate with someone with whom you are affectionate. Or perhaps you may choose to dress differently when you are going to be in the company of someone you love.

Interpretations of Intentionality Vary

Intentionality, or *the purposefulness of nonverbal codes* (Malandro, Barker, & Barker, 1989), has four possible interpretations. One possibility is *intentional nonverbal communication interpreted as intentional,* such as when you hug a friend. The hug is nonverbal, purposeful, and perceived as an intended message: I am so glad to see you. In this case, no misunderstanding occurs.

Another possibility is *an intentional code misperceived as having another intention,* such as when a man is reading the message printed on a woman's T-shirt and she covers her chest and quickly turns away. The reading of the shirt, a nonverbal code, is perceived as intentional lust. A third possibility is *an unintentional code perceived as intentional,* such as when someone forgets that the turn signal is on and another driver thinks that person intends to turn. A fourth possibility is *a code sent and received unintentionally,* such as when a man accidentally leaves a price tag on a new tie or a person wears mismatched socks. The code is noticed, but it is perceived as unintentional and discounted as meaningless.

In the study of nonverbal communication, the focus is on intentional nonverbal codes.

intentionality
The purposefulness of nonverbal codes.

What Are Nonverbal Codes?

Nonverbal codes are *codes of communication consisting of symbols that are not words, including nonword vocalizations.* Bodily movement, facial expression, the use of space, touching, vocal cues, and clothing and other artifacts are all nonverbal codes. Let us consider these systematic arrangements of symbols that have been given arbitrary meaning and are used in communication.

nonverbal codes
Codes consisting of symbols that are not words, including nonword vocalizations.

Cultural Note

Chinese, Japanese, and Koreans bow, and Thais bow their heads while holding their hands in a prayerlike position. The *bumi putra,* or Muslim Malaysians, have a greeting of their own: They shake hands as westerners do, but they follow up by touching their heart with their right hand to indicate that they are greeting you "from the heart."

Bodily Movement and Facial Expression

kinesics

The study of bodily movements, including posture, gestures, and facial expressions.

The study of posture, movement, gestures, and facial expression is called **kinesics,** a word derived from the Greek word *kinesis,* meaning movement. Some popular books purport to teach you how to "read" nonverbal communication so that you will know, for example, who is sexually aroused, who is just kidding, and whom you should avoid. Nonverbal communication, however, is more complicated than that. Interpreting the meaning of nonverbal communication is partly a matter of assessing the other person's unique behavior and considering the context. You don't just "read" another person's body language; instead, you observe, analyze, and interpret before you decide the probable meaning.

Assessing another person's unique behavior means that you need to know how that person usually acts. A quiet person might be unflappable even in an emergency situation. A person who never smiles may not be unhappy, and someone who acts happy might not actually be happy. You need to know how the person expresses emotions before you can interpret what his or her nonverbal communication means.

Considering the context means that the situation alters how you interpret nonverbal communication. Many people get talkative, candid, and sometimes stupid when they drink alcoholic beverages. Finding someone excessively friendly at a long party might be more attributable to the proof of the drinks than to anything else. People tend to be formally polite at ceremonies, emotionally unguarded in their homes, and excessively prudent when applying for a job.

To look more deeply into interpreting nonverbal communication, let us consider the work of some experts on the subject: Albert Mehrabian, Paul Ekman, and Wallace Friesen.

Mehrabian (1971) studied nonverbal communication by examining the concepts of liking, status, and responsiveness among the participants in communication situations.

NONVERBAL COMMUNICATION ON THE WEB

For some additional information on nonverbal communication, try contacting the Communication Institute for Online Scholarship (CIOS) by using any search engine and the key word, *nonverbal.*

1. *Liking* was often expressed by leaning forward, a direct body orientation (e.g., standing face to face), close proximity, increased touching, relaxed posture, open arms and body, positive facial expression, and eye contact (i.e., looking directly at the other person). For example, look at how a group of males act when drinking beer and watching a game on television, or watch newly matched couples in the spring.
2. *Status,* especially high status, is communicated nonverbally by bigger gestures, relaxed posture, and less eye contact. Male bosses sometimes put their feet up on their desks when talking to subordinates, but subordinates rarely act that way when talking to their boss.
3. *Responsiveness* in nonverbal communication is exhibited by moving toward the other person, by spontaneous gestures, by shifting posture and position, and by facial expressiveness. In other words, the face and body provide positive feedback to the other person.

Ekman and Friesen (1969) categorized movement on the basis of its functions, origins, and meanings. Their five categories include emblems, illustrators, affect displays, regulators, and adaptors.

1. *Emblems* are movements that substitute for words and phrases. Examples of emblems are a beckoning first finger to mean "come here," an open hand held up to mean "stop," and a forefinger and thumb together to mean "OK." Be wary of emblems; they may mean something else in another culture.
2. *Illustrators* accompany or reinforce verbal messages. Examples of illustrators are nodding your head when you say yes, shaking your head when you say no, stroking your stomach when you say you are hungry, and shaking your fist in the air when you say, "Get out of here." These nonverbal cues tend to be more universal than many of the other four categories of movement.
3. *Affect displays* are movements of the face and body used to show emotion. Watch people's behavior when their favorite team wins a game, listen to the door slam shut when an angry person leaves the

Instant Recall

room, and watch men make threatening moves when they are very upset with each other but don't dare fight openly.

4. *Regulators* are nonverbal moves that control the flow or pace of communication. Examples of regulators are starting to move away when you want the conversation to stop, looking at the floor or looking away when you are disinterested, or yawning and looking at your watch when you are bored.

5. *Adaptors* are movements that you might perform fully in private but only partially in public. For example, you might rub your nose in public, but you would probably never pick it.

Finally, Ekman and Friesen (1967) determined that a person's facial expressions provide information to others about how he or she feels, whereas the person's body orientation suggests how intensely he or she feels. Put facial expression and body orientation together, and your interpretation of nonverbal messages will become more accurate.

To illustrate the importance of nonverbal communication, consider the finding that audiences who can see the speaker understand more of the message than audiences who cannot see the speaker (Kramer & Lewis, 1951). Apparently, bodily movement and facial expression increase the ability to interpret meaning.

Space

Anthropologist Edward T. Hall (1966) introduced the concept of **proxemics,** *the study of the human use of space,* in his book *The Hidden Dimension.* This researcher and others, such as Werner (1987), have demonstrated the role space plays in human communication. Two concepts considered essential to the study of the use of space are territoriality and personal space:

proxemics

The study of the human use of space and distance.

1. *Territoriality* refers to your need to establish and maintain certain spaces as your own. In a shared dormitory room, the items on the common desk area mark the territory. On a cafeteria table, the placement of the plate, glass, napkin, and eating utensils marks the territory. In a neighborhood, it might be fences, hedges, trees, or rocks that mark the territory. All are nonverbal indicators that signal ownership.

2. *Personal space* is the personal "bubble" of space that moves around with you. It is the distance you maintain between yourself and others, the amount of room you claim as your own. Large people usually claim more space because of their size, and men often take more space than women. For example, in a lecture hall, observe who claims the armrests as part of their personal bubbles.

Hall (1966) was the first to define the four distances people regularly use while they communicate. His categories have been helpful in understanding the communicative behavior that might occur when two communicators are a particular distance from each other. Beginning with the closest contact and the least personal space, and moving to the greatest distance, Hall's four categories are intimate distance, personal distance, social distance, and public distance.

1. *Intimate distance* extends from you outward to 18 inches, and it is used by people who are relationally close to you. Used more often in private than in public, this intimate distance is employed to show affection, to give comfort, and to protect. Graves & Robinson (1976) and Burgoon (1978) say that intimate distance usually shows positive response because individuals tend to stand and sit close to people to whom they are attracted.

2. *Personal distance* ranges from 18 inches to 4 feet, and it is the distance used by most Americans for conversation and other nonintimate exchanges.

3. *Social distance* ranges from 4 to 12 feet, and it is used most often to carry out business in the workplace, especially in formal, less personal situations. The higher the status of one person, the greater the distance.

4. *Public distance* exceeds 12 feet and is used most often in public speaking in such settings as lecture halls; churches, mosques, and synagogues; courtrooms; and convention halls. Professors often stand at this distance while lecturing.

Distance, then, is a nonverbal means of communicating everything from the size of your personal bubble to your relationship with the person to whom you are speaking or listening. In fact, sex, size, and similarity seem to be among the important determiners of your personal space.

According to Argyle and Dean (1965), men tend to take more space because they are often bigger. Women take less space, and children take and are given the least space. Research by Addis (1966), Leventhal and Matturro (1980), and Snyder and Endelman (1979) shows that women exhibit less discomfort with small space and tend to interact at closer range. Perhaps because women are so often given little space, they come to expect it. Also, women and children in our society seem to desire more relational closeness than do men.

Your relationship to other people is related to your use of space (Guardo, 1969). You stand closer to friends and farther from enemies. You stand farther from strangers, authority figures, high-status people, physically challenged people, and people from racial groups different from your own. You stand closer to people you perceive as similar or unthreatening because closeness communicates trust.

The physical setting also can alter the use of space. People tend to stand closer together in large rooms and farther apart in small rooms according to Sommer (1962). In addition, physical obstacles and furniture arrangements can affect the use of personal space.

TRY ◄ ► THIS

Next time you go to a party, notice how the size of the room and the seating arrangement affect the way people are grouped and how they communicate.

The cultural background of the people communicating also must be considered in the evaluation of personal space. Hall (1963) was among the first to recognize the importance of cultural background when he was training American service personnel for service overseas. He wrote:

> Americans overseas were confronted with a variety of difficulties because of cultural differences in the handling of space. People stood "too close" during conversations, and when the Americans backed away to a comfortable conversational distance, this was taken to mean that Americans were cold, aloof, withdrawn, and disinterested in the people of the country. USA housewives

4.2 PROXEMICS AND COMMUNICATION

Fill in the blanks:

1. Personal space is the _____ people maintain between themselves and others.

2. _____ people and _____ tend to claim more personal space.

3. The study of the human use of space is known as _____.

4. _____ is the need to establish and maintain certain spaces as our own.

5. _____ distance is used most often in the workplace.

6. Most Americans maintain _____ distance when engaging in conversation.

Answers: 1. distance   2. Large/men   3. proxemics   4. Territoriality   5. Social   6. personal

muttered about "waste-space" in houses in the Middle East. In England, Americans who were used to neighborliness were hurt when they discovered that their neighbors were no more accessible or friendly than other people, and in Latin America, exsuburbanites, accustomed to unfenced yards, found that the high walls there made them feel "shut out." Even in Germany, where so many of my countrymen felt at home, radically different patterns in the use of space led to unexpected tensions. (Hall, 1963, p. 422)

Cultural background can result in great differences in the use of space and in people's interpretation of such use. As our world continues to shrink, more people will be working in multinational corporations, regularly traveling to different countries, and interacting with others from a variety of backgrounds. Sensitivity to space use in different cultures and quick, appropriate responses to those variations are imperative.

TRY ◀▶ THIS

Purposefully overstep someone's personal space and watch his or her reaction. Does the person become uncomfortable, move back, or not even notice?

Touching

tactile communication

The use of touch in communication.

Tactile communication is *the use of touch in communication.* Because touch always involves invasion of another's personal space, it commands attention. It can be welcome, as when a crying child is held by a parent, or unwelcome, as in sexual harassment, and our need for and appreciation of tactile communication starts early in life. Schutz (1971) observed:

> The unconscious parental feelings communicated through touch or lack of touch can lead to feelings of confusion and conflict in a child. Sometimes a "modern" parent will say all the right things but not want to touch the child very much. The child's confusion comes from the inconsistency of levels: if they really approve of me so much like they say they do, why don't they touch me? (p. 16)

Montagu (1971) points out that insufficient touching can lead to health disorders, such as allergies and eczema, speech problems, and even death. Researchers have found that untouched babies and small children can grow increasingly ill and die.

For adults, touch is a powerful means of communication (Fromme et al., 1989). Usually, touch is perceived as positive, pleasureful, and reinforcing.

Touch is a form of communication that is essential to our growth and development.

The association of touch with the warmth and caring that began in infancy carries over into adulthood. People who are comfortable with touch are more likely to be satisfied with their past and current lives. They are self-confident, assertive, socially acceptable, and active in confronting problems.

Touch is part of many important rituals. In baptism, the practice in many churches is as little as a touch on the head during the ceremony to as much as a total immersion in water. Prayers in some churches are said with the pastor's hand touching the person being prayed for. In fundamentalist Christian churches, the healer might accompany the touch with a mighty shove, right into the hands of two catchers. Physician Bernie Siegel (1990) wrote the following in his book on mind-body communication:

> I'd like to see some teaching time devoted to the healing power of touch—a subject that only 12 of 169 medical schools in the English-speaking world deal with at all . . . despite the fact that touch is one of the most basic forms of communication between people. . . . We need to teach medical students how to touch people. (p. 134)

Religion and medicine are just two professions in which touch is important for ceremonial and curative purposes.

TRY◀▶THIS

Think about how you use nonverbal communication. Are you comfortable touching and being touched? Do you frequently hug others or shake hands with others? Why or why not?

Touch varies within each co-culture. The findings relating touch with gender indicate that:

◆ Women value touch more than men do (Fisher, Rytting, & Heslin, 1976).

◆ Women are touched more than men from the sixth month on (Clay, 1968; Goldberg & Lewis, 1969).

◆ Women touch female children more often than they touch male children (Clay, 1968; Goldberg & Lewis, 1969).

◆ Men and their sons touch each other the least (Jourard & Rubin, 1968).

◆ Female students are touched more and in more places than are male students (Jourard, 1966).

◆ Males touch others more than females touch others (Henley, 1973–1974).

◆ Males may use touch to indicate power or dominance (Henley, 1973–1974).

On this last point, to observe who can touch whom among people in the workplace is interesting. Although fear of being accused of sexual harassment has stopped nearly all touch except for handshaking, the general nonverbal principle is that the higher-status individual gets to initiate touch, but touch is not reciprocal: The president might pat you on the back for a job well done, but in our society you don't pat back.

Further, both co-culture and culture determine the frequency and kind of nonverbal communication. People from different countries handle nonverbal communication differently—even something as simple as touch. Sidney Jourard (1968) determined the rates of touch per hour among adults from various cultures. In a coffee shop, adults in San Juan, Puerto Rico, touched 180 times per hour, while those in Paris, France, touched about 110 times per hour, followed by those in Gainesville, Florida, who touched about 2 times per hour, and those in London, England, who touched only once per hour. A more recent study indicates that North Americans are more frequent touchers than are the Japanese (Barnlund, 1975).

Touch sends such a powerful message that it has to be handled with responsibility. When the right to touch is abused, it can result in a breach of

Instant Recall

Write the correct letter from the choices below in each blank:

A. Women   **B. Men**   **C. Sons**   **D. Daughters**

1. _____ value touch more than _____ do.

2. _____ are more likely to use touch to indicate dominance.

3. _____ and their _____ touch each other the least.

4. _____ touch daughters more than they touch _____.

5. _____ students are touched more than _____ students.

Answers: 1. A, B   2. B   3. B, C   4. A, C   5. A, B

trust, anxiety, and hostility. When touch is used to communicate concern, caring, and affection, it is welcome, desired, and appreciated.

Vocal Cues

paralinguistic features

The nonword sounds and nonword characteristics of language, such as pitch, volume, rate, and quality.

vocal cues

All the oral aspects of sound except words themselves; part of paralinguistic features.

Nonverbal communication does include some sounds, as long as they are not words. We call them **paralinguistic features,** *the nonword sounds and nonword characteristics of language, such as pitch, volume, rate, and quality.* The prefix *para* means "alongside" or "parallel to," so *paralinguistic* means "alongside the words or language."

The paralinguistic feature examined here is **vocal cues,** *all the oral aspects of sound except words themselves.* Vocal cues include:

◆ *Pitch:* the highness or lowness of your voice.

◆ *Rate:* how rapidly or slowly you speak.

◆ *Inflection:* the variety or changes in pitch.

◆ *Volume:* the loudness or softness of your voice.

◆ *Quality:* the unique resonance of your voice, such as huskiness, nasality, raspiness, and whininess.

◆ *Sounds and silence:* such nonword sounds as *mmh, huh,* and *ahh* and pauses or absence of sound used for effect in speaking.

◆ *Pronunciation:* whether or not you say a word correctly.

◆ *Articulation:* whether or not your mouth, tongue, and teeth coordinate to make a word understandable to others (for example, a lisp).

◆ *Enunciation:* whether or not you combine pronunciation and articulation to produce a word with clarity and distinction so it can be understood. A person who mumbles has an enunciation problem.

These vocal cues are important because they are linked in our minds with a speaker's physical characteristics, emotional state, personality characteristics, gender characteristics, and even credibility.

According to Kramer (1963), vocal cues frequently convey information about the speaker's characteristics, such as age, height, appearance, and body type. For example, people often associate a high-pitched voice with someone who is female; someone who is younger; and someone who is smaller, rather than larger. You may visualize someone who uses a loud voice as being tall and large or someone who speaks quickly as being nervous. People who tend to speak slowly and deliberately may be perceived as being high-status individuals, or having high credibility.

TRY◀▶THIS

When you picture people you talk to on the telephone before meeting them, does your expectation of how they will look usually turn out to be accurate? What vocal cues did they use that led to your picture of how they would look?

A number of studies have related emotional states to specific vocal cues. Joy and hate appear to be the most accurately communicated emotions, whereas shame and love are among the most difficult to communicate accurately (McCroskey, Larson, & Knapp, 1971). Joy and hate appear to be conveyed by fewer vocal cues, and this makes them less difficult to interpret than emotions such as shame and love, which are conveyed by complex sets of vocal cues. "Active" feelings such as joy and hate are associated with a loud voice, a high pitch, and a rapid rate. Conversely, "passive" feelings, which include affection and sadness, are communicated with a soft voice, a low pitch, and a relatively slow rate (Kramer, 1963).

Personality characteristics also have been related to vocal cues. Dominance, social adjustment, and sociability have been clearly correlated with specific vocal cues (Bateson et al., 1956).

Although the personality characteristics attributed to individuals displaying particular vocal cues have not been shown to accurately portray the person, as determined by standardized personality tests, our impressions affect our interactions. In other words, although you may perceive loud-voiced, high-pitched, fast-speaking individuals as dominant, they might not be measured as dominant by a personality inventory. Nonetheless, in your interactions with

> ## COMMUNICATION CHALLENGE
>
> ### Clothes Communicate!
>
> Your clothing communicates who you are, what you value, and how you see yourself. Consider the clothing and jewelry you wear and what it might communicate about you. Keep a record for 3 or 4 days of all the clothing, jewelry, and other adornments you wear. After you have compiled this record, suggest why you made these choices and what these items might communicate to others. Finally, ask two friends what your clothing communicates to them. Consider the similarities or differences between your perceptions of your clothing and the perceptions of your friends.

such people, you may become increasingly submissive because of your perception that they are dominant. In addition, these people may begin to become more dominant because they are treated as though they have this personality characteristic.

Sex differences are also related to vocal cues. Men and women demonstrate different intonational patterns. For instance, many women tend to state declarative sentences with an upward inflection to suggest a question rather than a declaration (Eakins & Eakins, 1978).

Vocal cues can help a public speaker establish credibility with an audience and can clarify the message. Pitch and inflection can be used to make the speech sound aesthetically pleasing, to accomplish subtle changes in meaning, and to tell an audience whether you are asking a question or making a statement, being sincere or sarcastic, or being doubtful or assertive. A rapid speaking rate may indicate you are confident about speaking in public or that you are nervously attempting to conclude your speech. Variations in volume can be used to add emphasis or to create suspense. Enunciation is especially important in public speaking because of the increased size of the audience and the fewer opportunities for direct feedback. Pauses can be used in a public speech to create dramatic effect and to arouse audience interest. Vocalized pauses—*ah, uh-huh, um,* and so on—are not desirable in public speaking and may distract the audience. Far better than vocalized pauses is silence. One observer noted:

> Sometimes silence is best. Words are curious things, at best approximations. And every human being is a separate language. . . . [Sometimes] silence is best. (Hardman, 1971)

Clothing and Other Artifacts

objectics

The study of the human use of clothing and other artifacts as nonverbal codes; object language.

Objectics, or *object language,* refers to *the study of the human use of clothing and other artifacts as nonverbal codes.* **Artifacts** are *ornaments or adornments*

INTERPRETING NONVERBAL COMMUNICATION

Watch an animated web site without the sound. Experts argue that much of the meaning of discourse comes not from what is said but what is seen. Can you tell what is happening, what is being expressed, and what emotions are being portrayed by sight alone? Are any individuals in your class better at "reading the nonverbal" than others are?

we display that hold communicative potential, including jewelry, hairstyles, cosmetics, automobiles, canes, watches, shoes, portfolios, hats, glasses, tatoos, body piercings, and even the fillings in teeth. Your clothing and other adornments communicate your age, gender, status, role, socioeconomic class, group memberships, personality, and relation to the opposite sex. Dresses are seldom worn by men, low-cut gowns are not the choice of shy women, bright colors are avoided by reticent people, and the most recent Paris fashion is seldom seen in the small towns of mid-America.

Clothing and other artifacts play an important role in nonverbal communication.

artifacts

Ornaments or adornments we display that hold communicative potential.

These cues also indicate the time in history, the time of day, and the climate. Clothing and artifacts provide physical and psychological protection, and they are used for sexual attraction and to indicate self-concept. Your clothing and artifacts clarify the sort of person you believe you are (Fisher, 1975). They permit personal expression (Proctor, 1978), and they satisfy your need for creative self-expression (Horn, 1975). A person who exhibits an interest in using clothing as a means of expression may be demonstrating a high level of self-actualization (Perry, Schutz, & Rucker, 1983). For example, an actress who always dresses in expensive designer dresses may be showing everyone that she is exactly what she always wanted to be.

Many studies have established a relationship between an individual's clothing and artifacts and his or her characteristics. Conforming to current styles is correlated with an individual's desire to be accepted and liked (Taylor & Compton, 1968). In addition, individuals feel that clothing is important in forming first impressions (Henricks, Kelley, & Eicher, 1968).

Perhaps of more importance are the studies that consider the relationship between clothing and an observer's perception of that person. In an early study, clothing was shown to affect others' impressions of status and personality traits (Douty, 1963). People also seem to base their acceptance of others on their clothing and artifacts. In another early study, women who were asked to describe the most popular women they knew used clothing as the most important characteristic (Williams & Eicher, 1966).

TRY ◀ ▶ THIS

Observe others' clothing and determine what their choices tell you about their personality.

What Are Some Ways to Improve Nonverbal Communication?

You can improve your use of nonverbal communication by being sensitive to context, audience, and feedback.

The *context* includes the physical setting, the occasion, and the situation. In conversation, your vocal cues are rarely a problem unless you stutter, stammer, lisp, or suffer from some speech pathology. Paralinguistic features loom large in importance in small-group communication, where you have to adapt to the distance and to a variety of receivers. These features are, perhaps, most important in public speaking because you have to adjust volume and rate, you have to enunciate more clearly, and you have to introduce more vocal variety to keep the audience's attention. The strategic use of pauses and silence is also more apparent in public speaking than it is in an interpersonal context in conversations or small-group discussion.

The *audience* makes a difference in your nonverbal communication, so you have to adapt. When speaking to children, you must use a simple vocabulary and careful enunciation, articulation, and pronunciation. With an older audience or with younger audiences whose hearing has been impaired by too much loud music, you must adapt your volume. Generally, children and older people in both interpersonal and public-speaking situations appreciate slower speech. Also, adaptation to an audience may determine your choice of clothing, hairstyle, and jewelry. For instance, a shaved head, a ring in the nose or lip, and a shirt open to the navel do not go over well in a job interview—unless you are trying for a job as an entertainer.

Your attention to giving *feedback* can be very important in helping others interpret your nonverbal cues that might otherwise distract your listeners. For example, some pregnant women avoid questions and distraction by wearing a shirt that says, "I'm not fat; I'm pregnant"; such feedback prevents listeners from wondering instead of listening. Similarly, your listener's own descriptive feedback—quizzical looks, staring, nodding off—can signal you to talk louder, introduce variety, restate your points, or clarify your message.

Summary

In this chapter you looked at the role of intentional nonverbal codes in communication. People often have difficulty interpreting nonverbal codes because they use the same code to communicate a variety of different meanings, they use a variety of codes to communicate the same meaning, and they have different interpretations of intentionality.

Nonverbal codes consist of nonword symbols. Bodily movements and facial expression, personal space, touching, vocal cues, and clothing and artifacts are nonverbal codes. Kinesics is the study of bodily movements, including posture, gestures, and facial expression. Five categories of bodily movements are emblems, illustrators, affect displays, regulators, and adaptors. Proxemics is the study of the human use of space. Territoriality—our need to establish and maintain certain spaces of our own—and personal space—the amount of physical distance people maintain between themselves and other people—are important concepts of proxemics. Tactile communication is the use of touch in communication, and it is essential to our growth and development. Vocal cues are all of the oral aspects of sound except the words themselves; they include pitch, rate, inflection, volume, quality, enunciation, specific sounds (such as *huh, ah,* and *mmh*), and silence. Objectics, or object language, is our display of material things, including hairstyles, clothing, jewelry, and cosmetics. Our object language communicates our age, gender, status, role, socioeconomic class, group memberships, personality, and relation to the opposite sex.

You can solve some of the difficulties in interpreting nonverbal codes if you consider all the variables in each communication situation, consider all the available verbal and nonverbal codes, and use descriptive feedback to minimize misunderstandings.

Issues in Communication

This Issues in Communication narrative is designed to provoke individual thought or discussion about concepts raised in the chapter.

Peter Nelson, an American, was recently faced with a 6-hour layover in Taiwan's international airport. A long layover in any airport is usually a dreadful prospect, but in this case it was particularly difficult. Passengers transferring from one flight to another were banned from the shopping area. Additionally, there was only a single vending machine and a television tuned to Airport CNN.

Peter occupied much of his time "people watching." He sat in a high balcony over an area where outgoing passengers left their loved ones to board international flights. He noticed that when Chinese couples approached the boarding gate, the partners usually looked at each other (sometimes bowing slightly) and said a few words, then parted as one entered a gate where nonpassengers were not allowed. During 2 hours of observation, only one couple—a young Chinese male and a youthful American female—actually embraced, hugged, and kissed. Otherwise, couple after couple repeated the same ritual, with the partners usually not touching each other or occasionally touching with just a quick hand on the shoulder.

A second part of the ritual became apparent to Peter only after he had watched for a while. After passengers went through the passengers-only gate, their loved ones lingered behind a glass partition where they could see the passengers standing in line to receive boarding passes. During this time, the people in line never looked back at their loved ones, even though they sometimes waited in line for 5 or 10 minutes. Only before disappearing down the corridor to the airplane would a passenger turn to wave quickly to his or her loved one waiting behind the glass. Then both would turn and leave.

Only once during the 2-hour period that Peter was watching did the routine not play out this way, and that was with the Chinese male and American female who embraced and kissed before the man entered the passengers-only gate. Just like the other people, the American woman waited behind the glass partition as her Chinese companion waited in line for his boarding pass. When he finally got his boarding pass, he waved good-bye and then disappeared swiftly down the corridor. The woman, however, lingered and watched him disappear. When she turned to leave, Peter noticed tears rolling down her face.

Apply what you have learned about nonverbal communication as you ponder and discuss the following questions: In what ways are the nonverbal codes the Chinese use to say good-bye to their loved ones in an airport different from the ways Americans say good-bye in an airport? In general, how does culture influence nonverbal communication? (If you're aware of any specific examples not included in the chapter, be sure to state those too.) Compare the nonverbal communication you use when saying good-bye to a loved one with your nonverbal communication when waiting for your flight or when chatting with someone waiting for the same flight as you.

Additional Resources

Aguinis, H., Simonsen, M. M., & Pierce, C. A. (1998). Effects of nonverbal behavior on perceptions of power bases. *Journal of Social Psychology, 138*(4), 455–475.

Andersen, P. A., Guerrero, L. K., Buller, D. B., & Jorgensen, P. F. (1998). An empirical comparison of three theories of nonverbal immediacy exchange. *Human Communi-cation Research, 24*(4), 501–536.

Bailey, W., Nowcki, S., & Cole, S. P. (1998). The ability to decode nonverbal information in African American, African and Afro-Caribbean, and European American adults. *Journal of Black Psychology, 24*(4), 418–432.

Grammer, K., Kruck, K. B., & Magnusson, M. S. (1998). The courtship dance: Patterns of nonverbal synchronization in opposite-sex encounters. *Journal of Nonverbal Behavior, 22*(1), 27.

Tucker, J. S., & Anders, S. L. (1998). Adult attachment style and nonverbal closeness in dating couples. *Journal of Nonverbal Behavior, 22*(2), 109–125.

References

Addis, B. R. (1966). *The relationship of physical interpersonal distance to sex, race, and age.* Unpublished master's thesis, University of Oklahoma.

Argyle, M., & Dean, J. (1965). Eye-contact, distance, and affiliation. *Sociometry, 28,* 289–304.

Barnlund, D. C. (1975). Communicative styles of two cultures: Public and private self in Japan and the United States. In A. Kendon, R. M. Harris, & M. R. Key (Eds.), *Organization of behavior in face-to-face interaction.* The Hague: Mouton.

Bateson, G., Jackson, D. D., Haley, J., & Weakland, J. H. (1956). Toward a theory of schizo-phrenia. *Behavioral Science, 1,* 251–264.

Burgoon, J. K. (1978). A communication model of personal space violations: Explication and an initial test. *Human Communication Research, 4,* 129–142.

Clay, V. S. (1968). The effect of culture on mother-child tactile communication. *Family Coordinator, 17,* 204–210.

Douty, H. I. (1963). Influence of clothing on perception of persons. *Journal of Home Economics, 55,* 197–202.

Eakins, B. W., & Eakins, R. G. (1978). *Sex differences in human communication.* Boston: Houghton Mifflin.

Ekman, P., & Friesen, W. V. (1967). Head and body cues in the judgment of emotion: A reformulation. *Perceptual and Motor Skills, 24,* 711–724.

Ekman, P., & Friesen, W. V. (1969). The repertoire of nonverbal behavior: Categories, origins, usage, and coding. *Semintica 1,* 49–98.

Fisher, J. D., Rytting, M., & Heslin, R. (1976). Hands touching hands: Affective and evaluative effects of interpersonal touch. *Sociometry, 3,* 416–421.

Fisher, S. (1975). Body decoration and camouflage. In L. M. Gurel & M. S. Beeson (Eds.), *Dimensions of dress and adornment: A book of readings.* Dubuque, IA: Kendall/Hunt.

Fromme, D. K., Jaynes, W. E., Taylor, D. K., Hanold, E. G., Daniell, J., Rountree, J. R., & Fromme, M. L. (1989). Nonverbal behavior and attitudes toward touch. *Journal of Nonverbal Behavior, 13,* 3–14.

Goldberg, S., & Lewis, M. (1969). Play behavior in the year-old infant: Early sex differences. *Child Development, 40,* 21–31.

Graves, J. R., & Robinson, J. D. (1976). Proxemic

behavior as a function of inconsistent verbal and nonverbal messages. *Journal of Counseling Psychology 23,* 333–338.

Guardo, C. J. (1969). Personal space in children. *Child Development, 40,* 143–151.

Hall, E. T. (1963). Proxemics: The study of man's spatial relations and boundaries. In *Man's image in medicine and anthropology* pp. 422–445. New York: International Universities Press.

Hall, E. T. (1966). *The hidden dimension.* New York: Doubleday.

Hardman, P. (1971, September). Every human being is a separate language. *The Salt Lake Tribune.*

Henley, N. (1973–1974). Power, sex, and nonverbal communication. *Berkeley Journal of Sociology, 18,* 10–11.

Henricks, S. H., Kelley, E. A., & Eicher, J. B. (1968). Senior girls' appearance and social acceptance. *Journal of Home Economics, 60,* 167–172.

Horn, M. J. (1975). Carrying it off in style. In L. M. Gurel & M. S. Beeson

(Eds.), *Dimensions of dress and adornment: A book of readings.* Dubuque, IA: Kendall/Hunt.

Jourard, S. M. (1966). An exploratory study of body accessibility. *British Journal of Social and Clinical Psychology, 5,* 221–231.

Jourard, S. M. (1968). *Disclosing man to himself.* Princeton, NJ: Van Nostrand.

Jourard, S., & Rubin, J. E. (1968). Self-disclosure and touching: A study of two modes of interpersonal encounter and their inter-relation. *Journal of Humanistic Psychology, 8,* 39–48.

Kramer, E. (1963). The judgment of personal characteristics and emotions from nonverbal properties of speech. *Psychological Bulletin, 60,* 408–420.

Kramer, E. J. J., & Lewis, T. R. (1951). Comparison of visual and nonvisual listening. *Journal of Communication, 1,* 16–20.

Leventhal, G., & Matturro, M. (1980). Differential effects of spatial crowding and sex on behavior. *Perceptual and Motor Skills, 51,* 111–119.

Malandro, L. A., Barker, L., & Barker, D. A.

(1989). *Nonverbal communication*. New York: Random House.

McCroskey, J. C., Larson, C. E., & Knapp, M. L. (1971). *An introduction to interpersonal communication*. Englewood Cliffs, NJ: Prentice Hall.

Mehrabian, A. (1971). *Silent messages*. Belmont, CA: Wadsworth.

Montagu, A. (1971). *Touching: The human significance of the skin*. New York: Harper & Row.

Perry, M. O., Schutz, H. G., & Rucker, M. H. (1983). Clothing interest, self-actualization and demographic variables. *Home Economics Research Journal, 11,* 280–288.

Proctor, L. (1978). *Fashion and anti-fashion*. London: Cox and Wyman.

Schutz, W. C. (1971). *Here comes everybody*. New York: Harper & Row.

Siegel, B. S. (1990). *Peace, love and healing: Bodymind communication and the path to self-healing*. New York: Harper Perennial.

Snyder, C. R., & Endelman, J. R. (1979). Effects of degree of interpersonal similarity on physical distance and self-reinforcement theory predictions. *Journal of Personality, 47,* 492–505.

Sommer, R. (1962). The distance for comfortable conversation: A further study. *Sociometry, 25,* 111–116.

Taylor, L. C., & Compton, N. H. (1968). Personality correlates of dress conformity. *Journal of Home Economics, 60,* 653–656.

Werner, C. M. (1987). Home interiors: A time and place for interpersonal relationships. *Environment and Behavior: 19,* 169–179.

Williams, M. C., & Eicher, J. B. (1966). Teenagers' appearance and social acceptance. *Journal of Home Economics, 58,* 457–461.

2

Receiving Communication:
Empathic and Critical Listening

MOST OF US SPEND considerably more time listening each day than we do speaking. Part 2 consists of two chapters dedicated to listening, critical thinking, and mass communication.

Chapter 5, Listening and Critical Thinking, provides suggestions on how to improve your listening and critical thinking skills. Because much of the content of our communication comes from mass-media sources, Chapter 6, Mass Communication, is designed to help you become an intelligent consumer of mass media.

When you have read and thought about this chapter, you will be able to:

1. Differentiate between hearing and listening.

2. List some factors that interfere with effective listening.

3. Define *active, empathic,* and *critical listening.*

4. Understand why critical thinking is important.

5. Differentiate between observations and inferences.

6. Distinguish among types of evidence and between types of arguments.

7. Identify some fallacies that can occur during critical thinking and listening.

8. Utilize specific skills to improve your listening ability.

5

Listening and Critical Thinking

> **"It is the province of knowledge to speak and it is the privilege of wisdom to listen."**
>
> OLIVER WENDELL HOLMES

> **"I like to listen. I have learned a great deal from listening. Most people never listen."**
>
> ERNEST HEMINGWAY

L istening is our most used and least studied communication skill. In this chapter you will learn the difference between hearing and listening. You will learn about some of the factors that can interfere with listening and about three kinds of listening—active, empathic, and critical. Critical listening and thinking are also discussed together in greater detail. Finally, you will discover how to improve your own listening skills.

> **"I know that you believe you understand what you think I said, but I am not sure you realize that what you heard is not what I meant."**
>
> ANONYMOUS

S arah sat in the waiting room of the doctor's office fidgeting nervously. For several months she had been getting headaches every day, and they seemed to be getting worse as time went on. This week she had already missed two classes because her head ached so much. Her roommate, Rhonda, had scared her by saying that she knew of two people who died from brain cancer, and their only symptom had been bad headaches. By the time the doctor saw her, Sarah was almost in tears. In the examining room, the doctor smiled encouragingly and leaned forward in his chair while Sarah talked about her headaches. When she fell into an anxious silence, the doctor asked her a lot of questions and finally concluded that Sarah may simply need glasses. She made an appointment with an optometrist, and, sure enough, she was farsighted. Once she got used to her glasses, reading was much easier and her headaches disappeared.

Listening is an important key to successful communication—it is one of the primary ways in which we discover others, enrich our relationships, and broaden our knowledge. Being a good listener also involves evaluating the accuracy of the messages we hear. If Sarah had listened critically to the message her roommate gave her, she might not have worried so much. This chapter will help you develop your listening skills so that you can become a more competent communicator.

What Is Listening?

Have you ever had the embarrassing experience of having someone ask you a question during a conversation when you were only pretending to listen? You have no idea what the question was, so you have no idea what the answer should be. Have you had someone ask you to do something that was important to that person but unimportant to you—so you forgot to do it? The sounds can go into your ears, but that does not mean that your brain interprets those sounds; nor does it mean that your mind stores the message or that your body does what the message requested. Sometimes you hear, you listen, and you even understand the message, but you do not obey. The listening process is complicated. Much happens between the reception of sounds and an overt response by the receiver.

The process of listening is summarized in Figure 5.1. As the illustration shows, we receive stimuli, such as music, in the ear, where the smallest bones in the body translate the vibrations into sensations to the brain. The brain focuses on the sensations and gives them meaning. Your brain might, for example, recognize the name of the song or the fact that an unfamiliar artist is singing it. Your interpreted message is stored in your short-term or long-term recall for future use (Schab & Crowder, 1989). You might even be able to bring back the feelings and remember the person you were with the next time you hear that song.

hearing

The physiological act of receiving sound.

The first step in learning about listening is to understand the distinction between hearing and listening. **Hearing** is simply *the act of receiving sound.*

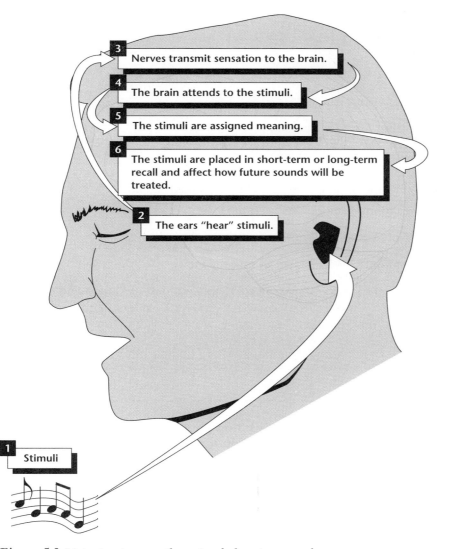

Figure 5.1 Listening is more than simply hearing sounds.

You can close your eyes to avoid seeing, cover your nose to avoid smelling, and shrink away to avoid touch, but your ears have no flaps to cover them. Their structure suggests that for your own protection, your ears should never be closed, even when you sleep. Because you cannot close your ears, you hear; you receive sounds. However, hearing is not the same as listening.

Listening is *the process of receiving and interpreting aural stimuli.* That is, listening is using your brain to help you understand the sounds you hear. Your brain helps you give meaning to the sounds. You hear with your ears; you listen with your brain.

listening

The process of receiving and interpreting aural stimuli.

Instant Recall

Match the correct letter from the choices below with each description:

A. **Hearing**	D. **Speaking**
B. **Listening**	E. **Listening to mass media**
C. **Writing**	F. **Reading**

_____ 1. The communication skill used the most and studied the least.

_____ 2. The communication skill used the least.

_____ 3. The physiological process of receiving sound waves.

_____ 4. The interpretation of sounds into meaning.

_____ 5. Americans spend 40 percent to 55 percent of their time doing this activity.

Answers: 1. B 2. C 3. A 4. B or E 5. B

How Much Do People Listen?

Think how much you listen every day. Because you are a student, you probably spend much of your time listening to professors. You might also listen to music or the news when you are walking or running, and you may both listen to and watch television each day. On the job, you listen to supervisors, sales associates, or customers. Some studies have come up with more specific answers to how much people listen.

A classic study of listening showed that Americans spend more than 40 percent of their time listening (Rankin, 1926). Weinrach and Swanda (1975) found that business personnel, including those with and without managerial responsibilities, spend nearly 33 percent of their time listening, almost 26 percent of their time speaking, nearly 23 percent of their time writing, and almost 19 percent of their time reading. When Werner (1975) investigated the communication activities of high school and college students, homemakers, and employees in a variety of other occupations, she determined that they spend 55 percent of their time listening, 13 percent reading, and 8 percent writing. Figure 5.2 shows how much time college students spend in various communication activities each day. According to these studies, you spend over half your time (53 percent) listening either to the mass media or to other people.

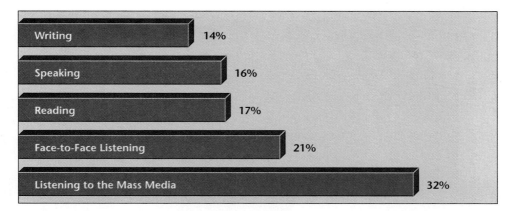

Figure 5.2 Proportions of time spent by college students in communication activities.

How Well Do People Listen?

You probably think you listen pretty well. Most of us do. However, the studies on listening consistently show that you are probably incorrect about how effectively you listen.

In general, immediately after being presented with a message, people are likely to recall only half of what they have heard. In a management setting, that loss occurs even when the persons being tested are forewarned that they will be tested on the content of the message. Tested 2 months later, the subjects recall only about one-quarter of the information (Nichols & Stevens, 1957). In an educational setting, students recall more information if they have been told that they will be tested and graded on the information (Smeltzner & Watson, 1984).

What Interferes with the Ability to Listen?

Many factors might contribute to listening difficulty. Three of the main barriers to effective listening are noise, your perceptions of others, and yourself.

Noise

The term **noise** refers to *interference in the communication process from external and internal sources.* An example of an external interference is physical distractions; examples of internal interference are mental, factual, and semantic distractions.

noise

Interference in the communication process from external and internal sources.

Listeners are sometimes distracted by noise and cannot listen to the speaker's message. Careful attention to the speaker allows listeners to avoid distractions.

physical distractions

All the stimuli in the environment that keep you from focusing on the speaker and the message.

mental distraction

An internal source of interference: the wandering of the mind when it is supposed to be focused on something.

factual distractions

A source of internal interference that occurs when you focus so intently on the details that you miss the main point.

Physical distractions are *all the stimuli in the environment that keep you from focusing on the speaker and the message.* The stimuli could be loud music, seductive perfume, bright lights, loud talking, or even an outrageous dress. All of these distractions from outside can keep you from fully absorbing a message that is directed at you.

One of the three internal sources of interference is mental distraction. A **mental distraction** is *the wandering of the mind when it is supposed to be focused on something.* You are supposed to be listening to your friend; instead, you are wondering how much she paid for that outfit. You are supposed to be listening to your supervisor, but you are still thinking about the disturbing call you just received. During a lecture, you are admiring an attractive face nearby. All of these are examples of mental distractions that interfere with high-fidelity listening.

TRY◄►THIS

What makes your mind wander when you are supposed to be listening? Does it happen more when you are tired or when you are well rested? See if you can analyze yourself to determine what distracts you.

A second internal source of interference is **factual distractions,** *which occur when you focus so intently on details that you miss the main point.* A student pilot had carefully listened to her instructor state all the rules about how far a small plane is supposed to stay from heavy cloud formations. Finding herself in a cloud, she accurately repeated to the flight instructor all the facts about cloud formations. Unfortunately, she had missed the main point, which was that small planes are supposed to stay outside cloud formations whenever possible.

A third internal source of interference is **semantic distractions,** *which occur when you overrespond to an emotion-laden word or concept.* Semantic distractions occur when you stop listening because you hear a word that slights you, your religion, your family, or your ethnic group. Consider the following example: The dean of a medical school, an African-American woman, participated in a search committee for a dean of engineering. In the opening discussions, an engineering faculty member who was well below her in rank, status, and pay exhibited a mixture of sexism and racism by acting as if he would decide whether her suggestions had merit. His implication that he would take her ideas under consideration, that he would decide whether she should be listened to, made the dean so angry that she threatened to leave the committee.

semantic distractions

A source of internal interference that occurs when you overrespond to an emotion-laden word or concept.

TRY◀▶THIS

What slights, slurs, or implications through word or gesture would cause you to stop listening and start distancing yourself from another person? What are the "red-flag" words that set you off and keep you from listening?

Perceptions of Others

Your capacity for listening can be limited by the speaker's status, the stereotypes you use to categorize others, and the sights and sounds associated with the speaker.

Status—*a person's social standing, rank, title, or value*—can affect listening. A private in the army may listen attentively to the captain, who outranks him, just as a patient might listen attentively to a physician who is providing postoperative advice. However, people tend not to listen critically to those whom they perceive as above them in social standing. **Critical listening** is *listening that challenges the speaker's message by evaluating its accuracy, meaningfulness, and utility.* People listen most critically to those whom they regard as equals because they feel they can argue and respond critically. Someone who is perceived as being below someone else in intelligence, social status, or economic standing may be asked little and heeded less. Thus, high-status individuals are often listened to uncritically, peers are listened to critically, and messages from underlings are rarely welcomed and even more rarely obeyed.

status

A person's social standing, rank, title, or value—can affect listening.

critical listening

A type of active listening that challenges the speaker's message by evaluating its accuracy, meaningfulness, and utility.

Stereotypes, which were discussed in Chapter 4, also affect your capacity for listening. People tend to listen to certain people about certain things. They treat individuals as if they are the same as all the others in a given category. For example, older people may not ask a younger person for his or her opinion because they perceive all younger people as having too little experience. Some people might dismiss anyone from other cultures because they don't think foreigners will be able to understand them. How often are women asked about cars and men asked about window coverings?

TRY ◀▶ THIS

Can you think of any categories of people to whom you are unlikely to listen? Can you think of categories of people to whom you are more likely to listen?

sights and sounds

What you see and hear affects listening.

Sights and sounds affect listening because *what you see and hear may determine whether or not you pay attention to a speaker.* If you are totally distracted by a woman with a ring in her lip or by a man with a tatoo on his cheek or a deep scar across his face, those sights will keep you from listening well. Some individuals have a terrible time talking with an unusually attractive person. Similarly, a strident voice, lisp, stammer, or mutter can keep you from listening to someone because you are so distracted by how the person sounds.

Yourself

Another obstacle to effective listening is yourself. You can become an obstacle to listening through egocentrism, defensiveness, and experiential superiority. After looking more closely at each of these obstacles, you will better understand how you can interfere with your own effective listening.

egocentrism

Excessive self-focus, which interferes with listening.

Egocentrism is *excessive self-focus,* or seeing yourself as the central concern of nearly every interaction with others. Egocentric people do not listen because the only thing that really matters to them is themselves. Anyone else's concerns are unimportant. In the following example, Sue, Judith's supervisor, has to get Judith's signature on some important papers that she forgot to sign; Sue walks down to Judith's office to get the signatures:

Sue: Hi, Judith; do you have a minute?

Judith: Sue, did you hear that I got the Laddlam account? That took a lot of time and effort. I must have worked on that for four months.

Sue: That's great, I'm sure you worked hard. Here are some . . .

Judith: And that wasn't even the best thing that happened to me this week. Do you remember the trouble I was having with the Salmon & Salmon account? Well, I certainly fixed that by . . .

An egocentric person is so self-centered that he or she neither listens to nor cares what the other person says.

Defensiveness is another characteristic of self that can reduce listening effectiveness. The term refers to *individuals' acting threatened, as if they must defend what they have said or done.* In the following example, two teenagers exhibit defensiveness when their father comes into the kitchen, which he has just cleaned after dinner, and finds bread crumbs and peanut butter smeared on the table. His teenage son and daughter are watching TV in the next room, well within hearing range:

defensiveness

An impediment to listening that occurs when individuals act threatened, as if they must defend what they have said or done.

Father: Who was in the kitchen after I cleaned it?

Children: *[Silence]*

Father: Ben, were you in the kitchen after I cleaned it?

Ben: I don't remember if I went in there or not.

Father: Becky, did you have a peanut butter sandwich after we finished dinner?

Becky: I don't even like peanut butter.

Father: Am I to assume that Mom came in here after dinner and after I cleaned the kitchen and that she made this mess?

Children: *[Silence]*

You may act defensively when you have done or said something you should not have. However, some people feel threatened or defend themselves vigorously even when they receive messages that were intended to be neutral or nonthreatening. In any case, defensiveness reduces listening capacity.

TRY ◄►THIS

Think about what makes you stop listening and start being defensive: comments about your appearance? your past? your job? your major? your grades? See if you can analyze yourself and determine what makes you defensive.

A third way you can impede your own listening capacity is by exhibiting **experiential superiority,** *looking down on others because their experience with life is not as good or as extensive as yours.* Following is an example, a dialogue between father and son:

experiential superiority

An impediment to listening that occurs when you look down on others because their experience is less extensive than yours.

Father: By the time I was your age, I had been working full-time for 5 years.

Son: Yes, but now things are more expensive, and jobs are hard to find.

Father: Are you kidding? I grew up during a major recession, when jobs were nearly impossible to find.

Son: Well, things aren't so great right now.

Instant Recall

Fill in the blanks:

1. A blaring television, worries about an upcoming exam, and a personal attack are all examples of _____.

2. You may act _____ when you say or do something you shouldn't have.

3. _____ people do not listen because all that matters to them is themselves.

4. People listen critically to those they regard as _____.

5. Looking down on others because their life experience is not as extensive as yours is _____ _____.

Answers: 1. Noise (or interference)   2. defensively   3. Egocentric   4. equals   5. experiential superiority

Feedback, which demonstrates active listening, may be verbal or nonverbal, positive or negative.

Father: I think you've been pampered all your life. You don't even know what real work is. In my day, kids were expected to work long hours for little pay.

The father never lets his son forget that he sees his experience as better than, more valuable than, and superior to that of his son.

Three Kinds of Listening: Active, Empathic, and Critical

Listeners engage in three kinds of listening: active, empathic, and critical. The following sections examine these forms of listening in more detail.

Active Listening

Active listening is *"involved listening with a purpose"* (Barker, 1971). Its opposite, passive listening, is listening to the radio, TV, or stereo while you study or wearing earphones when you walk, run, or exercise. Barbara (1957) described the difference between active listening and passive listening like this:

> In [active listening], the individual listens with more or less his or her total self—including his [or her] special senses, attitudes, beliefs, feelings, and intuitions. In [passive listening], the listener becomes mainly an organ for the passive reception of sound, with little self-perception, personal involvement, . . . or alive curiosity. (p. 12)

Valued in conversation, small-group discussion, and even question-and-answer sessions in public speaking, active listening is a communication skill worth learning.

Active listening is characterized by verbal and nonverbal feedback. **Feedback** consists of *the listener's verbal and nonverbal responses to the speaker and the speaker's message.* The feedback may be one of two kinds: positive or negative. **Positive feedback** consists of *verbal and nonverbal responses intended to affirm the speaker and the speaker's message.* Examples of nonverbal positive feedback are positive facial expressions, attentive looks, smiles, laughing, and leaning forward. Examples of verbal positive feedback are statements such as "I really liked your point about taxes," or "You made me think about this issue in an entirely new way." The usual result of positive feedback is that the speaker delivers a longer message, makes fewer errors, and is less defensive.

Negative feedback consists of *verbal and nonverbal responses intended to disconfirm the speaker and the speaker's message.* Nonverbally, negative feedback can consist of frowning and making negative facial expressions, turning the head and tilting the body away from the speaker, talking to others, reading the newspaper, decreasing eye contact, or responding with glassy-eyed indifference. Verbally, negative feedback could be "I don't understand your point," "You don't seem to know the facts," or "So what?" The usual result of negative feedback is that the speaker delivers a shorter message, makes more errors, and is more defensive.

active listening

Involved listening with a purpose.

feedback

The listener's verbal and nonverbal responses to the speaker and the speaker's message.

positive feedback

Verbal and nonverbal responses intended to affirm the speaker and the speaker's message.

negative feedback

Verbal and nonverbal responses intended to disconfirm the speaker and the speaker's message.

TRY ◀▶ THIS

Think about what kind of feedback you receive when you converse with others. What communication behavior is rewarded by your listeners? What communication behavior is punished? Has feedback altered the way you are today?

Cultural Note

The way a person actively listens can vary from culture to culture. College students in Finland, for example, listen carefully and take notes but do not respond overtly while being addressed by the professor. In fact, they remain quite expressionless. In some Native American bands and in some Hispanic groups, people avert their eyes when listening; but, in groups such as northern whites and blacks, people tend to maintain eye contact while actively listening.

Empathic Listening

empathic listening

A type of active listening in which you listen with a purpose and attempt to understand the other person.

empathy

The ability to perceive another person's world view as if it were your own.

Empathic listening, a form of active listening, is *listening with a purpose and attempting to understand the other person*. To distinguish between active listening and empathic listening may be easier if you remember that **empathy** is *the ability to perceive another person's world view as if it were your own*. The goal of empathic listening is to gain total understanding of the other person. Kenneth B. Clark (1980) explains empathy as

> the capacity of an individual to feel the needs, the aspirations, the frustrations, the joy, the sorrows, the anxieties, the hurt, indeed, the hunger of others as if they were his [or her] own. (p. 188)

The opposite of empathy is not hostility but neutrality. Few responses can be more punishing than indifference to your thoughts, feelings, and ideas. At least a hostile response indicates that the listener has interpreted what you said and reacted to it. An indifferent or neutral response signals to the speaker that the listener did not even care enough to respond—positively or negatively.

Some communication scholars see empathy as the centerpiece of communication. Bochner and Kelly (1974) described empathy as "the essence of all communicative processes." Howell (1982) observed that "empathic skills are central to competence in human interaction." Perhaps you already realize that a friend's or partner's ability to listen empathically is the very essence of your relationship.

The goal of empathic listening is *attempting* to understand someone else. Empathy and empathic listening do not necessarily involve knowing exactly how someone else feels. Every person feels differently about the loss of a loved one, the end of a relationship, the joy of a new job or promotion, the happiness of a birth or marriage, and the struggles of everyday life. You can never completely understand how another person feels about any of these

5.3 TYPES OF LISTENING

Match the correct letter(s) from the choices below with each description:

A. Passive listening   **B. Empathic listening**   **C. Critical listening**

_____ 1. You listen to music on the elevator as you talk with your friend.

_____ 2. Some scholars see this activity as the centerpiece of communication.

_____ 3. The defense attorney listens carefully to the prosecuting attorney making a case against her client.

_____ 4. You listen as a salesperson tells you why you should buy a car made in Korea.

_____ 5. These items describe two kinds of active listening.

Answers: 1. A   2. B   3. C   4. C   5. B and C

things because your experiences and those of another person will never be exactly the same. But our inability to duplicate feelings does not mean an inability to empathize. You can imagine how a person feels, identify with how you have felt in similar situations, and show the person you care with your look, your touch, and your concern. You can also be an empathic listener by adopting the Zen Buddhist notion of **mindfulness,** which Julia Wood (1997) describes as *being "fully engaged in the moment."* Mindful people clear their minds of other thoughts, especially distractions; focus their concentration on the other person; and recognize that mindfulness takes practice (Wood, 1997).

mindfulness
The state of being fully engaged in the moment.

Critical Listening

Critical listening is yet another kind of active listening: listening that challenges the speaker's message by evaluating its accuracy, meaningfulness, and utility. The underlying principle of critical listening is learning how to be skeptical, which requires questioning and analyzing what you are told. Much of what you hear is untrue, unproven, or pure speculation. For example, messages from people in advertising and sales are usually suspect because such occupations are typically profit-oriented, rather than interested in selling you something you really need. Today's "truth" can change by tomorrow as more, or different, information becomes available.

Critical listening and critical thinking really go hand in hand: You cannot listen critically if you do not think critically.

Critical Thinking and Listening

critical thinking

Analyzing and judging the accuracy of messages.

Like critical listening, **critical thinking** requires *analyzing and judging the accuracy of messages.* You can think critically without listening—you may think critically about something you've read or seen—but you cannot listen critically without also thinking critically.

Why Is Critical Thinking Important?

Critical thinking is central to your ability to be a skilled critical listener and an effective communicator. Indeed, everyone from educational theorists to business management writers thinks critical analysis is important to a person's development. At the top of the hierarchy of learning developed by Benjamin Bloom (1954) are the skills of problem solving and thinking. Educational theorist Jean Piaget (1948/1974) asserted that when people acquire knowledge by memorization, they do not have true knowledge; real knowledge is acquired when people construct ideas. Resnick and Klopfer (1989) said, "To know something is not just to have received information but also to have interpreted it and related it to other knowledge." Critical thinking is basic not only to education but to your ability to be an effective listener and your development as a competent communicator.

What Is Involved in Critical Thinking and Listening?

Critical thinking and listening involve identifying the source and analyzing the message. You might already be doing identification and analysis, but you may not be doing them very systematically.

Identify the Source

Whether you are thinking or listening critically, you need to consider the source of the message. For example, imagine that your friend, a biology major, tells you that you should eat peach pits because doing so will reduce the chance that you will die from your smoking habit. Do you believe your friend? What if a medical researcher tells you eating peach pits will reduce your chance of dying from smoking. Do you believe the researcher? Suppose a national survey of 100,000 people randomly selected and studied over a 20-year period with a $10 million grant from the National Institutes of Health indicates that you should eat peach pits. Now do you believe it?

TRY ◀▶ THIS

To whom do you listen? Whom do you turn to for accurate information? What makes you decide to whom you listen?

Identifying the source of a message is the crucial first step in deciding whether or not to listen to that message and act upon it. The key element is **source credibility,** or *the speaker's competence to make the claim, as perceived by the listeners.* You need to know if the issue is within the speaker's area of expertise. In the example above, the medical researcher is more credible than the biology major. You also need to determine if the message source is a respected expert who uses scientific methods to discover facts, if other experts can replicate the findings and support the claim, and if the claim seems to remain true over time. The proper skeptic asks who the speaker is, what the speaker knows, how the speaker discovered the information, and who else thinks the speaker is correct.

source credibility

The speaker's competence to make a claim, as perceived by the listeners.

Analyze the Message

message analysis

A step in critical thinking and listening that includes evaluating the process by which information or knowledge was discovered and evaluating the message itself.

The next step in critical thinking and listening is **message analysis,** which requires *evaluating the process by which information or knowledge was discovered and evaluating the message itself.* For instance, most reputable print, broadcast, and cable news sources rely on experienced and educated reporters who are expected to gather information from a variety of credible sources before their stories, or messages, are disseminated to the general public. This process for gathering information is more reliable than might occur before a message appears on the Internet. Anyone can post any kind of message on the Internet, regardless of source, credibility, or origin.

A reporter verifies messages before reporting them.

When evaluating the message itself, you should consider whether or not it is consistent with other known information. In science, a single discovery made through the scientific method can yield a "truth" that might last forever. In social science, "truth" needs to be rediscovered under ever-changing circumstances, and few of our knowledge bits have a long shelf life. Changing circumstances are exactly why you need to be skeptical. You must always be ready to revise your knowledge base as you gain new information that passes your critical judgment.

TRY ◄►THIS

What difference does it make how you gain information or knowledge? What are some procedures or processes used to gain information or knowledge? What procedures are you most likely to trust?

What Abilities Are Related to Critical Thinking?

An individual who thinks and listens critically must distinguish between observations and inferences; must be able to categorize evidence as emotional, logical, or personal; and must understand the various types of arguments.

observations

Descriptions based on phenomena that can be sensed— seen, heard, smelled, or felt.

first-person observation

Your description of what you sensed.

second-person account

Your (or someone else's) report of what another person observed.

inferences

Generalizations from or about information you have received through your senses.

Distinguish between Observations and Inferences

You may recall from Chapter 3 that **observations** are *descriptions based on phenomena that can be sensed—seen, heard, tasted, smelled, or felt.* A **first-person observation** is *your description of what you sensed;* a **second-person account** is *your (or someone else's) report of what another person observed.* A first-person observation would obviously be more credible than a second-person account, which may be altered during transmission.

As a critical thinker and listener, you need to distinguish between observations and **inferences,** or *generalizations from or about information you have received through your senses.* For instance, if you see a small child playing alone near a busy street, you make a first-person observation that a small child is playing alone near a busy street. But you may make any number of inferences. You might infer that the child is an orphan, that he or she is not loved or cared for, that the child will be injured or killed, or that the child should be legally removed from the parents.

Observations and inferences can be distinguished in a number of ways. Whereas inferences can be made before, during, or after observation, observations can occur only while something is being viewed. Whereas inferences go beyond that which is seen, observations do not. Interpretation is the goal of inferences, whereas reporting is the goal of observation. Finally, whereas observations are more likely to be agreed-upon by observers, inferences vary widely in the agreement they elicit from individuals (Brooks & Heath, 1989).

Categorize Emotional, Logical, and Personal Evidence

Arguments consist of *propositions and their justification.* A **proposition** is *a statement of what you believe,* whereas a **justification** is *all the evidence you have gathered that supports the proposition.* People who try to persuade others use three types of evidence: logic, emotion, and themselves.

When you engage in critical thinking, you need to distinguish among these types of evidence. Sometimes arguments combine elements of all three, but most evidence can be categorized as primarily emotional, primarily logical, or primarily personal. An **emotional proof,** or *pathos,* is *based on feelings or emotions.* An example is this declaration from a roommate: "I'm hungry. Let's order a pizza." A **logical proof,** or *logos,* is *based on reasoning.* An example of a logical proof is this advice from a neighbor: "Yes, you should landscape with eastern white pine because they grow fast and tall, will grow anywhere, and are resistant to disease." A **personal proof,** or *ethos,* is *based on the authority and knowledge of a credible source.* An example of a personal proof is this suggestion from an interior decorator: "You should use imported English polished cotton for your drapes."

As with any kind of evidence, you—as the critical thinker—have to decide the merit of the claims in the message. Some types of arguments you might receive are discussed below.

Types of Arguments

People engaged in critical thinking also must understand the types of arguments. Arguments can be classified as inductive or deductive.

Inductive Arguments

Inductive arguments are *those that move from specific instances to a generalization.* Taylor, Meyer, Rosegrant, and Samples (1989) suggested that "inductive thinking may also be called generalization" (p. 128). Here is an inductive argument concerning jogging:

> Jane is in great shape, and she jogs. (Observation)
>
> Bill looks terrific, and he jogs. (Observation)
>
> Kim's great muscle definition is from jogging. (Observation, Inference)
>
> Therefore, people who jog look good. (Generalization)

You critically evaluate inductive reasoning by deciding if the observations are accurate and if enough observations exist to justify the generalization. A

argument

A proposition and its justification.

proposition

As part of an argument, a statement of what you believe.

justification

As part of an argument, all the evidence you have gathered that supports the proposition.

emotional proof

Evidence based on feelings or emotions.

logical proof

Evidence based on reasoning.

personal proof

Evidence based on the authority and knowledge of a credible source.

inductive arguments

An argument that progresses from specific instances to a generalization.

person who says, "A teller at Bank ABC was very rude to me yesterday. All the tellers at Bank ABC are rude," has not made enough observations to justify a generalization.

Deductive Arguments

deductive argument

An argument that progresses from a general proposition to a specific instance.

syllogism

An argument with a major premise, a minor premise, and a conclusion.

accuracy

In evaluating a deductive argument, the truth or verifiability of the major and minor premises.

valid

In evaluating a deductive argument, the ability to logically derive a conclusion from its propositions.

Deductive arguments *move from a general proposition to a specific instance.* The entire three-part form of a deductive argument is called a **syllogism,** or *an argument with a major premise, a minor premise, and a conclusion.* Here is a deductive argument:

If you jog, you will look like you're in good shape. (Major premise)

Jane jogs. (Minor premise)

Therefore, Jane looks like she's in good shape. (Conclusion)

Deductive arguments are evaluated in two ways. One way is to judge the argument's **accuracy,** *the truth or verifiability of the major and minor premises.* The major premise in the example above is worth questioning because some people who jog do not look like they are in good shape. The minor premise is verifiable, but the truth of the conclusion is in jeopardy because Jane might have looked like she was in good shape *before* she started jogging. The second way to judge a deductive argument is to examine its structure, or arrangement. *If the conclusion can be logically derived from its propositions,* then the argument is said to be **valid.** For example, most people would agree with the following argument, which is both accurate and valid:

People who drive while they are intoxicated are more likely to have accidents than are those who drive only when they are not intoxicated.

Jack regularly drives while he is intoxicated.

Therefore, Jack is more likely to have an accident than are persons who do not drive while intoxicated.

The following argument, based on the same idea, includes propositions that are not true:

People who drive while they are not intoxicated are more likely to have accidents than are those who drive only when they are intoxicated.

Jill drives only while she is not intoxicated.

Therefore, Jill is more likely to have an accident than are those who drive while intoxicated.

Most people would not accept the general proposition that people who drive when they are not intoxicated are more likely to have an accident than are those who drive when they are intoxicated. The falsity of this major premise renders the entire argument false. However, the argument is valid in that it follows the valid form for an argument, symbolically represented as

$A < B$

$\underline{J < A}$

$\therefore J < B$

Unfortunately, speakers and writers rarely provide you with the structure of their thoughts. That you will receive a list of observations and inferred generalizations or that you will hear a syllogism is unlikely. Instead, you are likely to hear someone say, "You ought to go to Florida over spring break," a generalization with all the observations missing. To find out whether the generalization is worth heeding, you need to ask, "Why?" Then the speaker has to supply the observations, with which you may or may not agree: "Florida is warm in the spring." "The trip is inexpensive if we go together," and "Lots of students go to Florida during break." Then you can decide if you agree with the observations, the inferential leap, and the generalization.

Deductive arguments also are rarely heard in their full form. Instead, people tend to talk in **enthymemes,** or *parts of the entire argument, such as a premise or just the conclusion.* An example of an enthymeme is "Taxes are unjust" (the major premise of a deductive argument) or "This new 1 percent increase is unjust" (the conclusion of a deductive argument). You can mentally lay out the argument like this:

enthymemes

Parts of a deductive argument, such as a premise or a conclusion.

Sales taxes are unjust. (Major premise)

The 1 percent increase is a sales tax. (Minor premise)

Therefore, the 1 percent increase is unjust. (Conclusion)

Because the syllogism is correctly arranged, it is valid. However, you could certainly question the accuracy of the major premise that sales taxes are unjust.

The main point is that a critical thinker and listener usually needs to seek more information about a person's inductive and deductive arguments. Unfortunately, speakers in both public and interpersonal communication often assume that listeners agree with the unstated parts of their argument and that a listener mentally fills in the rest of the argument using his or her own observations or premises. Yet the listener's observations and premises may or may not be what the speaker had in mind. Don't be afraid to inquire about a speaker's intended meaning, because the intended meaning may make a difference in its acceptability.

Identify Types of Fallacies

Perhaps you have heard someone say, "That is a fallacious argument," but you were unsure what the term meant. A **fallacy** is *an argument that is flawed, that does not follow the rules of logic, and that is, therefore, not to be believed.* Actually, people use fallacies all the time, but as a critical thinker and listener you need to know how to recognize them and to know why you should discount them.

fallacy

An argument that is flawed, does not follow rules of logic, and therefore is not to be believed.

Hundreds of types of fallacies exist, many of them with fancy Latin names, but here you will examine 10 of the most common ones to help you become a better critical thinker and listener. To help you remember them, they will be placed in two categories: **fallacies of relevance,** which *are flawed because the conclusion is based on irrelevant premises,* and **fallacies of ambiguity,** which *are flawed because they contain a word or words with two or more meanings.*

Fallacies of Relevance

fallacies of relevance

Arguments that are flawed because the conclusion is based on irrelevant premises.

fallacies of ambiguity

Arguments that are flawed because they contain a word or words with two or more meanings.

argument against the person

A fallacy in which the person, rather than the issue at hand, becomes the focus.

appeal to the people

A fallacy that invites you to join the group and do something because "everyone is doing it"; also known as the *bandwagon effect.*

appeal to authority

A fallacy that occurs when a person offers information that is outside his or her area of expertise.

hasty generalization

A fallacy in which an inference is drawn from insufficient observation; also called a *premature generalization.*

1. An **argument against the person,** called *argumentum ad hominem* in Latin is, literally, *an "argument to the man" instead of to the issue.* This argument is also a propaganda device known as *name calling.* When you say "Beth is a jerk" in response to an argument with her about an issue, you are using an argument against the person. The argument is a fallacy, or a flawed argument, because it is irrelevant to the issue. Name calling is a sidetrack that does not logically follow from the argument. You can probably think of many examples yourself, but a few more are "He's such a racist," "She's a man hater," and "They're just rich snobs."

2. An **appeal to the people,** also known as the *bandwagon effect* in propaganda literature, *invites you to join the group and do something because "everyone is doing it."* Examples are buying beer from a microbrewery because that's what the in-crowd is drinking; eating at the country club because that's where the wealthy group gathers; or getting a motorcycle because that is what the "cool" people drive. This fallacy is particularly appealing to people who are concerned about keeping up with others. But remember that what "everyone is doing" can sometimes be unwise, so you should think critically about following this appeal, whether you hear it from your friends, politicians, or advertisers.

3. An **appeal to authority** occurs when *a person offers information that is outside his or her area of expertise.* An appeal to authority can sometimes be legitimate, such as when you ask a physician about your health, a mechanic about your car, or an old mariner about fishing. However, a physician selling cars, an actor selling windows, or a chemist commenting on race relations are examples of fallacious appeals to authority. Because none of these people are experts in these areas, their authority is false. Another variation is the "plain folks" approach: acting as if the speaker is just an ordinary person whose advice should be followed. As with the other examples, the flaw is that the "authority" is outside his or her field of expertise, or the ordinary person is not an expert in that particular subject.

4. A **hasty generalization** could be called a *premature generalization* because *you draw an inference before you have enough observations to justify it.* A woman once bitten by a dog mistrusts all dogs; a man once jilted by a woman vows never to date again.

5. **False cause**—referred to as *post hoc ergo propter hoc* in Latin—is *the fallacy of believing "after this; therefore, because of this."* Because one thing happened after another does not mean the first thing caused the second. For example, the oysters a woman ate before becoming pregnant did not cause her to become pregnant; or just because a man stayed up late watching television and had a headache the next day does not necessarily mean that staying up late watching television causes headaches. Causal links are tough to prove. Many people still disbelieve the long-established causal link between smoking and cancer.

6. **Begging the question,** which is also called a *circular argument,* is *based on using a conclusion that is also your premise.* For example, all educated people can speak competently in public. How is this "fact" known? Because all competent public speakers are educated. You argue that if all *A = B,* then all *B = A.* The argument may sound right, but it is circular, and the system is closed to outside inspection.

7. An **irrelevant conclusion** occurs when *evidence supports one conclusion but you make another.* For example, suppose you are in a particular organization and you are attempting to change outsiders' perceptions that the group is racist. You suggest some measures that would make membership in the group more appealing to other ethnic groups. After you have argued in favor of these measures for some time, you conclude that racism is a heinous crime against society. Most people would agree with this conclusion, but not because of your arguments, which do not provide evidence that racism is a heinous crime against society. Your conclusion, though applauded, remains irrelevant to your arguments or premises.

8. You commit the fallacy of **false alternatives** when you rely on "either-or" thinking which *suggests that only two alternatives are possible, and it often hints that one of the two is disastrous or to be avoided.* For instance, if you are campaigning for the presidency of your school's student council, you might assert that people are either for you or against you. Yet, in reality, many people may support some of your positions as well as some of your opponent's positions. This fallacy may be viewed more broadly as oversimplification. Generally, more than two alternatives exist in considering any matter.

Fallacies of Ambiguity

9. The **fallacy of equivocation** occurs when *you purposefully use the ambiguous qualities of language to your advantage or when you use two different meanings of the same word within a single context.* Some words are relative. For instance, the words *good, small, better, thin, big, worse,* and *tall* all need to be qualified or considered in context. A college professor may be the oldest person in her classroom but far from the oldest person at a family reunion. A member of Weight Watchers who has achieved his goal may be the thinnest person at

false cause

The fallacy of attributing the cause of something to whatever happened before it.

begging the question

A fallacy that occurs when you use a conclusion that is also your premise; also called a *circular argument.*

irrelevant conclusion

A fallacy that occurs when evidence supports one conclusion but you draw another one.

false alternatives

A fallacy which suggests that only two alternatives are possible and that one of the two is disastrous or to be avoided.

fallacy of equivocation

A fallacy that occurs when you purposefully use the ambiguous qualities of language to your advantage or when you use two different meanings of the same word within a single context.

Instant Recall

Fill in the blanks:

1. If an issue is within a source's area of expertise, that person is probably _____.

2. Critical thinking requires distinguishing between _____ and _____ .

3. "I feel sick to my stomach" is an example of a(n) _____ proof.

4. Inductive arguments move from _____ to a _____ .

5. In a valid argument the _____ can be logically derived from its _____.

Answers: 1. credible   2. observations/inferences   3. emotional   4. specific instances/generalization 5. conclusion/premises

---

the weekly meeting but not the thinnest person where he works. A person who is 5 feet 10 inches tall could be the tallest person among her group of friends but not the tallest person in her family. You equivocate when you note that someone is the oldest, the thinnest, or the tallest without specifying the context.

fallacy of division

A fallacy in which you argue that what is true of the parts must be true of the whole or that what is true of the whole must be true of the parts.

10. The **fallacy of division** has two forms: (1) *arguing that what is true of the parts must be true of the whole, and* (2) *arguing that what is true of the whole must be true of the parts.* An example of the first form is observing that one of the students in a class is highly motivated and concluding, on that basis, that everyone in the class is similarly motivated. An example of the second form is noting that a certain class has a particularly high cumulative grade-point average and assuming, therefore, that everyone in the class has similarly high grades. Both conclusions are fallacious.

You probably hear, or perhaps even use, some of these fallacies every day without realizing it. You now know how to recognize them, and, hopefully, you have a better understanding of why you should avoid these fallacies in your own speaking, and why you should discount them when you hear them from others.

Scholars have agreed for years that critical thinking and listening are important, but you don't have to be a scholar to realize their importance in your own life. If you are like most people living in the United States today, you are almost constantly bombarded with messages from a variety of sources. You can not possibly evaluate every message you receive, but your abilities as a critical thinker and listener will help you analyze the messages to which you attend.

Joseph N. Capella (1987), a professor at the University of Pennsylvania, identified some specific verbal and nonverbal behaviors associated with effective listening: eye gaze, posture, gestures, distance, dominance, involvement, the regulation of speaking turns, language choices, and the use of intimate questions. Let us consider each of these behaviors, as well as others associated with effective listening. You may wish to evaluate your own listening behavior to determine which of these you regularly demonstrate and which ones you want to add to your repertoire.

What Skills Are Associated with Effective Listening?

Verbal Skills

The notion of verbal components of listening may seem strange to you. You may reason that if you are engaged in listening, you cannot also be speaking. However, you encode and decode simultaneously, and you can make verbal responses while you are deeply involved in listening. To determine your current competence in this area, consider the skills you regularly practice:

1. *Invite additional comments.* Suggest that the speaker add more details or give additional information. Phrases such as "Go on," "What else?" "How did you feel about that?" and "Did anything else occur?" encourage the speaker to continue to share ideas and information.
2. *Ask questions.* One method of inviting the speaker to continue is to ask direct questions, requesting more in-depth details, definitions, or clarification.
3. *Identify areas of agreement or common experience.* Briefly relate similar past experiences, or briefly explain a similar point of view that you hold. Sharing ideas, attitudes, values, and beliefs is the basis of communication. In addition, such comments demonstrate your understanding.
4. *Vary verbal responses.* Use a variety of responses such as "Yes," "I see," "Go on," and "Right" instead of relying on one standard, unaltering response such as "Yes," "Yes," "Yes."
5. *Provide clear verbal responses.* Use specific and concrete words and phrases in your feedback to the speaker. Misunderstandings can occur if you do not provide easily understood responses. In the following example, the man's ambiguous responses to his wife's questions confuse the issue:

> **Wife:**   What time do you want dinner?
>
> **Husband:**   Well, I have to grind feed and do chores up north and vaccinate a sick steer.
>
> **Wife:**   The meat loaf and potatoes will take about an hour to bake.

Husband:	What time will Dan be home? Do you think he will have time to help me when he gets home?
Wife:	I don't know if Dan can help you, but I would like to know what time you want to eat.
Husband:	It will have to wait until I get all my work done.
Wife:	I guess I will have to figure it out for myself.

The husband in the preceding dialogue offers vague, general answers to the wife's questions. In the following dialogue, two roommates are discussing the end of a relationship, but the listener offers little clear feedback—the overused and ambiguous words are too general to supply the speaker with satisfaction:

Charlie:	I've just broken up with my girlfriend.
Fred:	Oh.
Charlie:	We've gone together for the past 3 1/2 years, and she just broke it off.
Fred:	That's something.

In both dialogues, the listeners fail to supply clear responses to the other communicator. If the husband in the first dialogue had answered his wife's questions directly, and if Fred had offered more specific comments, these conversations would have been greatly improved through active listening.

6. *Use descriptive, nonevaluative responses.* It is better to say, "Your car has a broken headlight, a burned-out taillight, and a dented fender," (descriptive) than to say, "That car of yours sure is a pile of junk" (evaluative). Trivializing or joking about serious disclosures suggests a negative evaluation of the speaker. Similarly, derogatory remarks are seen as offensive. Attempting to be superior to the speaker by stating that you believe you have a more advanced understanding suggests an evaluative tone. The conversation between Charlie and Fred that was begun earlier becomes worse as it continues. Not only does Fred respond with ambiguous comments, but he also appears to act superior to Charlie:

Charlie:	Hasn't this ever happened to you?
Fred:	No.
Charlie:	I thought you broke up with Jane.
Fred:	Yes, but that was different. You see, I broke it up, not her!

Charlie probably feels defensive because of Fred's act of superiority and demonstrates his frustration with the somewhat aggressive question about one of Fred's earlier relationships.

7. *Provide affirmative and affirming statements.* Comments such as "Yes," "I see," "I understand," and "I know" provide affirmation. Offering praise and specific positive statements demonstrates concern.

8. *Avoid complete silence.* The lack of any response suggests that you are not listening to the speaker. The "silent treatment" induced by sleepiness or lack of concern may result in defensiveness or anger on the part of the speaker. Appropriate verbal feedback demonstrates your active listening.

9. *Allow the other person the opportunity of a complete hearing.* When you discuss common feelings or experiences, avoid dominating the conversation. Allow the other person to go into depth and detail; allow the other person the option of changing the topic under discussion; allow the other person to talk without being interrupted. One woman reported the following conversation that she had with her roommate's brother. She stated that she felt very frustrated because she was unable to complete any of her thoughts and Jerry had not listened to her.

Jerry: So you and Maggie are going to move out of the house?

Char: Yeah, we're thinking about . . .

Jerry: Well, I think it's wrong. Have you talked with your folks about it?

Char: Yes, I talked to . . .

Jerry: Is it what they want?

Char: Yes . . .

Jerry: How do you know?

Char: Well, my mom said . . .

Jerry: What?

Char: *[Hesitating because of the continuing frustration she is feeling]* That it was up to me to make my own decisions about where I live.

Jerry: Well, that's not what she wants at all. She's just saying that because she knows that you are so headstrong and won't do what she wants anyway.

Char: I can't talk to you anymore about this now. I'll see you later.

Because of her frustration in this conversation, Char lowered her opinion of Jerry. After a number of similar conversations, she began to avoid him completely.

10. *Restate the content of the speaker's message.* Use repetition of key words, phrases, and ideas to demonstrate your understanding of the conversation. Such restatements should be brief.

11. *Paraphrase the content of the speaker's message.* Restate the speaker's message in your own words to determine if you understand the content of the message. Your goals in paraphrasing should be to completely understand the other person, rather than to disagree or to state your own point of view.

12. *Paraphrase the intent of the speaker's message.* People generally have a reason for making statements or disclosing information. Demonstrate your understanding of the speaker's intention by attempting to state that intention concisely in your own words.

Nonverbal Skills

Although you demonstrate active listening through the verbal skills previously listed above, the majority of your active-listening ability is shown through nonverbal communication. The following nonverbal skills are essential in your ability to demonstrate active listening. As you listen to another person, have a friend observe you to determine if you are practicing these skills:

1. *Demonstrate bodily responsiveness.* Use movement and gestures to show your awareness of the speaker's message. Shaking your head in disbelief, checking the measurements of an object by indicating the size with your hands, and moving toward a person who is disclosing negative information demonstrate appropriate bodily responsiveness.

2. *Lean forward.* By learning toward the speaker, a good listener demonstrates interest in the speaker. A forward lean suggests responsiveness as well as interest. In addition, learning places the listener in a physical state of readiness to listen to the speaker.

3. *Use direct body orientation.* Do not angle yourself away from the speaker; instead, sit or stand so that you are directly facing him or her. A parallel body position allows the greatest possibility for observing and listening to the speaker's verbal and nonverbal messages. When you stand or sit at an angle to the speaker, you may be creating the impression that you are attempting to get away or that you are moving away from the speaker. An angled position also blocks your vision and allows you to be distracted by other stimuli in the environment.

4. *Use relaxed, but alert, posture.* Your posture should not be tense or "proper," but neither should it be so relaxed that you appear to be resting. Slouching suggests unresponsiveness; a tense body position suggests nervousness or discomfort; and a relaxed position accompanied by crossed arms and legs, a backward lean in a chair, and a confident facial expression suggests arrogance. Your posture should suggest to others that you are interested and that you are comfortable talking with them.

5. *Establish an open body position.* Sit or stand with your body open to the other person. Crossing your arms or legs may be more comfortable, but that posture frequently suggests that you are closed off psychologically, as well as physically. In order to maximize your nonverbal message to the other person that you are "open" to him or her, you should sit or stand without crossing your arms or legs.

6. *Use positive, responsive facial expressions and head movement.* Your face and head will be the speaker's primary focus. The speaker will be observing you, and your facial expression and head movement will be the key. You can demonstrate your concern by nodding your head to show interest or agreement. You can use positive and responsive facial expressions, such as smiling and raising your eyebrows.

7. *Establish direct eye contact.* The speaker will be watching your eyes for interest. One of the first signs of a lack of interest is the listener's tendency to be distracted by other stimuli in the environment. For example, an instructor who continually glances out the door of her office, a roommate who glances at the television program that is on, or a business executive who regularly looks at her watch is, while appearing to listen, showing signs of disinterest. Try to focus on and direct your gaze at the speaker. When you begin to look around the room, you may find any number of other stimuli to distract your attention from the speaker and the message.

8. *Sit or stand close to the speaker.* Establishing close proximity to the speaker has two benefits. First, you put yourself in a position that allows you to hear the other person and that minimizes the distracting noises, sights, and other stimuli. Second, you demonstrate your concern or your positive feelings for the speaker. You probably do not stand or sit close to people you do not like, you do not respect, or with whom you do not have common experiences. Close physical proximity allows active listening to occur.

9. *Use vocal responsiveness.* Change your pitch, rate, inflection, and volume as you respond to the speaker. Making appropriate changes and choices shows that you are actually listening, in contrast to responding in a standard, patterned manner that suggests you are only appearing to listen. The stereotypical picture of a husband and wife at the breakfast table with the husband, hidden behind a newspaper, responding, "Yes, yes, yes" in a monotone voice while the wife tells him their son has shaved his hair, she is running off with the mail carrier, and the house is on fire provides a familiar example of the appearance of listening while one is actually far away from the speaker's message.

10. *Provide supportive utterances.* Sometimes you can demonstrate more concern through nonverbal sounds such as "Mmm," "Mmm-hmm," and "Uh-huh" than you can by stating, "Yes, I understand." You can easily provide supportive utterances while other persons are talking or when they pause. You are suggesting to them that you are listening but you do not want to interrupt with a verbalization of your own at this particular time. Such sounds encourage the speaker to continue without interruption.

Active listening requires a great deal of energy and sensitivity to the other person, but it is a reachable goal. The behaviors previously outlined should assist you in listening more actively to others.

Summary

In this chapter you have learned the difference between hearing and listening. Most people spend more time listening than using any other communication skill. Yet listening is usually the least studied communication skill. Physical, mental, factual, and semantic distractions interfere with listening, as can status, stereotypes, and what you see and hear others doing. You can even interfere with your own listening by acting egocentric or defensive or by exhibiting experiential superiority.

Active listening, or listening with a purpose, includes empathic and critical listening. Empathic listening involves attempting to understand another person. Critical listening requires evaluating a speaker's message for accuracy, meaningfulness, and usefulness.

Critical listening and critical thinking go hand in hand. The first step in critical thinking and listening is identifying the source and establishing the source's credibility; the second step is evaluating the message and the process by which the information was discovered. A critical thinker and listener must be able to distinguish between observations and inferences; categorize evidence as emotional, logical, or personal; and understand the difference between inductive and deductive arguments. Deductive arguments are evaluated for accuracy and validity; they may appear as complete syllogisms or incomplete arguments called enthymemes. Fallacies are errors that can take the form of argument against the person, appeal to the people, appeal to authority, hasty generalization, false cause, begging the question, irrelevant conclusion, false alternatives, equivocation, or division.

A number of specific verbal and nonverbal behaviors, discussed in this chapter, can positively affect your ability to listen.

Additional Resources

Active listening (1997). *Public Management,* 79 (12), 25–27.

Brownell, J. (1996). *Listening: Attitudes, principles, and skills.*

Boston: Allyn and Bacon.

Merker, H. (1994). *Listening.* New York: HarperCollins.

Weaver, J. B., III, & Kirtley, M. D. (1995). Listening styles and empathy. *Southern Communication Journal, 60*(2), 131–141.

Issues in Communication

This Issues in Communication narrative is designed to provoke individual thought or discussion about concepts raised in the chapter.

Harry and Brenda were in a big hurry to get to work. Harry hurriedly put the breakfast dishes in the sink while Brenda helped their daughter, Sally, into her coat. As they were on their way out the door to their separate cars, Brenda said, "I have to work late tonight, so you'll need to pick up Sally at day care." Harry responded without even thinking, "Yeah, okay." As he was shutting his car door, he heard Brenda yell, "And don't be late because they get really upset when parents are late to pick up their kids!" He waved, thinking, "That's Brenda for you—always overreacting." By the time Harry got to work, he had completely forgotten Brenda's request.

At 5:15 Harry was working at his desk—well, actually, he was talking with another guy about the Monday night football game—when his wife called. She was angry. The day care center had called her to ask why Sally hadn't been picked up yet. "Well," said Harry, "why didn't you pick her up?" Brenda was furious. "I told you this morning that I had to work late! I told you to pick up Sally, and you said you would. I also told you how angry they get when parents are late." By now Harry's friend was looking con-cerned, but Harry winked at him and waved him away. "I don't remember you saying that," he said to Brenda. "But I'll go right now."

Harry was 10 minutes away from Playtime Daycare, but in rush-hour traffic, the drive would take at least 20 minutes. When Harry arrived, Sally was crying because she was the only kid left in front of the school. The woman holding her hand said, "You are over half an hour late. Playtime closes at 5, but we cannot leave a child alone. Next time you're late, you'll be charged extra." Sally's caregiver was obviously mad at Harry, his daughter was clearly upset, and his wife would be reluctant to ask him to pick up Sally the next time she has a late meeting. Harry suddenly recalled their hurried conversation earlier that morning, and he realized Brenda had not been overreacting when she told him not to be late. He knew he was in hot water.

Apply what you have learned about listening as you ponder and discuss the following questions: How do people hear and not listen? What factors might have interfered with Harry's ability to listen? Explain how active, empathic, and critical listening could have been used to create a more positive scenario. What specific listening strategies could have been used to avoid this particular outcome?

References

Barbara, D. (1957). On listening—the role of the ear in psychic life. *Today's Speech, 5,* 12.

Barker, L. L. (1971). *Listening behavior.* Englewood Cliffs, NJ: Prentice-Hall.

Bloom, B. (1954). *Taxonomy of educational objectives: Handbook I. Cognitive domain.* New York: Longmans.

Bochner, A. P., & Kelly, C. W. (1974). Interpersonal competence: Rationale, philosophy, and implementation of a conceptual framework. *Speech Teacher, 23,* 289.

Brooks, W. D., & Heath, R. W. (1989). *Speech communication* (6th ed.). Dubuque, IA: Wm. C. Brown.

Capella, J. N. (1987). Interpersonal communication: Definitions and fundamental questions. In C. R. Berger & S. Chaffee (Eds.), *Handbook of communication science* (pp. 216–217). Newbury Park, CA: Sage.

Clark, K. B. (1980, February). Empathy: A neglected topic in psychological research. *American Psychologist, 35,* 188.

Howell, W. S. (1982). *The empathic communicator.* Belmont, CA: Wadsworth.

Nichols, R. G., & Stevens, L. A. (1957). Listening to people. *Harvard Business Review, 35,* 85–92.

Piaget, J. (1974). *To understand is to invent: The future of education.* New York: Viking. (Original work published 1948.)

Rankin, P. T. (1926). The measure of the ability to understand spoken language. *Dissertation Abstracts, 12,* 847.

Resnik, L. B., & Klopfer, L. E. (1989). *Toward the thinking curriculum: Current cognitive research.* Washington, DC: USA Association for Supervision and Curriculum Development.

Schab, F. R., & Crowder, R. G. (1989). Accuracy of temporal coding: Auditory-visual comparisons. *Memory and Cognition, 17,* 384–397.

Smeltzner, L. R., & Watson, K. W. (1984, Fall). Listening: An empirical comparison of discussion length and level of incentive. *Central States Speech Journal, 35,* 166–170.

Taylor, A., Meyer, A., Rosegrant, T. & Samples, B. T. (1989). *Communication* (5th ed.). Englewood Cliffs, NJ: Prentice-Hall.

Werner, E. K. (1975). *A study of communication time.* Unpublished master's thesis, University of Maryland.

Wood, J. T. (1997). *Communication in our lives.* Belmont, CA: Wadsworth.

When you have read and thought about this chapter, you will be able to:

1. Understand why the study of mass communication is important.

2. Define *mass communication* and understand it in the context of the communication process.

3. Recognize mass media's role in shaping our culture, behavior, and attitudes.

4. Differentiate among gatekeeping, agenda setting, and framing.

5. Understand the strengths and the limitations of some of the media industries.

6. Think more critically about the mass media.

6

Mass Communication and Media Literacy

This chapter discusses mass communication, in which "mediated" communication uses technology to address a larger audience. This communication form entertains, informs, and provides a forum for public debate. In this chapter you will learn the importance of studying mass communication. Mass communication is defined and explained in the context of the communication process. You will then explore the effects of mass media—how the media shape our culture and our attitudes, how they influence behavior, and how they perpetuate stereotypes. The strengths and weaknesses of five types of mass media are discussed, and you will learn how you can be a more critical consumer of mass media.

im, a reporter for a local news station, arrived to check out the scene: the cooling system of a cold-storage building had malfunctioned, and there were rumors that tons of butter had melted. As he surveyed the building and spoke to the owner, he decided that although there were pools of butter on the floor, the situation did not warrant coverage for the local six o'clock news. When the butter caught fire and homeowners living nearby were evacuated from their homes because of the acrid smoke, he changed his mind and began gathering more information for the story that would air in a few hours.

Rose sighed. She just wanted to relax in front of the TV after a grueling day at work, but she was tired of watching sitcoms about middle-class white couples who fought a lot and wives who were all thin and beautiful. As a Chinese American happily married to a Caucasian, Rose rarely saw anything on TV that accurately resembled her life. She turned off the television, tuned the radio to a classical station, and settled back on the couch to read.

Vera was supposed to meet a friend in Boston, so she got up early and started getting ready for her trip. The first thing she did was turn on the weather channel. It showed hurricane-strength winds and rain all along the coast. She called her friend to cancel their meeting; the ferries would not be running from Martha's Vineyard to the mainland during a storm like this. Perhaps next weekend would be better.

Why Should You Study Mass Communication?

mass communication

The process in which professional communicators using technological devices share messages over great distances to influence large audiences.

Many of the reasons for studying more personal forms of communication are also relevant to the study of mass communication. Perhaps the most important is that by understanding the process of mass communication, you will learn to think critically about the messages the media send us. You will become a more thoughtful media consumer. As a consumer of the media, and as a citizen of a world in which technology seems to be bringing people closer together, your responsibility is to understand how the media function and to develop the skills to interpret the significance of the products they offer. By understanding the nature and function of mass communication, you can begin to recognize the significance of the media and the role they play in shaping your understanding of the world.

What Is Mass Communication?

Wilson and Wilson (1998) define **mass communication** as *a process in which professional communicators using technological devices share messages over great distances to influence large audiences.* You can look at this definition in the context of the communication process, which involves a source, a channel, a message, a receiver, and feedback (Figure 6.1).

Mass communication can be delivered electronically.

In mass communication, a professional communicator is the **source,** *someone who shares information, ideas, or attitudes with someone else.* The source might be a television or newspaper reporter, an author, or an announcer. The technological devices are the **channels,** or *the means by which a message is sent.* For example, radio and television messages are transmitted via cable and satellite systems, and printed messages are transmitted via printing presses, computers, and, increasingly, via satellite. The **message** is *whatever the source attempts to share with another person.* In mass communication, the large audience comprises the **receivers,** *the people who are the intended recipients of the message.* Occasionally a receiver of the message will send **feedback** to the source, that is, a *response that allows the source to determine if the message was correctly understood.* In mass communication feedback can be conveyed through a letter to the editor, for instance, or a telephone call to a television station.

source

Someone who shares information, ideas, or attitudes with someone else; in mass communication the source is professional communicators.

channels

The means by which a message is sent; in mass communication, the channels are technological devices.

message

Whatever the source attempts to share with another person.

receivers

The people who are the intended recipients of the message.

feedback

A response that allows the source to determine if the message was correctly understood.

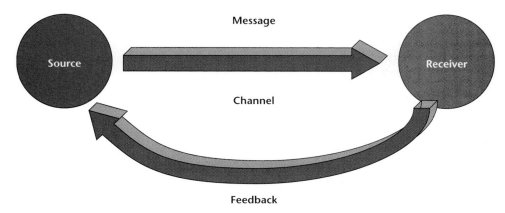

Figure 6.1 The communication process.

Fill in the blanks:

1.   The means by which a message is sent is the _____ or _____ _____.

2.   The receivers are the _____.

3.   Someone who shares information and ideas with someone else is the _____.

4.   _____ allows the source to determine if the message was correctly understood.

Answers: 1. channel/technological device   2. audience   3. source   4. Feedback

What Are the Effects of the Mass Media?

The mass media do much more than inform and entertain. They also shape our culture and our attitudes, influence behavior, and perpetuate stereotypes.

Shape Culture

culture

A set of beliefs and understandings a society has about the world, its place in it, and the various activities used to celebrate and reinforce those beliefs.

Because people depend on the mass media to inform them, the media play a major role in shaping our culture. **Culture,** in this context, is *a set of beliefs and understandings a society has about the world, its place in it, and the various activities used to celebrate and reinforce those beliefs.* How do media decisions about what is important influence our culture? Consider the influence of televised football on the American culture. The sense of "maleness" and competition that surrounds football supports the belief that men are supposed to be big, tough, and macho. The game subtly reinforces the notion that people can be anything they want if only they try hard enough, a distinct belief of the American culture. Indeed, as early as the nineteenth century, cheap paperback novels promoted the American virtues of working hard, getting an education, and pulling yourself up by the bootstraps. Such values have been repeated in radio programs, magazine stories, and television situation comedies so often they have become a part of our social fabric.

Men seem to bond around the sport of football.

Once you start to think this way, the significance of the mass media as "culture industries" becomes apparent. This viewpoint assumes two important concepts. First, the media are an arena for working out competing definitions of reality. Thus, the media become a debating ground for our system of values and beliefs. Second, the effects of the media are not simple, direct results but complex consequences interwoven in the cultural fabric. When you see the media as contributing to the culture, you can ask how they affect that culture on a societal level. The media use gatekeeping to determine what you see and read about; and agenda setting suggests how you should think about issues.

Gatekeeping

Gatekeeping is *the process of determining what news, information, or entertainment will reach a mass audience.* The term *gatekeeping,* coined by Kurt Lewin in 1947, describes the fact that news must travel through a series of checkpoints before it reaches the public (Wilson & Wilson, 1998). To see how gatekeeping works, consider what happens with a freeway accident involving a large truck and two cars. Gatekeeping first occurs when newspapers, for example, determine if the accident is serious enough to justify sending reporters to the scene. If reporters are sent to the scene, they will act as gatekeepers when they decide if a story should be written about it. If the story is written, it goes to a copy editor, who edits it, and then it may go to the city editor, who judges its importance. Such decisions are made every day in mass media—by a news director at a television station, an acquisitions editor at a book publishing company, and other gatekeepers. Thus, each day, a number of people control what you see and how you see it.

gatekeeping

The process of determining what news, information, or entertainment will reach an audience.

```
TRY ◀▶ THIS
```

Think about all the things you watched on television while growing up. What are some of the enduring lessons you learned from these shows?

Agenda Setting

Agenda setting simply means *choosing what topics an audience will read about and hear about.* According to Wilson and Wilson (1998), "The professional communicators working for the mass media set the news and information agenda for us" (p. 15). Although journalists attempt to serve as watchdogs of the political process, other forces also shape such agendas. Political and social agendas are both challenged and validated through the information and entertainment media. If the media deem a story or issue important, it will get media attention; if they perceive the story as unimportant, it will receive very little attention. Take the example of a suburban race for city council in which eight candidates are vying for five open seats on the council. The large city paper decides not to feature the contest because other breaking news is more important, and this race is just one of seven in the surrounding suburbs. The suburban paper gives the contest front-page coverage, but it provides the incumbents with slightly more coverage. On the other hand, a local magazine devotes equal space to all the candidates. The television station only mentions that the race is "impossible to predict." Agendas can vary greatly within a medium, and from one medium to another. Very few professional communicators, especially those involved in processing news stories, purposely slant the news to fit their own bias. They generally attempt to be objective and fair (Wilson & Wilson, 1998).

agenda setting

The process of selecting what topics an audience will read about and hear about.

framing

Taking a particular perspective on a story.

Shape Attitudes

Mass media move beyond the gatekeeping and agenda-setting functions by framing what you see, hear, and read. **Framing** means *taking a particular perspective on a story.* In a TV or radio broadcast or in a newspaper or magazine article the framing might consist of what parts of the story receive emphasis. Framing is even more obvious on the opinion pages of a newspaper, on the commentary portion of a broadcast, on news documentaries on television, on radio and TV talk shows, and in news magazines. The same story can get left-of-center treatment in *The Washington Post* and right-of-center treatment in *The Washington Times. The New York Times* reflects a somewhat liberal point of view, while *The Wall Street Journal* normally assumes a conservative stance. *Newsweek,* published by the same people who bring you *The Washington Post,* often drifts left of center, while *US News & World Report* lists to the right. As a student of communication studies, you need to know what biases already exist in what purport to be objective accounts of events. If the content of your daily communication comes from news sources that have a perspective of their own, you have a right to know that what you see, hear, and read has already been through a series of gatekeepers, has been chosen as part of the media's agenda, and has been framed to suggest how it is to be interpreted. Framing, then, is one way that mass media shape attitudes.

TRY ◀▶ THIS

Buy two newspapers from the same day or two news magazines from the same week or listen to the early-evening news and the late-evening news on different channels. What differences do you observe concerning which stories are covered, where they are placed, and how they are covered? Do you think your news source makes any difference in how you think and in what you discuss with others?

Influence Behavior

No issue better illustrates the influence of mass media on our actions than the issue of violence. Most people agree that violence is more prevalent in the United States than in most other countries, and many experts think they have proof that mass media is implicated in the burgeoning violence. A look at the research tells part of the story.

The 1968 National Commission on the Causes and Prevention of Violence, the 1972 Surgeon General's Report, the National Institute of Mental Health's 1982 study, the U.S. Attorney General's 1984 Task Force on Family Violence, and the American Medical Association's 1996 study all demonstrate a positive correlation between TV violence and aggressive behavior by the children and adults who watch it. The American Psychological Association compiled 1,000 commentaries, reports, and research studies on the impact of TV violence and found the same positive correlation between TV violence and aggressive behavior (Wilson & Wilson, 1998). Consider these examples:

- After the film *Fuzz* appeared on TV, at least two people were doused by gasoline and "flamed" just as delinquents did to a vagrant in the movie.

- After *The Deer Hunter* was broadcast on TV, with a scene showing men playing Russian roulette, 20 people died imitating the "game."

- Touchstone Films removed a video scene in which football players demonstrated their "courage" by lying in the middle of a highway at night—after several young men died imitating the scene (Wilson & Wilson, 1998).

But the influence of television isn't entirely negative. The American people have never known so much about political candidates, accidents, crime, crises, and weather than they do today. With the advent of 24-hour news and weather programs, you can find out the latest news, weather, and road reports whenever you wish.

Perpetuate Stereotypes

Julia Wood (1994), a communication professor at the University of North Carolina, provides an interesting picture of the world as depicted by the media: It is a world in which white males make up two-thirds of the population. The women are fewer in number perhaps because less than 10 percent live beyond 35. Those who do, like their male counterparts and the younger females, are nearly all white and heterosexual. In addition to being young, the majority of women are beautiful, very thin, passive, and primarily concerned with relationships and getting rings out of collars and commodes. There are a few bad, bitchy women, and they are not so pretty, not so subordinate, and not so caring as the good women. Most of the bad ones work outside the home, which is why they are hardened and undesirable. The more powerful, ambitious men occupy themselves with important business deals, exciting adventures, and rescues of dependent females, whom they often assault sexually (pp. 231 ff).

What Wood is talking about is the stereotypes that mass media perpetuate. Stereotypes often depict people who are not from the dominant culture, which, as you will learn in Chapter 9, is white, middle-class men. For example, consider the treatment of gays and lesbians in the movies. According to Richard Corliss (1996), homosexuals have primarily had a "nonperson status" in movies. Some movies, such as *The Birdcage* and *Philadelphia*, have portrayed gay men more sympathetically.

Similarly, when the media portray women, the women tend to fit cultural views of gender. Wood (1994) says women are depicted "as sex objects who are usually young, thin, beautiful, passive, dependent, and often incompetent and dumb. Female characters devote their primary energies to improving their appearances and taking care of homes and people" (p. 233). The good women, like Snow White and Sleeping Beauty, tend to be soft, tender, pretty, and passive. The bad women, like the wicked witch in *The Wizard of Oz* and Alex in the movie *Fatal Attraction*, are hard, cold, and aggressive. In films and in TV movies, it is unusual to find a man who is tender and cooks for the family or a woman who is a CEO. Instead, people are regularly portrayed in gender roles that are traditional, limiting, and unrealistic.

The point is that media portrayals do not necessarily reflect reality. Like the gatekeepers of the news, the movie moguls have an unwritten rule about how women and men must behave. Wood (1994) says, "The rule seems to be that a woman may be strong and successful if and only if she also exemplifies traditional stereotypes of femininity—subservience, passivity, beauty, and an identity linked to one or more men" (p. 241).

6.2 MASS-MEDIA CONCEPTS

Write the correct letter from the choices below in each blank on the left:

A. Gatekeeping   B. Agenda setting   C. Framing   D. Stereotyping

_____1. The city editor of the newspaper decided to emphasize the possible causes of the riot instead of simply listing the injured and the arrested.

_____2. The news director of the TV station laid out a plan to spend 3 minutes per night on the evening news showing what his reporters discovered about healthy citizens using handicapped parking placards that were stolen, fake, or belong to a relative or friend.

_____3. Asians are rarely seen on television programs except as martial-arts experts; Hispanics are usually depicted as crooks; and Arabs are usually shown as unshaven plotters.

_____4. The magazine editor delayed the story about investments until next month's issue, called for a rewrite and reduction of the risky-bond story, and placed the article about a new CEO for MegaCorp as the lead.

_____5. Thousands of photographs deemed likely to undermine home-front morale were censored from illustrated publications, newsreels, and films during World War II (Roeder, Jr., 1995).

Answers: 1. C   2. B   3. D   4. A   5. A or B

What Are the Mass Media?

The mass media include newspapers, books, magazines, journals, television, radio, motion pictures, videotapes, audiotapes, compact disks, and the Internet. This section briefly discusses newspapers, television, news magazines, the Internet, and professional journals, as these are the sources you are most likely to use when preparing for your public speech in class.

Newspapers

Freedom of the press has long been America's chief defense against government abuses of its citizens. Our oldest mass medium, newspapers are one of our most reliable sources of information. While generally very good at its mission, the American press has of late been accused of abuse of power. Books warn of the arrogance of the press (Fallows, 1999), a syndicated columnist notes that citizens now see the power of the press as replacing the dangers once posed by big government, and surveys place journalists rather low on the national hierarchy of valued professions. Nonetheless, newspapers have a long and distinguished history in this country. They have established coveted awards for excellence, such as the Pulitzer Prize, and they have exposed crimes, scandals, and corruption down through the decades.

In the past, every city had competing newspapers clamoring for the attention of readers who soaked up information in taxis, on commuter trains, on buses, and even in cars stuck in traffic. Gradually, however, afternoon papers failed and morning papers merged. Today many cities have only one newspaper. Circulation has plummeted, and figures indicate that the average age of readers is rising by the year. Currently, newspaper readers tend to be older; younger people seem to find print journalism unattractive. Nonetheless, newspapers remain one of the most informative, carefully edited, and insightful sources of information and analysis, but they must be read with a critical eye.

TRY ◄ ► THIS

Imagine what the print media will be like in the future. Do you think newspapers will become obsolete? What role do you think computer technology will play in print journalism?

Even highly credible newspapers make mistakes, so don't consider everything you read in the paper to be 100 percent reliable. For example, *The Cincinnati Inquirer* once ran a story critical of the Chiquita Banana Company, but the story was based largely on internal e-mail messages from the company. The newspaper later apologized for running a story based on an unreliable source, ran front-page retractions, and paid $10 million to the banana company. Among the most reliable newspapers are national publications such as *The Los Angeles Times, The New York Times,* and *The Washington Post.* Some good regional papers include *The Atlanta Constitution, The Miami Herald,* and *The St. Louis Post Dispatch.* Make sure you know which newspapers in your area are considered the most reliable and trustworthy.

Many newspapers are now available on the web, yet this has not led to the demise of the printed newspaper, as many once thought. Although newspaper readership has been diminishing for years, newspapers today continue to be a powerful and reliable source of information.

Television

Television news is currently
the most widely used source
of information about current
events. You probably get at
least some of your information from the 6 or 10 P.M.
news or from MSNBC's or
CNN's continuous news coverage. Like newspapers, commercial television stations report the news, but they must
also make a profit.

Today's TV news is
immediate and
continuous.

When you are watching
broadcast news, you should
recognize that the immediacy
of the news is much more a
factor with television than it is with newspapers and magazines, so skepticism
regarding breaking news is particularly important. Broadcast news stations will
often go immediately on the air with a breaking news story to "beat" competing
stations. Often, however, initial statements and inferences regarding events are
unclear or even incorrect. Indeed, sometimes the biggest, most important
events remain unsettled for years. Consider the assassination of Martin Luther
King, Jr., the assassination of President John F. Kennedy, and Flight 800 that
crashed over Long Island.

News Magazines

News magazines are better for in-depth treatment of recent events than are
newspapers and television. The disadvantage of news magazines is that the

e-note
www.

INTERNET GUIDE TO THE NETWORKS

ABC-TV: **www.abc.com**

CBS-TV: **www.cbs.com**

NBC-TV: **www.nbc.com**

Fox TV: **www.foxworld.com**

Information on programming and scheduling: **www.tvnet.com**

news they contain is not as immediate as that in newspapers and on television. National news magazines like *Time, Newsweek,* and *US News & World Report* are regarded as reliable sources. Other sources tend to be more liberal- or conservative-leaning and are not as objective.

Even though news magazines have more time than television broadcasts and newspapers to get the facts of a story straight, they too make mistakes. For example, *Newsweek* reported in its June 22, 1998, edition that the Rainforest Café posted a loss in the last quarter of 1997. In its July 6, 1998, edition, *Newsweek* ran a correction:

> In our June 22 article on the growing use of fantasy décor ("Our New Theme Song," BUSINESS), we reported that the Rainforest Café posted a loss in the last quarter of 1997. In fact, it made a profit in that quarter. Newsweek regrets the error. (p. 20)

So, it's important to remember that even the best sources sometimes make mistakes.

The Internet

Internet

A global network of interconnected computer networks.

Some of the most outrageous news comes from the **Internet,** *a global network of interconnected computer networks.* Matt Drudge, alleged journalist, provided the early news reports regarding the Lewinsky-Clinton scandal. Rumors run rampant on the Internet every time a dramatic or mysterious event occurs. The trouble with the Internet is that many of the web sites and alleged news sources offer little more than speculative gossip. With the exception of reputable newspapers and magazines, many sites have no gatekeeper—in other words, no one is checking the sites' information for accuracy and integrity.

Professional Journals

Every academic discipline has professional journals, as do professions such as law and medicine. Some journals have excellent reputations for advancing knowledge. For example, *The New England Journal of Medicine* (American) and *Lancet* (British) are regarded as highly reliable sources of information about advances in medicine. Generally, professional journals are good sources of information because they are carefully reviewed by editorial reviewers. However, all professional journals are not created equal. Every discipline has a hierarchy of journals in which the reputation is based on readership (in scholarly circles, less may be better), on rejection rates (the more articles rejected, the more selective the journal), or on the reputation and standing of the authors.

The downside of professional journals is that they are written for specialized audiences and often use jargon that is difficult for an ordinary person to understand. In addition, professional journals are often resistant to new ideas that run counter to established notions. Ideas that threaten the reviewers' carefully staked-out territories may never be printed. Such resistance to new ideas continues today in all professions, as boards of reviewers encourage articles consistent with their current beliefs and reject those that threaten established ideas. Regardless, professional journals are a good source of information because the information is collected by using established standards, is reviewed by experts, and is published only after being selected as the best thinking on the subject at the time.

How Can You Be a Critical Consumer of Mass Media?

Although a few suggestions on how to be a critical consumer of specific media were provided in the previous section, this section gives you tips to help you be a more critical consumer of mass media in general:

1. *Professional communicators make numerous decisions about what you see and how you see it.* Whether you're reading the newspaper or

Instant Recall

Match the correct letter from the choices below with each description:

A. Newspapers   **D. News magazine**
B. Television/radio   **E. Professional journals**
C. Internet

_____1. Fastest at getting news to the largest number.

_____2. Most thorough at collecting and editing news.

_____3. Most likely to have errors in reporting news.

_____4. Least likely to be known to the public.

_____5. Best source of news analysis.

Answers: 1. B (the Internet is fast but does not go to the largest number)   2. D   3. C   4. E   5. D

watching television, remember that someone else decided what should be covered (gatekeeping), whether the topic continues to be an important issue (agenda setting), and how the subject is presented (framing).

2. *Be careful of a "herd mentality" in news gathering in which certain stories are sensationalized.* Don't get all your information from one source or one medium. By using a number of sources, you can examine the differences among them regarding how a story is covered.

3. *Although the primary goal of newspapers, news magazines, and broadcast news is to inform the audience, each must also present the news in a way that brings in a profit.* The unfortunate result of these cross-purposes is that some sources will say almost anything to get someone to buy their publications or watch their broadcasts.

4. *Some publications have biases that affect their presentation of the news.* Be sure you are aware of any underlying biases in the publications you read.

5. *Learn what you can from media sources, but learn to think for yourself as well.* As a consumer of mass media, you should be wary of how much credence you attribute to what you see, hear, and read because all media are subject to human error and biases.

Summary

In this chapter you learned about mass communication, a process in which professional communicators using technological devices share messages over great distances to influence large audiences. Perhaps the most important reason for studying mass communication is that by understanding this process you learn to think critically about the messages the media send and you will become a more thoughtful consumer.

The mass media do much more than entertain and inform; they also shape our culture and our attitudes, influence behavior, and perpetuate stereotypes. Gatekeeping, agenda setting, and framing are three ways in which professional communicators control what you see, hear, and read in the mass media.

Forms of mass media include newspapers, books, magazines, journals, television, radio, motion pictures, videotapes, audiotapes, compact discs, and the Internet. Newspapers, television, news magazines, the Internet, and professional journals are likely sources to use when you are preparing to give a speech, but to use these sources effectively, you should follow this chapter's suggestions on how to be a more critical consumer of the mass media.

Additional Resources

Alexander, A., & Hanson, J. (1997). *Taking sides: Clashing views on controversial issues in mass media and society* (4th ed.). Guilford, CT: Dushkin/Brown & Benchmark.

Dodd, C. H. (1998). *Dynamics of intercultural communication* (5th ed.). New York: McGraw-Hill.

Dominick, J. R. (1999). *The dynamics of mass communication* (6th ed.). New York: McGraw-Hill.

Gorham, J. (Ed.). (1997). *Mass media 97/98.* New York: Dushkin/McGraw-Hill.

Montgomery, K. C. (1996, July–August). Children in the digital age. *American Prospect*, 69–74.

Walker, C. (1996, May). Can TV save the planet? *American Demographics*, 42–43, 46–48.

Wilson, J., & Wilson, S. L. (1998). *Mass media/mass culture* (4th ed.). New York: McGraw-Hill.

Corliss, R. (1996). The final frontier. *Time*, 66–68.

References

Dominick, J. R. (1999). *The dynamics of mass communication* (6th ed.). New York: McGraw-Hill.

Fallows, J. (1997). *Breaking the news: How the media undermine American democracy.* New York: Random House.

Roeder, Jr., G. H. (1995, Fall). Missing on the home front: Wartime censorship and postwar ignorance. *Phi Kappa Phi Journal,* 25–29.

Wood, J. T. (1994). *Gendered lives: Communication, gender, and culture,* (pp. 231–244). Newbury Park, CA: Wadsworth.

Wilson, J., & Wilson, S. L. (1998). *Mass media/mass culture* (4th ed.). New York: McGraw-Hill.

Issues in Communication

CULTURAL DEMOCRACY

This Issues in Communication narrative is designed to provoke individual thought or discussion about concepts raised in the chapter.

American television operates in a system that encourages producers to provide content that satisfies the largest number of viewers. Popularity is the notion behind cultural democracy. By watching a certain program on a certain channel at a certain time, we "vote" for that program. As a result, the content that gets the highest rating is the content that endures and is imitated. This approach assumes that the judgment of the TV audience is the best way to decide what content is of value.

This approach has intuitive appeal and seems consistent with the democratic ideals behind American society. That the cultural democracy concept is endorsed by many in the industry is not surprising.

Cultural democracy will inevitably lead to the lowest common denominator programs. Shows that titillate and excite will draw bigger ratings than shows that make people contemplate. Perhaps programmers have a duty to society at large to present content of value that may not get the highest ratings.

Parents who think that certain programs are undesirable for their children can choose not to watch, but this action may not communicate their feelings to program producers. Short of writing letters of protest and forming watchdog groups (things that most viewers do not do), cultural democracy allows little room for dissent.

Finally, cultural democracy discourages distinguishing between content that is popular yet trivial and content that is important but lacks mass appeal. If value and worth are associated with popularity, then the unpopular will be perceived as valueless no matter what its intrinsic merit. Popularity may not equal significance.

In today's ratings-driven television environment, to justify scheduling another clone of "Baywatch" or "Jerry Springer" is easy, because it's what the public wants. The question is: should TV programming be determined by popularity.

Apply what you have learned about mass communication as you ponder and discuss the following questions:

Although the cultural democracy concept is endorsed by many in the industry, is popularity the best way to decide what programming gets aired? Do producers have an ethical duty to look beyond the numbers? How can viewers register their dissatisfaction with current programming?

Communication Contexts:

Couples, Teams, and Cultures

PART 3 FOCUSES ON PEOPLE in pairs, teams, and cultures. This unit will increase your understanding of how people communicate in small groups, in interpersonal relationships, and with people from other cultures and co-cultures.

Chapter 7, Interpersonal and Family Communication, explores the nature of interpersonal relationships and how to improve communication within your interpersonal relationships.

Chapter 8, Intercultural Communication, looks closely at communication between people of different cultures and co-cultures, and provides specific strategies for improving intercultural communication.

Chapter 9, The Dynamics of Small-Group Discussion, covers small-groups—what they are and how they work.

Chapter 10, Group Leadership, Conflict and Problem Solving, examines leadership, effective group problem-solving, and decision making.

When you have read and thought about this chapter, you will be able to:

1. Define *interpersonal relationship*.

2. List some reasons we engage in interpersonal relationships.

3. Provide some examples of Knapp's relational stages.

4. Explain relational initiation, maintenance, and deterioration.

5. Reveal why self-disclosing is important.

6. Relate supportive and defensive behaviors to communication.

7. Explain how you can become a more effective communicator.

8. Explain how interpersonal communication functions in the family.

Interpersonal and Family Communication

"Seeing ourselves as others see us would probably confirm our worst suspicions about them."

FRANKLIN P. JONES

"It is those who have not really lived—who have left issues unsettled, dreams unfilled, hopes shattered and who have let the real things in life . . . pass them by—who are most reluctant to die. It is never too late to start living and growing."

ELIZABETH KUBLER-ROSS

Interpersonal relationships can be complicated and they sometimes require a lot of work, but by expanding your knowledge and learning new skills, you can improve your satisfaction within your interpersonal relationships. In this chapter you will learn that interpersonal relationships help you understand yourself, others, and your world; they can help you fulfill your needs and increase and enrich positive experiences. You will learn the stages of relational development, maintenance, and deterioration. Self-disclosure also will be explored in detail. Because conflict occurs in virtually all interpersonal relationships, you also will learn some methods of conflict resolution. Finally, you will look at interpersonal communication within the family.

"All happy families resemble one another; every unhappy family is unhappy in its own way."

TOLSTOY, IN *ANNA KARENINA*

M arla and Jess have been married for 25 years. When asked the secret to a lasting relationship, they hesitate a little before answering. Both say that they don't think there's a magical formula to a successful relationship but, rather, that a deep, lasting relationship requires good communication and a lot of hard work. They talk about how they thought their first date would be their last, but they're thankful that it wasn't. Marla and Jess think one reason they've stayed together so long is the rituals they've established through the years. For example, they dubbed Saturday nights their night out together, when they're both at work they talk to each other on the phone at least once during the day, and each year they celebrate their wedding anniversary by going away together for a weekend. Another factor has been their ability to adapt to changing roles within the family. For example, when Marla got a big promotion at work, Jess took on more responsibilities at home. But the most important factor has been their ability to communicate effectively with each other. The result is a more meaningful relationship than either could have imagined back on their first date.

The Nature of Interpersonal Relationships

The Definition of Interpersonal Relationships

interpersonal relationship

The association of two or more people who are interdependent, who use some consistent patterns of interaction, and who have interacted for an extended period of time.

On the simplest level, relationships are associations or connections. Interpersonal relationships, however, are far more complex. **Interpersonal relationships** may be defined as *associations between two or more people who are interdependent, who use some consistent patterns of interaction, and who have interacted for an extended period of time.* Let us consider the different elements of this definition in more detail.

First, *interpersonal relationships include two or more people.* Often, interpersonal relationships consist of just two people—a dating couple, a single parent and a child, a married couple, two close friends, or two coworkers. Interpersonal relationships can also involve more than two people—a family unit, a group of friends, or a social group.

Second, *interpersonal relationships involve people who are interdependent.* Interdependence refers to people's being mutually dependent on each other and having an impact on each other. Friendship easily illustrates this concept. Your best friend, for example, may be dependent on you for acceptance and guidance. You, on the other hand, might require support and admiration. When individuals are independent of each other, or when dependence occurs only in one direction, the resulting association is not defined as an interpersonal relationship.

Third, *individuals in interpersonal relationships use some consistent patterns of interaction.* These patterns may include behaviors generally understood across a variety of situations, as well as behaviors unique to the relationship. For example, a husband may always greet his wife with a kiss. This

Communication is central to the development of interpersonal relationships.

kiss is generally understood as a sign of warmth and affection. On the other hand, the husband may have unique nicknames for his wife that are not understood outside the relationship.

Fourth, *individuals in interpersonal relationships generally have interacted for some time.* When you nod and smile at someone as you leave the classroom, when you meet a girlfriend's siblings for the first time, or when you place an order at a fast-food counter, you do not have an interpersonal relationship. Although participants use interpersonal communication to accomplish these events, one-time interactions do not constitute interpersonal relationships. We should note, however, that interpersonal relationships may last for varying lengths of time—some are relatively short, and others continue for a lifetime.

The Importance of Interpersonal Relationships

Interpersonal relationships are essential for all of us. Five reasons we engage in interpersonal relationships are (1) to understand ourselves, (2) to understand others, (3) to understand our world, (4) to fulfill our needs, and (5) to increase and enrich positive experiences.

Understanding Ourselves

One way we come to understand ourselves is through our interactions with others. Three factors influence how we communicate with others in interpersonal situations: social class, social comparison, and special others.

We don't usually like to admit that our **social class,** *a group whose members share the same economic or social status,* can affect our view of others and ourselves. Consider this example: Sergei grew up in a blue-collar

social class

A group whose members share the same economic or social status.

family and is the first in his family to attend college. His grades in high school were so good that he received a scholarship to attend a private college. When Sergei got to college, he discovered that most of the students he met had parents in the white-collar professions. He had always been proud of how hard his parents and grandparents had worked to provide for him, but he suddenly found himself embarrassed by his background. As a result, Sergei kept to himself and didn't make many friends. He could endure the discomfort and unhappiness this situation brought him for only one semester. The following semester he transferred to a public university, where he met students from a variety of backgrounds. He felt more comfortable at this school, and he made many friends. Sergei's social class influenced not only what others thought of him but also what he thought of himself.

A second factor that influences interpersonal relationships is **social comparison,** or *evaluation of the self by comparing oneself to others.* For example, you find out at tryouts for the musical that some other contenders can dance and sing better than you can, or you notice that a colleague who started working for the firm at the same time you did has earned promotions more quickly. Social comparison occurs through verbal and nonverbal communication. When you meet someone, you might ask what the person does for a living or what his or her major is in college, you might look at what the person is wearing, or you might notice whether he or she has a firm handshake. Throughout the years, we gain more knowledge about what we do well, ordinarily, or poorly by comparing our behavior, performance, or productivity to that of others.

Finally, a third factor that influences interpersonal relationships is **special others:** *people who take a special interest in you, mentor you, or encourage you to be something more than you would have been otherwise.* A "special other" might be a teacher who said you were good at math, science, or literature; a coach who encouraged your gifts as an athlete; a choir director who gave you a solo; or a parent or grandparent who encouraged your creative side. In the workplace, the special other might be someone who trains you and serves as a mentor or progressively gives you more challenging responsibilities and promotes you. These special people play a large role in making you who you are, and they do this by communicating with you about your special attributes through verbal and nonverbal means. Such people shape not only how you see yourself but also how you communicate with and see others.

social comparison

Evaluation of the self by comparing oneself to others.

special others

People who take a special interest in you, mentor you, or encourage you to be something more than you would have been otherwise.

TRY ◄ ► THIS

Make a list of all your different "selves" and how each of your roles differs as a friend, boyfriend or girlfriend, son or daughter, sibling, or student.

Understanding Others

Interpersonal relationships also assist us in learning about others. Many times, we may feel we know people before we even have a relationship with them. We make judgments, draw inferences, and reach conclusions about others without really knowing very much about them. Professors Charles R. Berger and Richard J. Calabrese (1975) labeled this phenomenon the **uncertainty principle.** This principle simply suggests that *when we initially meet others and thus know little about them, we rid ourselves of this uncertainty by drawing inferences from the information with which we are presented.* Additionally, the urge to reduce uncertainty motivates further interpersonal communication.

Sometimes we want so much to have someone we like fit our own preconceived ideas that we see what we want to see in the person. When we actually involve ourselves in a relationship with that person, however, we may find that our initial reactions were inaccurate. For example, the quiet woman you work with who seems aloof may actually be a warm person who is introverted and shy. The large man you see on the street who has a stern expression on his face isn't necessarily mean; he may just be troubled about his wife's illness. Your friend's mother, who reacted coldly when you first met her, may actually just be intimidated by strangers.

People can be quickly stereotyped, categorized, and forgotten; however, we cannot learn about others through snap judgments and initial interactions. Interpersonal relationships allow us to continue to grow in our knowledge of other persons.

Understanding Our World

In addition to learning more about ourselves and about others through interpersonal relationships, we also learn more about our world—our environment. Our environment consists of other people, physical objects, events, and circumstances. Our knowledge of the environment comes largely through the interactions we have in our relationships. For example, who most greatly influences your future plans? How did you come to form your life philosophy? Your responses to these questions probably indicate that you learned about these people, ideas, and issues through your interpersonal relationships with acquaintances, friends, and family.

We often develop interpersonal relationships to *cope* with our environment. For instance, when we encounter everyday stresses, such as tough exams, pressuring parents, and confusing relationships with others, we need to feel someone is able to empathize. To discuss these difficulties with friends and to discover creative ways of handling them is reassuring. These relationships truly help us cope with our complex world.

Research done by Hawken, Duncan, and Kelly (1991) shows that college students who get involved with others tend to stay in college whereas those who are uninvolved tend to drop out. These researchers point out that "socially integrated students are more likely to live in a dormitory, have a

uncertainty principle

The principle which suggests that when we initially meet others and thus know little about them, we eliminate the uncertainty by drawing inferences from the information presented to us.

part-time job on campus, participate in clubs and social organizations, and declare an academic major earlier in their careers." Students appear to have the most difficulty establishing social integration in their first year at school, when 60 percent of the dropping out occurs.

Fulfilling Our Needs

According to William Schutz (1976), we have three basic interpersonal needs that are satisfied through interaction with others. These are (1) the need for **inclusion,** or *becoming involved with others;* (2) the need for **affection,** or *being cared for by others;* and (3) the need for **control,** or *the ability to influence others, our environment, and ourselves.* Although we may be able to fulfill some of our physical, safety, and security needs through interactions with relative strangers, we can fulfill the other needs only through our interpersonal relationships.

The interdependent nature of interpersonal relationships suggests that people mutually satisfy their needs in this type of association. Interdependence suggests that one person is dependent on another to have some need fulfilled and that the other person (or persons) is dependent on the first to have the same or other needs fulfilled. For example, a child who is dependent on a parent may satisfy that parent's need for control. The parent, on the other hand, may supply the child's need for affection in hugging, kissing, or listening to the child.

Complementary relationships—*those in which each person supplies something the other lacks*—provide good examples of the manner in which we have our needs fulfilled in interpersonal relationships. A romantic involvement between a popular male and an intelligent female is an example of a complementary relationship, since the woman may find herself involved in the social events she desires and the man may find himself increasingly successful in his classes. Another example of a complementary relationship is a friendship between an introverted individual and an extroverted one. The introvert may teach her friend to be more self-reflective or to listen to others more carefully, while the extrovert might, in exchange, encourage her to be more outspoken or assertive.

Our needs also may be fulfilled in **symmetrical relationships**—*those in which the participants mirror each other or are highly similar.* A relationship between two intelligent persons may reflect their need for intellectual stimulation. Two people of similar ancestry might marry in part to preserve their heritage.

Whether the other person or persons are similar to us or highly different, our needs are generally fulfilled through the relationships we have with them.

inclusion

The state of being involved with others.

affection

The emotion of caring for others and/or being cared for by them.

control

The ability to influence others, our environment, and ourselves.

complementary relationships

Relationships in which each person supplies something the other person or persons lack.

symmetrical relationships

Relationships between people who mirror each other or who are highly similar.

| TRY ◄ ► THIS |

Think about your friendship and dating relationships and determine whether they are symmetrical or complementary.

Increasing and Enriching Positive Experiences

We also enter into interpersonal relationships to increase and enrich positive experiences and/or to decrease negative experiences. One theory, the **cost-benefit theory,** suggests that *individuals will maintain a relationship only as long as the benefits of the relationship outweigh the costs* (Homans, 1961). Some of the benefits of a relationship include personal growth, improved self-concept, increased self-knowledge, assistance with particular tasks, greater resources, and an improved capacity for coping. The costs include time and energy spent on the relationship, psychological stress created by the relationship, perhaps physiological stress, and social limitations. According to the cost-benefit theory, if the costs begin to outweigh the benefits, we may decide to terminate the relationship. If the benefits appear to outweigh the costs, we may escalate relationship development.

Interpersonal relationships are not so simply translated into a cost-benefit model, however. More often, we engage in bargaining in our interpersonal relationships. **Bargaining** occurs when *two or more parties attempt to reach an agreement on what each should give and receive in a transaction between them.* Bargains may be explicit and formal, such as the kinds of agreements you reach with others to share tasks, to attend a particular event, or to behave in a specified way. Bargains may also be implicit and informal. For example, in exchange for receiving a compliment from him every day, you might agree not to tell embarrassing stories about your boyfriend in public. You may not even be aware of some of the implicit, tacit agreements you have with others with whom you communicate.

A study on interpersonal bargaining (Deusch & Kraus, 1962) identified three essential features of a bargaining situation:

1. All parties perceive the possibility of reaching an agreement in which each party would be better off, or no worse off, than if no agreement were reached.
2. All parties perceive more than one such agreement that could be reached.
3. All parties perceive the other or others to have conflicting preferences or opposed interests with regard to the different agreements that might be reached.

What are some examples of bargaining situations? You may want to go out with friends when your spouse would prefer a quiet evening at home. A woman might prefer to go hiking, whereas her husband is more eager to take a cruise. One person could use the word *forever* to mean a few days or weeks, whereas another assumes it refers to a much longer period of time. In each of these instances, the disagreement can be resolved through bargaining.

Thibaut and Kelley (1959) underlined the importance of bargaining in interpersonal communication:

> . . . Whatever the gratifications achieved in dyads, however lofty or fine the motives satisfied may be, the relationship may be viewed as a trading or bargaining one. The basic assumption running throughout our analysis is that

cost-benefit theory

A theory of interpersonal relationships which suggests that individuals will maintain a relationship only as long as the benefits of the relationship outweigh the costs.

bargaining

The process in which two or more parties attempt to reach an agreement on what each should give and receive in a relationship.

Complete the following statements:

1. Interpersonal relationships are defined as associations between two or more people who are _____.

2. When meeting someone for the first time, we draw inferences from physical data around us. This is known as the _____.

3. In a complementary relationship each person _____.

4. A relationship in which the participants mirror each other is called a _____.

5. Cost-benefit theory suggests that individuals will _____.

*Answers: 1. interdependent   2. uncertainty principle   3. supplies something the other lacks
4. symmetrical relationship   5. maintain relationships only as long as the benefits
outweigh the costs*

every individual voluntarily enters and stays in any relationship only as long as it is adequately satisfactory in terms of rewards and costs.

This statement emphasizes the central role of bargaining in interpersonal relationships and underlines the notion of cost-benefit analysis.

The Stages in Interpersonal Relationships

Communication and relationship development are symbiotic; that is, communication affects the growth of relationships, and the growth of relationships affects communicative behavior (Miller, 1976). Current theories on the growth of relationships rest on the original work of researchers Altman and Taylor (1973). These authors developed the **social penetration theory,** which explains the development and deterioration of interpersonal relationships through the exchange of intimate information. In essence, the theory states that *interpersonal exchanges move from superficial, nonintimate information transfers to more intimate information exchanges through the process of revealing personal information.* The amount of interaction increases as the relationship develops. Further, cost-reward considerations determine how quickly or slowly relationships develop. Dissolution, or depenetration, is the reverse process of development, or penetration.

social penetration theory

A theory that explains how relationships develop and deteriorate through the exchange of intimate information.

154

Relational Development

Professor Mark L. Knapp (1978) of the University of Texas expanded on Altman and Taylor's social penetration theory by identifying 10 interaction stages of interpersonal relationships. Professor Leslie A. Baxter (1979, 1982, 1983, 1984) and others have experimentally attempted to validate these stages. The model that Knapp presented generally appears valid. Furthermore, this developmental model helps organize and explain relational changes. The first five stages cover **relational development,** *the process by which relationships grow:*

1. **Initiating** is stage 1, *the short beginning period of an interaction.* This stage involves first impressions, the sizing up of the other person, and attempting to find commonality. An example is "scouting" at a party, where you might break off the initiating stage when you don't find what you are seeking in the person you have just met. If this first stage goes well, you might move to stage 2 in a first meeting.

2. **Experimenting** occurs when *the two people have clearly decided to find out more about each other, to quit scouting, and to start getting serious about each other.* This stage includes sharing personal information at a safe level: what music, people, classes, professors, and food you like or dislike. In a situation where you are "captive" in an airplane seat, are waiting for a concert to begin, or sit next to someone in a classroom for 3 or 4 months, this stage could start early and last for weeks.

3. **Intensifying** involves *active participation, mutual concern, and an awareness that the relationship is developing* because neither party has broken it off and both people are encouraging its development. The information exchanges get more personal and more intimate. Both are comfortable with each other, use private jokes and language, and express commitment.

4. **Integrating** means *the two start mirroring each other's behavior in manner, dress, and language.* They merge their social circles, designate common property, and share interests and values. They know more about each other than does anyone else, except long-term best friends, and others see them as a pair.

5. **Bonding** is *the final stage in relational development—the people in the relationship commit to each other.* They may exchange personal items as a symbol of commitment; they may participate in a public ritual that bonds them, as in the case of marriage; or they may vow to be friends for life and demonstrate that commitment by always being present at important points in each other's life. Living together, marrying, having children, buying a home, or moving together to another place are examples of bonding.

Relational Maintenance

Once individuals have bonded in a relationship, they enter a stage of **relational maintenance** in which they begin establishing *strategies for keeping*

relational development

In Knapp's model, the process by which relationships grow.

initiating

In Knapp's stages of relational development, the short beginning period of a relationship.

experimenting

In Knapp's relational development model, the stage in which partners attempt to discover information about each other.

intensifying

In Knapp's relational development model, the stage in which partners become more aware of each other and actively participate in the relationship.

integrating

In Knapp's relational development model, the stage in which partners start mirroring each other's behavior.

bonding

In Knapp's relational development model, the stage in which partners commit to each other.

relational maintenance

In Knapp's model, the process of keeping a relationship together.

the relationship together. Although Altman and Taylor, as well as Knapp, briefly considered relational maintenance, but not in much detail. Professor William Wilmot (1980) suggested that relationships stabilize when the partners reach a basic level of agreement about what they want from the relationship. In addition, relationships can stabilize at any level of intimacy, and even "stabilized" relationships may have internal movement.

Although we initially develop a relationship on the basis of such factors as attractiveness and personal charisma, we maintain relationships for different reasons. Maintained relationships invite certain levels of predictability, or certainty (Perse & Rubin, 1989). Indeed, we attempt to create strategies that will provide us with additional personal information about our relational partners (Berger & Kellermann, 1989). We are also less concerned with partners' expressive traits (e.g., being extroverted and spontaneous) and more concerned with their ability to focus on us through empathic, caring, and concerned involvement (Davis & Oathout, 1987). Indeed, as relationships are maintained, partners not only become more empathic but also begin to mirror each other's behavior.

Numerous other studies have explored what keeps a relationship together. Bruess and Pearson (1997) revealed in their study that the following seven rituals are important characteristics of long-term relationships:

1. *Couple-time rituals*—for example, exercising together or having dinner together every Saturday night
2. *Idiosyncratic/symbolic rituals*—for example, calling each other by a special name or celebrating the anniversary of their first date
3. *Daily routines and tasks*—for example, if living together, one partner might always prepare the evening meal and the other might always clean up afterward
4. *Intimacy rituals*—for example, giving each other a massage or, when apart, talking on the telephone before going to bed
5. *Communication rituals*—for example, getting together for lunch with a friend every Friday afternoon or going out to a coffee bar with a significant other
6. *Patterns, habits, and mannerisms*—for example, meeting her need to be complimented when going out for a fancy evening, and meeting his need to be reassured before family events
7. *Spiritual rituals*—for example, attending services together or doing yoga together in the evening

In another study, Pearson (1996) looked at couples who had been happily married for more than 40 years. She found that many of these marriages were characterized by stubbornness ("This marriage will succeed no matter what"), distortion ("She is the most beautiful woman in the world"), unconditional acceptance (regardless of faults), and the continuous push and pull of autonomy or independence versus unity or interdependence. Maintaining positive, satisfying relationships isn't easy, but the people who are the most satisfied with their relationships are probably those who have worked hardest at maintaining them.

Relational Deterioration

The last five stages identified by Knapp (1978) occur during **relational deterioration,** *the process by which relationships disintegrate:*

1. **Differentiating** occurs when *the two partners start emphasizing their individual differences instead of their similarities.* Instead of going to movies together, he plays basketball with his friends and she goes out with her friends. Some separate activities are healthy in a relationship but, in differentiation, the pulling apart is to get away from each other.
2. **Circumscribing** is characterized by *decreased interaction, shorter times together, and less depth to sharing.* The two people might go to public events together but do little together in private. Each person figuratively draws a circle around himself or herself, a circle that does not include the other person. The exchange of feelings, the demonstrations of commitment, and the obvious pairing are disappearing.
3. **Stagnating** suggests a *lack of activity, especially activity together.* Interactions are minimal, functional, and only for convenience. The two people now find conversation and sharing awkward instead of stimulating. During this stage, each individual may be finding an outlet elsewhere for developmental stages.
4. **Avoiding** brings *reluctance to interact, active avoidance, and even hostility.* The two former partners are now getting in each other's way, each seeing the other as an obstacle or a limitation. The amount of their talk may actually increase, but the content and intent are negative. Arguing, fighting, disagreeing, and flight mark their interactions.
5. **Terminating** occurs when *the two people are no longer seen by others or themselves as a pair.* They increasingly dissociate, share nothing, claim common goods as individual property, and give back or get rid of the symbols of togetherness. Divorce, annulment, and dissolution are manifestations of this stage, as are people who no longer live together, former friends who have nothing to do with each other, and roommates who take separate and distant quarters.

Knapp (1978) acknowledged that individuals do not progress in a linear way through the stages of development and deterioration (summarized in Table 7.1). He proposed that people move within stages to maintain their equilibrium or stability. In other words, people might behave in a way that is more characteristic of one stage even though they are generally maintaining the interaction patterns of another stage.

Similarly, individuals do not move through each of these stages with everyone they meet. Research shows that people base decisions to develop relationships on such factors as physical attractiveness, personal charisma, and communication behaviors (Friedman, Riggio, & Casella, 1988; Sabatelli & Rubin, 1986). In general, we are more likely to attempt to develop relationships with people who are attractive, emotionally expressive, extroverted, and spontaneous.

relational deterioration

In Knapp's model, the process by which relationships disintegrate.

differentiating

In Knapp's relational development model, the stage in which partners emphasize their individual differences rather than their similarities.

circumscribing

In Knapp's relational development model, the stage marked by a decrease in partners' interaction, time spent together, and depth of sharing.

stagnating

In Knapp's relational development model, the stage of deterioration marked by the partner's lack of activity, especially together.

avoiding

In Knapp's relational development model, the stage characterized by partners' reluctance to interact, active avoidance, and hostility.

terminating

In Knapp's relational development model, the stage of deterioration in which the partners are no longer seen as a pair by themselves or others.

TABLE 7.1	AN OVERVIEW OF INTERACTION STAGES	
PROCESS	STAGE	REPRESENTATIVE DIALOGUE
Coming Together	1. Initiating	"Hi, how ya doin'?" "Fine, You?"
	2. Experimenting	"Oh, so you like to ski. . . . So do I." "You do?! Great. Where do you go?"
	3. Intensifying	"I . . . I think I love you." "I love you too."
	4. Integrating	"I feel so much a part of you." "Yeah, we're like one person. What happens to you happens to me."
	5. Bonding	"I want to be with you always." "Let's get married."
Coming Apart	1. Differentiating	"I just don't like big social gatherings." "Sometimes I don't understand you. This is one area where I'm certainly not like you at all."
	2. Circumscribing	"Did you have a good time on your trip?" "What time will dinner be ready?"
	3. Stagnating	"What's there to talk about?" "Right. I know what you're going to say, and you know what I'm going to say."
	4. Avoiding	"I'm so busy, I just don't know when I'll be able to see you." "If I'm not around when you try, you'll understand."
	5. Terminating	"I'm leaving you . . . and don't bother trying to contact me." "Don't worry."

SOURCE: From *Interpersonal Communication and Human Relationships,* 3rd ed. by Mark L. Knapp and Anita L. Vangelisti, 1996, Boston: Allyn and Bacon. Copyright © 1996 by Allyn and Bacon. Reprinted by permission.

Self-Disclosure

To be a more effective communicator in an interpersonal relationship, you should be able to define self-disclosure to recognize its importance, to know its appropriate use, and to understand when it should be avoided.

What Is Self-Disclosure?

self-disclosure

The process of making intentional revelations about oneself that others would be unlikely to know.

As the relational development stages change, intentional revealing of personal information changes. **Self-disclosure** is *the process of making intentional revelations about oneself that others would be unlikely to know.* You do not have to tell someone you are petite or bald, but others won't know how often you exercise or your position on capital punishment unless you tell

7.2 IDENTIFYING RELATIONAL STAGES

  A. **Relational initiation**
  B. **Relational maintenance**
  C. **Relational deterioration**

Write the appropriate letter from the choices below in each blank on the left:

____1. Practicing rituals

____2. Experimenting by sharing "safe" personal information

____3. Circumscribing or shallow sharing

____4. Strategic planning for relational continuance

____5. Integrating by mirroring each other's behavior

Answers: 1. B   2. A   3. C   4. B   5. A

them. Self-disclosure can be as unthreatening as talking about your recent vacation or as difficult as confiding that your father is an alcoholic.

Why Is Self-Disclosure Important?

Self-disclosure is important for two reasons: It allows you to establish more meaningful relationships with others, and it allows you to develop a more positive attitude about yourself and others. Through self-disclosure, relationships grow in depth and meaning. If you use self-disclosure appropriately, your relationships will move from being fairly superficial to being deeper and more meaningful. When you self-disclose more to others, they will most likely disclose more to you. On the other hand, the inability to self-disclose can result in the end of a relationship. Without the opportunity for self-disclosure and active listening, relationships appear to be doomed to shallowness, superficiality, or termination.

Concerns about Self-Disclosure

Although self-disclosure is an aspect of interpersonal communication, people are often unwilling to self-disclose to others. In general, people are reluctant to self-disclose because they do not respect themselves or they do not trust others, or both. Even those individuals who are willing to self-disclose may have concerns such as (1) whom to disclose to, (2) what to disclose, and (3) how much to disclose.

To Whom Should I Disclose?

Although a surprising number of self-disclosures occur with fellow passengers on a bus, a train, or an airplane, people normally disclose important information about themselves to someone they want to know better. In fact, self-disclosure of low-risk information often occurs at the beginning of a conversation with someone you just met or are just becoming acquainted with. "What is your name?" "Where are you from?" or "What do you do?" are common opening questions. But to strangers you meet accidentally or at a party, for example, you should be wary about your revelations. Remember, self-disclosure involves *intentional* revelations, so you should self-disclose only to those people with whom you consciously choose to initiate or maintain a relationship.

What Should I Disclose?

When considering what to disclose, keep in mind that positive disclosures are more appropriate at the beginning of a relationship and that negative disclosures are best revealed to people you trust. You should also be aware that even positive disclosures can be negative if they overwhelm the unsuspecting recipient. For example, suppose in the first moments of a conversation with a new acquaintance you reveal, "I'm a Phi Beta Kappa graduate of Swarthmore, which is where I always wanted to go to school. My mom and dad met and fell in love there, although my mom never finished. She dropped out soon after she and my dad got married because she was pregnant. Times sure have changed haven't they? She ended up going back for her degree when she was in her midthirties . . ." To parcel the information out more slowly during the course of the conversation and to allow the other person to reciprocate would be more appropriate.

How Much Should I Disclose?

The answer to the question "How much should I disclose?" depends on who the recipient is, what your relationship is with that person, and what the consequences will be of revealing more information about yourself. For example, you can reveal much more to a long-term personal friend, partner, or spouse than you should to your new boss.

Gender Differences

Men and women have different reasons for choosing to self-disclose or for avoiding disclosure. One study suggested that men avoid self-disclosure to maintain control over their relationships whereas women avoid self-

report talk

Tannen's term for men's view of conversation as instrumental or as a way to demonstrate knowledge and reveal information.

disclosure to avoid personal hurt (Rosenfeld, 1979). Another investigation showed that men disclose more to strangers and casual acquaintances whereas women are more willing to disclose to intimates (Stokes, Fuehrer, & Childs, 1980). Research conducted by Deborah Tannen (1990) revealed that men prefer **report talk,** meaning they tend to *view conversation as instrumental or as a way to demonstrate knowledge and reveal information.* In contrast, women tend to prefer **rapport talk,** which means they *view conversation as a way to develop relationships, strengthen ties, and share experiences.* In general, a variety of factors play a role in why men and women choose to self-disclose. These factors are summarized in Table 7.2.

rapport talk

Tannen's term for women's view of conversation as a way to develop relationships, strengthen ties, and share experiences.

TABLE 7.2   GENDER DIFFERENCES IN SELF-DISCLOSURE

Underlying Factor	Gender Differences
Positive or negative nature	• Both sexes are equally likely to offer negative information. • Women offer more negative than positive information.
Cognitive or affective information	• Women offer more affective information than men.
Intimate or nonintimate information	• Women report that they disclose more intimate information than men. • In interactions, men set the pace of intimacies and women match the pace set by men.
Topics under discussion	• Men and women do not differ on the amount they self-disclose on nonintimate topics, such as politics. • Women self-disclose more on intimate topics such as sex and religion.
Sex of the target person	• Females prefer other females to whom to self-disclose. • In mixed-sex dyads, females and males do not self-disclose to a different extent.
Attractiveness of the target person	• In general, both women and men self-disclose more to an attractive person than to an unattractive person. • Attractiveness may be a more relevant variable for women than for men.
Interaction of attractiveness and the sex of the target person	• Both women and men self-disclose more to attractive individuals of the same sex. • Both women and men provide less negative self-disclosure to attractive persons of the opposite sex.
Attractiveness of the discloser	• Men who perceive themselves as attractive self-disclose more than men who perceive themselves as unattractive. • Women who perceive themselves as attractive self-disclose less than women who perceive themselves as unattractive.
Age of the discloser	• In general, women self-disclose more than men of all ages. • For both women and men, self-disclosure increases as they mature and become older.

(Continued)

TABLE 7.2 *CONCLUDED*	
Nonverbal behaviors	• Increased eye contact encourages self-disclosure in women but inhibits self-disclosure in men. • As the amount of personal space decreases among interactants, women self-disclose more while men self-disclose less. • For both women and men, increased touch is associated with increased self-disclosure. • Increased movement on the part of a male target of disclosure and decreased movement on the part of a female target of disclosure resulted in increased self-disclosure on the part of clients in a counseling setting.
Influence of sex-related variables	• For men, increasing levels of femininity and decreasing levels of masculinity are associated with an increasing level of self-disclosure. • For women, increasing levels of masculinity coupled with decreasing levels of femininity are associated with increasing levels of self-disclosure; however, the addition of masculinity to stationary levels of femininity is not associated with increased self-disclosure. • Homosexual men and heterosexual women are similar in self-disclosure behavior, while homosexual women and heterosexual men are not.

SOURCE: From *Gender & Communication,* 4th ed. by J. C. Pearson, R. L. West, and L. H. Turner. Reprinted by permission of The McGraw-Hill Companies.

Unwillingness to Self-Disclose

In the sections that follow you will examine the specific communication behaviors that are related to an unwillingness to self-disclose.

Defensiveness

Defensiveness is *the tendency to protect and support our ideas and attitudes against attack by others.* Defensiveness may occur when individuals receive negative feedback, and they may not listen effectively to others because of their defensive posture. Defensiveness may occur because individuals believe that the kind of person they are is not consistent with the kind of person they are supposed to be. In other words, a person's "real" self is discrepant from his or her "idealized" self. The difference between these two selves causes the person to feel uneasy because of the concern that he or she will show others the "real" self and be discounted.

Six behaviors have been identified as contributing to defensiveness (Gibb, 1961). These behaviors and their counterparts, which lead to a supportive communication climate, are listed in Table 7.3. Let us consider each of these categories in more depth:

1. *Evaluation* is the use of judgmental statements as opposed to *descriptive statements.* "You are doing failing work" is a highly evaluative statement that invites a defensive response. "Your paper was graded lower because of two run-on, two fused, and two incomplete sen-

defensiveness

The tendency to protect and support our ideas and attitudes against attack by others.

TABLE 7.3 DEFENSIVE VERSUS SUPPORTIVE COMMUNICATION BEHAVIORS	
DEFENSIVE BEHAVIORS	SUPPORTIVE BEHAVIORS
1. Evaluation	1. Descriptive statements
2. Control	2. Problem orientation
3. Strategy	3. Spontaneity
4. Neutrality	4. Empathy
5. Superiority	5. Equality
6. Certainty	6. Provisionalism

SOURCE: Based on Jack R. Gibb, "Defensive Communication," *Journal of Communication*, 11 (1961): 141–148.

tences" is a more descriptive statement. You will hurt fewer feelings and encounter fewer difficulties with others if you communicate with description and observation instead of evaluation.

2. *Control* refers to commands, statements that say others must do as you do or as you say. "If you would study as I do, you would get better grades" is an example of a control statement. The parallel supportive behavior is *problem orientation.* Problem orientation suggests that a number of alternatives are possible and that you and the other person can find a good solution together. "What do you think you can do to improve your grades?" or "What can I do to help you gain higher grades?" are examples of this method.

3. *Strategy* implies an element of manipulation in assuming a defensive posture toward others. The term *strategy* also suggests that an idea was generated for protection as a reason for one's behavior. Late for a lunch appointment, a defensive person might decide on a strategy that will cover the faux pas by saying, "I had a long-distance call that held me up for 10 minutes." The alternative supportive behavior, called *spontaneity,* suggests a more honest expression, such as, "I'm sorry I'm late. I don't have a great excuse; I just lost track of time. I apologize."

4. *Neutrality* reflects a lack of interest or concern for another person. Unresponsiveness or statements such as "I couldn't care less" or "That's your problem" are examples. On the other end of this continuum is *empathy,* in which you try to adopt the other person's perspective. "I know how you must feel" and "I have an idea what you could try" are examples of empathy.

5. *Superiority* implies that what you have to say is somehow better, more important, or more effective than what someone else has to say. "You will see that I am right" and "Glad to see that you are catching up" are examples of superiority. *Equality* is the supportive mode, in which the other person is treated as a respected human being. "None of us has all the answers" and "By working together we can both do better" suggest equality.

6. *Certainty* implies that you have all the answers and that others are simply at fault for not recognizing it. Your words sound like commandments, perfect and carved in stone. "I can't help it that those fools didn't vote for the best person—me" is an example of certainty. *Provisionalism,* at the other end of the continuum, suggests that you are not infallible, that you do not know who is at fault, and that a number of "right answers" are possible. "There were three strong candidates, and maybe I need to try harder next time" is an example of provisionalism. Some words that suggest provisionalism are *perhaps, maybe, might,* and *possibly.*

Defensiveness may be a regular response pattern resulting from strong negative feelings about self or may be a function of current statements from others. Occasional defensiveness in response to others' evaluative, controlling, strategic, neutral, superior, or certainty statements is a natural response. However, recognizing that you respond defensively may assist you in altering your behavior in these occasional circumstances.

TRY ◄►THIS

Think of times when defensiveness has caused fighting or other problems in your friendship or dating relationships. How did you overcome these problems?

We may dismiss occasional defensiveness that occurs on rare occasions, that occurs in response to another person's comments, or that is not overly destructive to effective communication. Regular defensiveness, however, can be a problem. Never being open and honest in communication can lead to shallow interpersonal relationships and a distrust of others. Further, regular defensiveness can lead to a communication climate in which people learn to expect such behaviors as evaluation, control, strategy, neutrality, superiority, and certainty. If you feel you use defensiveness as a regular response to others, you may want to consider ways to overcome your negative feelings about yourself to be free of the potential negative effects of defensiveness in your communication behavior.

Nonassertiveness

assertiveness

The ability to communicate feelings and ideas directly and honestly.

Whereas defensiveness should be avoided and supportiveness encouraged, **assertiveness,** *the ability to communicate feelings and ideas directly and honestly,* is desirable. People with strong self-concepts, high self-esteem, and good verbal skills do not invite others to speak for them, do not allow others to say what their feelings should be, and do not disregard their feelings and ideas. Marginalized, powerless, and timid people are the common victims of unassertiveness; they find the world always in others' control.

Assertive people own their feelings; that is, they are willing to disclose what they think and how they feel. Unassertive people avoid stating what they think. They might say, "Well, I've heard other people say they don't like him" or "Republicans believe in the pro-life position" instead of owning up to feelings and thoughts by declaring "I don't like him" or "I believe in the pro-life position." Assertive people tell others, even those with power over them, what their expectations, problems, and feelings are. Otherwise, the other person assumes that everything is satisfactory, and nothing is done about problems that need solutions and feelings that remain hurt.

People in service roles and helping professions—mothers, nurses, sales personnel, and human services workers—spend much of their time serving others without having many of their needs met. Service to others and even sacrifice are noble activities, but they are unhealthy if they inspire undermining, resentment, and anger. Everyone has rights, and assertive people act to support their rights. However, you also have to avoid being overly assertive or aggressive.

Aggressiveness is *assertiveness carried to an extreme, standing up for your rights at the expense of others and caring about your needs but no one else's.* Aggressiveness might help you get your way a few times, but ultimately others will avoid you and let their resentment show. Both aggressive and unassertive people may suffer from a negative self-concept. Both have trouble with self-disclosure. They may feel that they have to overpower others to get their way. Unfortunately, their intense competitiveness often denies them the acceptance they seek.

aggressiveness

Standing up for one's rights at the expense of others.

Interpersonal Communication with Friends

With millions of people in this world, how do you decide which few should be your friends? How are you attracted to them? Why do you cultivate relationships with them? How does communication figure into the equation?

First, let us examine how we select our friends. **Proximity,** or *location,* is obvious but important. You are probably not going to have friends from places you have never been. You are most likely to find your friends where you spend most of your time. For this reason, a roommate can easily become a friend. People who go to the same religious services, belong to the same social clubs, or are members of the same gang are most likely to become friends. People with the same major or in the same dormitory, cafeteria, car pool, or part of the seating chart are also likely candidates. To underline the potency of proximity, consider that changes in location (high school to college and college to job) often change friendship patterns.

Second, we select, from all the people we see, the ones we find high in **social attractiveness,** *a feature that takes three forms: task, social, and physical* (McCroskey & McCain, 1974). In other words, a person who is desirable to work with, who seems to have "social value" in that others also show interest

proximity

Term referring to location, distance, range between persons and things.

social attractiveness

A concept that includes physical attractiveness, how desirable a person is to work with, and how much "social value" the person has for others.

Instant Recall

in him or her, and who physically looks good to us is socially attractive (Pearson & Spitzberg, 1990). Because of perceptual differences, you will not be looking for the same person as everyone else. In fact, someone who is "too good looking" may be perceived as unattainable, as inviting too many competitors, or as too difficult to sustain a relationship with as a friend.

responsiveness

The idea that we tend to select our friends from people who demonstrate positive interest in us.

Responsiveness, *the idea that we tend to select our friends from people who demonstrate positive interest in us,* is another feature of attraction. Not everyone responds positively to us, but someone who does is likely to get our attention. Few characteristics are more attractive than someone who actively listens to us, thinks our jokes are funny, finds our vulnerabilities wonderful, and sees our faults as amusing. In short, we practically never select our friends from among those who dislike us.

similarity

The idea that our friends are usually people who like or dislike the same things we do.

Similarity, *the idea that our friends are usually people who like or dislike the same things we do,* is another feature of attractiveness. Our friends might look like us, act like us, or think like us. Whatever we consider most important is the similarity we seek, so some friends are bound by their interests, others by their ideology, and still others by their mutual likes and dislikes. A hard-core environmentalist is unlikely to be close personal friends with a developer, whereas the developer is likely to select friends from people in the same business, country club, and suburb. Thousands of people find their friends in the same circle where they work: clerical workers with clerical workers, managers with managers, and bosses with bosses. Similarity is a powerful attracter.

Complementarity is *the idea that we sometimes bond with people whose strengths are our weaknesses.* Whereas you may be slightly shy, your friend may be assertive, and she is assertive for you. A math-loving engineer may find friendship with a people-loving communication major, who takes care of the engineer's social life while the engineer helps his friend with math courses. Having a friend who is too much like you can result in competitiveness that destroys the friendship.

complementarity
The idea that we sometimes bond with people whose strengths are our weaknesses.

TRY◄►THIS

List the features of attractiveness of your best friend, your boyfriend or girlfriend, or your lover or spouse.

"We distinguish between friendships and acquaintanceships," according to one text on interpersonal communication, "on the basis of choice and of positive regard. We choose our friends; we do not accidently have friendships" (Palisi & Ransford, 1987; Wiseman, 1986). Another truism, relevant here, is the old statement "You can't make friends; you have to be a friend, and then others will make you a friend."

Friendship is characterized by a host of qualities. Friends are available, they share in your activities, they care about you and the relationship, they disclose personal information, they are loyal, and they demonstrate understanding (Pearson & Spitzberg, 1990). Notice that all these characteristics operate through verbal and nonverbal communication. You can show availability and loyalty only by physically demonstrating support for a friend. You can self-disclose and show understanding only by talking and listening. Communication between people is what friendship is all about.

One study summarized the findings on friendship:

> The most consistently held rules indicate that friends are expected to (1) share news of success with each other, (2) show emotional support for each other, (3) volunteer to help in times of need, (4) strive to make each other happy while in each other's company,(5) demonstrate trust in each other, and (6) stand up for each other in their absence. It seems that friendships do involve a certain degree of commitment and trust in each other's unconditional support. (Pearson & Spitzberg, 1990)

Improving Communication in Interpersonal Relationships

We all want to have successful interpersonal relationships. We want to be able to trust others and to self-disclose to them. We want to be able to handle conflict and to use conflict resolution techniques that are mutually satisfying. Nonetheless, countless people find themselves in dissatisfying and unhappy relationships.

The Possibilities for Improvement

Can you improve your communication in interpersonal relationships? Until relatively recently, many people felt that learning to relate more effectively to others was impossible. Today, most individuals feel such a possibility does exist. Are such changes easy? Generally, they are not. You should not expect that an introductory course in communication will solve all your relational problems. Self-help books that promise instant success will probably result only in permanent disillusionment. Courses on assertiveness training, relaxation techniques, and marital satisfaction provide only part of the answer.

If you wish to improve your communication within your interpersonal relationships, you must have a commitment to learning a variety of communication skills. You must understand the importance of perceptual differences among people, the role of self-concept in communication, the nature of verbal language, and the role of nonverbal communication. You must be willing to share yourself with others as you self-disclose, and you must be willing to attempt to understand other people through careful and conscientious listening. In addition, you must recognize that, even when you thoroughly understand these concepts and are able to implement them in your behavior, your interactions with others may not be successful. Communication is dependent on the interaction between two communicators, and one person cannot guarantee its success. Others may have conflicting goals, different perspectives, or less ability to communicate competently.

We do not communicate with our spouses at home in the same way we would communicate with them in a public situation.

Learning individual communication concepts and specific communication skills is essential to effective interaction. You also need to understand the impact of these skills. For example, you do not communicate at home the way you do in the classroom. Self-disclosure, which is especially appropriate and important within the family context, may be out of place in the classroom. Preparation and planning are important in an interview, but they may be seen as manipulative in a conversation between partners.

Behavioral Flexibility

In addition to being improved by an understanding of communication concepts, skills, and settings, our interactions may be greatly enhanced by an underlying approach to communication behavior called behavioral flexibility.

Behavioral flexibility is defined as *the ability to alter behavior in order to adapt to new situations and to relate in new ways when necessary* (Pearson, 1983). Behavioral flexibility allows you to relax and let your guard down when you are with friends or to be your formal self while interviewing for a job. The key to behavioral flexibility may be self-monitoring, always being conscious of the effect of your words on the specific audience in a particular context.

behavioral flexibility

The ability to alter behavior to adapt to new situations and to relate in new ways when necessary.

TRY◄►THIS

Define behavioral flexibility and determine to what degree you exhibit this trait.

Flexibility is important in a variety of fields. For example, biologists and botanists have demonstrated that extinction of certain living things occurs because of an organism's inability to adapt to changes in the environment. Psychologists have suggested that women and men who are **androgynous**—*who hold both stereotypically male and stereotypically female traits*—are more successful in their interactions than are people who are unyieldingly masculine or absolutely feminine. Flexibility in psychological gender roles is more useful than a static notion of what being a man or a woman means in our culture. For instance, if you are a single parent, you may be called upon to behave in a loving and nurturing way to your child, regardless of your sex. If your goal is to be a successful manager in a large corporation, you may have to exhibit competitiveness, assertiveness, and a task orientation, regardless of your sex. As you move from interactions with coworkers to interactions with family and friends, you may need to change from traditionally "masculine" behaviors to those that have been considered "feminine."

androgynous

A term used in reference to persons who possess stereotypical female and male characteristics.

Behavioral flexibility is especially important in interpersonal communication because relationships between people are in constant flux. For example, the family structure has gone through sharp changes in recent years. In addition, the United States has an increasing older population. Changes in the labor force also require new skills and different ways of interacting with others. People travel more often and move more frequently. Four million unmarried couples cohabit (Singletary, 1999). As a result of these types of changes, people may interact differently today than in the past.

What kinds of changes might you expect in your own life that will affect your relationships with others? You may change your job 10 or more times. You may move your place of residence even more frequently. You probably will be married at least once, and possibly two or three times. You probably will have one child or more. You will experience loss of family members through death and dissolution of relationships. You may have a spouse whose needs conflict with your needs. Other family members may view the world differently than you and challenge your perceptions. When your life appears to be most stable and calm, unexpected changes will occur.

TRY◄►THIS

List the major changes you have made in your life, and determine how each has led to changes in your communication.

How can behavioral flexibility assist you through life's changes? A flexible person has a large repertoire of behaviors upon which to draw. Such an individual is confident about sharing messages with others and about understanding the messages that others provide. The flexible person is able to self-disclose when appropriate but does not use this ability in inappropriate contexts. The flexible person can demonstrate listening skills, but is not always the one who is listening. The flexible person can show concern for a child who needs assistance, can be assertive on the job, can be yielding when another person needs to exercise control, and can be independent when called on to stand alone. The flexible person does not predetermine one set of communication behaviors he or she will always enact. The flexible person is not dogmatic or narrow-minded in interactions with others.

To remember that changes are not always negative is important. In fact, a great deal of change is positive. For instance, when you graduate from college, the changes that occur are generally perceived as positive. When you enter into new relationships, you generally encounter positive change.

But even when change is positive, it can be stressful. Gail Sheehy, author of *Passages: Predictable Crises of Adult Life* (1976), wrote:

> We must be willing to change chairs if we want to grow. There is no permanent compatibility between a chair and a person. And there is no one right chair. What is right at one stage may be restricting at another or too soft.

Interpersonal Communication in the Family

Our families are important to us. Your family may be the people with whom you are most frequently involved in interpersonal communication. Family theorist Sven Wahlroos (1983) observed, "The greatest happiness and the deepest satisfaction in life, the most intense enthusiasm and the most profound inner peace, all come from being a member of a loving family." At the same time, families are coming apart at historically unprecedented rates, and what constitutes a family has changed dramatically over the years.

COMMUNICATION CHALLENGE

Practicing Behavioral Flexibility

For each of the three situations given below, suggest how a behaviorally flexible person and a person who is not behaviorally flexible might respond:

1. You are a man who believes that women and men are different and that men should be the final arbiter of decisions. Your wife believes the two of you should reach decisions together by talking about the situation until a solution is determined. How might you respond to your wife if you were behaviorally flexible? How would you respond if you were behaviorally inflexible?

2. You are a woman who cares a great deal about children. As a consequence, you take a job in a day-care center. You find you form many attachments to the children who come each day, and you suffer a certain amount of anguish and sadness each time one of the children is moved to a different center. You try to resolve the problem by becoming even closer to the new children who enroll. However, you know this is no solution, since these children, too, will at some time leave the day-care center. What would you do if you were behaviorally flexible? What would you do if you were behaviorally inflexible?

3. You are a person who likes to date only one individual at a time. You have had several fairly long-term relationships, but each has ended with the other person gradually fading out of the picture. You do not know why others leave you, but you feel a certain amount of distress about not being able to maintain a relationship. What would you do if you were behaviorally flexible? What would you do if you were behaviorally inflexible?

This section examines the importance of interpersonal communication in family life. Beginning with a definition of *family,* you will explore different types of families, and, lastly, examine the six principles of effective communication that contribute to family satisfaction. Studying family communication will not only help you better understand your family members but, by learning to communicate more effectively, will also help them better understand you.

What Is the Definition of Family?

Families have changed dramatically in the past five decades. Jane Howard (1978) suggested that past conceptions of families are outdated; not only has the definition of family changed over the years, but it can vary from one family to another.

The various configurations of a family require a broad definition that includes all families in which people find themselves. Our definition of family is based on one set forth by Bochner (1976): A **family** is *an organized, naturally occurring, relational, transactional group, usually occupying a common living space over an extended time period and possessing a confluence of interpersonal images that evolve through the exchange of meaning over time.* This long definition needs to be examined in parts.

family

An organized, naturally occurring relational, transactional group, usually occupying a common living space over an extended time period and possessing a confluence of interpersonal images that evolve through the exchange of meaning over time.

Families Are Organized

Family members enact their roles within the family unit. Your role may be mother, sister, daughter, aunt, grandmother, father, brother, son, uncle, or grandfather. Families are also organized, in that the behavior among members does not occur in a random or unpredictable fashion. We generally can predict, within a range of possibilities, how family members will act and react to each other. For example, when a 6-year-old brother and 12-year-old sister are watching television together, you can predict they will probably disagree about which show to view. Similarly, the behavior of other family members can be predicted within a range of possibilities.

TRY◀▶THIS

What are some of the predictable behaviors that occur in your family? What behaviors tend to occur over and over again?

Families Are Naturally Occurring

Bochner (1976) suggested that families occur "naturally," which suggests that they are not artificially created. We do not choose our parents; however, we generally choose at least one or more members of our current families. For instance, if you are married, you probably chose your spouse. If you have adopted children, you chose them. If you have dissolved a previous marriage, you may have made choices about who would be in your current family too. Some choice is possible and inevitable. The limited choice about who is defined as a member of your family affects your interactions.

Families Are a Relational System

Relationships can be defined simply as associations or connections. However, relationships are far more complex than such a definition suggests. Silverman and Silverman (1963) explained:

Consider for a moment a passenger ship in New York harbor, whose destination is Southampton. It is a "ship," of course, because we choose to call it "a ship," and an entity because we define it as one. It is also, among other things, engines, cabins, decks, and dinner-gongs—these are some of its parts or components. If we were to rearrange the components, or lay them out side by side, the entity would no longer be a ship, but perhaps look more like a junk-yard. The "parts," then, may be said to "make up" the whole, but the whole is defined by these parts in a particular relationship, each one not only to those attached to it, but also to the whole itself.

Similarly, families are relationships that include the individual members, their associations with each other, and their connection with the whole unit.

Families Are Transactional

This notion suggests that members share with each other; all participants are actively engaged in the communicative process. Communication as a transactional process varies as a result of context and situation. For example, people would behave differently if they were placed in other families. Similarly, a family behaves differently when the members are in different places or when they are facing a traumatic experience rather than normal, day-to-day events.

Families Occupy a Common Living Space over an Extended Time Period

While most families occupy common living quarters, some families do not. Many individuals in families that contain two working adults have adopted a commuter marriage, which includes two separate living quarters.

Families Possess a Confluence of Interpersonal Images That Evolve over Time

Each of us gains an understanding of the world by interacting with others. In other words, we learn to stereotype others because people we trust or respect stereotype them. We learn to be open and to share our feelings with others because our family members behave in such a manner. We learn appropriate levels of intimacy, the amount of ambition to demonstrate, and the kind of future to expect largely on the basis of our interactions with our family members. As George Herbert Mead (1934) observed, one cannot separate the person from his or her society. Nor can you separate the individual from the family.

What Are the Different Types of Families?

This section examines the most common types of families in contemporary America and some of the unique communication problems and patterns that exist in these family forms.

Couples with no children are *a type of family that includes two adults and no children.* Families have fewer children today than they did in the past.

couples with no children

A family type that includes two adults and no children.

In addition, couples are waiting longer to have children, and some couples choose childlessness.

A **single-parent family** *has one adult and adopted, natural, step-, or foster children.* A single-parent family typically occurs when one parent dies or leaves the family unit; however, an increasing number of individuals choose to parent by themselves from the start. These single parents include women in their thirties or forties who have careers but do not wish to pass up parenting, as well as teenagers who may "overestimate the benefits of child-bearing" (McGee, 1982). Twenty-seven percent of America's families are single-parent (U.S. Census Bureau, 1998).

When *two unrelated adults share living quarters, with or without children,* the family unit is defined as a **cohabiting-couple household.** Nonmarital cohabitation is not a new phenomenon, but it has become more prevalent and more openly practiced by Americans in recent times. The research on unmarried-couple households has been largely limited to college students; however, cohabitation is not limited to those in college. Cohabitators may not really be experiencing a "trial" marriage as many suggest. The cultural demands and the role expectations placed on married couples may far outweigh the relational rules a cohabitating couple has established. Although a couple may feel they are creating lifetime relational patterns during cohabitation, the partners may find that these patterns are dramatically altered when they become husband and wife. Cohabitation appears to have its own unique set of characteristics, and the communication patterns that occur between cohabitators are not generalizable to all family types.

A **blended family**—*or reconstituted family, stepfamily, or remarried family*—*consists of two adults and step-, adoptive, or foster children.* This family type is also numerically increasing in our culture. Communication is very difficult in a blended family. Communication patterns have already been established within the previous families. Family histories are brought forward, and these must be revised as the blended family establishes its new identity.

Dual-worker families, *which include two working adults,* have also gotten more numerous in recent history. Norms concerning the appropriateness of wives working outside the home were reversed within a single generation. The dual-worker couple is a marital arrangement that may be based on economics, egalitarianism, and technology, among other factors. This family form calls into question basic assumptions concerning one's sex role and one's function within the family unit.

Nuclear families *have a breadwinning father, a homemaking mother, and resident children.* According to the U.S. Census Bureau (1998), only 8 million of America's 71 million families still have a father, a mother, and at least one child under 18. Since more than half of mothers work, fewer than 4 million nuclear families still exist.

In **extended families,** *not only parents and children are part of the family unit but also grandparents, aunts, uncles, cousins, and others.* Extended families, like nuclear families, no longer occur with the frequency they once did. Increased mobility encourages second and third generations to live in separate homes, even in separate states.

Communicating in the Family

Every family has different rules or norms governing its communication patterns. Complete the following exercise in order to determine the patterns in your family:

1. What communication topics can be discussed? _____
   _____

2. What topics cannot be discussed (for instance, sex, money problems, religious convictions, drug use)? _____
   _____

3. When can you communicate with others? _____
   _____

4. When can you not communicate with family members? _____
   _____

5. What emotions are you allowed to communicate (anger, hostility, sadness, hurt, joy, sorrow, fatigue, enthusiasm)? _____
   _____

6. What emotions are you not allowed to communicate? _____
   _____

7. In what verbal and nonverbal behaviors do you participate in your family that you rarely, or never, participate in outside of your family unit? _____
   _____

8. Do you have family secrets you are not allowed to discuss with others?
   _____
   _____

9. List some words you cannot use in your family (jargon, clichés, profanity, nicknames). _____
   _____

10. List some nonverbal behaviors you cannot use in your family (nonverbal behaviors that have a specific meaning in one of your membership groups, nonverbal behaviors that have a profane meaning within your family, etc.). _____
    _____

After you have completed this inventory, compare your list with that of a person you trust. Do you see similarities? Explain why your family unit has different communication patterns than does another family unit. To what extent do nationality, region of the country, and other co-cultural differences affect your family communication? Consider *who* the primary "rule maker" is in your family. Does this affect the communication patterns? What conclusions can you draw from this exercise?

What Are the Factors That Contribute to Family Satisfaction?

Although contemporary families are highly diverse, research points to six factors that can contribute to family satisfaction.

First, family satisfaction is related to family members' ability to favorably perceive the communicative behavior of the other family members. Families who positively interpret their members' communicative behavior are generally more satisfied than are families who do not interpret positively their members' behavior (Beach & Arias, 1983). This study suggests that people who view events more favorably consistently view both their family members' communicative behavior and their family satisfaction more favorably. Such a result may seem somewhat trivial; positive people are positively disposed across a variety of measures. However, the finding may also suggest that if we are concerned with increasing family satisfaction, one tack may be to increase an individual's overall positive outlook. If therapists and practitioners can improve people's perceptions of various aspects of their family members' behavior, they may find that an added benefit is more family satisfaction. The study suggests that people who intervene in distressed marriages may not only need to work on behavioral change but, perhaps more important, also need to work on changing the perceptions of that behavior.

Second, family satisfaction is related to family members' ability to provide both verbal and nonverbal messages to each other. In other words, communication, in and of itself, is related to family success. Families whose members talk to each other tend to be more satisfied than families whose members do not talk to each other. Open and interactive communication affects the quality of the family relationship (Birchler & Webb, 1977; Boyd & Roach, 1977). Overall family satisfaction is highly related to the family members' ability to discuss problems effectively and to share their feelings (Snyder, 1979). Wives who rate high on communication competence similarly state they have high levels of family satisfaction (Dersch & Pearson, 1986).

Engaging in rituals is one way that families communicate with each other. **Family rituals** are *the forms of symbolic communication that are systematically repeated and that contribute to family satisfaction* (Wolin & Bennett, 1984). For example, your family might always have a cookout on the Fourth of July, your Thanksgiving meal might include the same menu items each year, or special occasions might call for a specific restaurant or new clothing. Family rituals also include private codes that family members create to communicate with each other. One couple, for instance, always asked the question, "Was that 93 cents or 96 cents?" as a way to ease tension when they sensed a conflict might be erupting. Their query was based on her parents' constant bickering over trivial details such as a three-cent difference. Another family used the term "G-N,"—meaning "Glamour-No"—when they spotted someone wearing bizarre, ill-fitting, or unfashionable clothing.

family rituals

The forms of symbolic communication that are systematically repeated and that contribute to family satisfaction.

Family rituals, such as birthday parties and reunions, help keep families together.

TRY ◀▶ THIS

What are some rituals that are practiced in your family? What events and occasions are expected to be experienced by all members of the family?

Third, family satisfaction is related to family members' abilities to send messages that indicate understanding. Understanding and demonstrating understanding are both related to family satisfaction. Through identification and empathy, family members come to define themselves as a unit (Walster, Walster, & Berscheid, 1978). Building such a relationship is not possible without understanding.

Families mature as members become increasingly sensitive to each other's views and to their own views of other families (Reiss, Costell, Beckman, & Jones, 1980). Maturing families continue to integrate and reintegrate each individual's view into a common set of understandings and conceptions. Less healthy, adaptive, or satisfied families fail to reconcile the varying perceptions of their members. Sensitivity to the often-differing needs and views of family members and an ability to integrate them into a new structure may be essential for satisfaction among family members.

Fourth, family satisfaction is related to family members' ability to provide supportive and positive comments to each other. In general, satisfied families provide more positive, supportive, and agreement statements. This behavior extends to the nonverbal area as well and is even more apparent in family members' nonverbal cues. Nondistressed families provide fewer negative comments than do distressed families (Gottman, 1979; Noller, 1980; Pike & Sillars,

1985). Satisfied families are more likely to positively reinforce each other (Vincent, Friedman, Nugent, & Messerly, 1979). Nondistressed families also enjoy more humor and laughter (Riskin & Faunce, 1970). In a review of literature on agreement and disagreement, Riskin and Faunce (1970) prescribed that families should have more agreements than disagreements if they wish to be fully functioning. The communication behavior of dissatisfied families is characterized by defensiveness (Riskin & Faunce, 1970), quarreling, nagging, and argument (Thomas, 1977), aversive control and coercion (Vincent, Weiss, & Birchler, 1975), expressions of hostility (Billings, 1979), and attempts to humiliate and threaten (Jacobson, 1981).

Families that include a delinquent child use less positive and more negative interactions than do families that do not include a delinquent child (Alexander, 1973). Families with delinquent children include three times as many negative statements as do families without such children. Furthermore, the positive or negative nature of the comments appears to affect delinquency: Delinquent behavior decreased when a balance of positive and negative occurred, but it increased when more negative statements were offered (Stuart, 1971).

Fifth, family satisfaction is related to the family's ability to reach consensus, to resolve differences, and to avoid or minimize conflict. Agreement is a hallmark of satisfied families and a key to successful marriages. One area in which agreement may be essential is the family members' agreement about their relationship. Two researchers demonstrated that couples who share a similar definition of their relationship are likely to agree on more relational issues and to be more cohesive than are couples who do not share relational definitions (Fitzpatrick & Best, 1979). Another researcher suggested that marital satisfaction may be more highly related to the couple's ability to resolve their differences or to achieve consensus than to any other communicative behavior:

> Of all the relationship variables that could be selected for understanding marital satisfaction, the couple's ability to arrive at consensus in resolving differences may be of central importance. There are two ways in which a couple could arrive at consensus. One possibility is that they share normative conflict resolution rules transmitted culturally or from parental models. The other possibility is that they are able to construct their own decision rules. (Gottman, 1979)

Sixth, family satisfaction is related to family members' flexibility. Concepts such as flexibility and trust are salient in conflict resolution and in family satisfaction. Scanzoni and Polonko (1980) hypothesized a relationship between trust, risk-taking ability, fairness, and flexibility. They stated that, when one family member trusts another, the other member is more likely to increase his or her trust of the first family member, which will lead to mutual flexibility. Similarly, if one family member is fair to the second, the second is likely to be more flexible and, thus, viewed to be fair by the first.

Instant Recall

7.4 FAMILY COMMUNICATION QUESTIONS

Write T *for true or* F *for false in each blank on the left:*

_____1. The cohabiting-couple household is a "trial" marriage.

_____2. A blended family is just two previously divorced people who marry.

_____3. An extended family is a couple with children.

_____4. Humor and laughter are a sign of a healthy family.

_____5. Defensiveness is one of the signs of a distressed family.

Answers: 1. F   2. F   3. F   4. T   5. T

TRY ◀ ▶ THIS

How would you explain your family's level of satisfaction or dissatisfaction?

Summary

In this chapter, you learned about interpersonal relationships, one context in which people communicate with each other. Interpersonal relationships are associations between two or more people who are interdependent, who use some consistent patterns of interaction, and who have interacted for a period of time. Interpersonal relationships are established for a variety of reasons, including to understand more about ourselves, to understand more about others, to understand our world, to fulfill our needs, and to increase and enrich our positive experiences. Relationships go through definable stages of development, maintenance, and deterioration, which affect self-disclosure.

Self-disclosure consists of verbal and nonverbal intentional statements about ourselves that other people are unlikely to know. Self-disclosure is important in interpersonal relationships because, when you tell others about

179

yourself, you become closer to them and are able to establish more meaningful relationships. Self-disclosure also allows you to establish more positive attitudes about yourself and others. Women and men exhibit different self-disclosure patterns. Some people choose not to self-disclose because they have negative feelings about themselves or do not trust others, or both. Two communication behaviors related to an unwillingness to self-disclose are defensiveness and nonassertiveness.

Communication can be improved in interpersonal relationships, but this is not a simple matter. In addition to understanding communication concepts, skills, and settings, we need to develop behavioral flexibility. Behavioral flexibility is the ability to alter our behavior in order to adapt to new situations and to relate in new ways when necessary. Interpersonal relationships are constantly changing, and individuals who wish to be successful in them must demonstrate flexibility.

You also learned about interpersonal communication within the family. Families are organized, naturally occurring, relational, transactional groups, usually occupying a common living space over an extended time period and possessing a confluence of interpersonal images that evolve through the exchange of meaning over time. Among current family types are the couple with no children, single-parent families, cohabitating couples, blended families, dual-worker families, nuclear families, and extended families.

Researchers have studied satisfaction within the family unit. Six communicative behaviors are related to satisfaction: (1) the ability to perceive the communicative behavior of other family members favorably, (2) the ability to provide both verbal and nonverbal messages to each other, (3) the ability to send messages that indicate understanding, (4) the ability to provide supportive and positive comments to each other, (5) the ability to reach consensus, to resolve differences, and to avoid or minimize conflict, and (6) flexibility.

Each of us can improve communication in our families by practicing the communicative behaviors outlined in this text and in other well-researched material on interpersonal relationships. Changing our behavior is usually risky, but the rewards are well worth the effort.

Issues in Communication

This Issues in Communication narrative is designed to provoke individual thought or discussion about concepts raised in the chapter.

Paul Erdo was born in Budapest, Hungary. During his life he was never married, had no children, never held down a job for an extended period of time, had no hobbies, and did not own a home. Indeed, Erdo owned only an orange plastic bag and a shabby suitcase. From the age of 21 until he died in 1996 at age 83, Erdo almost never slept in the same bed for seven nights in a row. Instead, he lived mainly off friends, admirers, and colleagues. You see, Erdo was also a mathematical genius who wrote more than 1,500 academic papers and established himself as a world-class mathematician.

Erdo exhibited restless energy, gobbled amphetamines, and drank too much coffee. His biographer claims that he sent out more than 1,000 letters a year—all on the subject of mathematics. Although he held no job with any permanence, he was often asked to teach mathematics. A teaching assistant had to be assigned to him because of his habit of impulsively leaving his classroom to complete a proof on which he was working. Once scheduled for surgery, he was so agitated about losing time from mathematical proofs that the physician had to summon a mathematician to Erdo's hospital room to talk prime numbers with him. As Paul Erdo once said, "We mathematicians are all a bit crazy." (Jamison, 1998)

The story of Paul Erdo is a true one. Apply what you have learned about interpersonal communication as you ponder and discuss the following questions: What kind of interpersonal communication skills do you think Erdo possessed? What do you think it would be like to be his friend or acquaintance? How far do you think you would get in relational development? If he was a family member of yours, do you think you would be able to provide him with positive, supportive comments? How would your ability or inability to be supportive affect your family satisfaction?

SOURCE: Dominick, Joseph R. (1999) *The Dynamics of Mass Communication*, 6/e. New York: McGraw-Hill.

Additional Resources

Canary, D., & Dindia, K. (Eds.). (1998). *Sex differences and similarities in communication: Critical essays and empirical investigations of sex and gender in interaction.* Mahwah, NJ: Lawrence Erlbaum.

Dindia, K. (1997). Self-disclosure, self-identity, and relationship development: A transactional/dialectical perspective. In Steve Duck (Ed.), *Handbook of personal relationships* (2nd ed., pp. 411–426). Chichester, England: Wiley.

Dindia, K., Fitzpatrick, M. A., & Kenny, D. A. (1997). Self-disclosure in spouse and stranger interaction: A social relations analysis. *Human Communication Research, 23* (3), 388–412.

Duck, S. (Ed.). (1997). *Handbook of personal relationships: Theory, research and interventions* (2nd ed.). Chichester, England: Wiley.

Montgomery, B. M., & Baxter, L. A. (Eds.). (1998). *Dialogism and relational dialectics.* Mahwah, NJ: Lawrence Erlbaum.

Vanzetti, N., & Duck, S. (Eds.). (1996). *A lifetime of relationships.* Pacific Grove, CA: Brooks/Cole.

References

Alexander, J. F. (1973). Defensive and supportive communications in family systems. *Journal of Marriage and the Family, 35,* 613–617.

Altman, I., & Taylor, D. A. (1973). *Social penetration: The development of interpersonal relationships.* New York: Holt, Rinehart and Winston.

Baxter, L. (1979). Self-disclosure as a relationship disengagement strategy: An exploratory investigation. *Human Communication Research, 5,* 212–222.

Baxter, L. (1982). Strategies for ending relationships: Two studies. *Western Journal of Speech Communication, 46,* 223–241.

Baxter, L. (1983). Relationship disengagement: An examination of the reversal hypothesis. *Western Journal of Speech Communication, 47,* 85–98.

Baxter, L. (1984). Trajectories of relationship disengagement. *Journal of Social and Personal Relationships, 1,* 29–48.

Beach, S. R. H., & Arias, I. (1983). Assessment of perceptual discrepancy: Utility of the primary communication inventory. *Family Process, 22,* 309–316.

Berger, C. R., & Calabrese, R. J. (1975). Some explorations in initial interactions and beyond: Toward a developmental theory of interpersonal communication. *Human Communication Research, 1,* 98–112.

Berger, C. R., & Kellermann, K. (1989). Personal opacity and social information gathering. *Communication Research, 16,* 314–351.

Billings, A. (1979). Conflict resolution in distressed and nondistressed married couples. *Journal of Consulting and Clinical Psychology, 47,* 368–376.

Birchler, G. R., & Webb, L. J. (1977). Discriminating interaction behaviors in happy and unhappy marriages. *Journal of Consulting and Clinical Psychology, 45,* 494–495.

Bochner, A. A. (1976). Conceptual frontiers in the study of communication in families: An introduction to the literature. *Human Communication Research, 2,* 381–397.

Boyd, L., & Roach, A. (1977). Interpersonal communicating skills differentiating more satisfying from less satisfying marital relationships.

Journal of Counseling Psychology, 24, 540–542.

Davis, M. H., & Oathout, H. A. (1987). Maintenance of satisfaction in romantic relationships: empathy and relational competence. *Journal of Personality and Social Psychology, 53,* 397–498.

Dersch, C. R., & Pearson, J. C. (1986). *Interpersonal communication competence and marital adjustment among dual career and dual worker women.* Paper presented at the annual meeting of the Central States Speech Association, Cincinnati, OH.

Deusch, M., & Kraus, R. M. (1962). Studies of interpersonal bargaining. *Journal of Conflict Resolution, 6,* 52.

Fitzpatrick, M. A., & Best, P. G. (1979). Dyadic adjustment in traditional, independent, and separate relationships: A validation study. *Communication Monographs, 46,* 167–178.

Friedman, H. S., Riggio, J. R. E., & Casella, D. F. (1988). Nonverbal skill, personal charisma, and initial attraction.

Personality and Social Psychology Bulletin, 14, 203–211.

Gibb, J. R. (1961). Defensive communication. *Journal of Communication, 11,* 141–148.

Gottman, J. M. (1979). *Marital interaction: Experimental investigations.* New York: Academic Press.

Hawken, L., Duncan, R. L., & Kelly, L. (1991, Fall). The relationship of interpersonal communication variables to academic success and persistence in college. *Communication Quarterly,* 297–308.

Homans, G. C. (1961). *Social behavior: Its elementary forms.* New York: Harcourt Brace Jovanovich.

Howard, J. (1978). *Families.* New York: Simon & Schuster.

Jacobson, N. S. (1981). Behavioral marital therapy. In A. S. Gurman & D. P. Kniskern (Eds.), *Handbook of family therapy.* New York: Brunner/Mazel.

Jamison, K. R. (1998, August 2). A review of *The man who loved numbers: The odd story of Paul Erdo and his search for mathematical truth. The Washington Post,* pp. 1, 10.

Knapp, M. L. (1978). *Social intercourse: From greeting to goodbye.* Boston: Allyn and Bacon.

McCroskey, J. C., & McCain, T. A. (1974). The measurement of interpersonal attraction. *Speech Monographs, 41,* 267–276.

McGee, E. A. (1982). *Too little, too late: Services for teenage parents.* New York: Ford Foundation.

Mead, G. H. (1934). *Mind, self, and society.* Chicago: University of Chicago Press.

Miller, G. R. (1976). *Explorations in interpersonal communication.* Beverly Hills, CA: Sage.

Noller, P. (1980). Channel consistency and inconsistency in the communication of married couples. *Journal of Personality and Social Psychology, 39,* 732–741.

Palisi, B. J., & Ransford, H. E. (1987). Friendships as a voluntary relationship: Evidence from national surveys. *Journal of Social and Personal Relationships, 4,* 143–159.

Pearson, J. C. (1983). *Interpersonal communication: Clarity, confidence, concern.* Glenview, IL: Scott, Foresman.

Pearson, J. C. (1996). Forty-forever years? Primary relationships and senior citizens. In N. Vanzetti & S. Duck (Eds.), *A lifetime of relationships* (pp. 383–405). Pacific Grove, CA: Brooks/Cole.

Pearson, J. C., & Spitzberg, B. H. (1990). *Interpersonal communication: Concepts, components, and contexts*. Dubuque, IA: William C. Brown.

Perse, E. M., & Rubin, R. B. (1989). Attribution in social and parasocial relationships. *Communication Research, 16,* 59–77.

Pike, G. R., & Sillars, A. L. (1985). Reciprocity of marital communication. *Journal of Social and Personal Relationships, 2,* 303–324.

Reiss, D., Costell, R., Berkman, H., and Jones, C. (1980). How one family perceives another: The relationship between social constructions and problem-solving competence. *Family Process, 19,* 239–256.

Riskin, J., & Faunce, E. E. (1970). Family interaction scales: Discussion of methodology and substantive findings. *Archives of General Psychiatry, 22,* 527–537.

Rosenfeld, L. B. (1979). Self-disclosure avoidance: Why I am afraid to tell you who I am. *Communication Monographs, 46,* 63–74.

Sabatelli, R. M., & Rubin, M. (1986). Nonverbal expressiveness and physical attractiveness as mediators of interpersonal perceptions. *Journal of Nonverbal Behavior, 10,* 120–133.

Scanzoni, J., & Polonko, K. (1980). A conceptual approach to explicit marital negotiation. *Journal of Marriage and the Family, 42,* 45–56.

Schutz, W. (1976). *The interpersonal underworld.* Palo Alto, CA: Science and Behavior Books.

Sheehy, G. (1976). *Passages: Predictable crises of adult life.* New York: Dutton.

Silverman, S. L., & Silverman, M. G. (1963). *Theory of relationships.* New York: Philosophical Library.

Singletary, M. (1999, February 21). The color of money. *The Washington Post,* H1, H4.

Snyder, L. (1979). The deserting, nonsupporting father: Scapegoat of family nonpolicy. *Family Coordinator, 28,* 594–598.

Stokes, J., Fuehrer, A., & Childs, L. (1980). Gender differences in self-disclosure to various target persons. *Journal of Counseling Psychology, 27,* 192–198.

Stuart, R. B. (1971). Operant-interpersonal treatment for marital discord. *Journal of Consulting and Clinical Psychology, 33,* 675–682.

Tannen, D. (1990). *You just don't understand.* New York: Morrow.

Thibaut, J. W., & Kelley, H. H. (1959). *The social psychology of groups.* New York: Wiley.

Thomas, E. J. (1977). *Marital communication and decision making.* New York: Free Press.

Vincent, J. P., Friedman, L., Nugent, J., & Messerly, L. (1979). Demand characteristics in the observation of marital interaction. *Journal of Consulting and Clinical Psychology, 47,* 557–567.

Vincent, J. P., Weiss, R. L., & Birchler, G.

(1975). A behavioral analysis of problem solving in distressed and nondistressed married and stranger diads. *Behavior Therapy, 6,* 475–487.

Wahlroos, S. (1983). *Family communication.* New York: Macmillan.

Walster, E., Walster, G. W., & Berscheid, E. (1978). *Equity:*

Theory and research. Boston: Allyn and Bacon.

Wilmot, W. W. (1980). *Dyadic communication* (2nd ed.). Reading, MA: Addison-Wesley, 1980.

Wiseman, J. P. (1986). Friendship: Bonds and binds in a

voluntary relationship. *Journal of Social and Personal Relationships, 3,* 191–211.

Wolin, S., & Bennett, L. (1984). Family rituals. *Family Process, 23,* 401–420.

When you have read and thought about this chapter, you will be able to:

1. Explain why you should study intercultural communication.

2. Identify cultures and co-cultures.

3. Provide examples of co-languages.

4. Explain potential intercultural communication problems.

5. Identify characteristics of specific cultures and understand how to use them in communication situations.

6. Practice strategies for improving communication with people from other cultures and co-cultures.

8

Intercultural
Communication

This chapter introduces you to communication between cultures and co-cultures. Being an effective communicator means understanding and sharing with people from various racial, ethnic, and cultural backgrounds. The goal of this chapter is to increase your confidence in your ability to communicate with people from other cultures and co-cultures. The chapter stresses the importance of communicating in an ever-changing world. The chapter also explains cultures and co-cultures, as well as the types and functions of co-languages, identifies some of the characteristics of several cultures, and provides strategies for improving intercultural communication.

Anisa Puria's family is originally from India. Anisa was born there, but she lived there only until she was 3 years old, which is when Anisa and her family moved to the East African country of Tanzania. Now 18, Anisa and her family have lived in Tanzania ever since. Anisa is fluent in Hindi, English, and Swahili, the language of trade in East Africa. She still wears a sari (the traditional Indian dress) every day. Anisa is currently studying abroad in the United States. She isn't sure if it's the sari, her British accent, or her dark skin, but Anisa has noticed that white American students rarely speak to her unless she speaks to them first. They seem unfamiliar with where Tanzania is, and they seem confused that a person of Indian origin would be living in an African country.

Chris Johnson grew up in North Dakota, graduated from North Dakota State University, and currently works for Midwest Software, a rapidly growing software company. As a technical specialist, Chris is frequently sent to other countries where his company's software is being used. Although he's only 26, he's already been to Austria, Germany, France, and Denmark. While Chris knows his company's software inside and out, communicating with people from a variety of countries isn't always easy for him. The language barrier is one thing, but not knowing a country's customs also puts him at a disadvantage. The next time he has to travel to another country, Chris plans to do some research about that country's customs prior to leaving. He also thinks it would be a good idea to learn a few basic words of the country's native language—*hello, good-bye,* and *computer* would be a good place to start.

Perhaps you, too, would be reluctant to talk to someone like Anisa. Maybe, like Chris Johnson, you will one day find yourself having to communicate with people in other countries. If so, this chapter will help you feel more confident communicating with people from different cultures and co-cultures.

Why Is the Study of Intercultural Communication Important?

intercultural communication

The exchange of information between individuals who are unalike culturally.

Rogers and Steinfatt (1999) define **intercultural communication** as *"the exchange of information between individuals who are unalike culturally."* Not long ago, intercultural communication involved only missionaries, jet-setting business executives, foreign correspondents, and some national political figures. Now, however, developments in technology and shifts in demographics have created a society in which intercultural communication is inevitable. So one reason for the importance of studying intercultural communication is *our increasing exposure to people of other cultures and co-cultures.* More people are exposed to different cultures through war, commercial travel, and global economies, and more people are exposed to different co-cultures. It is highly likely that at some point in your life you will have to interact with people from different cultures and co-cultures. A second reason is *our economic need to relate to others.* Today we sell our corn and cars in Asia, and we buy coffee from Colombia, bananas from Costa Rica, and oil from Africa. A third reason is, *simply, our curiosity about others.* We are curious about people who don't look like us, sound like us, or live like us. We wonder why one woman always wears a long dress and veil, why another always walks five paces behind her spouse, why a man wears a turban, and why some people don't eat meat.

What Are Cultures and Co-cultures?

You have just learned that intercultural communication is the exchange of information between people of different cultures, but you may be uncertain about the definitions of culture and co-culture. **Culture** can be defined as *a system of shared beliefs, values, customs, behaviors, and artifacts that the members of a society use to cope with one another and with their world.* Transmitted from generation to generation through social learning, culture can also be seen as the mechanism that allows human beings to make sense of the world around them. Cultures include a wide variety of races, ethnic groups, and nationalities.

In the United States, a number of co-cultures exist based on language, race, religion, economics, age, gender, and sexual orientation. A **co-culture** is *"a group whose beliefs or behaviors distinguish it from the larger culture of which it is a part and with which it shares numerous similarities"* (DeVito, 1986). *Co-culture* is used here, rather than the more common term *subculture* because the latter implies that these groups are somehow inferior to the dominant culture. In the United States, where the dominant culture is white, upper-middle-class males, examples of co-cultures are Hispanics, adolescents, and lesbians. These people experience a lifestyle which differs from that of the dominant culture. Note that an individual can belong to a number of co-cultures. A person can be, for example, Hispanic, adolescent, and a lesbian.

Cultures and co-cultures mingle in America.

culture

A system of shared beliefs, values, customs, behaviors, and artifacts that the members of a society use to cope with one another and with their world.

co-culture

A group whose beliefs or behaviors distinguish it from the larger culture of which it is a part and with which it shares numerous similarities.

Co-languages

Language is often a crucial co-cultural feature. Obvious problems can occur when individuals are speaking different languages. Not as obvious are problems

co-languages

Specialized languages used by co-cultures to facilitate effective communication and to distinguish group members from nonmembers.

argot

The specialized language of disreputable underground co-cultures.

cant

The specialized language of nonprofessional, usually noncriminal, groups.

jargon

The technical language of a particular trade, profession, or group.

slang

Language derived from cant and argot that consists of terms widely known to the dominant culture but not acceptable for use in formal writing and speaking.

that occur when people use different **co-languages,** which are *specialized languages used by co-cultures to facilitate effective communication and to distinguish group members from nonmembers.* Within the larger society that uses a dominant language (which is English in the United States), a co-culture creates a specific language adapted to its specific experiences. As with the dominant language, co-languages change over time, but they always perform a necessary function. The following four examples of co-languages illustrate ways in which co-cultures communicate.

Argot

Argot is *the specialized language of disreputable underground co-cultures* (De-Vito, 1986), such as gangs, prisoners, drug dealers, prostitutes, pickpockets, and burglars. People like these, who live on the edges of society, have their own words for *prison, lawyers,* and the names of drugs. The general society is often exposed to this kind of language through television shows and movies that try to depict prison life or life on the streets.

Cant

Cant is *the specialized language of a nonprofessional (usually noncriminal) group* (DeVito, 1986). This group includes taxi drivers, truckers, noncommissioned military personnel, food servers, and dockworkers. Taxi drivers, for instance, have specialized terms for people who use the cab, for people who do not use the cab, for people who do not tip, and for people who flee without paying.

Jargon

Jargon is *the technical language of a particular trade, profession, or group.* Jargon differs from argot or cant in that it is a more technical and professional co-language. Computer scientists, physicians, investors, and lawyers, to name only a few, are noted for their use of jargon. Jargon projects experience, authority, and expertise.

Slang

Slang consists of *terms derived from argot and cant that are widely known to the dominant culture but are not acceptable for use in a formal setting, speech, or writing.* Popular slang terms have a short life span.

TRY◄►THIS

Make a list of some of the more common slang terms you use or hear often. At the end of the semester come up with another list, and compare the two to see if the terms have changed.

Physicians use jargon to communicate with each other about medicine and health.

What Are Some Potential Intercultural Communication Problems?

Intercultural communication is subject to all the problems that can hamper effective interpersonal communication. However, several additional problems may occur during intercultural interactions. Becoming aware of these issues can help you avoid them or reduce their effects. Keep in mind that although the barriers identified here can be problematic, they do not occur in every exchange.

Ethnocentrism

The largest problem that occurs during intercultural communication is that people bring an ethnocentric perspective to the interaction. **Ethnocentrism** is *the belief that your own group or culture is superior to all other groups or cultures.* You are ethnocentric if you see and judge the rest of the world only from your own culture's perspective. Some common examples include thinking that everyone should speak English, that people in the United States should not have to learn languages other than English, that the U.S. culture is better than Mexico's, or that the Asian custom of bowing is odd (Dodd, 1998). To some extent, each of us operates from an ethnocentric perspective, but problems arise when we interpret and evaluate other cultures by the norms and standards of our own. Generally, a lack of interaction with another culture fosters high levels of ethnocentrism and encourages the notion that one culture is somehow superior to another. Ethnocentrism can create defensiveness on the part of the person who is being treated as if he or she is somehow deficient or inferior.

In ethnocentrism you use your own culture as the measure that others are expected to meet, whereas in **cultural relativism** you *judge another person's culture by its own context.* Saying that the Asian custom of bowing

ethnocentrism

The belief that your own group or culture is superior to other groups or cultures.

cultural relativism

The belief that another culture should be judged by its context rather than measured against your own culture.

is odd overlooks the long history of bowing to one another as a sign of respect. To communicate effectively with people from different cultures, you need to accept people whose values and norms may be different from your own.

Stereotyping

stereotype

A generalization about some group of people that oversimplifies their culture.

Rogers and Steinfatt (1999) define a **stereotype** as *"a generalization about some group of people that oversimplifies their cultures."* In one way stereotyping is unavoidable. When you think of lawyers, physicians, gardeners, and homeless people, generalized images come to mind. Stereotyping becomes troublesome in communication when people make assumptions about an individual on the basis of simplified notions about the group to which he or she belongs—for example, assuming that the Asian student in your class probably doesn't speak good English or that the blonde, female guidance counselor is dim-witted. Such negative stereotypes are injurious to individuals and groups.

Allport (1958) noted that people are more likely to stereotype individuals and groups with whom they have little contact. It's easy to make unwarranted assumptions about people or groups; challenge yourself to learn more about people from cultures and co-cultures other than your own by getting to know them.

What Are Some Characteristics of Different Cultures?

Accepting that your own culture is not superior to another person's culture is one way to improve intercultural communication. Another way is by understanding some of the values and norms of other cultures. For example, say you are an American teaching in Japan (a *collectivist* culture). Your students' first assignment is to give a speech before the class. After you give them the assignment, they automatically form groups and each group selects a spokesperson to give the speech. In the United States (an *individualistic* culture), students would be unlikely to turn a public-speaking assignment into a small-group activity, unless specifically directed to do so. If you didn't know something about the norms and customs of the Japanese culture, you might have been totally baffled by your students' behavior.

In this section you will learn about the characteristics of six cultures: individualistic versus collectivist cultures, uncertainty-accepting versus uncertainty-rejecting cultures, and implicit-rule versus explicit-rule cultures. Keep in mind that the characteristics discussed below are general tendencies: They are not always true of a culture, nor are they true of everyone in a culture.

Instant Recall

8.1 INTERCULTURAL COMMUNICATION CONCEPTS

For each statement, indicate which concept is illustrated by writing the appropriate letter from the choices below in the blank on the left:

A. Stereotype   **B. Ethnocentrism**   **C. Cultural relativity**

_____1. "Praying five times a day is a time-honored religious practice of the Muslims."

_____2. "Wealthy senior citizens drive Cadillacs."

_____3. "North America's capitalist system yields a better economy than any other economy in the world."

_____4. "Your vagabond lifestyle tells me you must be an artist."

_____5. "Americans should learn something from Southeast Asian countries, which value the elderly much more than we do in the United States."

Answers: 1. C   2. A   3. B   4. A   5. C

Individualistic versus Collectivist Cultures

Much of what is known about individualistic and collectivist cultures comes from a study by Hofstede (1980) that involved over 100,000 managers from 40 countries. Neither China nor Africa was included in the study.

Individualistic cultures are *societies that value individual freedom, choice, uniqueness, and independence.* These cultures place "I" before "we" and value competition over cooperation, private property over public or state-owned property, personal behavior over group behavior, and individual opinion over what anyone else might think. In an individualistic society people are likely to leave the family home or the geographic area in which they were raised to pursue their dreams; their loyalty to an organization has qualifications; they move from job to job; and they may change churches that no longer meet their needs. Loyalty to other people has limits: Individualistic cultures have high levels of divorce and illegitimacy. According to the Hofstede (1980) study, the top-ranking individualistic cultures are the United States, Australia, Great Britain, Canada, and the Netherlands.

Collectivist cultures, on the other hand, *value the group over the individual.* These cultures place "we" before "I" and value commitment to family,

individualistic cultures

Cultures that value individual freedom, choice, uniqueness, and independence.

193

COMMUNICATION CHALLENGE

Interpret the Meaning of Common Sayings

Examine carefully the sayings below, and by yourself or with classmates determine whether they reflect a collectivist or an individualistic culture:

1. When spider webs unite, they can tie up a lion.
2. God helps those who help themselves.
3. The squeaky wheel gets the grease.
4. The ill-mannered child finds a father wherever he goes.

Answers: 1. An Ethiopian proverb, collectivist   2. An American saying, individualistic
3. An American saying, individualistic   4. An African saying, collectivist

SOURCE: L. A. Samovar, R. E. Porter, and L. A. Stefani, *Communication between Cultures*, 3rd ed. Belmont, CA: Wadsworth, 1998.

collectivist cultures

Cultures that value the group over the individual.

tribe, and clan; their people tend to be loyal to spouse, employer, community, and country. Collectivist cultures place a higher value on cooperation than on competition and on group-defined social norms and duties than on personal opinion (Coleman, 1998). An ancient Confucian saying captures the spirit of collectivist cultures: "If one wants to establish himself, he should help others to establish themselves first." The highest-ranking collectivist cultures are Venezuela, Pakistan, Peru, Taiwan, and Thailand (Hofstede, 1980).

Uncertainty-Accepting versus Uncertainty-Rejecting Cultures

uncertainty-accepting cultures

Cultures that tolerate ambiguity, uncertainty, and diversity.

uncertainty-rejecting cultures

Cultures that have difficulty with ambiguity, uncertainty, and diversity.

Uncertainty-accepting cultures *tolerate ambiguity, uncertainty, and diversity.* Some of these cultures already have a mixture of ethnic groups, religions, and races. They are more likely to accept political refugees, immigrants, and new citizens from other places. They are less likely to have a rule for everything and more likely to tolerate general principles. Uncertainty-accepting cultures include the United States, Great Britain, Denmark, Sweden, Singapore, Hong Kong, Ireland, and India (Hofstede, 1980). Interestingly, Singapore is a country that is more tolerant of uncertainty and diversity but has many rules, including one prohibiting chewing gum. This oddity should serve as a reminder that these characteristics are generalizations and, therefore, are not always found consistently in every culture.

   Uncertainty-rejecting cultures *have difficulty with ambiguity, uncertainty, and diversity.* These cultures are more likely to have lots of rules; more

likely to want to know exactly how to behave; and more likely to reject outsiders such as immigrants, refugees, and migrants who look and act different than they do. Among the most common uncertainty-rejecting cultures are Japan, France, Spain, Greece, Portugal, Belgium, Peru, Chile, and Argentina (Samovar, Porter, & Stefani, 1998).

Implicit-Rule versus Explicit-Rule Cultures

An **implicit-rule culture** is one in which *information and cultural rules are implied and already known to the participants.* For example, a traditional Arab woman knows one of the rules of her culture is that she is to walk a few paces behind her husband. People from an implicit-rule culture tend to be more polite, less aggressive, and more accommodating. Some implicit-rule cultures include the Middle East, Africa, and Latin America (Dodd, 1998).

An **explicit-rule culture** is one in which *information and cultural rules are explicit, procedures are explained, and expectations are discussed.* For example, in U.S. families, parents often discuss beforehand with their small children how the children are to act during a visit from someone of importance. People from an explicit-rule culture tend to be more combative, less willing to please, and less concerned about offending others. Some explicit-rule cultures are northern and western Europe and the USA (Dodd, 1998).

You might think about the difference between an implicit-rule culture and an explicit-rule culture in this way: In an implicit-rule culture the social rules are part of who and what you are. They are learned over time from others and are no more discussed than washing your hands or brushing your teeth are in America. In an explicit-rule country, rules are often developed, discussed, and negotiated as you go along.

Table 8.1 summarizes the characteristics of all six cultures discussed in this section. Most of the information is adapted from Carley Dodd's (1998) book entitled *Dynamics of Intercultural Communication.*

implicit-rule culture

A culture in which information and cultural rules are implied and already known to the participants.

explicit-rule culture

A culture in which information and cultural rules are explicit, procedures are explained, and expectations are discussed.

TABLE 8.1 SUMMARY OF CULTURAL CHARACTERISTICS

INDIVIDUALISTIC VS. COLLECTIVIST

INDIVIDUALISTIC CULTURES TEND TO:	COLLECTIVIST CULTURES TEND TO:
Value individual freedom; place "I" before "we."	Value the group over the individual; place "we" before "I."
Value independence.	Value commitment to family, tribe, and clan.
Value competition over cooperation.	Value cooperation over competition.
Value directness and clarity.	Value indirect communication.
Value telling the truth over sparing feelings.	Value "saving face" by not causing embarrassment.
Examples: United States, Australia, Great Britain, Canada, Netherlands	*Examples:* Venezuela, Pakistan, Peru, Taiwan, Thailand

UNCERTAINTY-ACCEPTING VS. UNCERTAINTY-REJECTING CULTURES

UNCERTAINTY-ACCEPTING CULTURES TEND TO:	UNCERTAINTY-REJECTING CULTURES TEND TO:
Be less threatened by ideas and people from outside.	Be threatened by ideas and people from outside.
Be willing to take risks in the face of uncertainty.	See uncertainty as a continuous hazard.
Avoid rules and seek flexibility.	Establish formal rules for behavior.
Dislike structure associated with hierarchy.	Prefer stability, hierarchy, and structure.
Prize initiative and doing things on one's own.	Seek agreement, consensus.
See truth as relative, and question authority.	Believe in absolute truths and expert authority.
Value individual opinion, general principles, and common sense.	Embrace written rules, planning, regulation, rituals, and ceremonies.
Examples: United States, Great Britain, Denmark, Sweden, Singapore, Hong Kong, Ireland, India	*Examples:* Japan, France, Spain, Greece, Portugal, Belgium, Peru, Chile, Argentina

IMPLICIT-RULE VS. EXPLICIT-RULE CULTURES

IMPLICIT-RULE CULTURES TEND TO:	EXPLICIT-RULE CULTURES TEND TO:
See cultural rules as implied, already known to participants.	See cultural rules as explicit; procedures are explained and discussed.
See an attack on an issue as an attack on the person; person and issue are perceived as one.	Person and issue are separate.
Prefer "saving face," the need to soothe an embarrassed or insulted person.	Expect communicators to be straightforward; people have to cope with embarrassment or insult.
Examples: Middle East, Africa, Latin America	*Examples:* Northern and western Europe, USA

Instant Recall

8.2 CULTURAL CHARACTERISTICS

Match the correct letter (or letters) from the choices below with each description:

A.	Collectivist culture	D.	Uncertainty-rejecting culture
B.	Individualistic culture	E.	Implicit-rule culture
C.	Uncertainty-accepting culture	F.	Explicit-rule culture

_____1. Values straight talk and emphasizes "I" over "we."

_____2. Is comfortable with new ideas, new people, and uncertainty.

_____3. Describes the dominant culture in the United States.

_____4. Discusses procedures and expectations.

_____5. Values cooperation and group-defined social norms.

_____6. Doesn't need to discuss cultural rules because participants know them already.

Answers: 1. B   2. C   3. B, C, and F   4. F   5. A   6. E

What Are Some Strategies for Improving Intercultural Communication?

Effective intercultural communication often takes considerable time, energy, and commitment. Although some people would like "10 easy steps" to effective intercultural communication, no foolproof plan is available. However, the strategies presented here should provide you with some ways to improve intercultural communication and, hopefully, avoid potential problems. Having some strategies in advance will prepare you for new situations with people from other cultures and co-cultures and will increase your confidence in your ability to communicate effectively with a variety of people.

1. *Conduct a personal self-assessment.* How do your own attitudes toward different cultures and co-cultures influence your communication with them? One of the first steps toward improving your

Japanese, Korean, and Thai cultures—to name a few—bow to show respect.

intercultural communication skills is an honest assessment of your own communication style, beliefs, and prejudices.

2. *Practice supportive communication behaviors.* Supportive behaviors, such as empathy, encourage success in intercultural exchanges; defensive behaviors tend to hamper effectiveness.

3. *Develop sensitivity toward diversity.* One healthy communication perspective holds that you can learn something from all people. Diverse populations provide ample opportunity for learning. Take the time to learn about other cultures and co-cultures before a communication situation, but don't forget that you will also learn about others simply by taking a risk and talking to someone who is different from you. Challenge yourself. You may be surprised by what you learn.

4. *Avoid stereotypes.* Cultural generalizations go only so far; avoid making assumptions about another's culture, and get to know individuals for themselves.

5. *Avoid ethnocentrism.* You may know your own culture the best, but that familiarity does not make your culture superior to all others. You will learn more about the strengths and weaknesses of your own culture by learning more about others.

code sensitivity

The ability to use the verbal and nonverbal language appropriate to the cultural or co-cultural norms of the individual with whom you are communicating.

6. *Develop code sensitivity.* Developing **code sensitivity** means learning to use *the verbal and nonverbal language appropriate to the cultural or co-cultural norms of the individual with whom you are communicating.* When communicating with someone, be sensitive to the verbal and nonverbal language of that person's culture or co-culture. The more you know about another's culture, the better you will be at adapting.

7. *Seek shared codes.* A key ingredient in establishing shared codes is **tolerating ambiguity,** or *being open-minded about differences,* while you determine which communication style to adopt during intercultural communication.

tolerating ambiguity

Being open-minded about differences.

8. *Use and encourage descriptive feedback.* Feedback encourages adaptation, and effective feedback is crucial in intercultural communication. During intercultural exchanges, both participants should be willing to accept feedback and exhibit supportive behaviors. Feedback should be immediate, honest, specific, and clear.

9. *Open communication channels.* Intercultural communication can be frustrating. One important strategy to follow during such interactions is to keep the lines of communication open.

Summary

In this chapter you learned what intercultural communication is and the importance of studying intercultural communication. All of us are increasingly exposed to people of other cultures and co-cultures, we have an economic need to relate to others, and we are curious about others.

Our culture influences communication. The experiences of co-cultures are vastly different from those of the dominant culture. The specialized language of a co-culture distinguishes members from nonmembers and facilitates effective communication between members. Argot, cant, jargon, and slang are all examples of co-languages.

Communication problems can be caused by ethnocentrism and stereotyping. An awareness of potential problems reduces cultural barriers before they become problems. Another way to reduce the cultural barriers that can occur is by learning about the norms and values of other cultures. The cultures discussed in the chapter are individualistic versus collectivist, uncertainty-accepting versus uncertainty-rejecting, and implicit-rule versus explicit-rule cultures.

Effective intercultural communication has no magic formula, but the chapter provides several strategies that may help you improve your communication skills.

In our changing world, an effective communicator must possess the skills to communicate with diverse cultures and co-cultures. You should now have a more complete understanding of the relationship between culture and communication.

Issues in Communication

This Issues in Communication narrative is designed to provoke individual thought or discussion about concepts raised in the chapter.

Two American women, Jennifer, the president of the World Communication Association (WCA), and Carla, the executive secretary, recently traveled to Seoul, Korea. They were in Korea to meet with the Korean Communication Association (KCA)—a predominantly male group of professors in the fields of language, literature, and linguistics—for the purpose of securing a formal invitation to bring the WCA to Korea the following year and getting the KCA to cohost the event. Jennifer and Carla's gracious host, a representative from the KCA, provided for all of their needs, including rides to and from the international airport and a complimentary stay at an exclusive hotel, where they were welcomed with fruit baskets and flowers. They were certain that this meant they would be invited to bring their organization to Korea next year.

The second evening they attended a business meeting, which included a formal dinner. Before the dinner was a cocktail hour, during which Jennifer and Carla met the distinguished Korean delegation, all of whom were professors. Jennifer and Carla were relieved that most of the professors spoke flawless English, since neither of them spoke Korean. No one was shy about talking with the American guests, and everyone seemed to be having a good time.

The seating at the meeting and dinner was assigned, with the Americans and the senior Korean professor at the head of the table, the host of the event on one side, and the rest of the professors around the outside of the table. While everyone else ate, the host, a high-status professor and entrepreneur, went systematically to six other male professors and engaged in brief, but seemingly serious, conversations with them.

The host started the meeting after the meal by asking Jennifer to say a few words. Jennifer talked about her organization's interest in exploring sites for next year's WCA conference, and she explained that Korea was one of three sites being considered. After Jennifer finished speaking, the host offered no opinion, nor did his expression offer any indication of his opinion. He simply began inviting the six individuals he had talked to during the meal to address the assembled group. Each of the six speakers said basically the same thing: "We are so glad you are here. We are pleased that you came to our country and are considering it as a site for your conference. It will be good to have you here in 3 years." Their message was obvious to Jennifer and Carla: Without actually saying the word *no*, the Koreans were clearly telling the two women that they were not welcome to bring the WCA conference to Korea next year. Jennifer and Carla were stunned. Until then, they had been fully expecting to receive the invitation they were seeking.

Apply what you have learned about intercultural communication as you ponder and discuss the following questions: How might the cultural differences between the Koreans and the Americans have affected their behaviors? What could Jennifer and Carla have done differently to prepare themselves for their visit? What specific strategies would you use in this situation?

Additional Resources

Dodd, C. H. (1998). *Dynamics of intercultural communication* (5th ed.). New York: McGraw-Hill.

Hecht, M. L., Collier, M. J., & Ribeau, S. A. (1993). *African American communication: Ethnic identity and interpretation.* Newbury Park, CA: Sage.

Hofstede, G. (1991). *Cultures and organization: Software of the mind.* London: McGraw-Hill.

Rogers, E. M., & Steinfatt, T. M. (1999). *Intercultural communication.* Prospect Heights, IL: Waveland Press.

Samovar, L., Porter, R. E., & Stefani, L. (1988). *Communication between cultures* (3rd ed.). Belmont, CA: Wadsworth.

World Factbook **www.odci.gov/cia/ publications/ 95 fact/index.html.**

References

Allport, Gordon W. (1954/1958). *The nature of prejudice.* Cambridge: Addison-Wesley/Garden City, NY: Doubleday.

Coleman, D. (1998, December 22). The group and self: New focus on a cultural rift. *The New York Times*, p. 40.

DeVito, J. A. (1986). *The communication handbook: A dictionary.* New York: Harper & Row.

Dodd, C. H. (1998). *Dynamics of intercultural communication* (5th ed.). New York: McGraw-Hill.

Hofstede, G. (1980). *Culture's consequences: International differences in work-related values.* Beverly Hills, CA: Sage.

Rogers, E. M., & Steinfatt, T. M. (1999). *Intercultural communication.* Prospect Heights, IL: Waveland Press.

Samovar, L. A., Porter, R. E., & Stefani, L. A. (1998). *Communication between cultures* (3rd ed.). Belmont, CA: Wadsworth.

When you have read and thought about this chapter, you will be able to:

1. Define *small-group communication* and state why it is important.

2. Recognize two main types of groups.

3. Describe the elements that help determine a group's culture.

4. Determine how gender and ethnicity affect small-group communication.

5. Describe how roles and norms develop in a group.

6. Identify three elements that create a group's climate.

7. Promote ethical group behavior.

chapter

9

The Dynamics of Small-Group Discussion

WITH GLORIA J. GALANES

"One finger cannot lift a pebble."

HOPI PARABLE

"We can never be sure that the opinion we are endeavoring to stifle is a false opinion; and if we were sure, stifling it would be evil still."

JOHN STUART MILL

"Even in those views we hold most strongly we may be mistaken."

JUDGE IRVING R. KAUFMAN

Small groups are everywhere. Families, work teams, support groups, study groups—all are examples of groups that form the foundations of our society. In this chapter, you will explore what small-group communication is and why it is important. You will learn about the two major types of groups; about the development of group culture, norms, and role structure; and about how to be an ethical group member. Because small groups are everywhere, you will have plenty of opportunities to practice what you learn in this chapter.

K evin works in the finance department of a major airline company. The head of the department values a team approach to tackling important issues, so Kevin frequently meets with his work team during the course of the day. Outside of work Kevin is also involved in a number of group activities. He sits on the board of his neighborhood association; he plays the guitar and jams weekly with friends; he goes out to lunch with four of his old college buddies each week; and he and his two sisters have been meeting to plan a party for his parents' thirtieth wedding anniversary.

Clearly, group activities are a big part of Kevin's life. Perhaps you didn't even realize until just now how prevalent they are in yours.

What You Should Learn about Small Groups

Small groups are the basic building blocks of our society, especially of organizations. Families, work teams, support groups, church circles, and study groups are all examples of the ways in which our society is built upon groups. In organizations, the higher up you go, the more time you will spend working in groups. For example, one report estimated that executives spend about *half* their time in business meetings (Cole, 1989).

Small groups are important for five reasons (Table 9.1). These reasons clarify why you will want to learn how to communicate effectively in small groups. First, humans need groups; membership in groups meets needs that we cannot meet for ourselves. William Schutz (1958), a psychologist who has studied group interaction, said that humans have needs for inclusion, affection, and control. Inclusion suggests that people need to belong to, or be included in, groups with others. As humans, we derive much of our identity, our beliefs about who we are, from the groups to which we belong. Starting with our immediate families and including such important groups as our church, mosque, or synagogue; interest groups; work teams; and social groups—all these help us define who we are. Affection, another essential need, means that we humans need to love and be loved, to know that we are important to others who value us as unique human beings. Finally, we have a

---

TABLE 9.1   WHY YOU SHOULD STUDY SMALL-GROUP COMMUNICATION

1. Humans need groups to meet needs they cannot meet as individuals.
2. Groups are everywhere.
3. Knowing how groups function and how to operate effectively in them will be a highly valued skill.
4. Working effectively in groups requires training.
5. The human need to contribute to society is powerful, and small groups are a means of participating in the democratic process.

American companies have come to realize how helpful groups can be in conducting their business.

need for control over our environment. We are better able to exercise such control if we work together in groups. One person cannot build a school, bridge, or new business. However, by working together in groups we *can* accomplish these and other complex tasks. We need others to meet our needs.

Second, groups are everywhere. You won't be able to escape working in them. For a moment, list all of the groups to which you currently belong, including informal groups such as study groups or your "lunch bunch." Students typically list between 8 and 10 groups, but sometimes as many as 20 or more and rarely fewer than 2. In corporate America, reliance on groups is even more prevalent and is expected to increase. Many American companies have discovered how helpful groups can be and have installed groups at *all* levels. For example, General Motors' successes with the Saturn subsidiary can be attributed in part to the involvement of groups at every point in the design, manufacture, and marketing of GM cars (Stroud, 1988). No matter what your occupational level, you are likely to find yourself in at least one work group.

The third reason is related to the second. Because group work is expected to increase in the future, particularly in business and industry, knowing how groups function and having the ability to operate effectively in them will be highly valued skills. If you expect to advance in the America of the future, you will have to know how to work in a group. In a national survey of 750 leading American companies, 71.4 percent of the respondents mentioned "ability to work in teams" as an essential skill for MBA graduates—more important by far than knowledge of quantitative and statistical techniques (DuBois, 1992). William Ouchi (1981) said that how well Americans counter competition will depend on how well we manage our work groups. So, if you plan to advance in your career, or if you just want to get anything done, you must learn how to participate as a member of a team.

Fourth, being an effective group or team member cannot be left to chance. Just because you are placed on a team doesn't mean you know how to work effectively in that team. As helpful as groups can be to any organization, they often fail because group leaders have not thought through exactly what they want the groups to accomplish or because group members have not been trained in how to behave appropriately as part of a team (Drucker, 1992). Effective group participation cannot be taken for granted. Group members need training to understand the dynamics of small-group interaction, which is much more complex than dyadic (two-person) interaction.

Finally, groups can be an important way for Americans to participate in the democratic process; thus they have the potential to help us achieve our ideals as a society. Because we can accomplish so much more in groups than we can as individuals, group participation can be an important vehicle through which we create and govern our society. A lone voice "crying in the wilderness" may have little effect, but a group of people working hard for a cause they believe in can make great changes. For example, in Springfield, Missouri, a recent controversy developed over where to locate a materials recovery facility (MRF) to handle the disposal of solid wastes. A task force assembled by the city council recommended construction of the MRF in a relatively undeveloped area. Residents near the proposed site objected, formed a neighborhood coalition to organize opposition to the MRF, distributed petitions, lobbied legislators, and conducted a public relations campaign to stop the MRF. Partly as a result of the coalition's efforts, the MRF proposal has been put on hold indefinitely. Every one of these entities—the city council, the task force, and the neighborhood coalition opposing the MRF—was composed of citizens exercising their right to participate in the democratic process. Every one was a small group trying to control its environment. This human need to contribute to something larger than ourselves cannot be underestimated:

> The basic ingredient cementing social cohesion is not the satisfaction of basic needs, but rather the availability for contribution. What best binds individuals to groups may not be so much the pressure to obtain necessities as the opportunities to give of oneself to something beyond merely self-interested acquisition. (Larkin, 1986)

People who give money, energy, and other resources live healthier, happier, more fulfilled lives and describe their lives as more meaningful than those who do not (Lawson, 1991). Groups facilitate giving because they enable people to participate directly in something greater than self. What better way to do this than through a group?

TRY◄►THIS

For the next week, keep a list of every group in which you interact, describe the type of group, and explain what needs are met by each group.

What Is Small-Group Communication?

Small-group communication *is the interaction of a small group of people to achieve an interdependent goal* (Brilhart & Galanes, 1998). The various elements of this definition imply several things.

First, *small* implies that each member of the group is aware of the other members of the group and reacts to each as an individual. Thus, *small* refers to members' mutual awareness of each other as individuals, not to absolute size. To illustrate the idea of mutual awareness, a class of 25 students may seem large on the first day of school but may come to seem like a small group by the end of the term. Typically, small groups contain at least 3 people, but they may have as many as 15 (rarely more) members.

We arbitrarily eliminate the dyad (two people) from this definition because small groups are fundamentally different from dyads. For example, if one member leaves a dyad, the dyad falls apart. However, members often leave small groups, sometimes to be replaced by new members, and the group itself continues. Clearly, small groups are different from dyads.

Members of a small group *interact* in such a way that each can influence and be influenced by the others. This interaction occurs through communication, which is usually face-to-face, but other channels of communication, such as over a computer network, qualify. The substance that creates a group and the glue that holds it together are the verbal and nonverbal communication that occurs among members. Even group members who communicate by electronic mail often convey nonverbal signals by using punctuation, such as exclamations for emphasis. In a small group, members continually send and receive messages. This constant sending and receiving is relatively spontaneous rather than prepared, as for a speech. The work of the group is accomplished through this communicative activity.

Finally, *interdependence* implies that one member cannot achieve the group's goal without the other members' achieving it also. For example, for one basketball player on a team to win a game while the other members lose is impossible. They *all* win or lose together. The success of one member is dependent on the success of all the members. This principle suggests that cooperation among members must exist. Even though members may disagree, at times vehemently, they must seek a joint outcome that will be satisfactory to all.

small-group communication

The interaction of a group of people, small enough to be perceptually aware of each other, to achieve an interdependent goal.

The Role of Communication in the Small Group

The definition of small-group communication just presented establishes *communication* as the essential process within a small group. Communication creates a group, shapes each group in unique ways, and maintains a group. In a way, a group is never fully created but is always in the process of being

structuration

The communicative process of forming and maintaining a small group through verbal and nonverbal communication that establishes the group's norms and rules.

created. This concept is known as **structuration,** *the process of forming and maintaining a small group through verbal and nonverbal communication that establishes the norms and rules governing members' behaviors.* The theory of structuration, developed by Poole, Siebold, and McPhee (1985, 1986), is quite complex. However, the main point is this: The *communication among members* is what creates group rules and operating procedures in the first place, and once they are established, communication tends to keep the rules and procedures in place (Poole, 1992).

As with other forms of human communication, small-group communication involves sending verbal and nonverbal signals that are perceived, interpreted, and responded to by other people. Group members pay attention to each other and coordinate their behavior in order to accomplish the group's assignment. Perfect understanding between the person sending the signal and those receiving it is never possible; in a group, members strive to have enough understanding to enable the group's purpose to be achieved.

Small-group communication differs from dyadic communication and from public communication in several important ways:

1. *Complexity.* Communication among small-group members is more complex than dyadic communication. For one person to tune in to the communicative signals of just one other person is difficult, and this process is complicated tremendously by the addition of even one person. Add several others, as in the typical five- to eight-person small group, and this process can lead to information overload. For example, in a dyad 1 interpersonal relationship is possible, but in a three-person group 9 unique relationships are possible and in a five-person group 25 such relationships exist.

2. *Purpose for communicating.* Humans communicate for many reasons, including to express one's self, to persuade, and to inform. In dyadic encounters, much communication occurs for the purpose of self-expression. Persuading and informing are important purposes for public communication. Although all these purposes are motives for communication in groups, another important purpose of communicating in groups is to accomplish tasks. Members must coordinate their efforts through communication to reach goals. Reaching goals, a purpose for dyadic communication or for public speaking, is often a defining purpose for small-group communication.

3. *Formality.* Small-group communication is more spontaneous and casual than public speaking, which is more formal and planned. In this regard, small-group communication is similar to dyadic communication. A public speaker has likely prepared a speech in advance by deciding what topics to address in what order, what evidence to present, what arguments to make, and how best to make them. Some shifting to accommodate the unique needs of the audience may occur, but a speech is generally a planned event. In small-group com-

munication, however, most remarks are spontaneous. Although group members may decide in advance what topics they want to bring up or may mentally rehearse what they want to say about them, usually they do not plan the exact wording. In addition, to predict exactly how others in the group will respond is impossible. Thus, in contrast to public speaking, to foresee the outcome of a small-group discussion is less predictable.

4. *Interchange of speaker and listener roles.* During public communication, the roles of the speaker and the audience members are relatively fixed: The speaker speaks and the audience listens. Even if the audience interrupts or asks questions after the speech, the speaker generally controls the flow of the discussion. In small-group communication, the roles of primary sender and primary receiver alternate frequently. For example, Mohammed makes a suggestion to his fellow group members. His remarks are short, in comparison with most speeches. After he finishes (or maybe even before), Sativa responds verbally and Mohammed becomes the receiver. The roles of sender and receiver shift quickly among members.

5. *Immediacy of feedback.* The example described in item 4 implies that in small groups feedback is immediate, whereas in public-speaking situations feedback is often delayed. A public speaker receives non-verbal feedback from an audience and may sense approval or disagreement, but usually does not know specific reactions and the reasons behind them. Unless audience members choose to communicate with a speaker immediately after a speech, or to write a letter in which they share their reactions, a public speaker may never know exactly what others think. In groups, a speaker often knows what the others think. To return to the previous example, Mohammed gives his suggestion and Sativa, frowning, says, "I don't think that's going to work at all." Tomas, with a puzzled expression, asks Mohammed to clarify a couple of points, which Mohammed does. Mary Beth leans forward to gain the group's attention and says, "I think Mohammed's idea will work well with two minor changes," and proceeds to modify Mohammed's suggestion to accommodate Sativa's disagreement. Each of these members has given immediate verbal and nonverbal feedback to the others.

6. *Creation of outcomes.* Because of the reasons discussed so far, in a public-speaking situation, the speaker is largely responsible for creating the speech and determining its outcome. In a small group, as the previous example illustrates, the group members themselves are mutually, equally responsible for creating the group's outcomes. The final outcome is a result of what Mohammed, Sativa, Tomas, and Mary Beth said and did during their group discussion. Thus, as with dyadic communication, all participants have an equal share in and an equal responsibility for what happens.

Instant Recall

Fill in the blanks:

1. Small-group communication is the _____ of a small group of people to achieve an _____ goal.

2. The process of forming and maintaining a small group through verbal and nonverbal behavior is known as _____.

3. Membership in groups meets _____ we cannot meet for ourselves.

4. Small-group communication involves sending _____ and _____ signals.

Answers: 1. interaction/interdependent   2. structuration   3. needs   4. verbal/nonverbal

How Should You Communicate in Groups?

If you, as a group member, are responsible, with the other members, for the outcomes of the groups to which you belong, what can you do to help achieve productive outcomes? The ability to speak fluently and with polish is not essential, but the ability to speak clearly is. You will help fellow group members understand you better by organizing your comments during small-group discussions.

1. *Relate your statements to preceding remarks.* Public speakers do not always have the opportunity to respond to remarks by others, but small-group members do. Your statement should not appear to come out of the blue. Clarify that your remark is relevant to the topic under discussion by linking your remark to the immediately preceding remark.

2. *Use conventional word arrangement.* When you speak, you should use conventional sentences so that people can understand you better. You have more latitude in written English, in which punctuation helps readers follow the thought and readers have time to think about what you have written.

3. *Speak concisely.* Don't be long-winded. During a speech, the audience expects the speaker to monopolize the floor, but during a small-group discussion, every member wants and deserves a turn.

4. *State one point at a time.* Sometimes this rule is violated appropriately, such as when one group member presents a report to the rest of the group. However, during give-and-take discussion, stating one idea at a time makes it easier for the group to discuss a topic effectively and for other members to respond directly to each topic.

The Types of Small Groups

Two major classifications of groups exist, depending on the reason the group was formed and the major human needs that it meets, as is shown in Figure 9.1. **Primary groups,** such as the family, are usually long-term and *exist to meet our needs for inclusion and affection (love, esteem).* Other examples of primary groups include your roommates, friends you socialize with regularly, and coworkers who regularly share coffee breaks. Even though primary groups exist mainly to provide love, affection, attention, and support for their members, such groups also have to solve problems and make decisions, although that is not their main goal. The tasks they perform are less important than their primary purpose of providing inclusion and affection. Primary groups are the main sources of our identity. Conversation in primary groups is usually informal and can appear very disorganized. Conversation is often an end in itself rather than the means to an end.

Secondary groups *are formed for the purpose of completing tasks, such as solving problems or making decisions.* Although secondary groups sometimes meet members' needs for inclusion or affection, their main purpose is to enable members to exercise power and control over their environment and others. In secondary groups, communication is the means to a task-related end. These groups enable people to accomplish more as part of a group than they could as individuals. They are the backbone of American business, educational, and governmental accomplishment. The various groups involved in the MRF controversy described earlier are examples of secondary groups. Learning how to interact in secondary groups is essential; so many decisions reached in secondary groups affect our lives. Unfortunately, all of us have had to suffer the consequences of poor decisions reached in such groups.

You are likely to find yourself involved in many different kinds of secondary groups. For example, most organizations get work done through **committees,** which are *small groups that have been given an assignment by*

primary groups

Groups whose main purpose is to meet our needs for inclusion and affection (e.g., a family).

secondary groups

Groups whose main purpose is completing a task (e.g., a committee).

committees

Task-oriented small groups that have been given an assignment by a person or an organization.

	Primary Groups	Secondary Groups
Major Needs Met	Inclusion, belonging, affection, love	Control, power, mastery, achievement

Figure 9.1 The two major types of groups and the principal needs they meet.

Japanese industry made extensive use of quality circles to improve the quality of Japanese goods.

either an individual or an organization. Assignments given to committees can range from gathering information and reporting it to carrying out a plan. Typical committees have 6 to 10 members, but sometimes committees can be quite large, up to 25 people or more. Many organizations are actually composed of layers of committees. This interlocking committee structure is typical of modern organizations, as shown in Figure 9.2.

In many business organizations, secondary groups such as quality control circles and self-managed work teams have very important functions. A **quality control circle,** sometimes shortened to *quality circle, is a small group of employees that meets regularly on company time to recommend improvements to products and work procedures.* Quality circles were developed after World War II through American and Japanese collaboration (Ruch, 1984). They took hold readily in Japan, which has a small-group-oriented culture. Japanese industry made extensive use of quality circles to improve the quality of Japanese goods. As a result, a Japanese label represents high quality. Quality circles were slower to be adopted in the United States, where managers feared that they would reduce management's power and labor union members feared that they were a ploy to increase production without compensating workers (Lawler & Mohrman, 1985). However, in recent years many U.S. companies have used quality circles to improve worker safety, create new products, save production costs, improve current products, and improve the quality of the work environment.

Self-managed work teams, also called *autonomous work groups,* are *groups of workers who are given the freedom to manage their own work.* For example, an automobile assembly team may be responsible for assembling a car from start to finish, as is done at Volvo and Saturn plants. Workers are free to select their own team leaders and sometimes to hire and fire their own

quality control circle

A small group of employees that meets on company time to recommend improvements in products and work procedures.

self-managed work teams

Groups of workers who have freedom to manage their own work, including deciding which member will perform which job in what order.

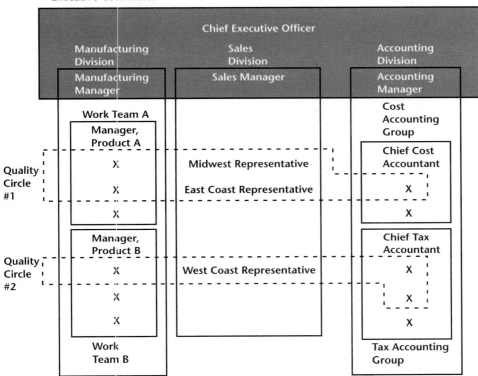

Executive Committee

Figure 9.2 A sample organization as an interlocking structure of small groups.

SOURCE: From Gloria J. Galanes and John K. Brilhart, *Communicating in Groups*, 3rd ed. Copyright © 1993 Times Mirror Higher Education Group, Inc. Reprinted by permission of The McGraw–Hill Companies.

members. They determine who will do what job and in what order. Members of self-managed work teams are often cross-trained so that each member can perform several tasks competently. This arrangement gives the team tremendous flexibility to use workers' skills most efficiently. Members of both self-managed work teams and quality control circles are usually more committed to their jobs than are other employees. They believe they are able to use more of their abilities and skills on the job and believe their work is more personally rewarding.

As you probably can tell, primary or secondary groups are not pure. Members of primary groups, such as families, engage in work, make decisions, and must cooperate to complete tasks. Members of secondary groups forge strong personal bonds and provide each other with affection and recognition. In fact, some of the best secondary groups are those with strong primary characteristics, where members feel appreciated and valued. Thus, both primary and secondary groups meet many needs in addition to the ones for which they were initially formed.

9.2 IDENTIFY THE TYPE OF GROUP

Write the correct letter from the choices below in each blank on the left:

A. **Primary group**   C. **Quality control circles**
B. **Secondary group**   D. **Self-managed work team**

_____ 1. Group with the specific purpose of recommending both product and procedural improvements.

_____ 2. Group that best meets our need for belonging and love.

_____ 3. Group that runs its own show by making decisions and being responsible for carrying them out.

_____ 4. Group that best meets our need for power, control, and achievement.

Answers: 1. C   2. A   3. D   4. B

Gender, Ethnicity, and Culture in Small Groups

gender

Characteristics of femininity and masculinity that are learned.

sex

Biological characteristics with which people are born.

Gender, *the learned characteristics associated with masculinity and femininity,* and ethnicity are considered co-cultures. Behaviors appropriate to each gender and ethnic group are learned. With little conscious effort we learn to become a female or male, an African American or a European American, in the same way we learn to become a salesclerk or a Protestant (Rubin, 1988). Research findings describing some effects of gender and ethnicity are described below (Pearson, West, & Turner, 1995). This information merely scratches the surface and is presented mainly to heighten your awareness of how much of our behavior is culturally transmitted.

In contrast to gender, **sex** refers to *the biological characteristics with which we are born.* Each culture or co-culture establishes "rules" for what is appropriate behavior for males and females. However, these gender rules have changed so much and so fast that past findings may not apply today, and they may not apply to you in particular.

Research about interpersonal communication suggests that males and females have different goals and rules for communicating. Lea Stewart and her colleagues suggested that male behavior signifies power and status whereas female behavior conveys subordination (Stewart, Stewart, Friedley, & Cooper, 1990). Women display more signs of immediacy (liking) and men more signs of potency (power). Women ask questions to keep a conversation going, but men ask questions for information. Maltz and Borker (1982) noted that men and women seem to have different rules about what constitutes friendly conversation, how to conduct such conversation, and what certain behaviors mean. For women, back-channel responses (i.e., saying things such as "Mm-hmm" and "I hear you" while another is talking) seem to mean "I'm paying attention to you; keep talking," but for men they seem to mean "I agree with you" or "I follow you so far." A male speaker receiving "Mm-hmms" from a woman is likely to believe she agrees with him, but a woman speaker receiving only occasional "Mm-hmms" from a man is likely to believe he is not listening.

In an early summary of research of male-female behavior in small groups, John E. Baird (1986) reported that women pay more attention to the relationships among group members whereas men are more instrumental, or task-focused. More recent research suggests differences, also. For example, Lynn Smith-Lovin and Charles Brody (1989) found that women interrupt men and women equally but that men interrupt women more often than they interrupt other men. In all-male groups, men interrupt to support each other; but the more women in the group, the less likely this is to occur. Men seem to consider sex to be related to status, whereas women do not.

Anthony Verdi and Susan Wheelan (1992) suggested that male-female differences are exaggerated. They found that all-male and all-female groups behave similarly to each other but mixed-sex groups behave differently. Although early findings showed that men talk more than women, Edward Mabry (1989) more recently found that women dominate group interaction and that men show subtle forms of resistance to a dominant presence of women. Georgia Duerst-Lahti (1990) found that women talk more often than men but for shorter periods.

Even though men and women behave similarly, their behavior is perceived differently. For instance, when women speak more tentatively in mixed-sex dyads, they are less influential with other women but more influential with men (Carli, 1990). In a study of trained and untrained mediators, the trained males and females behaved the same, but the untrained females were more controlling than the untrained males. However, the men, trained or not, were *perceived* as more controlling (Burrell, Donohue, & Allen, 1988).

Ethnicity is another important co-culture that affects communication rules and contributes to the development of group culture. Many people have had serious misunderstandings about what a particular communication behavior, performed by someone from another ethnic group, means. This section focuses on some of the communication differences between African Americans and European Americans because misunderstandings between these two cultural groupings have been particularly volatile.

African Americans and European Americans express themselves differently both verbally and nonverbally. Anita Foeman and Gary Pressley (1987) noted that African-American culture in the United States is an oral culture, with verbal inventiveness and playfulness highly valued. African Americans use the back channel to indicate interest and involvement in a discussion. Congregation members in African-American churches freely call "Amen," "Go ahead," or "That's right" to the minister as they would in a dialogue. Such responses are less frequent in most European-American churches. During a conflict, an African-American manager is more likely to confront the other individual directly, whereas a European-American manager is more likely to approach the problem indirectly. Consequently, some African Americans perceive European Americans as underreactive, and some European Americans see African Americans as overreactive. Degree of expressiveness differs, also. African Americans are both verbally and physically expressive (e.g., gesturing often), whereas most European Americans focus on verbal responses.

The African-American culture is more collective than the European-American culture. According to Foeman and Pressley (1987), African Americans strongly identify with other African Americans *as a group.* This communal structure helps offset the discrimination many African Americans still receive.

Finally, as we are increasingly part of a global community, to understand how our culture affects our behavior within small groups is important. Figure 9.3 provides a summary of the small-group behaviors valued in different cultures (Galanes, 1997). Keep in mind that we carry our cultural learning with us and that our individual cultural rules affect the joint culture we create in small groups.

The Development of Group Norms

norms

Informal rules for interaction.

The first time members meet as a group, they begin to establish the **norms,** or *informal rules for interaction,* that will eventually guide the members' behaviors. George Homans (1950) called a norm "an idea in the minds of the members of a group, an idea that can be put in the form of a statement speci-

- Conformity in small-group communication is more common in collectivist cultures (which value the group over the individual), such as Venezuela, Pakistan, Peru, and Taiwan.
- Competition and dissent are more common in individualistic cultures (which value freedom, choice, and independence), such as the United States, Australia, Great Britain, and Canada.
- A rigid hierarchy with a controlling group leader is preferred in uncertainty-rejecting cultures, such as India, Mexico, and the Philippines.
- Equality among group members, and use of first names, is preferred in uncertainty-accepting cultures, such as Israel, Australia, and New Zealand.
- Clear rules are expected in uncertainty-rejection cultures such as Japan and Greece.
- Flexible rules, high tolerance for ambiguity, and risk taking characterize uncertainty-acceptance cultures like Great Britain.
- Ambiguity and saving face is important in collectivist cultures like China, Korea, and Japan.

Descriptions of the various cultures are covered in greater detail in Chapter 8.

Figure 9.3 Cultural differences in small-group communication.

fying what the members . . . ought to do, are expected to do, under given circumstances." At first, the full range of human behavior is available to members. For example, they may greet each other formally ("Ms.," "Dr.," "Professor," and so forth) or they may speak informally and use first names. The initial pattern of behavior tends to set the tone for subsequent meetings and to establish the general norms that members will follow. Communication among members establishes the norms.

Most norms are not established directly. For example, if Sue comes late to a meeting and no one seems bothered, other members may get the message that coming on time to meetings is not necessary. By not saying anything to Sue, the group, without actually thinking about it or formally "deciding" it, has begun to establish a norm that members need not be on time.

The norms of any group tend to mirror the norms of the general culture or co-culture in which the group exists. For example, compare a small group of your college friends with a small group of your grandparents' friends. You and your friends use different language, dress differently, and act differently from the way your grandparents interact with their friends. Differences in age, class, status, and physical condition between these two co-cultures produce slightly different norms in groups formed from these co-cultures. As Susan Shimanoff (1992) stated,

> When group members come together for the first time, they bring with them past experiences and expectations regarding cultural and social rules and rules for specific groups they assume may be similar to this new group. It is out of these experiences and expectations as well as its unique interaction . . . that a particular group formulates its rules.

Norms often develop rapidly, without members consciously realizing what is occurring. They can be inferred by observing what members say and do. For example, behaviors that are repeated regularly (e.g., members always sit in the same seats) provide evidence of a norm. In addition, behaviors that are punished (e.g., one group member chastises another by saying, "It's about time you got here") indicate that a norm has been violated.

Members should pay attention to group norms to ensure that they are appropriate for what the group must accomplish. For example, sometimes an "overpoliteness" norm becomes established at a group's first meeting because members suppress disagreements or speak tentatively and ambiguously in an effort to be considerate. Later in a group's life, however, this behavior may be inappropriate because members need to challenge each other's thinking and express their opinions clearly. If the overpoliteness norm is entrenched, the group may never get around to doing its necessary critical thinking. Members should monitor norms to ensure that they are helpful, not harmful, to the group.

The Development of Role Structure

role

A position in a group that is part of an interlocking structure of other parts.

A **role** is *a position in a group that is part of an interlocking structure of other parts.* For example, plays and movies contain interlocking roles, each of which is a different character in the cast. Each character's role must fit within the play or movie structure. The same is true for groups. However, whereas in a movie the actor learns lines that are highly scripted, in a small group the "actor" (the group member) creates the role spontaneously, in concert with the other members. Just as an actor plays different roles in different scripts, individuals enact many diverse roles in the numerous groups to which they belong. For example, your role might be daughter or son in your main primary group; in a group of your best friends, you may be the good listener or the comedian; in yet another group, you may be the club treasurer or committee chair. You may be a leader in one group and play a supporting role in another. Whatever someone's role in a group, that role results from an interplay involving that member's personality, abilities, and communication skills, the talents of the other members, and the needs of the group as a whole.

The Types of Group Roles

formal role

An assigned role based on a member's position or title within a group.

Two major types of group roles are formal and informal. A **formal role,** sometimes called a *positional role,* is *an assigned role based on an individual's position or title within a group.* For example, Indira may be her service club's treasurer. As treasurer, she is expected to perform certain duties, such as paying the club's bills, balancing the checkbook, and making regular reports to the club about its financial status. These duties may even be specified in a job description for the position of treasurer. We also expect the person in a particular position to behave in certain ways. For example, what do you think Indira's fellow group members expect of her in addition to her assigned duties? Very likely they expect her to be well organized and to present her report clearly and concisely without wandering into topics irrelevant to the treasury.

An **informal role,** sometimes called a *behavioral role, is a role that is developed spontaneously within a group.* Informal roles strongly reflect members' personality characteristics, habits, and typical ways of interacting within a group. For example, Rich jokes around during fraternity meetings. He refuses to take anything seriously, cracks jokes that interrupt others, and calls members who work hard for the fraternity "overachievers." Rich's constant failure to take the group's job seriously has earned him the informal role of playboy in his group. In contrast, Jeff, one of the "overachievers," constantly reminds members about upcoming deadlines. His fraternity brothers have started calling him the group's timekeeper.

informal role

A role that is developed spontaneously within a group.

Role Emergence

Informal roles emerge by trial and error through the group's interaction. They are determined largely by the relative performance skills of the rest of the members. For example, well-organized Tamara, who likes structure and order, knows exactly how the group can accomplish its tasks and may try to structure the group's work: "I suggest we first make a list of all the things we need to do to finish our project." If no one else competes for the organizer role, and if the others think Tamara's structuring behavior is helpful to the group, the group members will reinforce and reward her statements and actions: "OK, Tamara, that sounds like a good idea." This reinforcement, in turn, encourages Tamara to perform more of those structuring behaviors.

On the other hand, members may perceive Tamara's attempts to structure the group as pushiness or bossiness and may discourage her: "What's the rush, Tamara? We have lots of time," or "Who died and made you queen, Tamara?" They may collectively support another member as the group's organizer. If Tamara is not supported as the group's organizer, she will search for another way to be valuable to, and valued by, the group. For instance, she may help clarify the proposals of the other members ("In other words, are you saying that . . . ?"). She might become the group's critical evaluator ("I think there are two major flaws with that proposal").

This example illustrates a major principle of small-group communication: *The role of each group member is worked out by the interaction between the member and the rest of the group and continues to evolve as the group evolves.* Every member needs to have a role that makes a meaningful contribution to the group. If one role doesn't work, the member will usually try to find another way to participate.

The Categories of Behavioral Functions

From these examples, you should be able to see that role comprises a set of behaviors that perform a function for the group. For formal roles, the set of behaviors is often specified in writing. For informal roles, the member performs the set of behaviors so regularly that others begin to expect it. Jeff's

Task Functions and Statements

Initiating and orienting: "Let's make a list of what we still need to do."
Information giving: "Last year, the committee spent $150 on publicity."
Information seeking: "John, how many campus muggings were reported last year?"
Opinion giving: "I don't think the cost of parking stickers is the worst parking problem students have."
Clarifying: "Martina, are you saying that you couldn't support a proposal that increased student fees?"
Evaluating: "Another thing that Toby's proposal would let us do is . . ."
Evaluating: "One problem I see with Cindy's idea is . . ."
Summarizing: "So we've decided that we'll add two sections to the report, and Terrell and Candy will write them."
Coordinating: "If Carol interviews the mayor by Monday, then Jim and I can prepare a response by Tuesday's meeting."
Consensus testing: "We seem to be agreed that we prefer the second option."
Recording: "I think we decided at our last meeting. Let me check the minutes."

Maintenance (Relationship-Oriented) Functions and Statements

Establishing norms: "It doesn't help to call each other names. Let's stick to the issues."
Gatekeeping: "Pat, you look like you want to say something about the proposal."
Supporting: "I think Tara's point is well made, and we should look at it more closely."
Harmonizing: "Jared and Sally, I think there are areas where you are in agreement, and I would like to suggest a compromise that might work for you both."
Tension relieving: "We're getting tired and cranky. Let's take a 10-minute break."
Dramatizing: "That reminds me of a story about what happened last year when . . ."
Showing solidarity: "We've really done good work here!" or "We're all in this together."

Self-Centered Functions and Statements

Withdrawing: "Do whatever you want; I don't care," or not speaking at all.
Blocking: "I don't care if we've already voted; I want to discuss it again!"
Status and recognition seeking: "I have a lot more expertise than the rest of you, and I think we should do it the way I know works."

Figure 9.4 Examples of task, maintenance, and self-centered statements.

fraternity relies heavily on his timekeeping duties and would be lost (at least temporarily) if he didn't perform them.

When you observe the roles people perform in groups, ask yourself what function is performed by those behaviors. The function, not the behavior itself, determines someone's role. For instance, Rich's joking would have a positive function if he joked occasionally to relieve tension during an argument. However, his constant and inappropriate joking performs the negative function of pulling the group off task. A member's behavior must be interpreted in the context of what else is happening in the group.

A number of classification schemes describe typical group functions that members' behaviors serve. One common scheme classifies behaviors by

9.3 BEHAVIORAL FUNCTION IN SMALL GROUPS

For each statement, identify which function is operative by writing the appropriate letter from the choices below in the blank on the left:

A. Self-centered function   **C. Task function**
B. Maintenance function

_____1. "Mario, I think that's a great idea. I don't know why we didn't think of that earlier."

_____2. "Whatever you want to do. It doesn't matter to me."

_____3. "Let's find out how much more it will cost the food service to open earlier in the morning and stay open later at night."

_____4. "Michael, I think you owe Tamara an apology for that comment. We really need to work together here if we're going to get this done."

Answers: 1. B   2. A   3. C   4. B

---

task functions

Behaviors in a group that are directly relevant to helping the group complete its assignment.

maintenance functions

Behaviors in a group that focus on the interpersonal relationships among members.

self-centered functions

Behaviors that serve the individual's needs at the expense of the group.

whether they perform task, maintenance, or self-centered functions. **Task functions** are *behaviors that are directly relevant to the group's task and that affect the group's output.* Their purpose is to focus group members productively on their assignment. **Maintenance functions** are *behaviors that focus on the interpersonal relationships among members;* they are aimed at supporting cooperative and harmonious relationships. Both task and maintenance functions are considered essential to effective group communication. On the other hand, **self-centered functions** are *behaviors that serve the needs of the individual at the expense of the group.* The person performing a self-centered behavior implies, "I don't care what the group needs or wants. *I* want . . ." Self-centered functions manipulate other members for selfish goals that compete with group goals. Examples of statements that support task, maintenance, and self-centered functions are shown in Figure 9.4. The list is not exhaustive; many more functions could be added.

These behavioral functions combine to create a member's informal role, which is a comprehensive, general picture of how a particular member typically acts in a group. An example of how individual functions combine to create a role is shown in Figure 9.5.

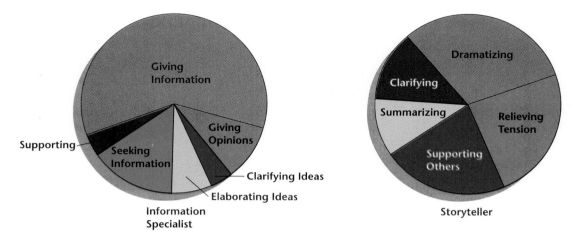

Figure 9.5 Behavioral functions combine to create roles.

SOURCE: Gloria J. Galanes and John K. Brilhart, *Communicating in Groups,* 2nd ed. Copyright © 1993 Times Mirror Higher Education Group, Inc. All Rights Reserved. Reprinted by permission.

The Networks of Communication

communication network

The pattern of message flow, or who talks to whom.

As the role structure develops in a group, so does the group's **communication network,** *the pattern of message flow (who actually speaks to whom in discussions).* The frequency and direction of communication both create and maintain the group's network. If Toshio calls the group's first meeting to order, the others may expect him to call all their meetings to order. If Andrea speaks frequently, she may find others looking (literally) to her for comment on each new issue. Quiet members may find themselves increasingly ignored. The type of network created in a group has an important bearing on group member productivity, cohesiveness, and satisfaction.

The most common types of networks are shown in Figure 9.6. Ideally, a small group of peers has an *all-channel network,* in which all participants are free to comment on a one-to-one basis with all others and with the group as a whole. Members do not need clearance from a central gatekeeping authority to speak; they can contribute while ideas are fresh in their minds without having to wait for someone's OK.

In both the *chain* and the *Y* networks, each member speaks only to one or two other members. Such networks are typical of hierarchical organizations with strict chains of command. For instance, the president may speak only to the vice-presidents, who speak to the division chiefs, who speak to the department managers, but department managers almost never speak directly to the president. Everyone must follow formal channels.

In a *wheel* network, all comments are directed toward one central person (usually the designated leader), who alone has authority to speak to the other members. Sometimes designated leaders inadvertently create wheel networks when they get into the habit of commenting after each person's remarks or

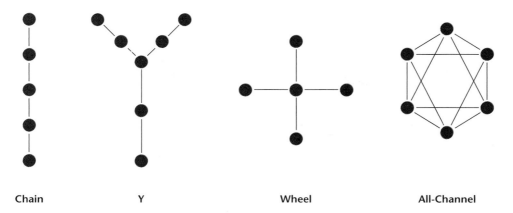

Chain   Y   Wheel   All-Channel

Figure 9.6 Communication networks.

restating what the other members say. The person in the center of the wheel can become overloaded with information, which may result in a severe bottleneck for the group. For certain types of tasks, the wheel can be faster than other networks. In the wheel and Y networks, the central members may be satisfied with the communication, but the other members usually are not.

Which is the best network? That decision seems to depend on the type of task and the time available to the group. Centralized networks such as the wheel, chain, and Y are often quicker and more accurate, especially for fairly simple problems, although members are usually less satisfied. The decentralized all-channel network seems to take more time but may, in fact, be quicker and more accurate for complex problems. The all-channel network generally produces higher member satisfaction as well (Shaw, 1964).

Group Fantasy

One of the most powerful ways by which a group establishes its individuality is through fantasy. Technically, **fantasy** refers to *the creative and imaginative shared interpretation of events that fulfills a group's needs to make sense of their experience and to anticipate their future* (Bormann, 1986). Fantasy, in this sense, does not mean fictitious or unreal. Instead, during certain periods of the group's interaction, rather than sticking to the group's immediate business, the members tell stories, relate past events, and share anecdotes. These fantasies play an important part in creating the group's unique identity. Although the talk of group members during fantasy may seem outside the group's real task, the stories may actually meet important psychological needs of the members.

A fantasy is introduced whenever a group member says something not directly related to the present task of the group. Often, fantasies stop there, but sometimes other *members pick up the story line and elaborate on it in a kind of group storytelling*. This is called a **fantasy chain**, first described by Robert

fantasy

The creative and imaginative shared interpretation of events that fulfills a group's need to make sense of their experience and to anticipate their future.

fantasy chain

A line of fantasies to which all (or most) group members contribute to create a kind of group storytelling.

Bales (1970). During a fantasy chain, members talk faster and louder and seem more excited than usual. Fantasy chains last from half a minute to half an hour, ending when one member gets the group back on task. This group storytelling can be creative and fun; more important, storytelling plays a central role in creating the group's culture (Peterson, 1987).

fantasy theme

The content, obvious or hidden, of a fantasy.

The content of a fantasy is called a **fantasy theme.** Fantasies have obvious, or manifest, themes and latent, or below-the-surface, themes that reveal the culture, values, and norms of the group. Often, fantasies have heroes and villains, plot lines, and a well-developed ethical structure that gives moral or psychological guidance to a group. To interpret the latent meaning of a fantasy, Bales (1970) suggested looking for a sudden insight rather than trying to analyze the fantasy systematically.

An example should clarify the concept of group fantasy. In the following short fantasy chain, the members of a group are working on their major project for the semester. Mary is taking notes for the group, when Louisa comments on her inch-long fingernails:

Discussion	Commentary
Louisa: Mary, I don't know how you can write anything with those nails! Don't they get in your way?	Louisa starts the fantasy chain; commenting about Mary's nails is clearly "off-task" behavior.
Mary: [Laughs] You like those? I had to figure out new ways to do things, but I like them!	
Grady: Gee, Mary those are dragon lady claws! I'll be staying out of your way!	Grady picks up the chain.
Manny: That's right, man; that's one lady I don't want to cross!	Manny adds his part.
Mary: [Still laughing] Oh, you don't have to worry; I'd only use them if you made me *really* mad! [She makes a catlike swiping motion at Manny and hisses like a cat.]	Mary's comment and behavior capture the playful nature of fantasy.
Louisa: That's right, Manny; you better not get on her evil side! You better do everything this lady asks you to do!	Louisa lightly touches on a possible meaning this fantasy may have for the group.
Grady: You've got fair warning, man. Say "Yes, Ma'am" when she gives you an assignment.	Grady's remark echoes Louisa's comment that Mary is a force to be listened to in the group.

In this segment, Louisa starts out by making an irrelevant comment about Mary's fingernails. After Mary's comment, Grady introduces the "danger" element, and Mary participates in expanding the image of herself as a danger-ous lady. When the guys talk about not crossing her, she assures them that they don't have to worry—unless they make her *really* angry. Louisa suggests what might make Mary angry (not doing what Mary wants), and Grady brings the group back to the task by mentioning the "assignment" for the project. What function has this fantasy served? The manifest theme of the fantasy is "Mary's long fingernails will be dangerous if she's angry." However, fantasy chains are relevant to the *present* group. In this sequence, the connec-tion between someone not doing an assignment and Mary being angry (and therefore "dangerous") is not a big stretch. The group seems to be establish-ing some standards for itself ("We will complete assignments") and some penalties for noncompletion ("Mary will be *really* mad!"). This fantasy says something about members' expectations and, very likely, about Mary's infor-mal role in the group. The fantasy helps build up the emerging culture of the group indirectly rather than directly and humorously rather than seriously.

Group Climate

Another important element that helps shape a group's culture is the **group climate,** which is *the emotional tone or atmosphere members create within the group.* For example, you have probably attended a group meeting where you could cut the tension with a knife. That atmosphere of tension describes the group's climate. Three factors that contribute heavily to group climate are trust, cohesiveness, and supportiveness.

group climate
The emotional tone or atmosphere that exists within a group.

Trust

Trust means that members believe they can rely on each other. If Joe says he'll have the membership report finished in time for the meeting, other members believe him. When Lorene disagrees with a suggestion, other mem-bers know she's trying to improve the group's output, not trying to backstab another member. When members trust each other, the group process can work in an ideal way. All members are free to attend to the group's task in-stead of trying to defend themselves.

Two types of trust are relevant to small-group communication. Having trust regarding the task means members can count on each other to get things done. A common source of conflict for many groups is having a member who doesn't contribute a fair share of the work, so the others have to pick up the slack. That makes members angry and the climate tense. Having interpersonal trust means that members believe the others are operating with the best interests of the group in mind and not from **hidden agendas,** *secret motives that individ-ual needs and wants ahead of the group.* When a trusted member disagrees with your suggestion, you usually feel free to explore the problem and are motivated to improve your idea. However, when a member you *don't* trust does the same thing, you may become defensive because you don't believe his or her motive is to help the group. This generally poisons good feelings, tearing the group apart. Not being able to trust other group members is one of the most serious prob-lems that even effective groups face (Larson & LaFasto, 1989).

hidden agendas
Secret motives that place individual needs and wants ahead of the group.

Cohesiveness

cohesiveness

The attachment members feel toward each other and the group.

Cohesiveness is *the attachment members feel toward each other and the group.* When a group is cohesive, members feel a strong sense of belonging to the group, they value their relationships with each other, and they consider the group attractive. Cohesive groups look and sound different from noncohesive groups. In cohesive groups, members sit close together and conform to the group's norms. They respond directly to each other and say positive things to and about each other.

Members of cohesive groups tend to communicate using one kind of "sensory metaphor" (Owen, 1985). For example, at first, various members indicate their understanding by saying "I see," "I hear you," or "I grasp that." Each of these metaphors for "I understand" refers to a different sense—sight, sound, touch. In cohesive groups, members tend to use the same sensory metaphor. For instance, if the *visual* metaphor is "chosen," members convey understanding with "I see," "I've got the picture," and "I've spotted a flaw." This happens subconsciously and indicates that members have influenced each other in subtle but significant ways.

Highly cohesive groups exhibit more open disagreement, probably because members trust each other enough to disagree openly on issues, facts, and ideas. Highly cohesive groups display more characteristics of primary groups (such as affection and inclusion) than do less cohesive groups (Barker, 1991). They have higher rates of interaction. Members are more satisfied with the group and its products. In addition, cohesive groups exert greater control over member behaviors (Nixon, 1979).

Cohesive groups cope more effectively with unusual problems, and their members work better as a team to meet emergencies. Usually, cohesive groups produce more than noncohesive groups, but if a group norm supports low production, they may produce less. One study found an optimum level of cohesiveness beyond which performance decreases (Kelly & Duran, 1985). Whether or not a cohesive group is productive also depends upon whether members accept their task. When the members support an organization's goals and are motivated and enthused about completing the task, they are productive (Greene, 1989). However, highly cohesive groups that are socially oriented rather than task-oriented may end up accomplishing nothing (Wood, 1989).

Although problems occur with highly cohesive groups that are socially oriented, cohesive groups are very satisfying to their members. In general, cohesiveness is desirable.

TRY ◄ ► THIS

Consider the most and least cohesive groups you have ever observed. List as many characteristics as you can recall of each one. In small groups or as a class, develop general principles that are associated with cohesiveness.

Supportiveness

A **supportive climate,** *an atmosphere of openness, is created when members care about each other and treat each other with respect* (Gibb, 1961). Members who are supportive foster trust and create cohesiveness. In a supportive climate, members feel safe to express themselves because they believe that others value their opinions. On the other hand, when members judge and attack each other, they create a **defensive climate,** *an atmosphere of tension in which members feel they must defend themselves from verbal or psychological attacks.* In this case, members spend so much energy defending themselves that little energy is available for productive and creative group work. Thus, a defensive climate robs the group of valuable ideas, energy, and enthusiasm.

Supportive and defensive climates are each created by what members say to each other and how they say it. Examples of defensive and supportive comments are presented in Figure 9.7.

supportive climate

An atmosphere of openness created by members' mutual respect and caring.

defensive climate

An atmosphere of tension in which members feel they have to defend themselves from verbal or psychological attacks.

Defensive Behaviors and Statements

Evaluation: Judging another person: "That's a completely ridiculous idea!"

Control: Dominating or insisting on your own way: "I've decided what we need to do."

Strategy: Manipulating: "Don't you think you should try it my way?"

Neutrality: Not caring about how others feel: "It doesn't matter to me what you decide."

Superiority: Pulling rank, maximizing status differences: "As group leader, I think we should . . ."

Certainty: Being a "know-it-all": "You guys are completely off base. I know exactly how to handle this."

Supportive Behaviors and Statements

Description: Describing your own feelings without making those of others wrong: "I prefer the first option because . . ."

Problem orientation: Searching for the best solution without predetermining what that should be: "We want to produce the best results and that may mean some extra time from all of us."

Spontaneity: Reacting honestly and openly: "Wow, that sounds like a great idea!"

Empathy: Showing you care about the other members: "Jan, originally you were skeptical. How comfortable will you be if the group favors that option?"

Equality: Minimizing status differences by treating members as equals: "I don't have all the answers. What do the rest of you think?"

Provisionalism: Expressing opinions tentatively and being open to others' suggestions: "Maybe we should try a different approach . . ."

Figure 9.7 Examples of defensive and supportive statements.

Being an Ethical Group Member

ethics

Rules or standards for right conduct or practice.

Ethics are *"rules or standards for right conduct or practice"* (*Random House Dictionary*, 1987). The unique nature of small groups requires attention to special ethical concerns regarding the treatment of speech, of people, and of information.

First, the field of communication strongly supports the value of free speech (Arnett, 1990), which is directly relevant to small-group communication. Many secondary groups are formed because several heads perform better than one, but that advantage will not be realized if group members are unwilling or afraid to speak freely in the group. An important ethical principle for small groups is that group members should be willing to share their unique perspectives. They should also refrain from saying or doing things that prevent others from speaking freely. Members who are trustworthy and supportive are behaving ethically.

Second, group members must be honest and truthful. In a small group, they should not intentionally deceive one another or manufacture information or evidence to persuade other members to adopt their point of view.

Third, group members must be thorough and unbiased when they evaluate information. Many decisions made in groups, from where to locate an MRF to whether it is safe to launch a space shuttle in cold weather, affect people's lives. Such decisions will be only as good as the information on which they are based and the reasoning the members use to assess the information. Group members must consider *all* relevant information in an open-minded, unbiased way by using the best critical thinking skills they can; otherwise, tragedies can result.

Finally, group members must behave with integrity. Members must be willing to place the good of the group ahead of their own goals. Some individuals cannot be team players because they are unable or unwilling to merge their personal agendas with those of the group. Groups are better off without such individuals. If you make a commitment to join a group, you should be the kind of team member who will benefit rather than harm the group. If you cannot in good conscience give a group your support, you should leave the group rather than to pretend to support the group while sabotaging it.

Summary

In this chapter, you learned how important small groups are and why you should understand the process of small-group communication. Groups are important because they help us meet needs we cannot meet alone. Groups are everywhere, and their importance is increasing. Groups can help us participate in the democratic process, but we must learn how to communicate effectively in them. Group communication is more complex and typically more task-oriented than dyadic communication. Compared to public speaking, group communication is less formal, the speaker and listener roles alternate frequently, feedback is immediate, and all members are jointly responsible for the group's outcomes. Primary groups meet our needs for affection, and secondary groups meet our needs for control.

Each group has a unique culture. Contributing to that culture are elements such as the norms and roles members develop, the networks created, the fantasies shared by members, and the group climate. Members' gender and ethnicity also affect the group's culture. However, gender and ethnic differences are learned behaviors and, thus, subject to change.

Norms and roles are created through interaction among members. Formal roles are associated with specific titles or positions, but informal roles emerge through interaction between a member and the rest of the group. Informal roles are based on members' behaviors and the functions they perform, including task, maintenance, and self-centered functions. Networks are created by members' patterns of interaction. Generally, all-channel networks are most productive and satisfying to members. Group culture also depends on the imaginative shared stories that members mutually create. Finally, culture is affected by group climate—the emotional atmosphere in a group—in particular, whether members trust each other, are cohesive, and support each other.

This chapter concluded with a discussion of the ethical behavior of group members. Valuable team members are willing to speak in the group and to refrain from doing things that prevent others from speaking freely, they are honest, they are unbiased and thorough when they evaluate information, and they always behave with integrity. Members who are unable to support the actions of a group should leave the group rather than fake support.

Issues in Communication

TEAMWORK AT PRI, INC.

This Issues in Communication narrative is designed to provoke individual thought or discussion about concepts raised in the chapter.

The senior manager of PRI, Inc., assigned five employees to prepare a presentation for a potential new client within 30 days. The presentation was to outline what PRI would do to launch a $250,000 grand opening of AutoMall, a giant discount car dealer that promised "no-haggle" sales of cars and trucks.

Samir, the assistant to the senior manager, was assigned to lead the group. During the 30 days that followed, Samir did very little to help the group: He attended only half of the scheduled meetings, and when he was there, he seemed preoccupied. Fortunately, Jayasankar and Sally assumed leadership responsibilities, assigned tasks, and kept the rest of the group on task and on schedule. Prior to the deadline, Jayasankar prepared all the financial estimates; Sally arranged for audio, video, and technical requirements; and Jason worked with Julie to create an impressive multiscreen video with surround sound to show the client what PRI could do to launch the new AutoMall. What about Samir? As the assigned leader of the group, Samir was responsible for the final presentation. Of course, Julie prepared the script for him.

On the day of the presentation Samir surprised everyone. Sounding polished and professional, he had obviously practiced his script. He made the work team, as well as PRI, look very good. The client was pleased, and 10 days later AutoMall signed a contract with PRI for the grand opening. Samir's supervisor, the senior vice-president of PRI, was so pleased that Samir received a bonus and the team received a plaque for their excellent work.

Apply what you have learned about the small-group process as you ponder and discuss the following questions: What type of group is this? What functions can be attributed to each of the group members? Although he seemed uninvolved in the process, did Samir help the group? What do you think the group climate was like for this group?

Additional Resources

Elmuti, D. (1996, March–April). Sustaining high performance through self-managed work teams. *Industrial Management, 38*(2), 4–9.

Frey, L. R. (1994, Spring). Introduction: Revitalizing the study of small group communication. *Communication Studies, 45*(1), 1–7.

Grob, L. M., Meyers, R. A., & Schuh, R. (1997, Summer). Powerful/powerless language use in group interactions: Sex differences or similarities? *Communication Quarterly, 45*(3), 282–304.

Roebuck, D. B. (1998, September). Using team learning in business and organizational communication classes. *Business Communication Quarterly, 61*(3), 35–50.

References

Arnett, R. C. (1990, Summer). The practical philosophy of communication ethics and free speech as the foundation for speech communication. *Communication Quarterly, 38,* 208–217.

Baird, J. E. (1986). Sex differences in group communication: A review of relevant research. *Quarterly Journal of Speech, 62,* 179–192.

Bales, R. F. (1970). *Personality and interpersonal behavior.* New York: Holt, Rinehart and Winston.

Barker, D. B. (1991, February). The behavioral analysis of interpersonal intimacy in group development. *Small Group Research, 22,* 76–91.

Bormann, E. G. (1986). Symbolic convergence theory and communication in group decision making. In R. Y. Hirokawa & M. S. Poole (Eds.), *Communication and group decision making* (p. 221 ff.). Newbury Park, CA: Sage.

Brilhart, J. K., & Galanes, G. J. (1998). *Effective group discussion* (9th ed.). Madison, WI: Brown & Benchmark.

Burrell, N. A., Donohue, W. A., & Allen, M. (1988). Gender-based perceptual biases in mediation. *Communication Research, 15,* 447–469.

Carli, L. L. (1990). Gender, language, and influence. *Journal of Personality and Social Psychology, 59,* 941–951.

Cole, D. (1989, May). Meetings that make sense. *Psychology Today, 23,* 14.

Drucker, P. (1992). *Managing for the future: The 1990s and beyond.* New York: Truman Talley Books/Dutton.

DuBois, C. C. (1992, September–October). Portrait of the ideal MBA. *The Penn Stater, 31.*

Duerst-Lahti, G. (1990, August). But women play the game too: Communication control and influence in administrative decision making. *Administration and Society, 22,* 182–205.

Foeman, A. K., & Pressley, G. (1987, Fall). Ethnic culture and corporate culture: Using black styles in organizations. *Communication Quarterly, 35,* 293–307.

Galanes, G. J. (1997). The dynamic of small group discussion. In J. C. Pearson & P. E. Nelson, *An introduction to human communication* (7th ed.). Dubuque, IA: Brown & Benchmark.

Gibb, J. R. (1961). Defensive communication. *Journal of Communication, 11,* 141–148.

Greene, C. N. (1989). Cohesion and productivity in work groups. *Small Group Behavior, 20,* 70–86.

Hill, B. (1997). *Internet directory for dummies: A reference for the rest of us.* Foster City, CA: IDG Books.

Homans, G. C. (1950). *The human group.* New York: Harcourt Brace Jovanovich.

Kelly, L., & Duran, R. L. (1985). Interaction and performance in small groups: A descriptive report. *International Journal of Small Group Research, 1,* 182–192.

Larkin, T. J. (1986). Humanistic principles for organizational management. *Central States Speech Journal, 37,* 37.

Larson, C. E., & LaFasto, F. M. J. (1989). *Teamwork: What must go right/what can go wrong.* Newbury Park, CA: Sage.

Lawler, E., & Mohrman, S. (1985, January–February). Quality circles after the fad. *Harvard Business Review,* 65–71.

Lawson, D. M. (1991). *Give to live: How giving can change your life.* LaJolla, CA: ALTI Publishing.

Mabry, E. A. (1989). Some theoretical implications of female and male interaction in unstructured small groups. *Small Group Behavior, 20,* 536–550.

Maltz, D. N., & Borker, R. A. (1982). A cultural approach to male-female miscommunication. In J. J. Gumperz (Ed.), *Language and social identity.* Cambridge: Cambridge University Press.

Nixon II, H. L. (1979). *The small group.*

Englewood Cliffs, NJ: Prentice-Hall.

Ouchi, W. (1981). *Theory Z: How American business can meet the Japanese challenge.* Reading, MA: Addison-Wesley.

Owen, W. F. (1985). Metaphor analysis of cohesiveness in small discussion groups. *Small Group Behavior, 16,* 415–426.

Pearson, J. C., West, R. L., & Turner, L. H. (1995). *Gender & communication* (3rd ed.). Madison, WI: Brown & Benchmark.

Peterson, E. E. (1987). The stories of pregnancy: On interpretation of small-group cultures. *Communication Quarterly, 35,* 39–47.

Poole, M. S. (1992). Group communication and the structuring process. In R. S. Cathcart & L. A. Samovar (Eds.), *Small group communication: A reader* (6th ed., pp. 147–157). Dubuque, IA: William C. Brown.

Poole, M. S., Siebold, D. R., & McPhee, R. D. (1985). Group decision-making as a structurational process. *Quarterly Journal of Speech, 71,* 74–102.

Poole, M. S., Siebold, D. R., & McPhee,

R. D. (1986). A structurational approach to theory-building in decision-making research. In R. Y. Hirokawa & M. S. Poole (Eds.), *Communication and group decision-making* (pp. 237–264). Beverly Hills, CA: Sage.

Random House dictionary of the English language (2nd ed., 1987). New York: Random House.

Rubin, B. D. (1988). *Communication and human behavior* (2nd ed.). New York: Macmillan.

Ruch, W. V. (1984). *Corporate communications: A comparison of Japanese and American practices.* Westport, CT: Quorum Books.

Schutz, W. C. (1958). *FIRO: A three-dimensional theory of interpersonal behavior.* New York: Rinehart.

Shaw, M. (1964). Communication networks. In L. Berkowitz (Ed.), *Advances in experimental social psychology* (Vol. 1, pp. 111–147). New York: Academic Press.

Shimanoff, S. B. (1992). Coordinating group interaction via communication rules. In R. S. Cathcart & L. A. Samovar (Eds.), *Small group communication: A reader* (6th ed., p. 225). Dubuque, IA: William C. Brown.

Smith-Lovin, L., & Brody, C. (1989, June). Interruptions in group discussions: The effects of gender and group composition. *American Sociological Review, 54*, 424–435.

Stewart, L. P., Stewart, A. D., Friedley, S. A., & Cooper, P. J. (1990). *Communication between the sexes: Sex differences and sex role stereotypes* (2nd ed.). Scottsdale, AZ: Gorsuch Scarisbrick.

Stroud, L. (1988, November 15). No CEO is an island. *American*, 94–97, 140–141.

Verdi, A. F., & Wheelan, S. A. (1992, August). Developmental patterns in same-sex and mixed-sex groups. *Small Group Research, 23*, 356–378.

Wood, C. J. (1989). Challenging the assumptions underlying the use of participatory decision-making strategies: A longitudinal case study. *Small Group Behavior, 20*, 428–448.

When you have read and
thought about this chapter,
you will be able to:

1. Define leadership.

2. Identify how leaders
   influence others.

3. Describe the major
   theoretical approaches to
   studying leadership.

4. Identify the criteria for
   effective group problem
   solving.

5. State the major steps in
   the Procedural Model
   of Problem Solving
   (P-MOPS).

6. Describe how group
   members can encourage
   creativity.

7. Reveal how conflict and
   problem solving are
   related.

8. Identify some methods of
   conflict resolution.

9. State the leader's role in
   problem solving.

10

Group Leadership, Conflict, and Problem Solving

WITH GLORIA J. GALANES

"Leaders must be strengthened in their determination to do new and bold things that must be done."

DR. ALBERT SCHWEITZER

"Without leadership there is no focus about which a number of individuals may cluster to form a group."

CECIL GIBB

"The successful organization has one major attribute that sets it apart from unsuccessful organizations: dynamic and effective leadership."

PAUL HERSEY AND
KENNETH BLANCHARD

Three topics that are essential for understanding small groups are leadership, problem solving, and conflict resolution. In this chapter you will learn how leaders influence others; the major theoretical approaches to studying leadership; the differences between problem solving and decision making; the criteria for effective problem solving; ways to manage conflict during the problem-solving process; and the leader's role in problem solving.

After 7 years as a sales representative, Britta Mae was promoted to manager, which meant supervising five of her former peers. As colleagues they all got along well, but she worried about how they would respond to her in her new role as their boss. She had always taken more of a leadership role anyway, but she was never in the position of being responsible for helping them achieve their sales goals.

Bill Kolinski's boss selected him to be the new team leader of a work group at a publishing company. The previous leader had quit the group because the team members were constantly bickering among themselves about how to tackle the issue at hand. Bill needed to find a way to increase cooperation and reduce conflict in the group to prove his leadership abilities to his boss.

Northern Utilities Power Plant No. 7 was faced with the complicated problem of how to get coal supplies from the West to the power plants in the East. Alexandra Barstead was asked to assemble a team to determine how to solve this problem quickly and inexpensively.

Britta, Bill, and Alexandra are faced with issues of leadership, conflict resolution, and problem solving. You, too, may one day find yourself faced with similar issues. This chapter will help you understand each of them, and it will also provide you with the tools you need to be a more effective group leader, to resolve group conflicts, and to solve group problems.

What Is Leadership?

Hackman and Johnson (1991) define **leadership** as *a process of using communication to influence the behaviors and attitudes of others to meet group goals*. Communication is at the heart of this process:

> Leadership is human (symbolic) communication which modifies the attitudes and behaviors of others in order to meet group goals and needs. (Hackman & Johnson, 1991, p. 11)

Leadership, then, is enacted through communication and persuasion, not through physical force or coercion. Furthermore, only influence designed to benefit the group can truly be termed *small-group leadership*. One member persuading another to sabotage a group goal is not considered leadership by this definition.

A **leader** is *a person who influences the behavior and attitudes of others through communication*. In small groups, two types of leaders are designated and emergent. A **designated leader** is *someone who has been appointed or elected to a leadership position* (e.g., chair, team leader, coordinator, or facilitator). An **emergent leader** is *someone who becomes an informal leader by exerting influence toward achievement of a group's goal but who does not hold the*

leadership

The process of using communication to influence the behaviors and attitudes of others to meet group goals.

leader

A person who influences the behavior and attitudes of others through communication.

formal position or role of leader. Emergent leaders are group members who become influential by behaving in ways that are helpful to the group and that are valued by the other members. Thus, *any* member of a group can provide leadership. In fact, groups work best when all members contribute skills and leadership behavior on behalf of the group.

Having a designated leader usually helps provide stability to a group. Groups with designated leaders accepted by the members have fewer interpersonal problems and often produce better outcomes than do groups without designated leaders (Hollander, 1978). Even in a group where leadership is shared among members, someone still must coordinate the flow of communication and the work of the members.

designated leader

Someone who has been appointed or elected to an official position of leadership.

emergent leader

Someone who becomes an informal leader by exerting influence in a group but does not hold the official position or title of leader.

TRY ◀▶ THIS

Think of the small-group leaders you have observed. Make two lists, one listing specific characteristics of the best leader and the other listing characteristics of the worst leader. Form groups of five or six and discuss your lists. Compile a master list of best and worst characteristics.

power

The ability to influence others.

The Sources of Influence (Power)

How do leaders, designated or emergent, gain their ability to influence others? A classic study by French and Raven (1981) identified five types of *interpersonal influence,* or **power:** reward, punishment, legitimate, referent, and expert.

Leadership is about communication, not personality or luck.

reward power

Power derived from the ability to give others tangible or intangible things they want and need.

punishment power

Power derived from the ability to withhold what others want and need.

coercion

A form of punishment that attempts to force compliance with hostile tactics.

legitimate power

Power by virtue of having a particular position or title.

referent power

Power based on others' admiration and respect.

charisma

An extreme type of referent power that inspires strong loyalty and devotion from others.

Leaders can exercise **reward power** *by giving followers things they want and need,* including tangible items such as money, material goods, and personal favors or intangible things such as special attention, acknowledgment and compliments. Leaders can use **punishment power** *by withholding these same items.* For example, a leader who frowns because a member has failed to complete an assigned task is administering a form of punishment. **Coercion** is a form of *punishment that attempts to force compliance with hostile tactics.* Genuine leaders should not resort to coercion, because it breeds resentment.

A leader has **legitimate power** *by virtue of title or position.* Legitimate leaders have the right to do certain things in groups that other members may not do, such as calling meetings, preparing the agenda, checking on the work of other members, and making assignments.

Referent power is *power based on others' admiration or respect.* When someone likes you, you have considerable influence over that person. **Charisma** is *an extreme type of referent power that inspires strong loyalty and devotion from others.* The more people are admired and respected, the more others copy their behavior, and the greater is their power to influence the group.

Leaders have **expert power** when *the other members value the leaders' knowledge or expertise.* For instance, if your group must conduct a panel discussion for class and you are the only one who has ever participated in a panel discussion, you have expertise the others value and, thus, can influence them because they respect your knowledge.

All members of a group have the ability to influence other members. For instance, all members, not just the designated leader, can reward others, withhold rewards, or have expertise potentially valuable to the group. In addition, a designated leader's influence usually stems from more than just legitimate power. Besides holding the title of leader, that person also has expertise, referent power, and so forth. In fact, if legitimate power is the leader's only source of influence, then someone else in the group with more broadly based power will probably emerge as a more influential informal leader. In short, all group members possess some sources of influence and can lead the group, even if they don't have the title of leader.

The Theoretical Approaches to Leadership

Since Aristotle's time, people have been interested in what makes a good leader. Is leadership something you are born with? Can you learn to be a leader? In this section, several approaches to understanding leadership are presented. The most useful current theories about leadership focus on the communication behaviors of individuals.

expert power

Power derived from knowledge or expertise valued by the group.

Trait Approaches

Trait approaches generally assert that *leaders are born, not made.* Originally, people believed that leaders possessed certain traits, such as intelligence, at-

10.1 LEADERSHIP AND SOURCES OF POWER

Write the appropriate letter from the choices below in each blank on the left:

A.	Designated leader	D.	Coercion
B.	Emergent leader	E.	Legitimate power
C.	Reward power	F.	Referent power

C 1. "Elect me and you will have better schools, more and better teachers, and a sanitation system to be proud of."

A E 2. "The president appointed me chair of the task force."

D 3. "You'll do it now, or your work with us is over."

B F 4. "She's never been the chair of the committee, but for years her support of the issues has been necessary for passage."

F 5. "We work hard for him, not because of the pay but because he is always so good to us."

Answers: 1. C   2. A or E   3. D   4. B or F   5. F

---

tractiveness, and size, that made them leaders. Some studies did find relationships between leadership and certain traits. For example, leaders tended to have higher IQs and were taller, more attractive, and larger than nonleaders (Stogdill, 1974). However, followers can also have these traits, and the leader is not necessarily the person in the group most endowed with any of these traits (the tallest or most intelligent). Current theorists dismiss the idea that leadership can be explained solely on the basis of traits.

More contemporary trait approaches examine personality characteristics that are more complex than simple traits. For example, the person who emerges as a group's leader is someone highly skilled at verbalizing ideas (Bormann, 1990; Geier, 1967). Several studies have found that complex traits, such as self-monitoring, are related to leadership emergence. **Self-monitoring** refers to *individuals' abilities to monitor, or pay attention to, both social cues and their own behavior* (Snyder, 1979). High self-monitors are sensitive to contextual cues, are socially perceptive, and can adjust their behaviors according to what seems needed at any given time. The ability to self-monitor is related to leadership emergence because high self-monitors seem better at adapting their behaviors to suit group needs (Zaccaro, Foti, & Kenny, 1991).

trait approaches

Approaches to studying leadership that focus on the leader's personal characteristics; they assume that leaders are born, not made.

self-monitoring

The degree to which individuals pay attention to social cues and adjust their behavior to fit.

239

Interestingly, female high self-monitors may not emerge as leaders because they pick up cues that female leadership is inappropriate and conform to other members' expectations. Low self-monitors can emerge as leaders in certain circumstances. Because they respond to their own internal cues rather than external ones from the other members, they may emerge as leaders when they personally have favorable attitudes about expressing leadership (Cronshaw & Ellis, 1991).

Verbal style is another characteristic associated with leadership emergence. In one study, members whose communicative style was quiet, tentative, or vague did not emerge as potential leaders (Baker, 1990). Instead, members who suggested procedures and helped organize the group emerged as leaders. Members with dramatic communication styles were perceived as helpful to the group, but they did not emerge as leaders.

Although the characteristics mentioned are often called traits, they are certainly complex traits that are associated with specific communication behaviors, such as paying attention to contextual cues or speaking clearly and directly. People whose communication behaviors help clarify the group's task and motivate other members are influential in groups.

Style Approaches

style approaches

Approaches to studying leadership that focus on the leader's pattern of behavior.

democratic leaders

Leaders who encourage members to participate fully in group decisions.

laissez-faire leaders

Nonleaders who take little or no initiative for structuring a group discussion.

autocratic leaders

Leaders who maintain strict control over group members.

Style approaches *to studying leadership focus on the pattern of behaviors leaders exhibit in groups.* Considerable research has examined three major styles of designated leaders: democratic, laissez-faire, and autocratic. **Democratic leaders** *encourage members to participate in group decisions,* even major ones: "What suggestions do you have for solving our problem?" **Laissez-faire leaders** are *nonleaders who take almost no initiative for structuring a group discussion* but may respond to questions: "I don't care; whatever you want to do is fine with me." **Autocratic leaders** *maintain strict control over their groups,* including making assignments and giving orders: "Here's how we'll solve the problem. First, you will . . ." Autocratic leaders ask fewer questions but answer more than democratic leaders; they make more attempts to coerce and fewer attempts to get others to participate (Rosenfeld & Plax, 1975).

Groups vary in the amount of structure and control their members want and need, but research findings about style have been consistent (Graen, Dansereau, & Minami, 1972; Jurma, 1978, 1979; Maier & Maier, 1957; Preston & Heintz, 1949; White & Lippett, 1960). Most people in the United States prefer democratic groups and are more satisfied in democratically rather than autocratically led groups.

The style approaches imply a single leadership style good for all situations. However, most scholars believe that the style should match the needs of the situation.

Contingency Approaches

Contingency approaches *to studying leadership assume that group situations vary, with different situations (contingencies) requiring different leadership* *styles.* In addition, a single group's situation will vary over time. Factors such as the type of task, the time available, and the skill of the members determine what type of leadership is most appropriate for a given situation. Most current researchers accept contingency assumptions. In this section, information about three contingency approaches is presented.

The Functions Approach

One contingency theory is the **functions approach,** which *assumes that groups have two main types of functions that must be performed for the group to be effective: task functions and interpersonal functions.* The functions approach is classified as a contingency theory because it assumes that the balance of task and interpersonal functions needed vary from group to group and from one time to another in the same group. For example, a group with a crisis on its hands and little time to solve it will need to concentrate on task-oriented functions, whereas a newly formed group whose goal is celebrating cultural diversity will need to pay careful attention to interpersonal functions such as harmony, respect, and support.

Many people have described several functions helpful to groups (Bales, 1950; Benne & Sheats, 1948). The following four functions emphasize the communicative focus of leadership (Fisher, 1985):

1. Leaders provide sufficient information, as well as the ability to process and handle a considerable amount of information.
2. Leaders enact a variety of functions needed within the group.
3. Leaders help group members make sense of decisions made and actions performed within the group by supplying good reasons for those actions.
4. Leaders focus on the here-and-now, stopping the group from jumping to unwarranted conclusions or finding formula answers too quickly.

Communication is central to leadership. One of the most important obstacles a group must overcome is the need to reduce a vast amount of complex and sometimes contradictory information to an understandable level (Weick, 1978). Group members must devise procedures for narrowing the number of plausible interpretations to find solutions. A basic function of the leader is to help the group find solutions by creating effective organizing procedures for problem solving.

The functions approach focuses on behaviors, not traits. This approach assumes that leadership consists of what people *do* for the group, not what they *are.* In addition, this approach assumes that the designated leader cannot, and should not, provide every function needed in the group. Instead, members can and should perform whatever functions the group needs. Thus, this approach encourages the designated leader to use the talents of all the members. The leader's unique function is to serve as the completer, to observe what needed functions are not being performed and to perform them or encourage others to do so (Schutz, 1979). This approach acknowledges that group leadership behavior is a property of the *group* and a product of the interaction among members and the designated leader.

contingency approaches

Approaches to studying leadership that assume that different leadership situations require different leadership behaviors.

functions approach

An approach to studying leadership that assumes groups have certain task and interpersonal functions that must be performed, but they may be performed by any member, not just the designated leader.

Situational Models

situational models

Models of leadership that encourage leaders to focus on specific factors within the group situation to determine the most appropriate leadership behaviors.

Situational models *encourage leaders to focus on certain aspects of a group situation to determine the best leadership approaches* and to adapt their behavior accordingly. Because of the infinite number of situational variables that could be considered, most models suggest that leaders focus on one or two key aspects of the situation. For example, the classic Hersey and Blanchard (1972, 1980) situational model of leadership suggests that leaders focus on group maturity—the extent to which group members are knowledgeable about the task, are motivated to complete it, and have developed into an effective team. According to this model, leadership behaviors can focus on the task, the interpersonal relationships among members, both, or neither. Groups at different maturity levels need different leadership behaviors. For example, a relatively inexperienced or unmotivated group needs a leader who focuses on task concerns, at least until members understand their task and objectives. As members become familiar with the task and the group begins to mature as a team, the leader should begin to increase relationship behavior. With even greater maturity, task behavior can be reduced; at full maturity, the leader can essentially allow the group members to run the group themselves, with little or no task or relationship activity from the leader.

This model suggests that a group's situation changes over time. Effective leaders can both assess a group's situation and adapt their behavior to fit the ever-changing needs of the group. Several studies, such as the self-monitoring studies described earlier, have found that leaders do adapt their behavior. Leaders adjust the amount of structure they provide in group discussions (Wood, 1977) and vary the amount of dominance and supportiveness they provide (Sorenson & Savage, 1989), and their interactions are more complex than the interactions of other members (Drecksell, 1984). Good leaders perceive the needs and goals of members and then adjust their behaviors to those needs (Kenny & Zaccaro, 1983).

Situational models generally focus on communicative behaviors. They conceive of small groups as puzzles, with each leadership piece having a unique shape in each puzzle. Trying to force a round piece into a square hole won't work. Thus, the most effective leadership for any group should fit that group's situation, and good leaders adjust their communication behavior to fit the group's situation.

The Communicative Competencies Approach

communicative competencies approach

An approach to leadership that focuses on how leaders exert influence by using specific communication skills and behaviors.

Communication scholars who adopt the **communicative competencies approach** have tried to *focus on the communicative behaviors of leaders as they exercise interpersonal influence* to accomplish group goals. They ask such questions as "What do effective leaders do?" The Communication Competency Model of Group Leadership, developed by Kevin Barge and Randy Hirokawa (1989), is one of the most comprehensive models to address this question. This model assumes that leaders help a group achieve its goals through communication skills (competencies). Two competencies include the task and interpersonal, or relationship, distinctions discussed earlier. Leaders must be flexible to draw from a personal repertoire of such competencies. Some of the most important leader competencies are described briefly here:

1. Effective small-group leaders are active communicators who encode ideas clearly and concisely. Emergent leaders speak frequently, although not necessarily the most frequently, in a group (Morris & Hackman, 1969). However, frequency of talk alone is not sufficient— its quality is essential (Russell, 1970). Leaders should speak clearly and fluently and be able to verbalize problems, goals, values, ideals, and solutions (Lashbrook, 1975).

2. Effective group leaders communicate a good grasp of the group's task. Their communication behaviors reveal extensive knowledge about the task, how to organize and interpret that knowledge, and what procedures will help get the job done.

3. Effective group leaders are skilled in mediating information and ideas supplied by all members. They are good at structuring disorganized or ambiguous information, at asking probing questions to bring out pertinent information, and at evaluating inferences and conclusions drawn from information (Fisher, 1985).

4. Effective group leaders express their opinions provisionally. Members do not like dogmatic leaders. Groups produce more and better alternatives if their leaders withhold their own opinions until later in a discussion instead of expressing them early (Anderson & Balzer, 1991). Groups whose leaders suspend their own judgments and encourage members to consider multiple viewpoints fully produce better solutions than other groups (Maier & Solem, 1952).

Effective leaders demonstrate appropriate communication skills.

5. Effective group leaders express group-centered concerns. Effective leaders do not act cocky or arrogant (Bennis & Nanus, 1985). They exhibit personal commitment to the group's goals in both word and deed, and they confront members who are more self- than group-centered (Larson & LaFasto, 1989).
6. Effective group leaders respect others when they speak. They are sensitive to nonverbal signals, and they are courteous.
7. Effective group leaders share rewards and credit with the group. Democratic leaders share rewards and punishments equally with the group (Rosenfeld, 1976), give credit to the group for accomplishments, and work to develop the leadership competencies of all members (Larson & LaFasto, 1989). They communicate their appreciation for the efforts of others.

The Distributed-Leadership Approach

distributed leadership

A leadership approach that expects each member, not just the leader, to take responsibility for the group by exerting appropriate influence.

Members and leader together are responsible for effective leadership in a group. **Distributed leadership** *explicitly acknowledges that each member is expected to perform the communication behaviors needed to move the group toward its goal.* Although it does not often happen, groups may even survive without a designated leader, like the long-term group studied by Eleanor Counselman (1991), which functioned without a designated leader but was not without leadership. Leadership functions, such as providing structure, setting group norms, and keeping the group on task, were performed by various members. Although this group is unusual, it supports an important point made earlier: Leadership is a property of the *group,* not of a single individual.

In fact, groups seem to be more productive when leadership behaviors are distributed. When Kevin Barge (1989) compared a leadership model in which the group leader was an active, directive influence to one in which all members engaged in the leadership process, he found that overall leadership activity, not the designated leader's activity alone, predicts overall group productivity.

Although most groups you are in have a designated leader, however, all members share leadership and responsibility for the group. This goal may be difficult to achieve, but it is a worthwhile goal. Ideally, all members should know something about group process so that they know what a group needs at any given time and can provide for those needs appropriately. Wise leaders encourage members to share in the leadership of the group.

Problem Solving

Many groups exist to solve problems. Group members must be both creative and critical to arrive at the best solutions. Groups are usually (but not always) better problem solvers than individuals, because several people can provide more information than one person. Groups also can supply more resources and collectively have a broader perspective. Group members can spot flaws in each other's reasoning. However, there are trade-offs. Group problem solving takes longer, and sometimes personality, procedural, or social problems in a group make work as a team difficult for members. Group problem solving is superior under certain conditions, such as when multiple solutions are equally appropriate, decisions must be acceptable to all the members, and the group has ample time to meet and discuss (Vroom, 1973). Groups are particularly well suited for **conjunctive tasks,** *for which no one member has all the necessary information but each member has some information to contribute. Individuals are often better at* **disjunctive tasks,** *which require little coordination and which can be completed by the most skilled member working alone* (Smith, 1989). Group problem solving is usually more effective when the process is systematic and organized because a group that does not have an overall plan for decision making is more likely to make a poor decision (Gouran & Hirokawa, 1986).

Problem Solving and Decision Making

Problem solving is *the process of moving from an undesirable present situation to a desirable goal by overcoming obstacles to that goal,* as depicted in Figure 10.1. For instance, if your organization is losing members (an undesirable present situation), increasing membership may be your goal. You face certain obstacles, such as lack of information about why members are quitting. The problem-solving process is a comprehensive procedure with several steps, including assessing the current situation, creating alternatives and

conjunctive tasks

Tasks for which no one group member has all the necessary information but each member has some information to contribute.

disjunctive tasks

Tasks with low coordination requirements that can be completed effectively by one member working alone.

problem solving

The process of moving from an undesirable present situation to a desirable goal by overcoming obstacles to that goal.

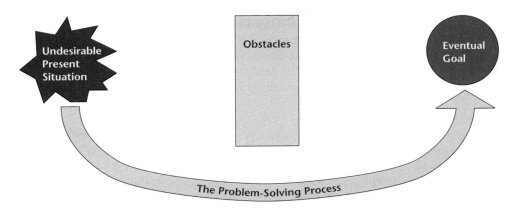

Figure 10.1 A model of the problem-solving process.

decision making

Choosing among alternatives.

charge

The group's assignment.

area of freedom

The limitations placed on a group as part of the group's charge.

evaluating them, selecting one or more, and implementing them. **Decision making** refers only to *the act of choosing among options* that already exist. The two processes are related, however, because many decisions are made in the process of problem solving. For example, a task force charged with designing a new campus union is a problem-solving group, but a screening committee selecting the best site for the union from among several preapproved sites is a decision-making group.

When a group is given its **charge,** or *assignment*, limits are placed on its ability to act. Those limits define the group's **area of freedom,** which is usually stated or implied in the charge. The charge specifies what a group is to do, whereas the area of freedom defines *the boundaries within which the group must work.* For instance, the task force designing a new campus union is given a financial limit it cannot exceed; the union must not cost more than $2 million. Both the charge and the area of freedom should be clear to all group members at the beginning of a problem-solving discussion.

Effective Group Problem Solving

good for transitions

If problem solving is to be effective, the group must meet three major criteria. First, the group must be organized. If it isn't, essential business that should be taken care of will not occur or may not be fully completed. Second, the group must be creative. Members must extend their individual thinking to come up with innovative ideas. Finally, the group must manage conflict appropriately so that the group is helped, not hurt, by differences of opinion. Each of these steps is discussed in greater detail below.

I. Organizing Problem-Solving Discussions

Groups using systematic procedures solve problems more effectively and have higher-quality discussions than do groups that do not use systematic procedures (Brilhart, 1966; Gouran, Brown, & Henry, 1978). Following a structured procedure often reminds discussants of something they forgot to

helps sets

do (such as analyze the problem thoroughly) in an earlier stage of problem solving and suggests logical priorities (Poole, 1983a, 1983b). An effective problem-solving process starts with an appropriate discussion question, includes an explicit discussion of the criteria the group will use to judge potential solutions, and follows a systematic problem-solving procedure.

examples in box on p.249

Wording the Discussion Question   Problem-solving groups typically handle three basic types of discussion questions. *Questions of fact* deal with whether something is true or can be verified. *Questions of value* ask whether something is good or bad, better or worse. Cultural and individual values and beliefs are central to the questions of value. *Questions of policy* ask what action should be taken. The key word *should* is either stated or implied in questions of policy. Examples of each type of question are presented in Figure 10.2.

Instant Recall

10.2 STYLES AND APPROACHES IN SMALL GROUPS

Complete the following statements:

1. The three major styles of designated leaders are _____, _____, and _____.

2. According to the functions approach _____ functions and _____ functions must be performed for a group to be effective.

3. "What do effective leaders do?" is a question that might be asked of someone who has adopted the _____ approach.

4. Distributed leadership acknowledges that each member is expected to perform the _____ behaviors needed to move the group toward its _____.

5. Problem solving involves moving from an _____ situation to a _____ goal, whereas decision making refers to choosing among _____ that already exist.

Answers: 1. democratic/laissez-faire/autocratic   2. task/interpersonal   3. communicative competencies   4. communication/goal   5. undesirable/desirable/options

---

Regardless of the type of discussion question guiding a problem-solving group, the leader must state the question appropriately. Well-stated questions are clear, are measurable, and focus on the problem rather than on a solution. First, the language and terminology should be concrete rather than abstract. If ambiguous terms such as *effective, good,* or *fair* are used, providing examples helps each group member have as close to the same meaning as possible. Figure 10.3 gives examples of how abstract terms can be made more concrete. Second, a well-stated discussion question helps group members know when the solution has been achieved. For example, a task force charged with "completing a report by May 15 on why membership has dropped from 100 to 50 members" knows exactly what it is to do by what deadline. Finally, a group should start its problem solving with a problem question rather than a solution question. **Problem questions** *focus on the undesirable present state and imply that many solutions are possible.* They do not bias a group toward one particular option. **Solution questions,** on the other hand, *slant the group's discussion toward one particular option.* They

problem questions

Group discussion questions that focus on the problem and imply that many solutions are possible.

solution questions

Group discussion questions that bias discussion because they focus the group's attention on a particular solution instead of the problem.

Fact

How has the divorce rate changed in the past 15 years?
How many Hispanic students graduate from high school each year?
What percentage of college students graduate in 4 years?
How often, on average, does a person speak each day?
What occupations earn the highest annual incomes?

Value

Why should people seek higher education?
How should Americans treat international students?
Does our legal system provide "justice for all"?
How should young people be educated about AIDS?
What is the value of standardized tests for college admission?

Policy

What courses should students be required to take?
Should the state's drunk driving laws be changed?
What are the arguments for and against mandatory retirement?
Should the United States intervene in foreign disputes for humanitarian reasons?
What advantages should government provide for businesses willing to develop in
   high-risk areas of a city?

Figure 10.2 Questions of fact, value, and policy.

"I think Ms. Brown is a **good lawyer** because she is *very credible*. She *knows the law*
   and always comes up with novel arguments that her opposing lawyers can't
   counter."

"Our solution for the parking problem has to be **effective.** I mean, it has to *reduce
   parking complaints, eliminate the amount of driving around looking for a space that
   happens now,* and *not cost the university any money*."

"I think **weapons** should be made illegal. I mean, *guns are really dangerous* in the
   wrong hands, and you can't tell me that people need *semiautomatic assault rifles* to
   hunt with."

Figure 10.3 Making abstract concepts more concrete.

may inadvertently cause a group to ignore creative or unusual options because they blind members to some alternatives. Examples of problem and solution questions appear in Figure 10.4.

criteria

Standards against
which a group's
solution or decision
is evaluated.

Discussing Criteria **Criteria** are *the standards by which a group must judge potential solutions.* For example, a solution's likely effectiveness ("Will it work?"),
acceptability ("Will people vote for our proposal?"), and cost ("Does this option
keep us within the budget?") are common criteria groups use. Group members
should discuss and agree on criteria before adopting a solution. Because criteria are based on the values of group members, two members, each using rational tools of decision making, can arrive at different conclusions. The more

Problem Questions	VS	Solution Questions
How can we reduce complaints about parking on campus?		How can we increase the number of parking spaces in the campus lots?
What can we do to increase attendance at our club's activities?		How can we improve publicity for our club's activities?
How can we make National Avenue safer to cross?		How can we get the city council to reduce the speed limit on National Avenue?

Choose an example ⇐

Figure 10.4 Problem questions versus solution questions.

Absolute Criteria (*must* be met)	Important Criteria (*should* be met)
Must not cost more than $2 million.	Should be centrally located.
Must be wheelchair accessible.	Should have stage space for concerts.
Must include flexible space that can be arranged in different ways	Should be attractive to all campus constituencies, including traditional and nontraditional students, faculty, and staff.

⇐ *Choose 1*

Figure 10.5 Absolute criteria versus important criteria for a new student union.

similar group members are—in age, gender, ethnicity, background, attitudes, values, and beliefs—the easier they can agree on criteria.

Two kinds of criteria are common. **Absolute criteria** are *those that* must *be met; the group has no leeway.* **Important criteria** are *those that* should *be met, but the group has some flexibility.* Group members should give the highest priority to criteria that *must* be met. Ideas that do not meet absolute criteria should be rejected, and the rest ranked on how well they meet important criteria. Examples of absolute and important criteria are presented in Figure 10.5.

Keeping the Problem-Solving Discussion Organized Effective problem solving does not happen by accident. If a group wants to solve a problem or make a decision effectively, certain events must occur during the discussion. The following functions are essential: a comprehensive analysis of the group's current situation, a clear understanding of what the group wants the solution to achieve, a complete survey of the available options, a thorough evaluation of the positive and negative aspects of those options, and appropriate use of high-quality information during the process (Hirokawa, 1992). The quality of a group's output depends on how well these criteria are met (Hirokawa & Rost, 1991). The single biggest error made by groups that reach faulty solutions is the failure to discuss thoroughly one or more of these steps.

absolute criteria

Criteria that *must* be met; the group has no leeway.

important criteria

Criteria that *should* be met if at all possible, but the group has some flexibility.

What problem-solving procedure a group uses does not seem to matter (Brilhart & Jochem, 1964; Hirokawa, 1983; Poole & Doelger, 1986), but using *no* structural pattern definitely seems to hurt the group's problem-solving ability (Bayless, 1967; Larson, 1969). Apparently, using a systematic problem-solving procedure helps ensure that addressing the essential functions is not left to chance. Thus, groups using systematic procedures are more likely to be effective problem solvers (Hirokawa, 1985). Systematic procedures help groups tap into members' critical thinking skills and knowledge.

Several models exist to help groups engage in systematic problem solving. Many of these models are based on the **reflective thinking model** of philosopher John Dewey (1910). Based on Dewey's model, the Procedural Model of Problem Solving (P-MOPS) incorporates the essential functions discussed earlier. The model is designed to help groups engage in critical thinking by keeping problem-solving discussions orderly so that the group is less likely to omit an important step in the problem-solving process. In addition, the model can be modified for a number of different kinds of problems.

The acronym **P-MOPS** has a double purpose: The letters simplify remembering both the full name of the model—Procedural Model of Problem Solving—and its main purpose—to *help groups "mop up" all necessary functions for high-quality problem solving.* The model's systematic structure can be adjusted to suit whatever contingencies a group faces. P-MOPS encourages the leader and members to construct a written outline with specific questions about all issues the group must consider so that no important contingency is overlooked. The model is not a rigid formula but a guide to encourage thorough problem solving. Whether your group uses P-MOPS or another procedural guideline, displaying the steps during discussion and keeping visual records of the discussion (such as with flip charts) help members keep on track. The five major steps in P-MOPS are listed in Figure 10.6 and are described as follows:

I. *What is the nature of the problem facing us?* The group makes a thorough assessment of the problem, including what is unsatisfactory, what led to the undesirable situation, what members ultimately desire, and what the

reflective thinking model

A problem-solving model developed by philosopher John Dewey that is based on his assessment of how individuals solve problems.

P-MOPS

An acronym for Procedural Model of Problem Solving, a structured, flexible procedure groups can use to ensure that no important step needed for effective problem solving is missed.

I. Problem description and analysis: "What is the nature of the problem facing the group?"

II. Generation and elaboration of possible solutions: "What might be done to solve the problem we've described?"

III: Evaluation of possible solutions: "What are the probable benefits and possible negative consequences of each proposed solution?"

IV. Consensus decision: "What seems to be the best possible solution we can all support?"

V. Implementation of the solution chosen: "How will we put our decision into effect?"

Figure 10.6   The steps in P-MOPS.

obstacles to that goal might be. Focusing on the problem before thinking about how to solve it is essential. What would you say if your doctor recommended surgery without first making a thorough examination? Problem analysis encourages group members to develop a shared image of the problem, to stay on track, and to develop solutions that address the real issues, rather than just the symptoms.

II. *What might be done to solve the problem?* Having many ideas from which to choose increases the chance that good ideas will be included among the choices. Writing down ideas where all can see them prevents losing ideas and may trigger new ones. Such procedures can help a group develop creative options during this step.

III. *What are the probable benefits and possible negative consequences of each proposed solution?* Once the problem has been thoroughly analyzed and alternatives have been described, the group is ready to evaluate the alternatives. The pros and cons of each solution must be explored. Every member must feel free to express opinions openly and honestly if this step is to work optimally.

IV. *What is the best possible solution we can all support?* If a decision seems to have emerged during the evaluation of the alternatives, the discussion leader should test for consensus ("We all seem to agree that our second option is the one we prefer. Am I understanding everyone correctly?"). Sometimes members find ways of combining or modifying options to refine them during this step.

V. *What will we do to put our solution into effect?* The final step involves implementing the solution. That may mean planning how to present the final recommendations to a parent organization (including deciding who will make the report and in what form) or actually carrying out the plan developed (for example, buying the materials needed and implementing the plan).

P-MOPS helps ensure that a group meets its critical thinking function, which is one of the main jobs of group problem solving. Another important aspect of group problem solving is creativity.

good transition

Encouraging Group Creativity

One of the most important jobs a leader has is to encourage group creativity. *One procedure that encourages creativity* is **brainstorming,** a technique that originated in the advertising industry to help develop imaginative advertising campaigns (Osborn, 1975). Critical evaluation kills creativity, so the main rule of brainstorming is "no evaluation," at least during the brainstorming process. Evaluation of the ideas takes place *after* the group has exhausted its options, such as during step III of P-MOPS. The four steps in brainstorming are:

1. *The group is given a problem to solve.* The problem can vary from specific ("What shall we name our new sports car?") to highly abstract ("How can we increase commuter student participation in student

brainstorming

A technique to help groups increase the number of creative options available by suspending judgment or evaluation.

activities?"). Sometimes group members prepare ahead of time. For example, a team brainstorming names for a new pudding first ate some of the pudding, then talked about its taste and what it reminded them of, and then brainstormed over 500 possible names.

2. *Members of the group are encouraged to generate as many solutions as possible.* Four guidelines are essential:

    a. No evaluation is permitted—no criticism of, laughing at, or negative reactions to any ideas.

    b. The group strives for quantity—the more ideas listed, the better.

    c. The group encourages innovation—unusual, wild, and crazy ideas are sought.

    d. The group encourages "hitchhiking"—members are asked to add to or modify others' ideas.

3. The group charts *all ideas so that the entire group can see them.* All ideas are written down on a chalkboard, marker board, or large sheets of paper plainly visible to all members of the brainstorming team, because looking at the posted ideas often triggers new ones. The listed ideas can later be used to write meeting minutes.

4. The group evaluates *all ideas at a different session.* After the brainstorming technique has been used to generate a long list of possible solutions, critical thinking is used to evaluate each idea, possibly to modify or improve on some of them, and to retain for consideration only those ideas that meet essential criteria. Sometimes a different group evaluates the ideas created by the brainstorming group. If the same group does the evaluating, it should take a physical break to let members switch mental gears from creative to critical thinking.

Many other specialized procedures and techniques help groups improve creative and critical thinking or help with other aspects of group discussion. P-MOPS and brainstorming help with two of the most essential discussion functions.

Managing Conflict in Small-Group Problem Solving

conflict

Expressed disagreement between people who are interdependent.

groupthink

The failure of a group to evaluate its options thoroughly and critically because members fail to express their disagreement.

Conflict is *an expressed struggle between people who must work together* (such as group members) *but whose goals or values are incompatible* (Hocker & Wilmont, 1991). Not only is conflict inevitable in small groups; it is desirable. Disagreement is a natural by-product when members with different perceptions, goals, and values try to discuss an issue or a problem. Conflict is at the heart of effective problem solving and decision making because it can improve group creativity and critical thinking. The saying "If two people perceive things in exactly the same way, one of those people is unnecessary" underscores the value of disagreement. Group members who are doing their jobs well *should* disagree. *The failure of a group to evaluate its options thoroughly and critically because of its failure to express disagreement* is called **groupthink** and can seriously damage a group's problem-solving process (Janis, 1983). However, conflict must be managed appropriately for the group to realize its benefits.

Substantive conflict, also called *intrinsic* conflict, is *disagreement over ideas, meanings, issues, and other matters pertinent (intrinsic) to the task of the group* (Guetzkow & Gyr, 1954). The basis of effective decision making and problem solving is how ideas, proposals, evidence, and reasoning are challenged and critically examined. Managed well, substantive conflict helps a group. **Affective conflict,** or *extrinsic* conflict, stems from *personal dislikes and power struggles* that have nothing to do directly with the group's task (Guetzkow & Gyr, 1954). Affective conflict is harmful to the group.

Capitalizing on Conflict for the Good of the Group   Although affective conflict may be better left unexpressed, substantive conflict cannot be of benefit unless it is made available to the group. The following guidelines help members capitalize on conflict for the good of the group:

1. *Express disagreement.* Failing to confront disagreements reduces satisfaction with the group and interferes with the decision-making and problem-solving processes. Not speaking up deprives the group of potentially valuable information.
2. *Stick with the issue at hand.* Deal directly with the issue under discussion, and do not bring up side issues (Kreps, 1990).
3. *Express disagreements with sensitivity.* Do not try to push others' emotional buttons. Monitor the effects of your statements on others and adjust your communication appropriately.
4. *Disagree with an idea, but do not ever criticize the person.* Express disagreement without devaluing the person with whom you disagree. Otherwise, you risk establishing a defensive climate that discourages honest discussion.
5. *Base your disagreement on evidence and reasoning, rather than rumor, innuendo, or emotion* (Kreps, 1990).
6. *React to disagreement with a spirit of inquiry, not defensiveness.* If someone disagrees with you, do not react as though you have been attacked personally. Listen actively to your fellow members' remarks. Clarify any misunderstandings and work together to discover a mutually acceptable solution. Make conflict work for, rather than against, the group.
7. *If someone persists in attacking you, stay calm.* This conflict may be one of your biggest challenges. First, do not let another's attacks intimidate you into being silent. Instead, confront the attacking member calmly, explaining how you feel and what you want: "I resent your personal attacks and I think they are inappropriate. I am willing to listen to your objections, but I want you to stop your attacks now." The attacker may apologize and calm down. If this doesn't work, ask for the group's intervention: "Do others think that personal attacks are acceptable behavior?" The other members, who probably are as uncomfortable as you, may now be encouraged enough to support you.

substantive conflict

Conflict over ideas, meanings, issues, and other matters pertinent to the group's task.

affective conflict

Conflict that stems from personal dislikes and power struggles.

Managing Conflict Whether conflict helps or harms the problem-solving process depends on how it is managed. Three general conflict management styles exist: the nonconfrontation, control, and solution-oriented styles (Putnam & Wilson, 1982). Each is appropriate under certain circumstances.

nonconfrontation

The passive conflict management style in which the individual gives in or avoids disagreement.

Nonconfrontation is *a passive conflict management style in which the group member who disagrees says nothing at all or quickly gives in to another member.* This style is appropriate only when the problem is unimportant, the risks of making a poor decision are slight, or when the relationship is genuinely more important than the outcome.

control

A highly aggressive conflict management style in which one person tries to win at all costs.

Control is *a highly aggressive conflict management style in which one person tries to win at all costs.* This approach can cause hard feelings in a group, but it is appropriate when you believe strongly about something and you perceive your needs will not be acknowledged or accommodated with other approaches.

solution orientation

A cooperative and assertive conflict management style that encourages conflicting parties to search jointly for a mutually acceptable solution.

Solution orientation is *a cooperative and assertive conflict management style that encourages all conflicting parties to work together for a solution that meets everyone's needs as fully as possible.* This approach is always appropriate but can take a lot of time. Solution-oriented outcomes often last because all members have their most important needs met. Sometimes members try to negotiate solutions that fully meet everyone's needs but are unable to arrive at such ideal solutions. In those cases, they may have to compromise, and each member gives up something. However, compromise can be an effective outcome when members feel that what they have given up is fair in comparison to what others have given up.

TRY ◄►THIS

Have you ever experienced small-group conflict? What method was used to resolve it? Was it effective?

The Leader's Role in Problem Solving

The leader's role in problem-solving discussions is important because the leader can ensure that the important discussion functions are performed. The following guidelines for leaders help promote effective problem-solving discussions:

1. *Make sure everyone knows the purpose of each meeting, the group's charge, and its area of freedom.* Members should have been informed of these by a meeting notice, but a brief reminder helps members focus on the task. In addition, members may have questions, so addressing them early may save time and prevent misunderstandings later.

10.3 PROBLEM SOLVING AND CONFLICT RESOLUTION

Write T *for true or* F *for false in each blank on the left:*

_____1. The Power Method of Problem Solving (P-MOPS) is a problem-solving model based on John Dewey's work.

_____2. Groupthink is a failure to express disagreement, and it can damage the problem-solving process.

_____3. *Substantive* conflict emerges from power struggles, while *affective* conflict stems from disagreements over issues.

_____4. A control approach to managing conflict is characterized by one person trying to win at all costs.

_____5. Each of the three conflict management styles is appropriate under certain circumstances.

Answers: 1. F   2. T   3. F   4. T   5. T

2. *Suggest procedures to follow.* If the group uses **P-MOPS** or any other discussion procedure, make sure everyone knows the steps. Provide a handout or put the steps on a board or chart visible to everyone.
3. *Ask a clear, measurable problem question to focus initial discussion.*
4. *Keep the discussion goal-oriented.* Summarize each major problem-solving step as it is completed.
5. *Make sure everyone has an equal opportunity to speak, with no one either dominating or withdrawing.*
6. *Stimulate creative thinking.* Use brainstorming or other creativity-enhancing techniques. Defer the evaluation of ideas until members exhaust ideas.
7. *Stimulate critical thinking.* After a group has done its creative thinking, encourage members to evaluate information completely. See that all proposed solutions are tested thoroughly before they are accepted as final group decisions.
8. *Promote teamwork and cooperation.* Establishing a climate of trust does more than anything else to develop cooperation and teamwork among members. Watch for and challenge harmful norms, role patterns, or hidden-agenda items that seem to conflict with group goals and with creating a trusting, supportive environment. Focus arguments on facts and issues, not on personalities.

Cultural Note

Our culture influences our behaviors, so the fact that several researchers have found that culture also plays a role in how we resolve conflict is not surprising:

- Elsayed-Ekhouly and Buda (1996) found that executives from Egypt, Saudi Arabia, Kuwait, and United Arab Emirates used more of an integrating and avoiding style compared to U.S. executives, who used more of an obliging, dominating, and compromising style.
- Gire (1997) confirmed that Nigerians, from a collectivist culture, preferred negotiation to a greater extent than did Canadians, from an individualistic society.
- Tinsley (1997) found that Americans prefer an "integrated individual interests" approach to conflict resolution whereas in the Chinese culture "relational bargaining," a Confucian approach to conflict, is more common.
- Chiu, Wong, and Kosinski (1998) looked at the conflict resolution styles of 96 Chinese and 89 Japanese managers from collectivist cultures that embrace traditional Confucian values. Their research showed that while the approaches of all the managers to resolving conflict were very similar, the Japanese managers tended to employ more assertive styles than did those from the People's Republic of China.

Summary

This chapter covered three important topics essential for understanding how small groups function: leadership, problem solving, and conflict resolution. Leadership is the exercise of interpersonal influence via communication to achieve group goals. A leader is someone who exercises influence. Designated leaders are appointed or elected to official leadership positions, whereas emergent leaders are informal leaders who are influential because their behaviors are useful to the group. Leaders' (and members') ability to influence stems from five power types: reward, punishment, legitimate, expert, and referent power. Numerous theoretical approaches study leadership. Trait approaches assume leaders are born, not made. Style approaches focus on the democratic, autocratic, and laissez-faire behaviors of leaders. Contingency approaches, including the functions, situational and communication competencies approaches, assume that different leadership situations require different leadership styles. The communicative competencies approach examines the communication behaviors leaders use. Distributed leadership suggests that both members and leaders are responsible for the group and should perform whatever leadership functions a group seems to need at any given time.

Problem solving is a comprehensive procedure that moves a group from an undesirable present situation to a desired goal by overcoming obstacles. Problem solving includes analyzing the problem, creating and evaluating alternatives, and choosing and implementing the agreed-upon alternative. Decision making involves only the selection of an alternative.

Effective group problem solving requires that a group be creative, systematic, and thorough in its problem-solving approach. First, the group's discussion should be initiated with a clearly worded problem question, which focuses on problem analysis, rather than a solution question, which may bias a group toward a particular option. Criteria, or standards for evaluating the solution, should be discussed and agreed upon by all members. Then the group's discussion should be kept organized by using a systematic problem-solving procedure such as the Procedural Model of Problem Solving (P-MOPS), which can be tailored to fit a group's unique circumstances. Creativity can be encouraged by using procedures such as brainstorming, in which the group's critical thinking is temporarily suspended so that a variety of options can be developed without fear of judgment.

Conflict, which is inevitable during problem-solving discussions, can be helpful to a group if it is used to promote effective critical thinking. Substantive conflict over issues and ideas can be especially helpful to a group, but affective conflict stemming from power and personality clashes is harmful. Whether conflict helps a group depends on how it is managed. Nonconfrontation, a passive style, prevents group members from receiving the full benefit of members' careful reasoning. Control, an aggressive, competitive style, tries to win no matter what and can tear a group apart. Solution orientation, an assertive, cooperative style, encourages conflicting members to search for a mutually acceptable solution but can take a long time. Each of the three major conflict management styles is appropriate in certain circumstances.

The leader's role helps determine whether group problem solving is effective or not. Although the members also are responsible for the group's ultimate output, the leader can facilitate effective problem solving by making sure the important problem-solving functions are performed.

Issues in Communication

This Issues in Communication narrative is designed to provoke individual thought or discussion about concepts raised in the chapter.

You are the chair of the newly formed Campus Speaker Committee, a student organization that selects campus speakers. The funding for speakers selected by the committee comes from a wealthy, respected alumnus who wants more controversial speakers to speak to students on campus. The alumnus gave the school a $50,000 endowment earmarked for this purpose. However, his endowment is contingent upon students' ability to choose speakers without interference from faculty and administration.

The Campus Speaker Committee has selected Representative Baker, a Republican member of Congress who is actively involved in a number of controversial political issues and is an alumnus of your college. The board of trustees for the college is thrilled with the choice of a conservative speaker, but many students on campus have given the announcement a lukewarm reception. Three days before the speaker's scheduled visit, an article in the student newspaper reveals that Representative Baker was a member of a white supremacist group when he was in college. The article reports that the white supremacist group still exists, and it lists the group's web site, which is full of racist statements.

Many students and faculty are now denouncing the Campus Speaker Committee for inviting such a person. The trustees and the school's president downplay the representative's former involvement in the group and continue to support his speaking on campus. The committee now must meet to decide whether or not to revoke Representative Baker's invitation to speak on campus.

Apply what you have learned about leadership, decision making, problem solving, and conflict resolution as you ponder and discuss the following questions: As the chair, what leadership style would be most conducive to helping the committee members reach a decision? Which theoretical approaches to leadership might help you reach a decision about the best approach to take? How will you use the three criteria essential for effective group problem solving to reach a decision? How will you deal with any conflict that arises as the committee members discuss the options?

Additional Resources

Crawford, L. (1997). Conflict and Tao. *Howard Journal of Communications, 8*(4), 357–370. Exegesis of an ancient Chinese text along with other sources to explore "what philosophical Taoism can teach about managing interpersonal conflict."

International Journal of Conflict Management. This English language professional journal contains many articles about conflict management across cultures.

Samovar, L. A., Porter, R. E., & Stefani, L. A. (1998). *Communication between cultures* (3rd ed.). Belmont, CA: Wadsworth. See, especially, chap. 7, Cultural influences on context: The business setting, pp. 175–197.

Tinsley, C. (1998). Models of conflict resolution in Japanese, German, and American cultures. *Journal of Applied Psychology, 83*(2), 316–323.

References

Anderson, L. E., and Balzer, W. K. (1991). The effects of timing of leaders' opinions on problem-solving groups: A field experiment. *Group and Organization Studies, 16,* 86–101.

Baker, D. C. (1990, Winter). A qualitative and quantitative analysis of verbal style and the elimination of potential leaders in small groups. *Communication Quarterly, 38,* 13–26.

Bales, R. F. (1950). *Interaction process analysis.* Cambridge, MA: Addison-Wesley.

Barge, J. K. (1989, Fall). Leadership as medium: A leaderless group discussion model. *Communication Quarterly, 37,* 237–247.

Barge, J. K., & Hirokawa, R. Y. (1989). Toward a communication competency model of group leadership. *Small Group Behavior, 20,* 167–189.

Bayless, O. L. (1967). An alternative model for problem solving discussion. *Journal of Communication, 17,* 188–197.

Benne, K. D., & Sheats, P. (1948). Functional roles of group members. *Journal of Social Issues, 4,* 41–49.

Bennis, W., & Nanus, B. (1985). *Leaders: The strategies for taking charge.* New York: Harper & Row, 1985.

Bormann, E. G. (1990). *Small group discussion: Theory and practice* (3rd ed.). New York: Harper & Row.

Brilhart, J. K. (1966). An experimental comparison of three techniques for communicating a problem solving pattern to members of a discussion group. *Speech Monographs, 33,* 168–177.

Brilhart, J. K., & Jochem, L. M. (1964). Effects of different patterns on outcomes of problem-solving discussions. *Journal of Applied Psychology, 48,* 175–179.

Chiu, R. K., Wong, M. M., & Kosinski, Jr., F. (1998). Confucian values and conflict behavior of Asian managers: A comparison of two countries. *Social Behavior and Personality, 26*(1), 11–22.

Counselman, E. F. (1991, May). Leadership in a long term leaderless group. *Small Group Research, 22,* 240–257.

Cronshaw, S. F., & Ellis, R. J. (1991). A process investigation of self-monitoring and leader emergence. *Small Group Research, 22,* 403–420.

Dewey, J. E. (1910). *How we think.* Boston: D. C. Heath.

Drecksell, G. L. (1984). *Interaction characteristics of emergent leadership.* Unpublished doctoral dissertation, University of Utah.

Elsayed-Ekhouly, S. M., & Buda, R. (1996, January). Organizational conflict: A comparative analysis of conflict styles across cultures. *International Journal of Conflict Management, 7*(1), 71–80.

Fisher, B. A. (1985). Leadership as medium: Treating complexity in group communication research. *Small Group Behavior, 16,* 167–196.

French, J. R. P., & Raven, B. (1981). The bases of social power. In D. Cartwright & A. Zander (Eds.), *Group dynamics: Research and theory* (3rd ed.). New York: McGraw-Hill.

Geier, J. C. (1967). A trait approach to the study of leadership in small groups. *Journal of Communication, 17,* 316–323.

Gire, J. T. (1997, January). The varying effect of individualism-collectivism on preference for methods of conflict resolution. *Canadian Journal of Behavioral Science, 29*(1), 38–43.

Gouran, D. S., Brown, C., & Henry, D. R. (1978). Behavioral correlates of perceptions of quality in decision-making discussions.

Communication Monographs, 45, 62.

Gouran, D. S., & Hirokawa, R. Y. (1986). Counteractive functions of communication in effective group decision-making. In R. Y. Hirokawa and M. S. Poole (Eds.), *Communication and group decision-making.* Beverly Hills, CA: Sage.

Graen, G., Dansereau, G., & Minami, T. (1972). Dysfunctional leadership styles. *Organizational Behavior and Human Performance, 7,* 216–236.

Guetzkow, H., & Gyr, J. (1954). An analysis of conflict in decision-making groups. *Human Relations, 7,* 367–382.

Hackman, M. Z., & Johnson, C. E. (1991). *Leadership: A communication perspective.* Prospect Heights, IL: Waveland Press.

Hersey, P., & Blanchard, K. (1972). *Management of organizational behavior: Utilizing human resources* (2nd ed.). Englewood Cliffs, NJ: Prentice Hall.

Hersey, P., & Blanchard, K. (1980). So you want to know your leadership style? In P. V. Lewis & J. Williams, *Readings in organizational communication* (pp. 219–234). Columbus, OH: Grid Publishers.

Hirokawa, R. Y. (1983). Group communication and problem-solving effectiveness: II. An investigation of procedural functions. *Western Journal of Speech Communication, 47,* 59–74.

Hirokawa, R. Y. (1985). Discussion procedures and decision-making performance. *Human Communication Research, 12,* 203–224.

Hirokawa, R. Y. (1992). Communication and group decision-making efficacy. In R. S. Cathcart & L. A. Samovar (Eds.), *Small group communication: A reader.* Dubuque, IA: William C. Brown.

Hirokawa, R. Y., & Rost, K. M. (1991, November). *Effective group decision making in organizations: A field test of the vigilant interaction theory.* Paper presented at the meeting of the Speech Communication Association, Atlanta, GA.

Hocker, J. L., & Wilmont, W. W. (1991). *Interpersonal conflict* (3rd ed.). Dubuque, IA: William C. Brown.

Hollander, E. P. (1978). *Leadership dynamics.* New York: Free Press.

Janis, I. L. (1983). *Groupthink: Psychological studies of policy decisions and fiascoes* (2nd ed.). Boston: Houghton Mifflin.

Jurma, W. E. (1978). Leadership structuring style, task ambiguity and group members' satisfaction. *Small Group Behavior, 9,* 124–134.

Jurma, W. E. (1979). Effects of leader structuring style and task-orientation characteristics of group members. *Communication Monographs, 46,* 282.

Kenny, D. A., & Zaccaro, S. J. (1983). An estimate of variance due to traits in leadership. *Journal of Applied Psychology, 68,* 678–685.

Kreps, G. L. (1990). *Organizational communication* (2nd ed.). New York: Longman.

Larson, C. E. (1969). Forms of analysis and small group problem solving. *Speech Monographs, 36,* 452–455.

Larson, C. E., & LaFasto, F. M. J. (1989). *Teamwork: What must go right/what can go wrong.* Newbury Park, CA: Sage.

Lashbrook, V. J. (1975, December). *Gibb's interaction theory: The use of perceptions in the discrimination of leaders from nonleaders.* Paper presented at the meeting of the Speech Communication Association, Houston, Texas.

Maier, N. R. F., & Maier, R. A. (1957). An experimental test of the effects of "developmental" vs. "free" discussions on the quality of group decisions. *Journal of Applied Psychology, 41,* 320–323.

Maier, N. R. G., & Solem, A. R. (1952). The contributions of a discussion leader to the quality of group thinking: The effective use of minority opinions. *Human Relations, 5,* 277–288.

Morris, C. G., & Hackman, J. R. (1969). Behavioral correlates of perceived leadership. *Journal of Personality and Social Psychology, 13,* 350–361.

Osborn, A. (1975). *Applied imagination.* New York: Scribner's.

Poole, M. S. (1983a). Decision development in small groups: II. A study of multiple sequences in decision making. *Communication*

Monographs, 50, 224–225.

Poole, M. S. (1983b). Decision development in small groups: III. A multiple sequence model of group decision development. *Communication Monographs, 50,* 321–341.

Poole, M. S., & Doelger, J. A. (1986). Developmental processes in group decision-making. In R. Y. Hirokawa & M. S. Poole, *Communication and group decision-making* (pp. 35–61). Newbury Park, CA: Sage.

Preston, M. G., & Heintz, R. K. (1949). Effectiveness of participatory versus supervisory leadership in group judgment. *Journal of Abnormal and Social Psychology, 44,* 344–345.

Putnam, L., & Wilson, C. (1982). Communication strategies in organizational conflict: Reliability and validity of a measurement scale. In M. Burgoon (Ed.), *Communication yearbook 6.* Beverly Hills, CA: Sage.

Rosenfeld, L. B. (1976). *Now that we're all here . . . relations in small groups.*

Columbus, OH: Charles E. Merrill.

Rosenfeld, L. B., & Plax, T. B. (1975). Personality determinants of autocratic and democratic leadership. *Speech Monographs, 42,* 203–208.

Russell, H. C. (1970, April). *Dimensions of communicative behavior of discussion leaders.* Paper presented at the Central States Speech Convention.

Schutz, W. C. (1979). The leader as completer. In R. S. Cathcart & L. A. Samovar (Eds.), *Small group communication: A reader* (3rd ed.). Dubuque, IA: William C. Brown.

Smith, H. W. (1989). Group versus individual problem solving and type of problem solved. *Small Group Behavior, 20,* 357–366.

Snyder, M. (1979). Self-monitoring processes. In L. Berkowitz, *Advances in experi-mental social psychol-ogy* (12th ed.). New York: Academic Press.

Sorenson, R. L., & Savage, G. T. (1989). Signaling participation through relational communication:

A test of the leader interpersonal influence model. *Group and Organization Studies, 14,* 325–354.

Stogdill, R. M. (1974). *Handbook of leadership: A survey of theory and research.* New York: Free Press.

Tinsley, C. H. (1997). Understanding conflict in a Chinese cultural context. In R. J. Lewici et al. (Eds.), *Research on negotiation in organizations* (Vol. 6, pp. 209–225). Greenwich, CT: JAI Press.

Vroom, V. H. (1973). A new look at management decision-making. *Organizational Dynamics,* 66–80.

Weick, K. (1978). The spines of leaders. In M. McCall & M. Lombardo (Eds.), *Leadership: Where else can we go?* (pp. 37–61). Durham, NC: Duke University Press.

White, R. K., & Lippett, R. (1960). Leader behavior and member ration in three "social climates." In D. Cartwright & A. Zander, *Group dynamics: Research and theory* (2nd ed.). Evanston, IL: Row, Peterson.

Wood, J. T. (1977). Leading in purposive discussions: A study of adaptive behaviors. *Communication Monographs, 44,* 152–165.

Zaccaro, S. J., Foti, R. J., & Kenny, D. A. (1991). Self-monitoring and trait-based variance in leadership: An investigation of leader flexibility across multiple group situations. *Journal of Applied Psychology, 76,* 308–315.

Fundamentals of Public Speaking:

Preparation and Delivery

PART 4 CONSISTS OF SIX CHAPTERS dedicated to various aspects of public communication: Chapter 11, Topic Selection and Audience Analysis; Chapter 12, Finding Information and Establishing Credibility; Chapter 13, Organizing Your Speech; Chapter 14, Communication Apprehension, Delivery, and Visual Resources; Chapter 15, The Informative Speech; and Chapter 16, Persuasive and Presentational Speaking. An appendix, at the end of the text, provides a quick overview of how to interview for information and employment.

When you have read and thought about this chapter, you will be able to:

1. Brainstorm and do personal inventories to identify speech topics.

2. Evaluate possible topics to determine topic involvement.

3. Show how to narrow a general topic for a 5-minute speech.

4. Analyze an audience by using all four levels of audience analysis.

5. Provide an example of a belief, an attitude, and a value.

6. Recognize the difficulty of changing beliefs, attitudes, and values.

7. Develop strategies for adapting yourself and your message to an audience.

11

Topic Selection and Audience Analysis

This chapter focuses on topic selection and audience analysis. Often, finding something to speak about seems difficult because you have so many choices. The overall goal of this chapter is to teach you techniques that will make you more comfortable with the process of selecting a topic and analyzing your audience, which in turn will start you on a path toward being a more effective and confident public speaker. This chapter will provide you with techniques for quickly determining a speech topic appropriate to both you and your audience, for analyzing and adapting your message to your audience, and for limiting your topic.

Rosita was worried. Her teacher had assigned her first speech, and she had only 1 week to prepare for it. The first two days after the assignment she found herself pondering topic ideas whenever she had a spare moment, but she didn't use any of the techniques her teacher suggested for selecting a topic.

On the third day, she started getting a little nervous about the impending deadline, so she decided to sit down and do some brainstorming. She had some success with that, but she figured it wouldn't hurt to try conducting a personal inventory as well. After coming up with several topic ideas, Rosita decided to sleep on it for a night before making a final decision about which topic was best for her.

On the fourth day, Rosita decided she would speak about "the health benefits of yoga." Since she had been taking a yoga class for over a year and had read a lot about yoga, Rosita knew it was a topic that she was both interested in and knowledgeable about. She had already sufficiently narrowed down the topic, so she knew her research wouldn't take too much time. Although she got off to a slow start, Rosita managed to get her speech done on time, and it even generated some positive comments from her classmates.

This chapter will help you avoid the worry Rosita experienced when faced with the prospect of selecting a speech topic.

How Do I Select a Topic?

In this section, you will examine two methods for selecting a speech topic: individual brainstorming and personal inventories. Then you will read about the importance of evaluating your involvement in and knowledge of a subject.

Individual Brainstorming

brainstorming

Naming as many ideas as a group or an individual can within a limited period of time.

Brainstorming is *thinking of as many topics as you can in a limited time so that you can select one topic that will be appropriate for you and your audience.* While group brainstorming can be a useful technique for selecting a topic for group discussion, individual brainstorming can be an equally effective way to find a topic for your public speech. Indeed, this technique can help you generate many speech topics. Most students find this method more productive than trying to think of just one topic for their speech.

You'll find individual brainstorming to be relatively quick and easy. First, give yourself a limited time—say, 5 minutes—and without trying to think of fancy titles or even complete thoughts, write down as many topics as you can. When your time is up, you should have a rough list of possible ideas or topics for your speech. This step can be repeated if you want an even larger list from which to choose. Second, select the *three* items from your list that are the most appealing to you as topics for your speech. Third, from those three topics choose the *one* that you think would be most appealing to both you and your audience.

Personal Inventories

Another way to find a topic for your speech is to conduct **personal invento-ries,** *surveys of your reading and viewing habits and behaviors.* You make choices every time you read, watch a television or movie, or surf the Internet. You can learn more about your own interests by examining carefully what you choose to read, what you like to watch, and which web sites you find most appealing. What kinds of books do you read? A person who reads only science fiction exhibits quite different interests than someone who prefers bi-ographies. Do you go to the movies or rent videos? The person who watches international movies reveals different interests than the person who watches horror films and musicals.

Public speaking starts with the self—with what you know, have experi-enced, or are willing to learn. Self-analysis, through personal inventories, can help you assess the areas in which you are qualified to speak.

Your personal inventories of viewing, reading, and using the Internet are just three rough indications of your interests. You may also wish to conduct inventories of your hobbies, leisure activities, and talents, the music you listen to, the organizations you belong to, the plays you attend, the jobs you've had, the elective courses you've taken, or the courses you've taken for your major.

Personal inventories should help you identify your own interests and preferences—including some of which you may not have been fully aware. Finding out how the topic relates to you is an early step in topic selection; how the topic relates to the listeners is a later consideration. Now you are ready to assess your personal involvement in and knowledge of the topic.

personal inventories

A speaker's surveys of his or her reading and viewing habits and behavior to discover what topics are of personal interest.

TRY ◀▶ THIS

Look around your room and determine what your possessions, decorations, and the way in which they are arranged say about you, your habits, and your interests.

Involvement in the Topic

After you have selected a possible topic area, you should evaluate the topic to see if you have the appropriate involvement in and knowledge of the subject. **Involvement** is simply a measure of *the importance of a topic to the speaker.*

Your brainstorming and personal inventories might have shown that you have an interest in many topics. However, you may not be involved in those particular areas. For example, you could be interested in sports because they allow you a kind of escape from everyday concerns, but you might not be highly involved in sports. How can you tell the difference between mere inter-est and involvement? What difference does it make whether a speaker is in-volved in a topic?

involvement

The importance of the topic to the speaker; determined by the strength of the feelings the speaker has about the topic and the time and energy the speaker devotes to that topic.

The selection of a topic for a public speech may emerge from your own interests or experiences.

One measure of involvement is how much time you put into a topic area. What if you find, through brainstorming and conducting personal inventories, that one of your interests is computers? You could probably consider yourself involved in computers if you spend time around them, learn how they work, read articles about them, and spend time in computer shops to see what new hardware and software are available. The amount of time you spend with your topic is, then, one measure of your involvement. *A second measure of involvement is how much effort you expend on a particular interest.* The person who is really involved in politics is much more than a passive observer. That person knows the candidates and politicians, works on campaigns, helps bring out the voters, reads about politics, talks with other interested persons, and joins groups with a similar interest. Involvement, then, is measured by the time and effort you commit to your subject.

Determining whether or not a speaker is involved in a speech topic is easy. An involved speaker speaks with conviction, passion, and authority. The involved speaker gives many verbal and nonverbal indications of caring about the topic. The person who is only trying to fulfill an assignment cannot convey the sense of involvement so important in public speaking. Usually, you will find that the speaker who really cares about the topic being discussed is often successful at getting you involved in the topic as well.

TRY ◄►THIS

For 2 days track how you spend your time on-line. How does the time you spend at your computer reflect your interests?

Knowledge of the Topic

After you have selected a topic area and determined your own involvement in the subject, you need to assess your personal knowledge of the subject. What do you know about the subject that can be communicated to your audience? Your knowledge about the topic comes primarily from three sources: yourself, other people, and such resources as books, films, magazines, television, newspapers, and your computer.

11.1 TOPIC SELECTION

Fill in the blanks:

1. Two measures of involvement in a topic are how much _____ and _____ go into that topic.

2. Brainstorming is thinking of as many topics as you can in a _____ _____.

3. After you have selected a topic area and have determined your own involvement in the subject, you need to assess your _____ _____ of the subject.

4. One way to find a topic for your speech is to conduct _____ _____, or surveys of your habits and behaviors.

Answers: 1. time / effort   2. limited time   3. personal knowledge   4. personal inventories

First, determine what you know about your subject from *your own experience*. Do you have experience that has not been shared by many other people? Have you raised children, worked at interesting jobs, served in the armed forces, traveled to unusual places, or done things that few can claim?

After determining what you know about a topic from your personal experience, you should turn to *other people* who might know more about the topic than you do. You can make your speech stronger by talking to people in your community or at your college or university who are knowledgeable about your topic. A telephone call, personal interview, or e-mail exchange can often provide you with some ideas and quotations for your speech that will show you cared enough about the subject to bring your audience current, expert information.

You can also bolster your knowledge of a topic by turning to *resources* such as magazines, books, films, newspapers, computer-accessed information services, and television. These resources can help you fill in information about your topic that you do not already know, and they will increase your credibility as a speaker.

Remember that when you get information from another person or from a resource, you must credit that person or resource. In other words, you must tell your audience that you got the information from someplace other than your own personal experience.

Robert M. Smith, of Alma College in Michigan, suggests there are four benchmarks in selecting a topic. First is whether the speaker can handle the topic. Second is whether the topic is appropriate, given the audience's age and educational, political, and religious characteristics. Third is the occasion. Can the speaker fit the selected topic into the class and the time limits? Finally, a speaker must consider if he or she can find the available information within the deadline. Can the information be gathered within the week or month you have to complete the assignment?

How Do I Narrow My Topic?

Brainstorming techniques and personal inventories can yield topic areas appropriate for you, but they may be too broad. A personal inventory may show that a speech on the topic of small-business administration is a good one for you, but it could take days or weeks to deliver because so much information is available on the subject. The advantage of starting with a very narrow topic is that it renders much information on the subject irrelevant. Only a small amount of the available information will be related to your narrowed topic; thus, your research will be highly focused, and you will not end up spending a lot of time obtaining information you cannot use.

The most common way to narrow a topic is to make it more specific and concrete. The small-business administration topic, for instance, can be narrowed to health care administration in your part of the country. You may even find it necessary to narrow the topic further, such as administration in hospitals or leadership in facilities for those with eating disorders. After carefully considering the audience's interests in the various kinds of small-business administrations, you might end up delivering a speech on the administrative hierarchy in the city's psychiatric wards.

One method of narrowing a topic is suggested by the small-business administration example just described. An abstract category discovered through brainstorming or personal inventories can be narrowed by listing smaller categories directly related to that topic. The abstract topic "college," for example, might yield the following smaller categories directly related to it:

- Application process for state colleges
- Application process for out-of-state schools
- Where to apply for financial aid
- On-campus residence
- Programs of study

A slightly different approach to narrowing a topic involves taking a broad category, such as music, and listing as many smaller topics as you can that are at least loosely related to that topic:

- The development of country/western music

- The influence of rock music on our youth
- Rap artists
- Music therapy
- Why any good song sounds bad in an elevator
- Music education at the elementary school level
- The history of the mandolin
- Country singers who serve as role models

The list of more specific and concrete topics can be extended until you have a large number from which to choose.

How will you know if your topic is narrow enough? There is no easy answer. Several things to consider are (1) the amount of information available on the narrowed topic, (2) the amount of information that can be conveyed within the time limits for the speech, and (3) whether or not the narrowed topic can be discussed with enough depth to keep audience members interested and increase their knowledge.

The advice in these sections on how to find and narrow a topic should help you choose a topic for your speech. If all these suggestions fail, you may wish to examine the potential speech topics in Table 11.1. These topics came from successful student speeches. Another idea worth considering is to generate a similar list of current topics with your classmates.

TABLE 11.1 POTENTIAL SPEECH TOPICS

AIDS protection	Death sentence	Birth control	Hazards of smoking
Cancer prevention	Pro-life/Pro-choice	Spouse abuse	Spirituality
Dealing with stress	Drug testing	Homelessness	Environmental consciousness
Diabetes	Choosing a computer	Getting in shape	How to lose weight
Child support	What is a "liberal"?	Lab animals	Decriminalizing drugs
Guns in schools	Women's rights	Donating organs	Drinking and driving
Organ donation	Child adoption	Foods to avoid	Effective study habits
The drinking age	The best jobs	Victims' rights	Greenhouse effect
Date rape	Crime rates	Financial aid	Your country of origin
Immigration rules	Cholesterol	Suicide	Living with roommates
Donating blood	Vitamins	TV violence	Big brothers/Big sisters
Alcoholism	Voting	Recycling	Choosing software
Service learning	Marriage	Pets	Gun control

How Do I Analyze My Audience?

Audience analysis is *the collection and interpretation of data on the demographics, attitudes, values, and beliefs of the audience obtained through observation, inferences, questionnaires, or interviews.* Why should you analyze your audience? Especially, why should you analyze your audience if it consists of your own classmates? Before we start talking about *how* to analyze an audience, we need to explain *why* we analyze an audience.

audience analysis

The collection and interpretation of data on the demographics, attitudes, values, and beliefs of the audience obtained by observation, inferences, questionnaires, or interviews.

Let us say you are going to give an informative speech on interest rates. Would you give that speech to a beginning communication class that consisted mainly of business majors in the same way as you would if the class consisted mainly of arts and sciences majors? Let us say you are going to give a persuasive speech on abortion. Would it matter to you that the audience consisted of many persons whose religious beliefs prohibited abortion? In short, how would you know the majors, religious beliefs, and interests of your audience unless you analyzed the audience?

Audience analysis is similar to target marketing in advertising and public relations. Analysis can be as simple as "eyeballing" a group to estimate age, gender, and race or as complicated as polling people to discover their predispositions on your topic. The information that follows is designed to make you more insightful about how you approach an audience and to invite you to think carefully about the people to whom you speak so that you can be as effective as possible.

Four Levels of Audience Analysis

To begin, we will survey four levels of audience analysis. The categories are called *levels* because the first is relatively easy and the last is more difficult to understand and to use. In that sense, the levels are like grade levels in school: The ideas and concepts increase in difficulty. The four levels begin with the distinction between captive and voluntary audiences.

Level 1: Captive and Voluntary Audiences

captive audience

An audience that has not chosen to hear a particular speaker or speech.

A **captive audience,** as the name suggests, is *an audience that has not chosen to hear a particular speaker or speech.* The teacher of a required class addresses a captive audience. A disc jockey who broadcasts commercial announcements between the songs you want to hear addresses a captive audience. Similarly, a student who addresses fellow students in a required speech class is addressing a captive audience.

Why should a public speaker distinguish a captive from a voluntary audience? One reason is that a captive audience has not chosen to hear from you or about your subject—you may have to motivate the participants to listen. Another is that captive audiences are **heterogeneous,** *characterized by many differences among individuals.* The speaker must adapt the topic and the content of the speech to a wider range of information and to more diverse atti-

heterogeneous

Characterized by many differences among individuals.

Classroom speakers generally face a captive audience.

tudes toward the subject. One of the advantages of a captive audience is that it gives the speaker an opportunity to present ideas to people who, under ordinary circumstances, might never have heard the information or the point of view embodied in the speech.

The **voluntary audience** *chooses to listen to the particular speaker or speech.* The most important characteristic of the voluntary audience is that the participants have a need or desire to hear the speech. The people who go to listen to a politician are usually sympathetic to the speaker's ideas. The students who stop to hear a traveling evangelist speak on the campus lawn may be curious about, or perhaps even committed to, the speaker's religious beliefs. The advantage of a voluntary audience is that the speaker addresses an audience that is more **homogeneous;** that is, *audience members are more like one another.* Addressing a captive audience is like attempting to attract new customers to a product; addressing a voluntary audience is like attempting to please customers who have previously purchased the product. A speaker is helped by knowing whether the audience is voluntary or captive because the nature of the audience affects the topic, rationale, approach, and goal of the speaker.

The task of determining the character of an audience is important. A specific example can demonstrate its complexity: At first, you might guess that a congregation is a voluntary audience—people choose to attend a particular church to hear a particular minister. What about the children in the congregation? Did they choose to hear the sermon, or did their parents make them go to church? What about some of the husbands and wives? How many people are present because their spouses wanted them to come along? To what extent did social pressures persuade some of these people to attend church? Did the audience members really know what the minister was going to say, or are they captives of the message that is being delivered?

voluntary audience

A collection of people who choose to listen to a particular speaker or speech.

homogeneous

Characterized by similarities among individuals.

Demographic
characteristics reveal
important informa-
tion about an
audience.

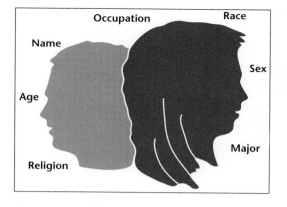

Even this first level of audience analysis is more challenging than it appears. The minister of a congregation addresses an audience that is in some ways voluntary and in some ways captive, so the minister must adapt the message to those differences.

How can you, in your class, make the distinction between a voluntary audience and a captive audience? You may find that your audience is more captive than voluntary—the members of the audience did not enroll in the class to hear you or your speech. On the other hand, they are there to learn how to give and to listen to speeches. You may have to adapt to your audience by ensuring that the students know why *you* are speaking to *them* about *this* particular subject. You will actually find yourself more dependent than most speakers on the voluntary audiences. They know from experience and investigation what their audience wants to hear. You will probably have to learn about your audience through the methods suggested in this chapter.

Level 2: Demographic Analysis

demographic
analysis

The collection and
interpretation of
data about the
characteristics of
people, excluding
their attitudes,
values, and beliefs.

The term *demographics* literally means "the characteristics of the people." **Demographic analysis** is *the collection and interpretation of data about the characteristics you write on forms: name, age, sex, hometown, year in school, race, major subject, religion, and organizational affiliations.* Such information can be important to public speakers by revealing the extent to which they will have to adapt themselves and their topics to an audience.

A closer look at one item might demonstrate the importance of demographic information about an audience. Let us see what the effect might be of your audience's majors. Suppose you plan to speak about the cost of littering in your state. Your audience consists of 21 students: 7 have not chosen a major subject, 3 are mathematics majors, 4 are biology majors, 6 are majoring in business administration, and 1 is an English major. This information gives you no reason to assume that any of them know much about littering, but you can assume that 9 to 13 audience members have a basic understanding of numbers: The business majors may have a better understanding of costs than the others, and the students majoring in math and science may find the cost-benefit approach attractive as well.

If you add more demographic information to that small bit of information, then you can find even more to guide you. Does your college attract students who are likely to be concerned about the expense of littering? Is your audience likely to be knowledgeable about rural or urban littering? Do any students in your audience belong to organizations concerned about conservation? Whatever your topic, the demographic characteristics of your audience can imply the audience's receptiveness to your topic.

Public speakers usually rely heavily on demographic information. Politicians send personnel ahead to find out how many blue-collar workers, faithful party members, elderly people, union members, and hecklers they are likely to encounter. They want to know how many and what kinds of cultural and co-cultural groups are likely to be present. They consult opinion polls, population studies, and reliable persons in the area to discover the nature of a prospective audience. Conducting a demographic analysis of your class can serve a similar purpose—analysis will help you design a speech better adapted to your audience.

Level 3: Audience Interest in and Knowledge of the Topic

As you move up the levels of audience analysis, the information you are asked to discover becomes more difficult to find. On level 3, your task is to determine the degree of **audience interest,** *the relevance and importance of the topic to an audience,* and the level of **audience knowledge,** *the amount of information the audience already has about the topic.* How familiar is your audience with the topic? This question is important because if your audience is disinterested in or unfamiliar with your topic, you will have to generate that interest in your speech.

One means of determining an audience's interest in and knowledge of a topic is to consider the "age" of the topic. Age and familiarity are closely related because the longer a topic has been around and the more recently it has gained importance, the more likely the audience is to know about it. Your classmates may know much about a topic that has been a burning issue in the student newspaper, but they may not know a great deal about nuclear fusion, power satellites, or the latest fashions. A topic that is old to a 45-year-old person can be new to a 19-year-old student. If you are addressing classmates of mixed ages, you would have to adapt both to persons who are familiar with the topic and to those who are not. Fortunately, old topics have new variations. Like people, topics live, change, and die—some have long and varied lives, whereas others pass quickly.

How can you gauge the audience's interest in and knowledge of your topic? One way to find out is to ask questions. You can ask demographic questions to help assess audience interest in your topic. The audience members' ages, majors, and organizational memberships can suggest their familiarity with, knowledge of, and interest in your topic. Ask your fellow students before and after classes, in the hallways and the cafeteria. Ask them in writing through a questionnaire, if your instructor encourages that kind of analysis. You can even ask for an indication of interest during your speech, by asking your classmates to raise their hands in response to such questions as these: How many of you watch television news? How many of you have been to Washington, DC? How many of you have read an unassigned book in the past 3 months?

audience interest

The relevance and importance of the topic to an audience; sometimes related to the uniqueness of the topic.

audience knowledge

The amount of information the audience already has about the topic.

Level 4: The Audience's Attitudes, Beliefs, and Values

attitude

A predisposition to respond favorably or unfavorably to a person, an object, an idea, or an event.

An **attitude** is *a predisposition to respond favorably or unfavorably to a person, an object, an idea, or an event.* The attitudes of audience members can be assessed through questionnaires, by careful observation, or even by asking the right questions. If your audience comes from a place where many attitudes, beliefs, and values are shared, your audience analysis may be easy. For example, a speech about safe sex would be heard in some colleges with as much excitement as a speech on snails; however, at other colleges, the same speech could be grounds for dismissal. Attitudes toward politics, sex, religion, war, and even work vary in different geographic areas and co-cultures. Regardless of the purpose of your speech, the attitudes of audience members will make a difference in the appropriateness of your topic. Some examples of attitudes follow:

Pro-war	Pro-business	Pro-technology
Antigovernment	Antimaterialism	Antiviolence
Anti-gun control	Pro-choice	Pro-tax
Pro-conformity	Anti-intellectual	Pro-diversity
Antipollution	Pro-life	Anti-immigrant
Anti-immigration	Antiexercise	Antigambling
Pro-animal rights	Pro-conservation	Pro-HMO

belief

A conviction; often thought to be more enduring than an attitude and less enduring than a value.

A **belief** is *a conviction.* Beliefs are usually considered more solid than attitudes, but our attitudes often spring from our beliefs. Your belief in good eating habits may lead to a negative attitude toward overeating and obesity and to a positive attitude toward balanced meals and nutrition. Your audience's beliefs make a difference in how the participants respond to your speech. They may believe in upward mobility through higher education, in higher pay through hard work, in the superiority of the family farm, in a lower tax base, or in social welfare. On the other hand, they may not believe in any of these ideas. Beliefs are like anchors to which our attitudes are attached. To discover the beliefs of an audience, you need to ask questions and to observe carefully. Some examples of beliefs follow:

Hard work pays off.	The Bible is God's word.
Taxes are too high.	Women are discriminated against.
Anyone can get rich.	The world gets better and better.
There is an afterlife.	Work comes before play.

value

A deeply rooted belief that governs our attitude about something.

A **value** is *a deeply rooted belief that governs our attitudes.* Both beliefs and attitudes can be traced to a value we hold. (Relationships among attitudes, beliefs, and values are illustrated in Figure 11.1.) Learned from childhood through the family, church, school, and many other sources, values are often

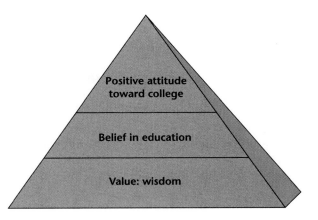

Figure 11.1 Relationships among attitudes, beliefs, and values.

so much a foundation for the rest of what we believe and know that they are not questioned. Sometimes we remain unaware of our primary values until they clash. For example, a person might have an unquestioned belief that every individual has the right to be and do whatever he or she wishes—basic values of individuality and freedom—until it comes to homosexuality. Sexual orientation as an aspect of individual freedom may clash with the person's value of individuality. The following are examples of values:

Marriage	Salvation	Beauty
Love	Equality	Law and Order
Friendship	Wisdom	Privacy
Courage	Happiness	Family
Freedom	Independence	Competition
Patriotism	Peace	Compassion
Religion	Loyalty	Faithfulness

The values held by your audience and the order in which the audience members rank these values can provide important clues about their attitudes and beliefs. A speaker who addresses an audience without knowing the values of the audience members is taking a risk that can be avoided through careful audience analysis.

Three Methods of Audience Analysis

This section examines three ways of analyzing an audience. The three methods are based on your observations of the audience, your inferences, and your questions and their answers.

Instant Recall

11.2 AUDIENCE ANALYSIS

Write the appropriate letter from the choices below in each blank:

A. Captive audience
B. Voluntary audience
C. Homogeneous audience
D. Demographic analysis
E. Attitudes, beliefs, and values
F. Heterogeneous audience

1. High school students listening to a speech in a required English course are considered a _____.

2. The audience is antigovernment. Its members think that government has too much control over their lives and that individual privacy is very important. This statement is an example of _____.

3. A group of Young Republicans is generally considered a _____.

4. A Republican legislator speaking to the Young Republicans is speaking to a _____.

5. You spent all morning collecting and interpreting data about the group you will be speaking to. This is an example of _____.

Answers: 1. A   2. E   3. C   4. B or C   5. D

Method 1: Observation

observation

Seeing and sensing the behavior and characteristics of an audience.

Effective public speakers must engage in active **observation,** *seeing and sensing the behavior and characteristics of their audience.* An effective lawyer selects an audience by questioning prospective jurors. The lawyer asks questions designed to discover prejudice, negative and positive attitudes, beliefs, and values. Later, as the witnesses testify, the lawyer observes their verbal and nonverbal behavior and decides which arguments, evidence, and witnesses are influencing the jurors. Evangelists know, from their many sermons, which Bible verses, parables, and testimonials bring sinners to the altar. People who speak on behalf of business associations, unions, political parties, colleges, and the underprivileged have usually spent years watching others and learning which approaches, arguments, and evidence are most likely to be accepted by an audience.

TRY ◀▶ THIS

Before each class, write down speech and demographic observations about the people sitting around you.

COMMUNICATION CHALLENGE

Ranking Values

Rank order five of the following values in their order of importance to you. If you can persuade some of your classmates, or the entire class, to do this as well, you will have information that will help you prepare your speech.

__ Wisdom	__ Equality	__ Fame
__ A comfortable life	__ Wealth	__ Health
__ A world at peace	__ Leisure	__ Love
__ Freedom	__ Security	__ Beauty
__ Maturity	__ Fulfillment	__ Relational satisfaction

How does your ranking compare to your classmates? What other values might help you with your speech?

SOURCE: Robert L. Heath, "Variability in Value System Priorities as Decision-Making Adaptation to Situational Differences," in *Communication Monographs*, 43: 325–333. © 1976 Speech Communication Association. Reprinted by permission of National Communication Association.

You can learn to observe your class. For every speech you give, you might listen to 20 or 25 given by others. You have a unique opportunity to discover your classmates' responses. Do they respond well to speakers who come on strong and authoritatively or to speakers who talk to them like equals? Do they like speeches about work, leisure, or ambition? Do they respond well to numbers and statistics, stories and examples, graphs and posters, or pictures and slides? As a listener in the classroom, you have a unique opportunity to observe your own and your classmates' responses to a variety of speakers.

You can also observe some demographic characteristics of your classmates: age, gender, race, and group affiliations (from athletic jackets and fraternity or sorority pins). You can see how your classmates respond to a speaker who keeps his or her eyes on the audience and how they respond to

The public speaker must consider differences in values among audience members.

one who depends heavily on notes. You can observe whether you and the audience respond favorably when the speaker is deeply involved in the speech. Every speech you hear will, in some way, indicate the speaker's attitudes, beliefs, and values.

Even though your audience may be more captive than most, you have an advantage over most public speakers. How many public speakers have an opportunity to hear every one of their listeners give a speech? Instead of sitting back like a passive observer, take advantage of the situation by listening actively, taking notes about each speaker's characteristics, and recording the audience's responses. You can analyze your audience continually by careful observation during a round of speeches.

Method 2: Inference

inference

A tentative conclusion based on some evidence.

To draw an **inference** is to draw *a tentative conclusion based on some evidence.* We draw an inference when we see someone dressed in rags and tentatively conclude the person is homeless. Our inferences are often accurate—we infer from a man's wedding band that he is married, from the children tugging at his sleeve he is a father, and from the woman holding his arm that she is his wife. We are basing these inferences on thin data, but they are probably correct. However, inferences can also be incorrect. The more evidence on which an inference is based, the more likely it is to be true.

You can base inferences on the observed characteristics of your audience, on demographic information, and on the information taken from questionnaires. You can draw inferences either indirectly or directly. An indirect way to draw inferences is by observation. You might, for example, find that 85 percent of the students at a particular university hold part-time jobs (an observation). You might infer that the school is expensive, that financial aid is limited, or that the cost of area housing is high. You might also infer, from your limited information, that most of the students in this school value their education, are exceptionally well motivated, or believe in saving money for future plans.

A more direct way to gather data on which to base inferences is to ask questions. You could, for example, ask either orally or in writing how many students in the class have part- or full-time jobs; how many are married, have families, have grown children; how many plan to become wealthy; whether they were raised in an urban or a rural setting; and how many have strong religious ties. The answers to these questions would provide valuable information about your audience.

To illustrate how this method works, let us examine one question, one answer, and some inferences that could be drawn from the information. The question is: How many students in your class are married? The answer may be 15 out of 25. From this data, several inferences can be drawn. First, the students are probably older than the average person enrolled in college. Second, they may be part-time students who are also raising a family or holding a job. Finally, they are motivated and mature enough to prepare for a class and handle a marriage and home. These inferences can assist you in preparing the content of your speech. For example, if your strongest inference is that these individuals are also raising a family, certain topics will hold greater interest than others. Such topics as setting priorities and saving money for the future may engage this audience. Conversely, a speech about dorm food, intermural athletics, or study abroad may be met with disinterest.

Method 3: The Questionnaire

A more formal way to collect data on which you can base inferences is to ask your audience to fill out a **questionnaire** consisting of *written questions developed to obtain demographic and attitudinal information*. Demographic information can be easily gathered and summarized from questions similar to those that follow:

questionnaire

A set of written questions developed to obtain demographic and attitudinal information.

_____1. I am   (*a*) a first-year student.
              (*b*) a sophomore.
              (*c*) a junior.
              (*d*) a senior.
_____2. I am   (*a*) under 18.
              (*b*) 18–21 years old.
              (*c*) 22–27 years old.
              (*d*) over 27.
_____3. I am   (*a*) single.
              (*b*) married.
              (*c*) divorced or separated.
              (*d*) widowed.
_____4. I have (*a*) no children.
              (*b*) one child.
              (*c*) two children.
              (*d*) more than two children.

The audience members do not have to identify themselves by name to provide this information. Keeping the questionnaires anonymous encourages honest answers and does not reduce the value of the information.

Attitudinal information can be collected in at least three ways. *One way is to ask questions that place audience members in identifiable groups,* as these questions do:

_____5. I (*a*) am active in campus organizations.
        (*b*) am not active in campus organizations.
_____6. I see myself as (*a*) conservative.
                    (*b*) liberal.
                    (*c*) independent.
_____7. I see myself as (*a*) strongly religious.
                    (*b*) moderately religious.
                    (*c*) unreligious.

A second method of gaining attitudinal information is to ask people to rank values, such as hard work, higher education, high pay, and security. People's ranking of their values can suggest additional information about their attitudes and beliefs.

COMMUNICATION CHALLENGE

Attitudinal Scale

Next to each word or phrase, indicate your attitude toward it by writing in the appropriate number: (1) strongly favor, (2) mildly favor, (3) neutral, (4) mildly disfavor, or (5) strongly disfavor.

____ a.	Internet censorship	____ h.	Alcohol consumption
____ b.	Recycling	____ i.	Welfare
____ c.	Gun control	____ j.	Military
____ d.	Minority groups	____ k.	Recreational drugs
____ e.	Divorce	____ l.	Religion
____ f.	Government controls	____ m.	Telemarketing
____ g.	Women's rights	____ n.	The U.S. president

Compile data that indicate the attitudes within your class on one of these topics. What does this information tell you about how to approach your audience about this topic?

The third method of collecting data about people's attitudes involves listing word concepts that reveal attitudes and then asking respondents to assess their attitudes toward these specific issues. One way to do this is to use an attitudinal scale like the one in the Communication Challenge above. The reactions to these and similar words or phrases can provide information that will help you approach your audience successfully. For example, if most persons in your audience are neutral to mildly favorable toward abortion, then your speech advocating abortion could be designed to raise their attitudes from mildly favorable to strongly favorable. If the responses are negative, then you may have to work just to move your audience closer to a mildly disfavorable attitude or toward neutrality.

How Do I Adapt to the Audience?

Analysis of an audience yields information about your listeners that enables you to adapt yourself and your verbal and nonverbal codes to that audience. A speech is not a message imposed on a collection of listeners; a speech is negotiated between a speaker and an audience and is designed to inform, entertain, inspire, teach, or persuade that audience. This negotiation is based on your analysis of your audience.

An important question to consider in adapting to an audience is, "How do I adapt to an audience without letting the audience dictate my position?" The answer is that you do not analyze the audience to discover your own po-

11.3 METHODS OF AUDIENCE ANALYSIS

Write T *for true or* F *for false in each blank on the left:*

_____ 1. Listening to your classmates' speeches and observing their nonverbal behavior in class is one kind of audience analysis.

_____ 2. If you observe that most people in your audience speak English as one of their multiple languages, you could draw an inference that the audience is mainly foreign born.

_____ 3. Audience members are more likely to tell the truth about themselves if they do not have to place their names on the questionnaire.

_____ 4. Asking audience members to indicate their response to word concepts on a scale is a way of assessing attitudes.

Answers: 1. T   2. T   3. T   4. T

sition but to discover theirs—how much do they know about the topic? What approach is most likely to persuade persons with their attitudes, beliefs, and values? Finding out, for example, that an audience is likely to be utterly opposed to your position is not an indication that you should alter your position on the issue. Instead you may have to adopt a more gradual approach to changing your listeners than you would have liked to use. Similarly, discovering that the audience is even more ignorant of the topic than you thought only indicates you will have to provide more background or more elementary information than you had originally planned. In short, you have to adapt yourself, your verbal and nonverbal codes, your topic, your purpose, and your supporting materials to the particular group of people you will face during your speech.

Adapting Yourself

In public speaking, the speaker also has to adjust to information about the audience. Just as the college senior preparing for a job interview adapts to the interviewer in dress, manner, and language, the public speaker prepares for an audience by adapting to its expectations. How you look, how you behave, and what you say should be carefully adjusted to an audience you have learned about through observation, experience, and analysis.

Adapting Your Verbal and Nonverbal Codes

The language you use in your speech, as well as your gestures, movements, and even facial expressions, should be adapted to your audience. Does your experience, observation, and analysis of the audience's attitudes indicate your language should be conversational, formal, cynical, or technical? Does your analysis indicate your listeners like numbers and statistics? Do your observations indicate you should pace the stage or stand still behind the lectern? Does your analysis indicate you should not use taboo words in your speech lest you alienate your group, or does the audience like a little lively language?

Adapting Your Topic

Public speakers should be permitted to speak about any topic that fits the assignment. In the classroom, at least, you should select a topic that relates to you. Remember, you will be giving your speech to an audience of classmates; therefore, the topic you select must be adapted to them. Audience analysis is a means of discovering the audience's position on the topic. From information based on observation, description, and inference, you have to decide how you are going to adapt your topic to this audience.

Audience analysis can tell you what challenges you face. If you want to speak in favor of physician-assisted suicide and your audience analysis indicates the majority of your listeners are opposed to that position, you need not conclude the topic is inappropriate. You may, however, adapt to the members of your audience by starting with a position closer to theirs. Your initial step might be to make audience members feel less comfortable about their present position so that they are more prepared to hear your position.

Your analysis might indicate your audience already has considerable information about your topic. You then may have to adapt by locating information the audience does not have. For example, you may want to deliver an informative speech about the latest world crisis, but your analysis may indicate the audience is not only already interested but also has sufficient information of the sort you planned to offer. You can adapt your topic by shifting to the area of the subject about which the audience is not so well informed: What is the background of the situation? What are the backgrounds of the personalities and the issues? What do the experts think will happen? What are the possible consequences?

Adapting Your Purpose

You should also adapt the purpose of your speech to your audience. Teachers often ask students to state the purpose of a speech—what do you want your audience to know, understand, or do? To think of your speech as one part of a series of informative talks your audience will hear about your topic may help. Your listeners have probably heard something about the topic before, and they are likely to hear about the topic again. Your particular presentation is just one of the audience's exposures to the topic.

Still, the immediate purpose of your speech is linked to a larger goal. The goal is the end you have in mind. Some examples of immediate purposes and long-range goals will illustrate the difference. The following are examples of the immediate purposes and long-range goals of an informative speech:

Immediate Purpose	**Long-Range Goal**
1. After listening to this speech, the audience should be able to identify three properties of printers.	1. To increase the number of people who will read articles and books about printers.
2. After listening to my talk, the audience should be able to name six expressions that are part of the street language used by urban African Americans.	2. To help the listeners understand and appreciate the language used by some African American students

The following are examples of the immediate purposes and long-range goals of a persuasive speech:

Immediate Purpose	**Long-Range Goal**
1. After my presentation, the audience should be able to state three positive characteristics of the candidate for mayor.	1. To have some of the audience members vote for the candidate at election time.
2. After my speech, the audience should be able to explain the low nutritional value of two popular junk foods.	2. To dissuade the listeners from eating junk food

You should note that an immediate purpose has four essential features. First, it is highly specific. Second, it includes the phrase *should be able to*. Third, it uses an action verb such as *state, identify, report, name, list, describe, explain, show,* or *reveal*. Fourth, it is stated from the viewpoint of the audience. You are writing the purpose as an audience objective.

The more specific your immediate purpose, the better you will be able to determine whether you have accomplished it. You should also use audience analysis to help you discover whether your purpose is appropriate. Suppose half the people in your class are going into fields in which a knowledge of food and nutrition is important. They already know more than the average person about nutritional values. Consequently, to deliver a speech about junk food may be inappropriate. To speak to a group of athletes about the importance of exercise may be unwise. You should adapt your purpose to the audience members by considering the level of their information, the novelty of the issue, and the other factors discussed in this chapter.

Adapting Your Supporting Materials

Your personal knowledge, your interviewing, your library research, and your Internet search should provide more material for your speech than you can use. Again, audience analysis helps you select materials for your audience. Your analysis might reveal, for example, that your classmates disrespect authority figures. In that case, you might be wasting your time informing them of the surgeon general's opinion on smoking; your personal experience or the experience of some of your classmates might be more important to them than an expert's opinion. On the other hand, if your audience analysis reveals that parents, teachers, pastors, and other authority figures are highly regarded, you may want to quote physicians, research scientists, counselors, and health-service personnel.

strategic choices

What you choose to do in your speech, from the words to the arguments.

As a public speaker, you should always keep in mind that the *choices you make in selecting a topic, choosing an immediate purpose, determining a long-range goal, organizing your speech, selecting supporting materials, and even creating visual aids are all* **strategic choices.** All of these choices are made for the purpose of adapting the speaker and the subject to a particular audience. The larger your supply of supporting arguments, the better your chances of having effective arguments. The larger your supply of supporting materials, the better your chances of providing effective evidence, illustrations, and visual aids. Your choices are strategic in that they are purposeful. The purpose is to choose, from among the available alternatives, the ones that will best achieve your purpose with the audience.

Summary

This chapter has two purposes: to help you select and narrow a speech topic appropriate for you and your audience and to help you analyze and adapt to your audience.

Brainstorming and personal inventories are two methods of topic selection. Your involvement in and knowledge of a topic are two aspects of a topic that can help you evaluate its appropriateness for you. Once you have chosen a topic, to narrow it to fit the subject, audience, and time allowed is important.

To discover if a topic is appropriate, you have to analyze your audience at four levels. Level 1 distinguishes between voluntary and captive audiences. Level 2 is demographic analysis, which evaluates the characteristics of the audience members. Level 3 analyzes the audience's interest in and knowledge of a topic. Level 4 determines the audience's attitudes, beliefs, and values.

Three methods of analyzing an audience are observation, inference, and questionnaires. Observation involves actively watching your audience and learning from its behavior. Inference uses data to draw tentative conclusions about an audience—conclusions that may make the audience's response more predictable. Questionnaires can be used to garner demographic and attitudinal information about the audience.

Adapting to an audience after audience analysis requires that you carefully adapt yourself, your verbal and nonverbal codes, your topic, your purpose, and your supporting materials to that group of people.

Issues in Communication

This Issues in Communication narrative is designed to provoke individual thought or discussion about concepts raised in the chapter.

Mary Reich is the new dean of students at Central University. Among her many responsibilities is speaking to student groups on campus. Kerri, a member of one of the sororities on campus, asked Mary if she'd be willing to appear at an event to speak about the university's initiatives to address the drinking epidemic among college students. At the time she was asked, Mary was preoccupied with some other work and she didn't inquire about any of the details. Since the event was a few weeks away, she planned to contact Kerri closer to the event and get the necessary details. Although she penned the event into her daily scheduler, Mary got wrapped up in her many new job responsibilities and forgot about the speech until the day before the event.

Despite her best intentions, Mary hadn't made time to contact Kerri before the event. She recalled that she was to talk about the university's initiatives to cope with the drinking epidemic on campus, and she had her assistant find out where she needed to be. She wasn't worried about the speech itself because she had public-speaking engagements all the time and was well versed in the subject matter. She was proud of the work the university had done to address the drinking crisis on campus.

When Mary got to the event, she was surprised to see many people she recognized as representatives of student government. She didn't see any of the leaders from the school's sororities and fraternities. Kerri came up to Mary to thank her for coming to speak to the student government. "We're quite interested in hearing what you have to say. We're concerned that the administration has gone too far without seeking the input of student government," Kerri said. Unfortunately, Mary didn't realize that Kerri was also a student government representative. She knew Kerri was in a sorority, so she had made the assumption that she would be speaking to fraternity and sorority members. Now, instead of speaking to an audience who was receptive to the University's initiatives, she had to stand before a hostile group, and she wasn't sure she was prepared for that.

Apply what you have learned about audience analysis as you ponder and discuss the following questions: What steps could Mary have taken to better prepare for her speech? How do you think she'll adapt her speech given what she knows about her audience? In what ways would her speech have been different if she really was speaking to fraternity and sorority members?

Additional Resources*

ABC News, **www. abcradioet.com.** Like audio better than text? This source puts the news in your ear instead of your eye with RealAudio newscasts and hourly updates.

Best News on the Net, **www.NovPapyrus. com/news.** Want more information on your subject? This web site links you to first-rate newspapers, wire services, and broadcast news.

Electronic Newsstand, **www.enews.com.** Need a topic? This on-line source has articles from consumer magazines. Look at the "Need to Read" archive or move to the "Monster Links" to more on-line publications.

Paul, N, **www/nando. net/prof/poyntger/ chome.html.** Interested in news groups? This is the site of an on-line publication,

"Computer-Assisted Research: A Guide to Tapping Online Information," which provides ideas for using news groups and other on-line services.

U.S. News Online, **www.usnews.com/ usnews.** Need deeper background to flesh out your speech? This source has "News You Can Use" on popular topics, breaking news, and background stories.

---

*From M. McGuire, L. Stilborne, M. McAdams, and L. Hyatt, *The Internet Handbook for Writers, Researchers, and Journalists.* New York: Guilford, 1997.

When you have read and thought about this chapter, you will be able to:

1. Identify four sources of information for a speech.

2. Recognize when you must cite sources and use oral footnotes.

3. Identify different types of supporting materials and understand how to use them in your speech.

4. Define *source credibility* and understand its importance in public speaking.

5. State four important aspects of credibility.

6. Utilize methods for establishing your credibility as a speaker.

12
Finding Information and Establishing Credibility

"Knowledge is the only instrument of production that is not subject to diminishing returns."

J. M. CLARK

"You can't build a reputation on what you are going to do."

HENRY FORD

"In the future everyone will be world-famous for fifteen minutes."

ANDY WARHOL

This chapter is designed to prepare you for presenting your first public speech by discussing where you can find information for your speech and how you can be more believable when you present your speech. First, you will learn about the sources and supporting materials you can use, as well as how to use them in your speech. The next section of the text explores speaker credibility, including four important aspects of credibility—competence, trustworthiness, dynamism, and co-orientation. Several research studies on credibility are then summarized, and ethical considerations are discussed.

This summer John is teaching medieval history to ninth-graders. During the first few lectures, John could see the students' eyes beginning to glaze over; he knew he was losing his audience, so he decided to change tactics. John asked the students questions and gave them time to research the answers on their own. What would you find in the home of a serf, a knight, or a noble? What did women, soldiers, and merchants wear? Could the daughter of a titled father marry the son of a wealthy but untitled merchant? The students shared what they had found during their research and seemed much more interested in the topics.

One day a student shared information he had found on the Internet, and another student contradicted this information with statistics she had found in a magazine article. John had not anticipated a situation like this, but he was glad for the opportunity to teach students the importance of verifying the credibility of their sources. Their next assignment was to research the information further and decide whose information was correct. The students were not only learning about medieval history but about information and source credibility as well.

As John's students found, many different sources of information are available to you. This chapter is designed to help you find reliable sources and supporting materials for your topics. You will also learn about the importance of developing credibility as a public speaker and about your ethical obligations in public speaking.

What Information Sources Can You Use?

Information sources for your speech include your personal experiences, written and visual resources, the Internet, and other people. Let us examine each of these sources.

Personal Experiences

personal experience

Your own life as a source of information for your speech.

The first place you should look for materials for the content of your speech is within yourself. Your **personal experience,** *your own life as a source of information,* is something about which you can speak with considerable authority. One student had been a "headhunter," a person who finds employees for employers willing to pay a premium for specific kinds of employees. This student gave a speech from his personal experience concerning what employers particularly value in employees. Another student had a brother who was mentally challenged and who died at age 9. She gave a speech about individuals who are mentally challenged and how they are treated in our society. Your special causes, jobs, and family can provide you with firsthand information that you can use in your speech.

However, you should ask yourself critical questions about your personal experience before you use it in your speech. Some of your experiences may be too personal or too intimate to share with strangers or even classmates. Others may be interesting but irrelevant to the topic of your speech. You can evaluate your personal experience as *evidence*, data on which proof may be based, by asking yourself the following questions:

1. Was your experience typical?
2. Was your experience so typical that it will bore an audience?
3. Was your experience so atypical that it was a chance occurrence?
4. Was your experience so personal and revealing that the audience may feel uncomfortable?
5. Was your experience one that this audience will appreciate or from which this audience can learn a lesson?
6. Does your experience really constitute proof or evidence of anything?

To consider the ethics of using your personal experience in a speech is also important. Will it harm others? Is the experience firsthand (your own), or is it someone else's experience? Experience that is not firsthand is probably questionable because information about others' experiences often becomes distorted as it is transmitted from one person to another. Unless the experience is your own, you may find yourself passing along a falsehood.

Written and Visual Resources

A second source of material for your speech is **written and visual resources**—*magazines, journals, newspapers, books, broadcasts, and documentaries that can be consulted for information, arguments, and evidence for your speech.* Magazines, journals, and newspapers may be particularly important resources for your speech, as they will provide the most recent information available on your subject. To locate articles on a given topic, you will have to check the periodical indexes in your school's library, which are available in book form and on computerized databases, such as *ERIC*. Your library is likely to have several indexes; depending on your topic, some you might start with are *The Reader's Guide to Periodical Literature*, the *Education Index*, the *Social Sciences Index*, and the *Index to Humanities. The Reader's Guide to Periodical Literature* will provide you with articles on just about any subject, but they are largely from popular magazines. If you're interested in scholarly articles on your topic, you will have to turn to one or more other indexes. Some of these are listed in Table 12.1, but many others are available. Be sure to check with a librarian if you are uncertain about which index will lead you to the articles that are most appropriate for your subject matter.

If you're using the printed version of an index, you simply look up a given topic to find a listing of all the articles recently published on that subject. You can explore the topic further by using key words related to your topic. For example, if your topic is *cocaine*, you could also look under *drugs, law enforcement, international regulation, medicine,* and *crime*.

Key words are also used to locate articles through on-line databases. You simply type the key word (or words) related to your subject, and the database

written and visual resources

Books, newspapers, magazines, broadcasts, and documentaries consulted for information, arguments, and evidence for a speech.

TABLE 12.1 WRITTEN RESOURCES FOR THE PUBLIC SPEAKER

GENERAL INDEXES TO PERIODICALS
New York Times Index (author, subject)
Reader's Guide to Periodical Literature
  (author, subject)
Social Sciences and Humanities Index
  (author, subject)

SPECIAL INDEXES TO PERIODICALS
Art Index (author, subject)
Bibliographic Index (subject)
Biography Index (subject)
Biological and Agricultural Index (subject)
Book Review Index (author, title)
Communication Abstracts (subject)
Index to Legal Periodicals (author, subject)
Psychological Abstracts (author, subject)

SPECIALIZED DICTIONARIES
Partridge, Eric. *A Dictionary of Catch Phrases.*
  1992.
Partridge, Eric. *A Dictionary of Clichés. 1993.*
Webster's New World Dictionary of Computer
  Terms. 1988.

SPECIALIZED ENCYCLOPEDIAS
Adams, J. T. *Dictionary of American History. 7* vols.
Encyclopedia of the Social Sciences. 15 vols.
Encyclopedia of World Art.
Grove's Dictionary of Music and Musicians. 9 vols.
Harris, Chester W. *Encyclopedia of Educational*
  Research.
Hastings, James. *Interpreter's Dictionary of the Bible.*
  4 vols.
McGraw-Hill. *Encyclopedia of Science and*
  Technology. 15 vols.
Munn, Glenn G. *Encyclopedia of Banking and*
  Finance.
The New Grove Dictionary of Music and Musicians.

YEARBOOKS
Americana Annual
Facts on File
Information Please Almanac
New International Year Book
Statesman's Year-Book
Statistical Abstract of the United States
World Almanac and Book of Facts

will produce all the relevant articles. Some databases even provide abstracts, or summaries, of the articles.

The following list, as well as Table 12.1, provides additional sources of information that you may find helpful. Do not limit yourself to just these sources, however, as they are merely some of the references you may be able to use in preparing your speech:

1. Frequently used yearbooks include the *World Almanac,* the *Book of Facts, Facts on File,* and the *Statistical Abstract of the United States.* These sources contain facts and figures about a wide variety of subjects, from population to yearly coal production. The encyclopedias contain short bibliographies and background material about many topics. Among the popular encyclopedias are the *Encyclopedia Americana* and the *Encyclopaedia Britannica.*

2. Sourcebooks for examples, literary allusions, and quotations include Bartlett's *Familiar Quotations,* George Seldes' *The Great Quotations,* Arthur Richmond's *Modern Quotations for Ready Reference,* and *Respectfully Quoted,* a dictionary of quotations requested from the congressional research service.

3. Biographies of famous persons can be found in *Who's Who in America, Current Biography,* and the *Dictionary of American Biography* (deceased Americans).

4. Newspaper files are helpful, especially if your college has *The New York Times,* one of the few newspapers that has an index. Newspapers tend to be most useful for recent information.

5. Professional journals, which are also indexed, are collected by many libraries. You can find articles about communication, psychology, sociology, economics, chemistry, mathematics, and many other subjects.

6. Many modern libraries own volumes of material on microfilm. Media resource centers on campuses have lists of slides, films, and other visual materials.

Still another resource important to the public speaker is the **card catalog,** which is *a source of information about materials in a library.* Many libraries today have a **computer catalog**—*an electronic source of the same information*—but some still have only card catalogs, and some maintain both systems. The card catalog lists materials in the library by author, title, and subject, and these categories are usually cross-indexed. The card provides the book's call number, which tells you where to find the book on the shelves, and it sometimes includes a brief description of the material.

The computer catalog is similar to the card catalog in that it has call numbers and entries arranged by author, subject, and title. However, using the computer catalog is much more efficient than using the card catalog. When you are conducting a search on a topic, the computer helps you narrow your search—something a card catalog cannot do. You begin by typing a word or phrase, such as *mass media and violence;* the computer will then display a list of all the subtopics related to mass media and violence. When you select a subtopic from those displayed, a list of the books related to that specific topic will appear. From this, you can learn not only the title of the books and where they're located but also whether or not they're checked out and, if they are, when they're due back. Sometimes a brief summary about the book is included.

If you select a speech topic that you are already involved in or knowledgeable about, you may not have to read a large number of books. On the other hand, if the subject is truly of interest to you, you may want to read several of the books. Usually, to check out several of the best books on the topic and to read them selectively for the information most usable to you in your speech is sufficient. Such information is usually quotations and evidence or proof that supports your position on the issue.

Regardless of the source you're using, to take good notes, to record the information accurately and precisely, and to credit the author in your speech when you deliver it is important. Making notes on an index card or separate piece of paper usually helps (Figure 12.1). In addition to recording information about the topic, be sure to include data about the source: the author, title, publisher, place of publication, date of publication, and page reference.

Don't forget that you can also use information from television news and documentaries, films, and tapes. An effective public speaker learns rapidly where to find good supporting materials.

card catalog

A source of information about materials in a library.

computer catalog

An electronic source of information about materials in a library.

> George F. Will, "Fetuses as Carolinians," *Newsweek* (June 8, 1998), p. 78.
>
> The Supreme Court refused to review (let stand) a South Carolina Supreme Court decision that says the state's child abuse law includes unborn children. (p. 78)
>
> George Will says, "In *Roe v. Wade* the court based constitutional law on biological nonsense, asserting that a fetus is 'potential life.' " (p. 78)
>
> The South Carolina attorney general prosecutes pregnant cocaine addicts for neglect and, sometimes, manslaughter. (p. 78)

Figure 12.1 Index card: A speaker's notes from a magazine. Notice that the speaker has included not only all publication information but page numbers, direct quotes, and paraphrased information.

Citing Sources

When you write an outline, compose a manuscript speech, or deliver a speech, you are expected to indicate where you found your information. Two reasons exist for this expectation: (1) A rule of scholarship dictates that any ideas that are not your own must be credited to the person whose ideas they are, and (2) writers and speakers must be able to verify what they say. What if a speaker claims that homosexuality is entirely hereditary? Your first response might be, Who says? The speaker might reveal a source. You might come up with 10 other sources who disagree. Citing sources, crediting others for ideas that originated with them, and challenging sources and the credibility of authors are important aspects of speech composition, delivery, and criticism.

In your written outline or manuscript, you can cite sources in a number of different ways, including the styles suggested by the *Publication Manual of the American Psychological Association* and the *MLA Handbook for Writers of Research Papers.* Your instructor should let you know what style you are expected to use and should provide details on how to use it.

oral footnote

An abbreviated manuscript footnote that tells the audience where you found your information.

When you are presenting your speech, you will be expected to provide **oral footnotes,** which are *abbreviated manuscript or outline footnotes that tell the audience where you found your information.* In a speech, the footnotes would sound like this:

"According to the secretary of labor. . ."

"A recent *Newsweek* article by conservative columnist George Will pointed out that . . ."

"*The Athens Messenger* reported that an angry burglary victim is organizing . . ."

"Dean Singleton from Education agrees that the future for entry-level teachers will be . . ."

In other words, in a speech, the speaker indicates that the information or idea came from a magazine, a journal, a newspaper, a book, the Internet, or an interview by providing a signal to the audience that the material came from another source.

Instant Recall

Oral footnotes for an Internet source are very much like oral footnotes for a book or periodical, except no one expects you to cite the specific World Wide Web address, which is known as a **URL,** or *uniform resource locator.* So you might say, "According to the April 19th edition of the on-line *New York Times,* Harold Nichols said . . ." This lets your audience know where on the Internet your information came from without actually providing a specific address. Regardless of which source you use, anyone who hears your speech has a right to request specific details about where you found your information. So it is important that you have these details in front of you when you give your speech.

The importance of citing sources in written and spoken discourse cannot be understated. *The use of someone else's ideas or words without credit* is an offense called **plagiarism.** In many colleges and universities, plagiarism is punishable by measures as serious as expulsion; outside the classroom, it can result in disgrace, fines, and even jail. Do not forget to reveal where you got your information: You have an ethical and legal obligation to do so.

The Internet

Many students now use the **Internet,** *a network of interconnected computer networks,* to find information for their speeches. The part of the Internet that you are most likely to use in your research is the **World Wide Web (WWW),**

URL

Uniform resource locator; the address of a web site.

plagiarism

The use of someone else's ideas or words without credit.

Internet

A network of interconnected computer networks.

World Wide Web (WWW)

The part of the Internet that links together all the individual web sites, hence the term *web.*

COMMUNICATION CHALLENGE

Oral Footnotes

Convert the following source information into oral citations:

1. Statistics downloaded on November 12 and found in the *Statistical Abstract of the United States* at **www.census.gov/stat_abstract.**

   Oral citation: _____

   _____

2. An article by Jeffrey Weld, "Attracting and Retaining High-Quality Professionals in Science Education," from *Phi Delta Kappan* magazine, March 1998, on pages 536–539.

   Oral citation: _____

   _____

   _____

hyperlink

A link in a web document that leads to another web site or to another place within the same document.

which *links together all the individual web sites.* It is called the "web" because it contains many sites linked together; users can travel from one site to another by clicking on hyperlinks. A **hyperlink** is *a link in a WWW document that leads to another web site or to another place within the same document.* The web is like a "multimedia encyclopedia containing over 200 million items" from simple text pages to color pictures, video clips, and audio programs (Gregory, 1999, p. 116). One problem with using the web is that it can be difficult to navigate. Dominick (1996) said, "Some have described using the Internet as trying to find your way across a big city without a map. You'll see lots of interesting stuff but you may never get to where you're going" (p. 346). Indeed, it's easy to get sidetracked and to feel somewhat overwhelmed when you're searching for information on the web, but there are ways to make your search easier. Some of these are discussed below.

The Internet invites rapid information searches.

web browser

A tool for viewing pages on the web; e.g., Netscape, Mosaic, and Internet Explorer.

Locating Information on the Web

Following are a few basic procedures for locating material on the World Wide Web:

1. Begin by connecting to the Internet, and clicking on your **web browser,** *a tool for viewing pages on the WWW.* Common web browsers are Netscape, Mosaic, and Internet Explorer.

TABLE 12.2 WWW LINKS TO OTHER SITES

You can find information on the Internet without using search engines. Specific web sites have been created by people who researched the WWW and compiled links to other sites. Typical categories include communications, humanities, medicine, travel, leisure, and government organizations. You can browse the categories and use the hyperlinks to log on to particular sites that interest you.

Web sites featuring compilations of links are particularly useful to the public-speaking student. For instance, let's say you are thinking about giving a speech on the environment. You can log on to the Argus Clearinghouse site (listed below) to see if it contains a list of web sites pertaining to the environment.

The three web sites listed below are good places to start:

◆ WWW Virtual Library: **lib.org.** This site lists many different web sites in 14 categories.
◆ Galaxy: **galaxy.einet.net/galaxy.html.** Called "the professional's guide to a world of information," this site provides links to web sites and articles published on the Internet.
◆ The Argus Clearinghouse: **www.clearinghouse.net/index.html.** This site not only lists web sites by category but also describes each site and rates it on the basis of quality, reliability, and design.

2. If you have the URL, or address, of the web site you are looking for, you can enter it in the box at the top of the page. Be careful not to add spaces or capital letters unless they are part of the address. Web sites that are designed as a guide to other sites are particularly useful for public-speaking students. A list of a few such sites is presented in Table 12.2.

3. If you do not have an address, you will need to use a **search engine,** *a program on the Internet that allows users to search for information.* Here are a few search engines you may want to try:

◆ Yahoo!: **www.yahoo.com**
◆ Alta Vista: **www.altavista.digital.com**
◆ Encyclopedia Britannica Internet Guide: **www.ebig.com**
◆ Excite: **www.excite.com**
◆ Lycos: **www.lycos.com**
◆ HotBot: **www.hotbot.com**
◆ MetaFind: **www.metafind.com**

search engine

A program on the Internet that allows users to search for information.

4. Once you get to a search engine's **home page,** *the first page on a web site, to which supporting materials are linked,* you can use a search engine in one of two ways: Either (1) click on one of the several categories listed, or (2) enter a key word (or words) into the search box, and then click the "search" button. For example, if you're using the first method to look for information on your speech topic, the increased popularity of the herb St. John's Wort, you would start by clicking on "health" on the home page (Figure 12.2), and then click on "alternative medicine" when the page with the list of subcategories

home page

The first page on a web site, to which supporting materials are linked.

appears (Figure 12.3). If you're using the second method, you would disregard the general subject listings on the home page, and start by typing in key words associated with your topic, for example, *St. John's Wort.* Of course, you can also use both methods.

bookmark

A feature of most web browsers by which important links can be saved in a file without having to look up the URL.

5. Although there are differences between the different search engines, some general tools can be used to narrow your search regardless of the search engine you're using (Table 12.3).

6. If you're using your own computer, you can save your favorite sites as **bookmarks,** *a feature of most web browsers in which important links can be saved in a file without having to look up the URL.*

TRY ◀▶ THIS

Use one of the search engines to find out as much information as you can about AIDS. Start by clicking on the category "Health," and go from there. Then return to the search engine's home page, and start another search by entering "AIDS and children" in the search box. Now what do you come up with? How does narrowing the topic help you manage the list of sites that come back to you?

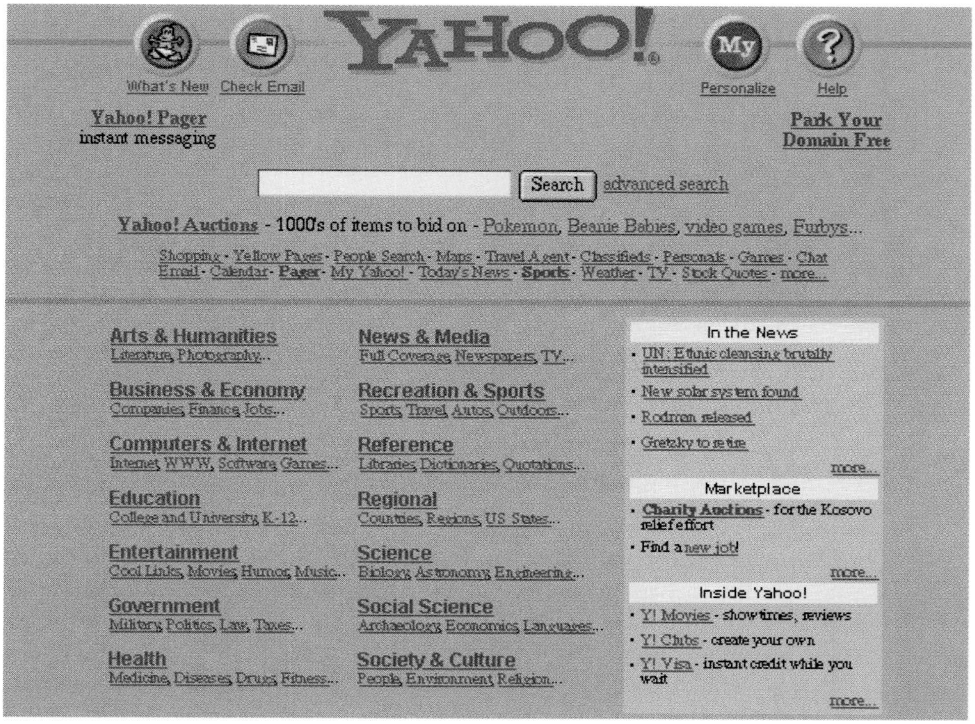

Figure 12.2 The home page of Yahoo!, a search engine. Notice that each topic area in bold is a hyperlink to more information on the subject.

QUOTATIONS ON THE WEB

www.motivatcus.com: The quotes at this site are motivational, inspirational, and positive.

cyber-nation.com/victory/quotations: Quotes here are listed by subject and author; a search option is also available. You can even sign up to receive a quote by e-mail every day.

startpage.com/html/quotations.html: This site lists quotes by subject and author, and it also includes links to other quotation web sites.

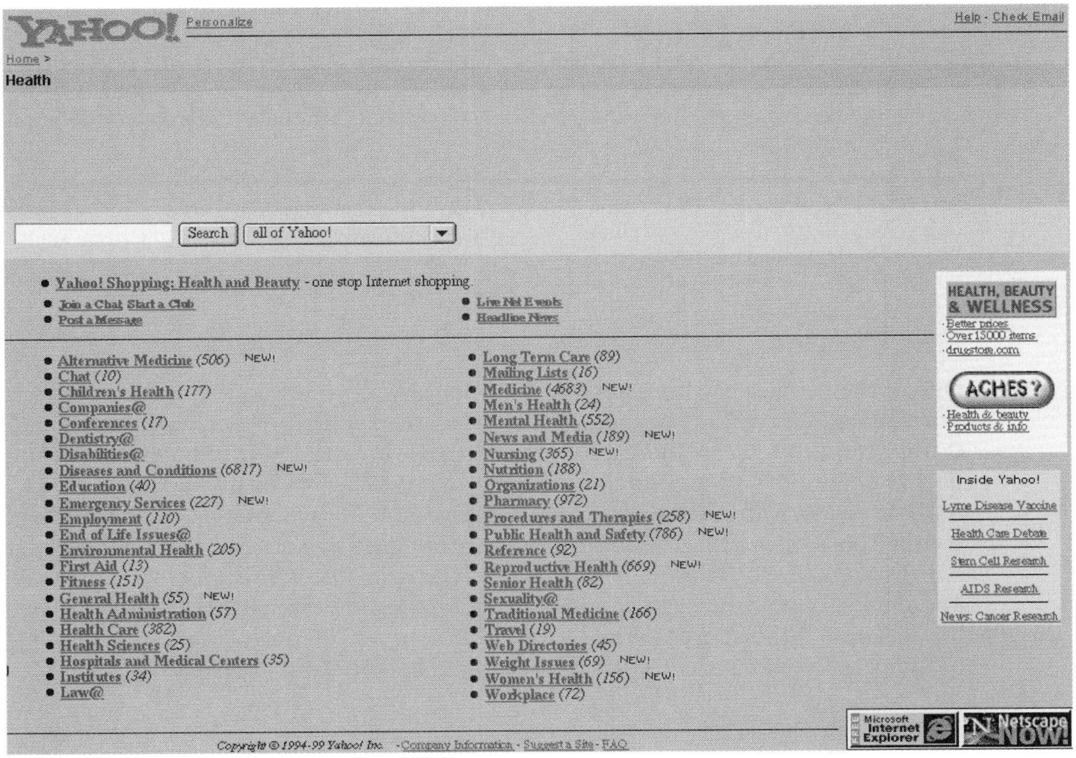

Figure 12.3 If you click on "Health" on the Yahoo! home page, you get to this display of topics on health, all of which link to other sources of information.

TABLE 12.3 TOOLS FOR NARROWING YOUR WWW SEARCH

◆ *Quotation marks:* Add these to your words or phrases to more closely define your intentions. For example, a multiword phrase in quotation marks tells the search engine to list only sites that contain words in that exact order.

◆ *Plus (+) or minus (–) signs:* Typed directly in front of a word or phrase, a plus sign indicates that the word or phrase must appear in the search results (e.g., herbs +St. John's Wort); a minus sign indicates that the word or phrase should *not* be included in the search results (herbs –Ginseng).

◆ *Boolean operators* (AND, OR, AND NOT, NEAR and parentheses):

   (a) Similar to the plus sign, AND indicates that the documents found must contain all the words joined by the AND operator. For example, to find documents that contain the words *herbs* and *St. John's Wort,* you would enter this: herbs AND St. John's Wort.

   (b) Using OR indicates that documents found must contain at least one of the words joined by OR.

   (c) AND NOT is used like the minus sign described above. It indicates that the documents found cannot contain the word that follows the term AND NOT.

   (d) NEAR finds words that appear within 5 to 30 words of one another (each search engine has a different range).
      Note that for all the boolean operators to work, they must appear in capital letters and with a space on each side.

   (e) Finally, parentheses are used to group portions of Boolean queries together for more complicated queries.

◆ Title search: Doing a title search allows you to restrict searches to the title portion of web documents. For example, if you type "title:St. John's Wort" or "t:St. John's Wort," the search engine will retrieve only documents that have the words *St. John's Wort* in their title.

SOURCE: Netscape's Net Search Tips (http://home.netscape.com/escapes/search/tips_general.html?cp=ntserch); Hamilton Gregory, *Public Speaking for College and Career,* 5th ed. (New York: McGraw-Hill, 1999).

One Caution

One of the problems with using the Internet for information is that this source is unregulated. The information may be biased, or just plain wrong, because no authority monitors the content of the sites. How do you determine what information is accurate and credible? Ultimately, you will have to make that decision. Ask yourself whether someone would have reason to present biased information. If at all possible, verify the information through other sources, such as newspaper or magazine articles. If it is a scholarly article, check for a list of references, and if a list of references is provided, try to determine if the list is credible by verifying some of the sources. Finally, credible sources often provide the credentials of the person who wrote the article or of people who were involved in it.

People Sources

One student wanted to do his speech on a topic in which he was involved, but almost every source he located through the library's reference works had

12.2 USING THE INTERNET

Fill in the blanks:

1. The _____ _____, _____ is the part of the Internet that links all the web sites together.

2. To locate information on your speech topic, you will have to use a _____ _____ if you do not know specific _____.

3. A _____ _____ is a tool for viewing pages on the web.

4. _____ or _____ signs can be used in front of a word or phrase to narrow your search.

Answers: 1.World Wide Web   2. search engine/URLs (or addresses)   3. web browser
4. plus/minus

been vandalized. Most of the written sources in newspapers, magazines, and journals had been cut out by someone who had researched the topic earlier. The student was so angry that he stormed into his professor's office, ready to quit the course. "What is the point of trying to write well-prepared speeches if the information isn't even available in the library?" he asked.

The student was asked to do one thing before dropping the course: See the director of libraries about his complaint. The director of libraries not only made an appointment with the student but showed considerable interest in the student's complaint. The director was chairing a task force for 16 colleges and universities that were delving into the problem of mutilation, the destruction of library holdings by students. The director spoke to the student for an hour. She gave him facts, figures, arguments, and ideas about the mutilation of library holdings. The student ended up delivering an excellent speech—not on the topic he had originally planned but on the problem of library mutilation and what to do about it.

The point is that speakers often overlook the most obvious sources of information—the people around them. You can get information for your speech from personal experience, written and visual resources, the Internet, *and* from other people. The easiest way to secure information from other people is to ask them in an informational interview.

Finding People to Interview

As a person who needs information about a particular topic, your first step is to find the person or persons who can help you discover more about it. Your instructor might have some suggestions about whom to approach. Among the easier and better sources of information are professors and administrators

The speaker who uses facial expression, gestures, movements, and voice to make a point exhibits dynamism.

who are available on campus. They can be contacted during office hours or by appointment. Government officials, too, have an obligation to be responsive to your questions. Even big business and industrial concerns have public relations offices that can answer your questions. Your object is to find someone, or a few people, who can provide you with the best information in the limited time you have to prepare your speech.

Conducting the Interview

An interview can be an important and impressive source of information for your speech—if you conduct the interview properly. After you have carefully selected the person or persons you wish to interview, you need to observe these proprieties:

1. *On first contact with your interviewee or the interviewee's secretary, be honest about your purpose.* For example, you might say, "I want to interview Dr. Schwartz for 10 minutes about the plans for student aid for next year so that I can share that information with the 20 students in my public-speaking class." In other words, to reveal why you want to talk to the person is good. To reveal how much of the interviewee's time you need to take is also good, and to keep the interview short is smart. If your interviewee wants to give you more time than you requested, that should be his or her choice. To be deceptive about why you want to talk to the person, or to not reveal why you want to talk is unwise, because you want the interviewee to trust you.

2. *Prepare specific questions for the interview.* Think ahead of time about exactly what kind of information you will need to satisfy yourself and your audience. Keep your list of questions short enough to fit the time limit you have suggested to the interviewee.

3. *Be respectful toward the person you interview.* Remember that the person is doing you a favor. You do not need to act like Mike Wallace on *60 Minutes.* Instead, dress appropriately for the person's status, ask your questions with politeness and concern, and thank your interviewee for granting you an interview.

4. *Tell the interviewee you are going to take notes so you can use the information in your speech.* If you are going to tape-record the interview, you need to ask the interviewee's permission, and you should be prepared to take notes in case the interviewee does not wish to be recorded. Even if you record the interview, to take notes as a backup in case something happens to the tape or tape recorder is a good idea.

5. *When you quote the interviewee or paraphrase the person's ideas in your speech, use oral footnotes to indicate where you got the information.* For example, "According to Dr. Fred Schwartz, the director of financial aid, the amount of student financial aid for next year will be slightly less than it was this year."

Sometimes the person you interview will be a good resource for additional information. For example, if the interviewee is an expert on your topic, he or she may be able to lead you to other people or to additional written resources for your speech. Remember, too, that how you behave before, during, and after the interview is a reflection on you, the class you are taking, and even your college or university.

What Supporting Materials Are Appropriate?

Now that you know where to look for information, the next step is locating **supporting materials,** *information you can use to substantiate your arguments and to clarify your position.* In this section you will examine examples, surveys, testimonial evidence, numbers and statistics, analogies, explanations, and definitions. Some of these supporting materials are used as evidence or proof; others are used mainly for clarification or amplification.

supporting materials

Any information used to support an argument or idea.

Examples

Examples, *specific instances used to illustrate your point,* are among the most common supporting materials found in speeches. Sometimes a single example helps convince an audience; at other times, a relatively large number of examples may be necessary to achieve your purpose. For instance, the argument that a university gives admission priority to out-of-state students could be supported by showing the difference between the numbers of in-state students and out-of-state students who are accepted, in relation to the number of students who applied in each group. Likewise, in a persuasive speech

examples

Illustrations drawn from specific instances.

designed to motivate everyone to vote, you could present cases in which several more votes would have meant a major change in admission.

You should be careful when using examples. Sometimes an example may be so unusual that an audience will not accept it as evidence or proof of anything. A student who refers to crime in his hometown as an example of the increasing crime problem is unconvincing if his hometown has considerably less crime than the audience is accustomed to. A good example must be plausible, typical, and related to the main point it before to be effective in a speech.

Two types of examples are factual and hypothetical. A *hypothetical* example cannot be verified like a *factual* example can. The length of the example determines whether it is brief or extended. The following is an example of a brief factual example:

> According to the May 1999 issue of *Motor Trend,* the Mercedes-Benz M-Class is the "most technologically sophisticated sports/utility vehicle."

Here is an extended hypothetical example:

> An example of a good excuse for a student's missing class is that he or she has a serious auto accident on the way to class, ends up in the hospital, and has a signed medical statement from a physician to prove hospitalization for a week. A poor excuse for a student's missing class is that the student, knowing beforehand when the final examination will be held, schedules a flight home for the day before the exam and wants an "excused absence."

The brief factual example is *verifiable,* meaning it can be supported by a source that the audience can check. The extended hypothetical example is not verifiable and is actually a composite of excuses.

Surveys

surveys

Studies in which a limited number of questions are answered by a sample of the population to discover opinions on issues.

Another source of supporting materials commonly used in speeches is **surveys,** *studies in which a limited number of questions are answered by a sample of the population to discover opinions on issues.* Surveys are found most often in magazines or journals and are usually seen as more credible than an example or one person's experience because they synthesize the experience of hundreds or thousands of people. Public opinion polls fall into this category. One person's experience with alcohol can have an impact on an audience, but a survey indicating that one-third of all Americans abstain, one-third drink occasionally, and one-third drink regularly provides better support for an argument. As with personal experience, you should ask some important questions about the evidence found in surveys:

1. *How reliable is the source?* A report in a professional journal of sociology, psychology, or communication is likely to be more thorough and more valid than one found in a local newspaper.
2. *How broad was the sample used in the survey?* Was it a survey of the entire nation, the region, the state, the city, the campus, or the class?

3. *Who was included in the survey?* Did everyone in the sample have an equally good chance of being selected, or were volunteers asked to respond to the questions?

4. *How representative was the survey sample?* For example, *Playboy*'s readers may not be typical of the population in your state.

5. *Who performed the survey?* Was it a nationally recognized survey firm, such as Lou Harris or Gallup, or was it the local newspaper editor? Was it performed by professionals such as professors, researchers, or management consultants?

6. *Why was the survey done?* Was it performed for any self-serving purpose—for example, to attract more readers—or did the government conduct it to help establish policy or legislation?

Testimonial Evidence

Testimonial evidence, a third kind of supporting material, is *written or oral statements of others' experience used by a speaker to substantiate or clarify a point.* One assumption behind testimonial evidence is that you are not alone in your beliefs, ideas, and arguments: Other people also support them. Another assumption is that the statements of others should help the audience accept your point of view. The three kinds of testimonial evidence you can use in your speeches are lay, expert, and celebrity.

Lay testimony is *statements made by an ordinary person that substantiate or support what you say.* In advertising, this kind of testimony shows ordinary people using or buying products and stating the fine qualities of those products. In a speech, lay testimony might be the words of your relatives, neighbors, or colleagues concerning an issue. Such testimony shows the audience that you and other ordinary people support the idea. Other examples of lay testimony are proclamations of faith by fundamentalist Christians at a church gathering and statements about the wonderful qualities of their college by alumni at a recruiting session.

Expert testimony is *statements made by someone who has special knowledge or expertise about an issue or idea.* In your speech, you might quote a mechanic about problems with an automobile, an interior decorator about the aesthetic qualities of fabrics, or a political pundit about the elections. The idea is to demonstrate that people with specialized experience or education support the positions you advocate in your speech.

Celebrity testimony is *statements made by a public figure who is known to the audience.* Celebrity testimony occurs in advertising when someone famous endorses a particular product. In your speech, you might point out that a famous politician, a syndicated columnist, or a well-known entertainer endorses the position you advocate.

Although testimonial evidence may encourage your audience to adopt your ideas, you need to use such evidence with caution. An idea may have little credence even though many laypeople believe in it; an expert may be quoted on topics well outside his or her area of expertise; and a celebrity is

testimonial evidence

Written or oral statements of other people's experience used by the speaker to substantiate or clarify points.

lay testimony

Statements made by an ordinary person that substantiate or support a point of view.

expert testimony

Statements made by someone who has special knowledge or expertise that support a point of view.

celebrity testimony

Statements made by a public figure that support a point of view.

often paid for endorsing a product. To protect yourself and your audience, you should ask yourself the following questions before using testimonial evidence in your speeches:

1. Is the person you quote an expert whose opinions or conclusions are worthier than most other people's opinions?
2. Is the quotation about a subject in the person's area of expertise?
3. Is the person's statement based on extensive personal experience, professional study or research, or another form of firsthand proof?
4. Will your audience find the statement more believable because you got it from this outside source?

Numbers and Statistics

A fourth kind of evidence useful for clarification or substantiation is numbers and statistics. Because numbers are easier to understand and digest when they appear in print, the public speaker has to simplify, explain, and translate their meaning in a speech. For example, instead of saying, "There were 323,462 high school graduates," say, "There were over 300,000 graduates." Other ways to simplify a number like 323,462 would be to write the number on a chalkboard or poster or to use a comparison, such as "Three hundred thousand high school graduates are equivalent to the entire population of Lancaster."

statistics

Numbers that summarize numerical information or compare quantities.

Statistics, *numbers that summarize numerical information or compare quantities,* are also difficult for audiences to interpret. For example, for an audience to interpret a statement such as "Honda sales increased 47 percent" is difficult. Instead, you could round off the figure to "nearly 50 percent," or you could reveal the number of sales this year and last year. You can also help the audience interpret the significance with a comparison such as "That is the biggest increase in sales experienced by any domestic or imported car dealer in our city this year."

You can greatly increase your effectiveness as a speaker if you illustrate your numbers by using visual aids, such as pie charts, line graphs, and bar graphs. You can help your audience by both saying and showing your figures. You also can help your audience visualize statistics by using visual imagery. For example, "That amount of money is greater than all the money in all our local banks," or "That many discarded tires would cover our city 6 feet deep in a single year." You can use numbers and statistics for support and substantiation if you can think of creative ways to help your audience simplify them, place them in a context, and translate them into their language. Your responsibility as a speaker is to help the audience understand your figures. Your responsibility as a listener is to seek clarification if you do not understand the meaning or significance of figures used in a speech.

analogy

A comparison of things that are basically unalike.

Analogies

Another kind of supporting material used in public speeches is analogies. An **analogy** is *a comparison of things in some respects, especially in position or* *function, that are otherwise dissimilar.* For instance, human beings and bees are different, but one could draw a comparison of the two different groups by pointing out that in many ways human beings are like bees. Some people are like queen bees, which are pampered and cared for by others; drones do nothing and yet are cared for; and workers seem to do all of the labor without any pampering. Similarly, analogies can be used to show that Roman society is analogous to American society and that a law applied in one state will work the same way in another.

An analogy also provides clarification, but it is not proof because the comparison inevitably breaks down. Therefore, a speaker who argues that American society will fail just as Roman society did can carry the comparison only so far because the form of government and the institutions in the two societies are quite different. Likewise, you can question the bee-human analogy by pointing out the vast differences between the two things being compared. Nonetheless, analogies can be quite successful as a way to illustrate or clarify.

Explanations

Explanations are another important means of clarification and persuasion that you will often find in written and visual sources and in interviews. An **explanation** *clarifies what something is or how it works.* A discussion of psychology would offer explanations and answers, as well as their relation to the field. How does Freud explain our motivations? What is *catharsis,* and how is it related to aggression? What do *id, ego,* and *superego* mean?

A good explanation usually simplifies a concept or an idea by explaining it from the audience's point of view. William Safire (1980), once a presidential speechwriter and now a syndicated columnist, provided an explanation in one of his columns about how the spelling of a word gets changed. In his explanation, he pointed out that experts who write dictionaries observe how writers and editors use the language. "When enough citations come in from cultivated writers, passed by trained copy editors," he quotes a lexicographer as saying, "the 'mistake' becomes the spelling" (Safire, 1980, p. 3C). You may find, too, that much of your informative speaking is explanation.

explanation

A means of clarification by simplifying, amplifying, or restating.

Definitions

Some of the most contentious arguments in our society center on **definitions,** or *determinations of meaning through description, simplification, examples, analysis, comparison, explanation, or illustration.* Experts and ordinary citizens have argued for years about definitions. For instance, when does art become pornography? Is withdrawal of life-support systems euthanasia or humanitarian concern? How you define a concept can make a considerable difference.

Definitions in a public speech are supposed to enlighten the audience by revealing what a term means. Sometimes you can use definitions that appear in standard reference works, such as dictionaries and encyclopedias, but it is

definitions

Determinations of meaning through description, simplification, examples, analysis, comparison, explanation, or illustration.

often even more effective to simply try to explain the word in language the audience will understand. For example, say you use the word *subcutaneous hematoma* in your speech. *Subcutaneous hematoma* is jargon used by physicians to explain the blotch on your skin, but you could explain it in this way: "*Subcutaneous* means 'under the skin,' and *hematoma* means 'swelled with blood,' so the words mean 'blood swelling under the skin,' or what most of us call a 'bruise.' "

Evidence and Proof

evidence

Data or information from which you can draw a conclusion, make a judgment, or establish the probability of something occurring.

Supporting material in your speech can be nearly anything that provides backing for your argument. It can be as simple as "I know this works because I did it myself" or as complex as a 50-page report by a government body. Evidence is both stronger and narrower than supporting material. As indicated at the beginning of the chapter, **evidence** is *data or information from which you can draw a conclusion, make a judgment, or establish the probability of something occurring.* In the legal system, strict rules govern what may or may not be used as evidence. In public speaking, the rules are considerably looser, but common sense still applies. For instance, a single example is supporting material and it is probably even evidence, but a single example is usually insufficient evidence on which to base a claim. Evidence is often described as being strong or weak. The statement "This works for me" is weak evidence compared with "This has worked for millions of people."

proof

Evidence that is sufficient to convince an audience of the truth of a claim.

If supporting material can be considered nearly anything that supports a contention and if evidence is seen as something stronger on which a conclusion or judgment can be based, then proof is the strongest type of support. **Proof** is *evidence that is sufficient to convince your audience of the truth of a claim.* Sufficient evidence could be a single example or hundreds of experiments. Evidence becomes proof when the audience accepts it.

How can you handle evidence in a speech so that it will be regarded as proof? The central concern is knowing what kind of, and how much, evidence will convince an audience that your assertions are true. Some audiences—for example, students grounded in math, business, and economics—are partial to statistics and numerical treatments of a topic. Other audiences are actually repelled by numbers and respond more favorably to long, dramatic stories or examples. The amount of evidence used is also an important consideration. Sometimes, one example proves the point; other times, all the examples in the world would be insufficient to prove your point.

No rules govern how much or what kind of evidence should be used in your speech, but standard ways exist for presenting evidence in a speech. First, you need to be highly selective about which evidence you use in your speech to support your claims. You need to choose the evidence that is most important to you and your audience. Second, you need to make a statement—either before or after, or both before and after, the evidence—that reveals what you are trying to prove. Many names for this kind of statement exist—argument, assertion, proposition, claim, and main point. Regardless of the name, the statement is a claim that invites evidence or proof.

12.3 IDENTIFYING SUPPORTING MATERIALS

Write the correct letter from the choices below in each blank on the left:

A. **Testimony**   D. **Examples**   G. **Surveys**
B. **Statistics**   E. **Evidence**   H. **Definitions**
C. **Explanation**   F. **Supporting materials**   I. **Analogies**

_____ 1. These may be the most common type of supporting material.

_____ 2. This supporting material is identified with celebrities, laypeople, and experts.

_____ 3. These provide clarification but are not proof because they inevitably break down.

_____ 4. These are considered to be more credible than examples or personal experience.

_____ 5. This supporting material becomes proof when the audience accepts it.

Answers: 1. D   2. A   3. I   4. G   5. E

The important point to remember about proof is that it is perceived differently by different people. The speaker is responsible for demonstrating the truth or probability of a claim. Intelligent analysis of the audience helps the speaker to discover which evidence will be perceived as proof.

Now that you know how to find information and use it in your speech, you may be wondering how believable and effective your audience will consider you. The section that follows provides guidance on how to be a more credible public speaker.

What Is Source Credibility?

More than 2,300 years ago Aristotle (1941) noted that a speaker's "character may almost be called the most effective means of persuasion he possesses." Since that time, scholars have continued to study the importance of the source, or speaker, because they correctly believe that *who* says something determines *who* will listen.

In the public-speaking classroom, you are the source of the message. You need to be concerned about your **source credibility,** *the audience's perception of your effectiveness as a speaker.* You may feel that you do not have the

source credibility

The audience's perception of a speaker's effectiveness.

313

same credibility as a high public official, a great authority on a topic, or an expert in a narrow field. That may be so, but you can still be a very credible source to your classmates, colleagues, or friends. A teacher may be credible to her students; a father may be credible to his child; a lawyer may be credible to her clients. The same teacher, however, may not be credible in her family; the father may not be credible in the office; and the lawyer may not even be credible to her peers.

To understand the concept of source credibility, you must first recognize that it is not something a speaker possesses, like a suit of clothes. Instead, the audience determines credibility. Like beauty, credibility "is in the eye of the beholder" (Rosnow & Robinson, 1967).

A speaker's credibility depends in part on who the speaker is, the subject being discussed, the situation, and the audience. Have you served in the armed forces overseas? You may have earned the right to speak on the pros and cons of supporting yourself. Have you grown up in another country? You may have earned the right to speak on another country's culture, food, or social customs.

Similarly, you might be more credible to some audiences than you are to others—your classmates might find you credible but the local teamsters union might not. The personality characteristics of the audience members also affect their response to your message and to you as a source of that message (Wood & Kallgren, 1988). Some people are more inclined to respond positively to a speaker simply because he or she is attractive, whereas others focus on the content of the speech.

How do we gain credibility with an audience? The answer is that public speakers earn the right to speak. They earn the right through their lives, experiences, and accomplishments. As one person observed, "Before you express yourself, you need a self worth expressing." You may have earned the right to speak on a number of subjects. Have you worked in a fast-food restaurant? You may have earned the right to comment on the quality of fast food and service. Have you raised children? You may have earned the right to speak on the problems and pleasures of family life. Think about it. What have you experienced, learned, or lived through that has earned you the right to speak?

Four Aspects of Credibility

What do audience members perceive that gives them the idea a speaker is credible? If individuals in the audience base credibility on judgments, what is the basis for those judgments? On what will your classmates be rating you when they judge your credibility? According to research, four of the most important aspects of credibility are competence, trustworthiness, dynamism, and co-orientation (Tuppen, 1974).

Competence

competence

The degree to which the speaker is perceived as skilled, reliable, experienced, qualified, authoritative, and informed; an aspect of credibility.

The first aspect of credibility is **competence,** *the degree to which a speaker is perceived as skilled, qualified, experienced, authoritative, reliable, and informed.* A speaker does not have to live up to all these adjectives; any one, or a few, might make the speaker credible. A machinist who displays her metalwork in a speech about junk sculpture as art is as credible as a biblical scholar who is demonstrating his ability to interpret scripture. They have different bases for their competence, but both can demonstrate competence in their own areas of specialization.

Words, visual aids, and an air of authority convey your own competence as a speaker. What can you build into your speech that will help the audience see and understand the basis of your authority? What experience have you had that is related to the subject? What training or knowledge do you have? How can you suggest to your audience that you have earned the right to speak about the subject? The most obvious way is to tell the audience the basis of your authority or expertise, but a creative speaker can think of dozens of ways to hint and suggest competence without being explicit, without seeming condescending, and without lying.

A speaker also signals competence by knowing the substance of the speech so well that he or she can deliver it without reading from note cards, without unplanned or vocalized pauses, and without mispronounced words. The speaker who knows the technical language in a specialized field and who can define the terms for the audience is signaling competence. The speaker who can translate complex ideas into language the audience can understand, who can find ways to illustrate ideas so that the audience can comprehend, and who is familiar with people who know about the subject and with books and articles about the subject signals competence.

Trustworthiness

The second aspect of credibility is **trustworthiness,** *the degree to which a speaker is perceived as honest, fair, sincere, friendly, honorable, and kind.* These perceptions are also earned. We judge people's honesty by both their past behavior and our present estimates. Your classmates will judge your trustworthiness when you speak in front of them. How do you decide whether or not other speakers in your class are responsible, sincere, dependable, or just? What can you do to help your audience perceive you as trustworthy?

You may have to reveal to your audience why you are trustworthy. Have you held jobs that demanded honesty and responsibility? Have you been a cashier, a bank teller, or a supervisor? Have you given up anything to demonstrate you are sincere? The person who pays his or her own way through college ordinarily has to be very sincere about education, and the person who chooses a lower-paying job because he or she feels a sense of public service is displaying sincerity about the job. Being respectful of others' points of view can be a sign of fairness, and being considerate of other people can be a sign of kindness and friendliness. What can you say about yourself that will show your trustworthiness?

Dynamism

The third aspect of credibility is **dynamism,** *the extent to which an audience perceives the speaker as bold, active, energetic, strong, empathic, and assertive.*

trustworthiness

The degree to which the speaker is perceived as honest, fair, sincere, honorable, friendly, and kind; an aspect of credibility.

dynamism

The extent to which the speaker is perceived as bold, active, energetic, strong, empathic, and assertive; an aspect of credibility.

Audiences value behavior described by these adjectives. Perhaps when we consider their opposites—timid, tired, and meek—we can see why dynamism is attractive. People who exude energy and show the spirit of their convictions impress others. Watch the television evangelists and ministers and note how dynamic they look and sound. You can learn to do the same. Evidence indicates that the audience's perception of your highly dynamic qualities will enhance your credibility.

Dynamism is exhibited mainly by voice, movement, facial expression, and gestures. A person who speaks forcefully, rapidly, and with considerable vocal variety; a speaker who moves toward the audience, back behind the lectern, and over to the visual aid; and a speaker who uses facial expression and gestures to make a point are all exhibiting dynamism. What can you do with your voice, movement, facial expressions, and gestures to show the audience you are a dynamic speaker?

Co-orientation

co-orientation

Also known as common ground, it is the degree to which the speaker's values, beliefs, attitudes, and interests are shared with the audience; an aspect of credibility.

Co-orientation, also referred to as *common ground*, is the *sharing of values, beliefs, attitudes, and interests.* It involves telling the audience members explicitly how you agree with them. This kind of information sharing is not just demographic—sharing similarities about hometowns, family sizes, and so on—but ideological as well. That is, the speaker tells the audience which ideas he or she has in common with the audience. For example, Jesse Jackson, an African American, used co-orientation when he spoke to over 4,000 mostly white, rural southeastern students and community members. He persuaded hundreds of students to register to vote by talking about how both the inner-city poor and the rural poor in their area share similar problems of illiteracy, illegitimate births, unemployment, drug dependency, bad schools, and poverty. An informative speech may require a minimal amount of co-orientation. However, a persuasive speech requires that the speaker go beyond areas of complete agreement into areas in which the speaker is trying to make a case for acceptance of his or her point of view on the issue.

Examples of student speeches in which the speaker used co-orientation include speeches about student housing, dormitory food, and honors societies. The student who spoke about student housing complained about the use of three-person rooms in the dormitories. He knew the majority of the students in the class had suffered through a year or two of such living conditions, and he established common ground by simply recounting some of his experiences in trying to study, entertain, and sleep in a three-person room. The student who spoke about the low quality of dormitory food knew most of the audience members had tasted it. She brought in a tray of dormitory food to remind them, and this established common ground. The student who spoke about honors societies was in an honors section full of students who had received invitations to join various honors societies. Unfortunately, most of the societies met only once and cost a high fee to join. The speaker established common ground by recounting a shared experience of receiving such letters and of being uncertain whether to join.

You don't have to be a national figure like Jesse Jackson to establish source credibility with an audience. Some speakers know so much that audiences listen; others are so dynamic that audiences listen; and still others inspire so much trust that audiences listen. You need to determine what you can do or say that will invite the audience to perceive you as credible.

Research Findings about Increasing Credibility

Credibility can be achieved before, during, or after a public speech. A speaker can have a reputation before arriving at a hall; that judgment can be altered during the presentation; and the evaluation can change again long after the speech has ended. You might think that some speakers are great before you hear them. Then their dull presentation reduces their credibility. In the weeks after the speech, your evaluation of such speakers might rise again because you discover that their message has given you new hope. In other words, credibility is not static—it is always in flux, always alterable.

Nor is credibility something a speaker always possesses. It depends on topics, audiences, and situations. This feature makes the concept of source credibility a challenging one to public speakers. These comments about the changing nature of credibility are intended as a caution in interpreting the research findings that follow.

Most of the studies that try to measure the effect of a speaker's message on an audience indicate that highly credible speakers change audience opinions more than speakers whose credibility is poor (Rosnow & Robinson, 1967). At least when the speech is delivered, a person perceived as credible can seek and achieve more changes of opinion (Karlins & Abelson, 1970). However, as time passes, an interesting phenomenon called the **sleeper effect** occurs (Hovland & Weiss, 1967). Apparently, *the source of the speech and the message become separated in the listener's mind*—"I don't remember who said this, but . . ." The result of this separation of source and message is that the message loses impact as audience members later forget they heard it from a highly credible speaker. The speaker with little credibility benefits from the opposite effect. As time passes, the audience forgets the source of the information, and the message gains impact. In one study, 3 or 4 weeks after a speech, a highly credible speaker and a speaker with little credibility were about even with respect to their ability to change opinions.

sleeper effect
A change of audience opinion caused by the separation of the message content from its source over a period of time.

The lesson for the public speaker is that the effect of credibility may be short-lived. In most speech classes, several weeks or more may elapse between your presentations. In between, your classmates are exposed to other speakers and speeches. They need reminders of your credibility. We like to think audiences remember us and our speeches, but it is sometimes difficult for students to remember a speech they heard the day before yesterday, much less weeks earlier. Effective speakers remind the audience of their credibility. Remind your audience about your major subject, your special interest in the topic, your special knowledge, or your special experience. Credibility decays over time and must be renewed if you want to have the maximum effect on your audience.

The following generalizations and conclusions are based on a summary of nearly 30 years of credibility studies (Thompson, 1967):

♦ The introduction of a speaker by another person can increase the speaker's credibility. The credibility of the person making the introduction is as important to the speaker's credibility as what is said in that introduction. Your credibility may also be enhanced if the audience believes your introducer is highly credible. A close friend introducing you can reveal information that could enhance or harm your credibility. To be safe, the speaker should always provide the introducer with information that could potentially increase credibility by showing the speaker's competence, trustworthiness, dynamism, or co-orientation. Your introducer can make evaluative statements about you that might sound self-serving were you to say them.

♦ The way you are identified by the person introducing you also can affect your credibility. Students who are identified as graduate students are thought to be more competent than those identified as undergraduates. Graduate students are also seen as more fair-minded, likeable, and sincere (Andersen & Clevenger, 1963). It is possible, therefore, that your identification as a sophomore, junior, or senior might affect your credibility with an audience.

♦ The perceived social status of a speaker can make a difference in credibility. Speakers of high status are consistently rated as more credible than speakers of low status. Even more striking is the finding that listeners judge credibility and status during the first 10 or 15 seconds of the speech (Harms, 1961). Probably the audience receives a barrage of clues about the speaker at the very beginning of the speech. They see how the speaker is dressed and make judgments about the speaker's appearance.

♦ The organization of your speech can affect your credibility. Students who listen to a disorganized speech think less of a speaker after the speech than they did before the speech (Sharp & McClung, 1966). This judgment by the audience may be based on its expectations. In the public-speaking classroom, students expect good organization; when they perceive a speech as poorly organized, they lower their evaluation of the speaker. The lesson from this study is clear: A speaker should strive for sound organization, lest he or she lose credibility even while speaking.

♦ A speaker whose delivery is considered effective—whose use of voice, movement, and gesture is effective—can become more credible during a speech (Thompson, 1967). A payoff exists for the student who practices a speech and who learns to be comfortable enough in front of an audience to appear natural, confident, and competent.

♦ Nonfluencies—breaks in the smooth and fluid delivery of the speech—are judged negatively. Vocalized pauses, such as "mmh" and "ahh" are nonfluencies. Another kind of nonfluency is the repetitive use of certain words and phrases, such as *well, like,* and *you know* at every transition. These nonfluencies decrease the audience's ratings of competence and dynamism but do not affect the speaker's trustworthiness (Thompson, 1967).

Ethical Considerations

As you have learned, credibility is a perceptual variable that is not based on external, objective measures of competence, trustworthiness, dynamism, and co-orientation. However, you retain an ethical obligation to project a true image of yourself to your audience, to actually be the sort of person you purport to be. The well-known cliché "You can fool all of the people some of the time" may be accurate, but an ethical communicator avoids "fooling" anyone.

To determine if you are behaving ethically, answer the following questions:

1. *Are your speech's immediate purpose and long-range goal sound?* Are you providing information or recommending change that would be determined worthy by current standards? Attempting to sell a substandard product or to encourage people to injure others would clearly not be sound; persuading people to accept new, more useful ideas and to be kinder to each other would be sound.
2. *Does your end justify your means?* This time-honored notion suggests that communicators can have ethical ends but may use unethical means of bringing the audience to a particular conclusion. What are some of the ethical considerations you should make in presenting your message? Professor Stephen E. Lucas (1989) offered four suggestions:
   a. Be well informed about your subject.
   b. Be honest in what you say.
   c. Use sound evidence.
   d. Use valid reasoning.

Credibility does lie in the audience's perception of you, but you also have an ethical obligation to be the sort of person you project yourself to be. In addition, you must consider the influence of your message on the audience. Persuasive speeches, particularly, may make far-reaching changes in others' behaviors. Are the changes you are recommending sound and consistent with standard ethical and moral guidelines? Have you thoroughly studied your topic so that you are convinced of the accuracy of the information you are presenting? Are you presenting the entire picture? Are you using valid and true arguments? In short, are you treating the listeners in the way you wish to be treated when someone else is speaking and you are the listener? The Golden Rule applies to the communication situation.

Summary

This chapter focused on how to find information for the content of your speech and how to use that information once you have found it. Sources to consider when gathering information for a speech include your personal experiences, written and visual resources, the Internet, and other people. Personal experiences are something you can discuss with authority, but you must take care to evaluate personal experiences as evidence.

Written and visual resources can lead you to important information on a wide variety of topics, but certain tools are needed to locate them. To locate periodicals, you should become familiar with the periodical indexes in book form and on computerized databases such as ERIC. Card catalogs and computerized catalogs are used most often to locate books. Explaining where you found your information through written footnotes, when writing an outline or manuscript, and oral footnotes, when presenting your speech, helps you avoid charges of plagiarism and enhances your credibility.

Interviewing other people is another way to obtain information for your speech. The interviewee can provide expert information, quotations, and examples, and sometimes he or she can lead you to other experts or additional written resources.

Supporting material is information you can use to substantiate your arguments and to clarify your position. The supporting materials discussed in this chapter are examples, surveys, testimonial evidence, numbers and statistics, analogies, explanations, and definitions.

Evidence refers to data or information from which you can draw a conclusion, make a judgment, or establish the probability that something will occur. Proof is sufficient evidence to convince your audience that what you say is true. Knowing what kind of, and how much, evidence will be regarded as proof is an important consideration for a speaker. Knowing how to select and organize a claim and its evidence so that the audience will accept it as proof is also important.

This chapter also explored the concept of source credibility by examining what qualities people seek in a speaker and how they judge a speaker's worthiness. The four dimensions of source credibility are competence, trustworthiness, dynamism, and co-orientation. High-credibility speakers have an initial advantage in changing audience opinion. To be a competent speaker, you should establish common ground with the audience. As a speaker, your credibility can be influenced by who introduces you and how you are introduced. A speaker's status, organization, and delivery also can influence credibility.

Issues in Communication

This Issues in Communication narrative is designed to provoke individual thought or discussion about concepts raised in the chapter.

Sally Crawford, a freshman, worked hard on her persuasive speech. She decided her speech topic would be about the newly reported dangers of food dyes since she thinks many people use it and are unaware of its dangers. She felt she was qualified to talk about the topic because she had recently learned about the possible correlation between cancer and the use of food dye in her introductory nutrition course and because she had recently declared nutrition as her major. Although Sally thought she had already learned enough about the topic from her course, she interviewed her nutrition professor, Dr. Capra, for the speech. Dr. Capra, though very knowledgeable on the topic, also heads a consumer awareness group opposed to the unnecessary use of food additives.

The speech she delivered was impassioned and well organized. She felt she accomplished what she had set out to do: to persuade her audience of the dangers of food dye through her competence as a speaker, her dynamic delivery, and her ability to convince her listeners that this topic was relevant to their lives. When her instructor asked the class for feedback, Sally was surprised and discouraged to hear that very few of her classmates had been convinced. Many of her classmates said that although she appeared to be competent, they did not consider her very trustworthy because her primary source of information was clearly biased. In Sally's effort to be dynamic and persuasive, she had neglected some necessary components of establishing her credibility, and she had not been as thorough as she could have been when she was gathering information.

Apply what you have learned about information and source credibility as you ponder and discuss the following questions: Do you think Sally's audience was fair? What additional sources could Sally have used for her speech? What could she have done differently to establish herself as a more credible source? What kinds of supporting materials might Sally have used to improve the effectiveness of her speech?

Additional Resources

Hollihan, T. A. & Baaske, K. T. (1998). *Arguments and arguing: The products and process of human decision making.* Prospect Heights, IL: Waveland Press. Fine texts for learning how to use claims, evidence, and proof.

Larson, C. U. (1998). *Persuasion: Reception and responsibility* (8th ed.). Belmont, CA: Wadsworth Publishing Co. This text includes a good chapter on source credibility, pp. 289–306.

Ross, R. S. (1994). *Understanding persuasion* (4th ed.). Englewood Cliffs, NJ: Prentice Hall. This text includes fine chapters on source credibility (pp. 92–107) and on constructing an argument (pp. 110–135).

References

Andersen, K., & Clevenger, T., Jr. (1963). A summary of experimental research in ethos. *Speech Monographs, 30,* 59–78.

Aristotle. (1941). Rhetoric. In R. McKeon (Ed.), *The basic works of Aristotle* (1, 1356a, ll. 12–14) (W. R. Roberts, Trans.). New York: Random House.

Dominick, J. R. (1996). *The dynamics of mass communication* (5th ed.). New York: McGraw-Hill.

Gregory, H. (1999). *Public speaking for college and career* (5th ed.). New York: McGraw-Hill.

Harms, L. S. (1961). Listener judgments of status cues in speech. *Quarterly Journal of Speech, 47,* 168.

Hovland, C. I., & Weiss, W. (1967). The influence of source credibility on communicator effectiveness. In R. L. Rosnow & E. J. Robinson (Eds.), *Experiments in persuasion* (pp. 9–24). New York: Academic Press.

Karlins, M., & Abelson, H. I. (1970). *Persuasion.* New York: Springer.

Lucas, S. E. (1989). *The art of public speaking* (3rd ed.). New York: Random House.

Rosnow, R. L., & Robinson, E. J. (Eds.). (1967). *Experiments in persuasion.* New York: Academic Press).

Safire, W. (1980, November 30). When a mistake becomes correct, and vice versa. *Des Moines Sunday Register,* p. 3C.

Sharp, H., Jr., & McClung, T. (1966). Effects of organization on the speaker's ethos. *Speech Monographs, 33,* 182–183.

Tuppen, C. J. (1974). Dimensions of communicator credibility: An oblique solution. *Speech Monographs, 41,* 253–260.

Thompson, W. N. (1967). *Quantitative research in public address and communication.* New York: Random House.

Wood, W., & Kallgren, C. A. (1988). Communicator attributes and persuasion: Recipients' access to attitude-relevant information in memory. *Personality and Social Psychology Bulletin, 14,* 172–182.

When you have read and
thought about this chapter,
you will be able to:

1. Reveal the functions of an
   introduction.

2. State some creative ways
   to fulfill these functions.

3. Identify some outlines
   useful to the public
   speaker.

4. Apply the principles of
   outlining.

5. Name the functions of the
   body of a speech.

6. Distinguish among the
   possible organizational
   patterns.

7. Explain why a speech
   needs transitions and
   signposts.

8. Reveal the functions of a
   conclusion for a speech.

13

Organizing Your Speech

In this chapter you will learn how to organize your speech. You will examine the three main parts of a speech: introduction, body, and conclusion. You will learn the functions of each part and how to effectively organize the content. Understanding the parts of a speech, their functions, and how to organize the content is essential to becoming a successful public speaker.

Jenny shifted impatiently in her chair. This hour had been the longest class period she ever experienced. Today was Brian's day to give a speech, and he had chosen to talk about how it is possible, statistically speaking, to never see two identical snowflakes. Jenny had lost interest in the first few minutes of the speech; she didn't particularly care why scientists or mathematicians thought that no two snowflakes were alike, and she couldn't see how this was relevant or important to her life. Brian had made matters worse by reading his entire speech, never once looking up from his manuscript, and he even went 15 minutes beyond his allotted time. Jenny felt that the class period had been a complete waste of time, and she kept thinking of all the homework she could've been doing instead of sitting there, listening to a deadly boring and pointless speech. She made a vow to improve her own speaking skills so that her listeners could never accuse her of wasting their time or boring them to death.

Like Jenny, none of us would want to be in Brian's shoes. If Brian had given more attention to the parts and functions of a speech, he would have been more aware of whether his speech would be relevant or interesting to his audience.

The Introduction

introduction

The first part of the speech; its function is to arouse the audience and to lead into the main ideas presented in the body.

The **introduction** is *the first part of your speech*. The opening is important because audiences use the introduction to "size up" a speaker. In the first few sentences, and certainly in the first few minutes of a speech, audience members decide whether or not to listen to you. They also decide whether your topic is important enough to warrant their consideration. In those crucial minutes early in the speech, you can capture your audience's attention and keep it, or you can lose it—perhaps for the remainder of the speech. This section of the chapter is devoted to helping you compose the best possible introduction—one that will grab your audience's attention and keep their minds on your topic.

Following are the five functions of an introduction:

1. Gain and maintain audience attention
2. Arouse audience interest in your topic
3. State the purpose of your speech
4. Establish your qualifications for speaking on the topic
5. Forecast the development and organization of your speech

These five functions are not necessarily fulfilled in this order. Gaining audience attention often comes at the beginning, but it is an important function throughout the speech. Forecasting the speech's organization often comes toward the end of an introduction, but it does not have to be the last item.

Several of the functions of the introduction can be fulfilled by using the same words in the speech. For example, you could start your speech with

The introduction of a public speech gains and maintains audience attention.

TRY ◀ ▶ THIS

List the five functions of an introduction. Make sure the introduction of your speech performs these functions.

words that both gain attention and establish your credibility to speak on a certain topic: "I have been in fast-food sales for the better part of 10 years, so I want to talk with you about minimum-wage 'careers.'"

To assist you in composing an introduction for your public speech, this section systematically explores the five functions and presents some examples.

Gaining and Maintaining Audience Attention

This section suggests ways to gain and maintain audience attention. Perhaps these suggestions will inspire you to think of even better ideas for your own speech. Remember, these suggestions are not just a bag of tricks you perform for dramatic effect. Instead, you gain and maintain the audience's attention by involving your audience in your topic.

1. *Bring to the speech presentation the object or person about which you are going to speak.* A student speaking on health foods brings a tray full of health foods, which he shares with the audience after the speech; a student speaking on weight lifting brings her 250-pound

friend to demonstrate the moves during the speech; or a student demonstrating the fine points of choreography shows the dancing talents of six friends as a small part of the presentation.

2. *Invite your audience to participate.* Ask questions and invite audience members to raise their hands and answer; teach the audience first-aid techniques by having them do some of the techniques with you; or have audience members move their chairs closer together for your speech about overcrowded housing.

3. *Let your clothing relate to your speech.* A nurse talking about the dangers of acute hepatitis wears a nurse's uniform; a construction worker dons a hard hat; or a private security officer wears a uniform and badge.

4. *Exercise your audience's imagination.* Have the audience members close their eyes and imagine they are standing on a ski slope, standing before a judge on a driving-while-intoxicated charge, or entering the warm waters of Hawaii when Cleveland is freezing.

5. *Start with sight or sound.* Examples include 1 minute of music from a speaker, a poster-size picture showing the horrors of war, and the sounds of forest birds chirping in the cool dawn. One student gave a powerful speech on motorcycle safety. He showed slides as he talked about the importance of wearing a helmet while driving or riding on a motorcycle. Only one item appeared in color on each slide: a crushed or battered helmet that had been worn by someone who lived through a motorcycle accident.

6. *Arouse audience curiosity.* One student began his speech by saying, "A new sport has hit this state, yet it is a national tradition. Held in the spring of the year in some of our most beautiful timbered areas, this sport is open to men and women alike. It is for responsible adults only and requires common sense and patience. This sport of our grandparents is . . ." Naturally, by this time, the audience is very curious about the student's topic and anxious to hear more.

7. *Role-play.* A student invites an audience member to pretend to be a choking victim. The speaker then "saves" the victim by using the maneuver she is teaching the audience. Speakers themselves can, for example, play the role of a mechanic fixing a small engine, a nurse showing how to take vital signs, or an architect selling a proposal. Audiences can be asked to play the roles of people whose cars will not start, of paramedics learning what to do in the first few minutes with an accident victim, or of a board of directors considering a new building.

8. *Show a few slides or a very short film or video.* A football player speaking on violence in that sport shows a short video of a punt return while he points out which players were deliberately trying to maim their opponents with faceguards—as they have been taught to do; a Chinese student shows a few slides of her native land; or a student speaking on city slums presents a mind-grabbing sequence of 12 slides showing homeless people in doorways, rats in a child's room, and a family of 10 people living in three rooms.

9. *Present a brief quotation, or have the audience read something you have provided.* You can put your audience in the mood for your speech by using a few lines from a popular song, quoting inspiring words from T. S. Elliot, Ghandi, or Malcolm X, or citing a particularly eloquent statement by a pundit, news person, or entertainer. One enterprising student handed every class member an official-looking letter right before his speech. Each letter was a personalized summons to court for a moving violation that was detected by a police-owned spy camera at a busy intersection.

10. *State striking facts or statistics.* Examples include "Scientists have discovered the bones of a 17-million-year-old apelike creature, a creature that could be the common ancestor of the great apes and human beings" (Bones found, 1983), or "Women under 50 years of age could reduce their heart attacks by 65 percent by simply quitting smoking, according to a study in the *Journal of the American Medical Association*" (Research notes, 1983).

11. *Self-disclosure.* Tell audience members something about yourself—related to the topic—that they would not otherwise know: "I took hard drugs for 6 years"; "I was an eagle scout"; "I earn over $50,000 a year—legally."

12. *Tell a story, a narration.* Example: "I want to tell you about Tiow Tan, a friend of mine. Tan was a big success at South High: he lettered in track and football, and he had the second-highest grades in our senior year. Tan was just as good in college: he had a 3.5 GPA, drove a Corvette, and was selected for a student internship with IBM. But you read about my friend Tan in last week's newspaper. Maybe you didn't know who he was, but he was the one who died in a car wreck with his girlfriend on Route 340. They were killed by a drunken driver." If you choose to use narration, you should indicate to your audience whether the story is hypothetical or an actual account.

The preceding 12 suggestions for gaining and maintaining audience attention certainly are not the only possibilities, but they have all been tried successfully by other students. Your introduction should not simply imitate what you read in this book; instead, think of ideas of your own that will work best for you and your audience.

Some words of caution about gaining and maintaining attention: No matter what method you use for gaining audience attention, avoid being overly dramatic. One professor had a harrowing experience in class. She was writing down some comments about a speech when the next student rose to deliver his speech. She heard a horrifying groan and looked up to see the student on the floor with his whole leg laid open and bleeding. The other students leaped up and surrounded the injured student while the professor ran to the office to call for emergency assistance. The student had planned to give a speech on first aid and had borrowed a plastic leg wound in living color from the student health center. He had a bag of simulated blood on his stomach, which he squeezed rhythmically so that it would spurt like a severed artery. Unfortunately for the student, his attention-getting action introduction was too realistic. Instead of capturing the audience's attention, he managed to get the participants so upset that they were in no mood to listen to any more speeches that day.

Always make sure your attention-getting strategy is related to your topic. Some speakers think every public speech must start with a joke. Starting with a joke is a big mistake if you are not good at telling jokes or if your audience is not interested in hearing them. Jokes can be used in the introduction of a speech if they are topically relevant, but they are just one of hundreds of ways a speaker can gain attention. Another overused device is writing something such as "S-E-X" on the chalkboard and then announcing your speech has nothing to do with sex but that you wanted to get the audience's attention. Again, the problem with this approach is that the attention-getting strategy has nothing to do with the topic.

TRY◄►THIS

List the 12 ways to gain and maintain audience attention. Think of other ways that pertain to your speech topic.

Arousing Audience Interest

The second function of an introduction is to arouse audience interest in the subject matter. The best way to arouse audience interest is to show clearly how the topic is related to the audience. A highly skilled speaker can determine how to adapt almost any topic to an audience. Do you want to talk about collecting coins? Thousands of coins pass through each person's hands every year. Can you tell your audience how to spot a rare one? If you can arouse the audience's interest in currency, you will find it easier to encourage them to listen to your speech about the rare coins you have collected. Similarly, speeches about your life as a mother of four, a camp counselor, or the manager of a business can be linked to audience interests. The following is a good example of relating the topic to the audience; it occurred in a student speech on drinking and driving:

> Do you know what the leading cause of death is for people who attend this college? Some of you might think it is a disease that causes the most deaths—cancer, heart attacks, or AIDS. No, the leading cause of death among students at this college is car accidents. Not just ordinary car accidents, but accidents in which the driver has been drinking.

The speaker related her topic to the audience by linking a national problem to her own college. She prepared the audience to receive more information and ideas about this common problem.

Instant Recall

Stating the Purpose

The third function of an introduction is to state the purpose of your speech. Why state the purpose? Informative speeches invite learning, and learning is more likely to occur if you reveal to the audience what you want them to know. Consider the difficulty of listening to a history professor who spends 50 minutes telling you every detail and date related to the Crusades. Observe how much easier it is to listen to a professor who begins the lecture by stating what you are supposed to learn from it: "I want you to understand why the Crusades began, who the main participants were, and when the Crusades occurred."

The following are some examples of statements of purpose:

"Today I will tell you three ways to make your car last longer."

"What I want you to remember from my speech is why our national debt is costing a billion dollars per day."

"You will learn in this presentation several methods of protecting your credit card from crooks."

In speaking, as in teaching, audience members are more likely to learn and understand if you are clear about what is expected from them. That goal can be accomplished by stating the purpose in the introduction. However, sometimes in a persuasive speech you may wish to delay giving a statement of purpose until you have set the stage for audience acceptance. Under most circumstances, though—and especially in informative speeches—you should reveal your purpose in your introduction.

Establishing Your Qualifications

The fourth function of an introduction is to describe any special qualifications you have to enhance your credibility. You can talk about your experience, your research, the experts you interviewed, and your own education and training in the subject. Although you should be wary about self-praise, you need not be reserved in stating why you can speak about the topic with authority. The following is an example of establishing credibility through self-disclosure.

> I am a Catholic girl and I have a Baptist boyfriend. Our different religions have challenged us both but have strengthened, rather than weakened, our relationship because we have to explain our faiths to each other. With that in mind, I'd like to share with you the similarities between two seemingly different religions.

Forecasting Development and Organization

The fifth function of an introduction is to forecast the organization and development of the speech. The forecast provides a brief outline of your organization, a preview of the main points you plan to cover. Audience members feel more comfortable when they know what to expect. You can help by revealing your plan for the speech. Are you going to discuss a problem and its solution? Are you going to make three main arguments with supporting materials? Are you going to talk for 5 minutes or for 20? Let your audience know what you plan to do early in your speech. Two forecasts follow. Are they adequate in forecasting organization and development?

> Follow my advice this evening and you can earn ten dollars an hour painting houses, barns, and warehouses. First, I will show you how to locate this kind of work. Next, I will teach you how to bid on a project. And, last, I will give you some tips on how to paint well enough to get invited back.

> My purpose is to help you understand your own checking account. I will help you "read" your check by explaining the numbers and stamps that appear on the face; I will help you manage your checking account by showing you how to avoid overdraw charges; and I will demonstrate how you can prove that your check cleared.

The Body

Most speakers begin composing their speeches with the body rather than the introduction. The order used in composing a speech differs from the order used in delivering a speech because the speaker needs to know the content of the speech to write an effective introduction.

The **body** of a speech is *the largest portion of the speech, in which you place your arguments and ideas, your substantiation and examples, and your proofs and illustrations.* Since you usually do not have time to state in a speech everything you know about a subject, you need to decide what information to include and what information to exclude. Since the material you will use may not all be of equal importance, you need to decide where in the body to place it—first, last, or in the middle. Selecting, prioritizing, and organizing are three skills that you will use in developing the body of your speech.

Just as the introduction of a speech has certain functions to fulfill, so does the body. Following are the main functions of the body:

1. Increase what an audience knows about a topic (informative speech)
2. Change an audience's attitudes or actions about a topic (persuasive speech)
3. Present a limited number of arguments and/or ideas
4. Provide support for your arguments and/or ideas
5. Indicate the sources of your information, arguments, and supporting materials

You already know something about organization. Every sentence you utter has organization. The words are arranged according to rules of syntax for the English language. Even when you are in conversation, you organize your speech. The first statement you make is often more general than that which follows. For instance, you might say, "I don't like DeMato for Congress," after which you might say why you don't like DeMato. You probably don't start by stating a specific fact, such as DeMato's voting record, her position on health care, or her torrid love life. Likewise, when we compose a speech, we tend to limit what we say, prioritize our points, and back them as necessary with substantiation—all organized according to principles we have either subconsciously learned (as in the rules of syntax for language) or consciously studied (as in the rules of organization).

TRY ◀▶ THIS

List the experience, skills, and knowledge that make you qualified to speak on your topic.

The Principles of Outlining

An **outline** is *a written plan that uses symbols, margins, and content to reveal the order, importance, and substance of your speech.* An outline shows the

body

The largest part of the speech, which contains the arguments, evidence, and main content.

outline

A written plan that uses symbols, margins, and content to reveal the order, importance, and substance of a speech.

Use word processing to create an outline.

sequence of your arguments or main points, indicates their relative importance, and states the content of your arguments, main points, and substantiations. The outline is a simplified, abstract version of your speech.

Why learn outlining? First, outlining is a skill that can be used to develop written compositions, to write notes in class, and to compose speeches. Second, outlining teaches important skills, such as selecting the information and ideas most important for you and your audience; discriminating between what is more important and less important; and placing arguments, ideas, and support in a structure that will encourage learning and behavioral change. A third advantage is that an outline encourages you to speak conversationally. Some of the best speakers learn how to deliver their speeches from an outline, instead of having every word written out in a manuscript. Useful, important, and readily applicable in a speech communication class, outlining is an overall organizational plan that you need to understand.

The outline form is versatile and relatively easy to learn as long as you keep a few principles in mind. *The first principle of outlining is that all the items of information in your outline should be directly related to your purpose and long-range goal.* The **immediate purpose** is *what you expect to achieve with your speech today.* You might want the audience to be able to distinguish between a row house and a townhouse, to rent a particular video, to sign a petition, or to talk with others about a topic. All of these purposes can be achieved shortly after the audience hears about the idea. The **long-range goal** is *what you expect to achieve by your message in the days, months, or years ahead.* You may be talking about a candidate 2 months before the election, but you want your audience to vote a certain way at that future date. You may want to push people to be more tolerant toward persons of your race, gender, sexual preference, or religion, but tolerance is more likely to develop over time than instantly—so it is a long-range goal.

immediate purpose

What you expect to achieve on the day of your speech.

long-range goal

What you expect to achieve over a time period longer than the day of your speech.

The second principle of outlining is that the outline should be an abstract of the speech you will deliver. It should be less than every word you speak but should include all important points and supporting materials. Some instructors say an outline should be about one-third the length of the actual speech, if the speech were in manuscript form. However, you should ask what your instructor expects in an outline, because some instructors like to see a very complete outline whereas others prefer a brief outline. Nonetheless, the outline is not a manuscript but an abstract of the speech you intend to deliver, a plan that includes the important arguments or information you intend to present.

The third principle of outlining is that the outline should consist of single units of information, usually in the form of complete sentences that express a single idea. The following example is incorrect because it expresses more than one idea in more than one sentence:

I. Gun control should be used to reduce the number of deaths in the United States that result from the use of handguns. Half of the deaths from handguns occur because criminals use them to commit murder.

The same ideas can be outlined correctly by presenting a single idea in each sentence:

I. Government regulation of handguns should be implemented to reduce the number of murders in this country.
   A. Half of the murders in the United States are committed by criminals using handguns.
   B. Half of the handgun deaths in the United States are caused by relatives, friends, or acquaintances of the victim.

The fourth principle of outlining is that the outline should indicate the importance of an item with an outlining symbol. In the example, the **main points,** or *most important points, are indicated with Roman numerals,* such as I, II, III, IV, and V. The number of main points in a 5- to 10-minute speech, or even a longer speech, should be limited to the number you can reasonably cover, explain, or prove in the time permitted. Most 5-minute speeches have from one to three main points. Even hour-long speeches must have a limited number of main points because audiences seem unable to remember more than seven main points.

Subpoints, *the points supporting the main points, or those of less importance, are indicated with capital letters,* such as *A, B, C, D,* and *E.* Ordinarily, two subpoints under a main point are regarded as the minimum if any subpoints are to be presented. As with the main points, the number of subpoints should be limited; otherwise, the audience may lose sight of your main points. A good guideline is to present two or three of your best pieces of supporting material in support of each main point.

The fifth principle of outlining is that the outline should provide margins that visually indicate the relative importance of the items. The larger the margin on the left, the less important the item is to your purpose. However, the margins are coordinated with the symbols explained previously; thus, the main points have the same left margin, the subpoints have a slightly larger

main points

The most important points in a speech; indicated by Roman numerals in an outline.

subpoints

The points in a speech that support the main points; indicated by capital letters in an outline.

left margin, the sub-subpoints have a still larger left margin, and so on. A correct outline with the appropriate symbols and margins looks like this:

Topic: Conservative speakers & freedom of speech
Immediate purpose: Persuade students to listen to controversial speakers—without heckling.

Conservative Speakers Face "Heckler's Veto"

Introduction
I. The USA's principle of free speech is being threatened today by the very people who should be that principle's greatest supporters—lawyers and students.
   A. Lawyers have assailed Supreme Court Justice Clarence Thomas's address to the National Bar Association.
   B. Boisterous students, aggressive administrators, and an uncharacteristically benign faculty at Columbia University assailed the right of free speech for conservative luminaries.
   C. My purpose is to introduce civility to campus speeches by encouraging my fellow students to understand the true meaning of freedom of speech in the USA.

Body
II. Supreme Court Justice Clarence Thomas has points of view objectionable to blacks and whites, but he, like all Americans, has the right to speak and be heard.
   A. *The New York Times* reported that Thomas "accepted the invitation [from the ABA] with alacrity even though he knew he would confront an audience with many critics" (quoted in Yardley, 1998).
   B. According to Jonathan Yardley (1998, August 3) of *The Washington Post,* Thomas's speech was "angry, bitter and pugnacious" (p. D2).
   C. Nonetheless, Thomas is right about his right to be heard.
      1. Voltaire said, "I disapprove of what you say, but I will defend to the death your right to say it," a sentiment widely shared by free speech advocates.
      2. Yardley (1998) argues that " 'liberalism' as now defined in too many quarters is a synonym for ideological conformity and intolerance of dissent" (p. D2).
      3. A cardinal principle among earlier liberals was that everyone has a right to be heard, especially those who articulate unpopular ideas.
III. At Columbia University a conference on "Conservative Ideas in Higher Education" was disrupted by unruly students, closed off even to those who had paid to attend, and moved outside to Morningside Park, where at least one speaker was unable to complete his remarks because of the loud heckling.
   A. According to Nat Hentoff (1998), the dean of students at Columbia confined the meeting to Columbia University students only "to ensure the safety of our students" (p. A19).

B. The *Columbia Spectator,* the student newspaper, reported that the rules for admission to the conference produced an "effective ban," according to Hentoff (1998).

IV. Freedom of speech was not intended to protect the popular, the desired, and the politically correct; instead, freedom of speech only makes sense as a right to protect minority opinion, unpopular positions, and even hateful rhetoric.

A. Communication students should be defenders of the right to free speech because that right is the very basis of the communication discipline.

B. Communication students should recognize that challenging, debating, and even vigorous criticism are better armaments in the arena of ideas than are room closings, shouting down, and the "Heckler's Veto" (Hentoff, 1998).

Conclusion

V. While Clarence Thomas and the conservative speakers at Columbia University were treated disrespectfully, communication students should remember the two examples as reminders that they should be defenders of the right of free speech.

*The sixth principle of outlining is that the items should appear in **parallel form,** consisting of complete sentences, clauses, phrases, or words, but not a mixture of these.* Hacker (1995) in her text on writing, says, "Readers expect items in a series to appear in parallel grammatical form" (p. 63). The same could be said of listeners. Most teachers prefer an outline consisting entirely of complete sentences because such an outline reveals more completely the speaker's message. An outline like the one above on free speech is composed entirely of complete sentences; it is an example of parallel form because no dependent clauses, phrases, or single words appear in the outline. To clarify the idea of parallel form, you should note the differences between the following two examples (with the incorrect example shown first):

parallel form

The consistent use of complete sentences, clauses, phrases, or words in an outline.

I. Three measures of educational quality are college entrance exams, teacher-pupil ratios, and expenditures per pupil.

A. College entrance tests are higher in some states than in others.
   1. Top SAT states—New Hampshire, Oregon, and Vermont
   2. Top ACT states—Minnesota, Wisconsin, and Iowa
B. Teacher-pupil ratios:
   1. Connecticut and Wyoming tied for first.
   2. Others in the top 10: New York; Washington, DC; New Jersey; Oregon; Delaware; Maryland; Rhode Island; and Massachusetts.
C. Expenditures per pupil . . .

The example above is incorrect because it mixes sentences (A, B1) and non-sentences (A1, A2, and B2) instead of consistently using one form—complete sentences—as illustrated in the outline below, based on information from the U.S. secretary of education (Bell, 1984):

Topic: Measures of educational quality
Immediate purpose: To inform the audience of criteria used to measure educational quality

Measuring Quality in Our Schools

Introduction
  I. An informed electorate and parents in the know need to recognize and understand how the experts are determining the quality of our schools.
     A. Three measures determine quality: college entrance exams, teacher-student ratios, and expenditures per student.
     B. States differ markedly on how they score by these measures.

Body
  II. The first measures of educational quality are the two most often used college entrance exams, the ACT (American College Test) and the SAT (Scholastic Aptitude Test).
     A. Minnesota, Wisconsin, and Iowa were the top-scoring states on the ACT.
     B. Oregon, New Hampshire, and Vermont scored highest on the SAT.
  III. The second measure of educational quality is the teacher-student ratio or how many students each teacher teaches.
     A. Connecticut and Wyoming tied for first place on this dimension.
     B. Massachusetts, Rhode Island, Maryland, Delaware, Oregon, New Jersey, Washington, DC, and New York were among the top 10.
     C. Expenditures per pupil . . .

This example of correct parallel form uses complete sentences throughout; the outline is parallel because it repeats the same or similar forms throughout the composition.

TRY ◄►THIS

List the principles of outlining, and apply those principles when you make an outline.

The Development of a Rough Draft

Before you begin composing your outline, you can save time and energy by (1) selecting a topic that is appropriate for you, for your audience, for your purpose, and for the situation; (2) finding arguments, examples, illustrations, quotations, and other supporting materials from your experience, from written and visual resources, and from other people; and (3) narrowing your topic so that you can select the best materials from a large supply of available items.

Once you have gathered materials consistent with your purpose, you can begin by developing a **rough draft** of your outline, *a preliminary organization of the outline*. The most efficient way to develop a rough draft is to choose a limited number of main points important for your purpose and your audience.

rough draft
The preliminary organization of the outline of a speech.

Next, you should see what materials you have from your experience, from written and visual resources, and from other people to support these main ideas. You need to find out if you have any materials that support your subpoints—facts, statistics, testimony, and examples. In short, you assemble your main points, your subpoints, and your sub-subpoints for your speech, always with your audience and purpose in mind. What arguments, illustrations, and supporting materials will be most likely to have an impact on the audience? Sometimes speakers get so involved in a topic that they select mainly those items that interest them. In public speaking, you should select the items likely to have the maximum impact on the audience, not on you.

Composing an outline for a speech is not easy. Even professional speechwriters may have to make important changes to their first draft. Some of the questions you need to consider as you revise your rough draft follow:

1. Are my main points consistent with my purpose?
2. Are my subpoints and sub-subpoints subordinate to my main points?
3. Are the items in my outline the best possible ones for this particular audience, for this topic, for me, for the purpose, and for the occasion?
4. Does my outline follow the principles of outlining?

Even after you have rewritten your rough draft, you would be wise to have another person—perhaps a classmate—examine it and provide an opinion about its content.

The next outline (based on a speech by Smith, 1998) is an example of what a rough draft of a speech looks like:

Topic: Sex and persuasion
Statement of purpose: To discourage sexual activity among teenagers

Introduction
 I. Teenagers have sex for the wrong reasons.
   A. Alcohol & sexual activity.
   B. Statistics on sexual activity now and in the past.
   C. Forecast of reasons: peers, family and school.

Body
 II. Adolescents pushed by peers to have sex.
   A. The influence of friends.
   B. Rewards for having sex.

III. Family influence on adolescent sex.
    A. Parental power and premarital sex.
    B. Parents talking with teens about sex.
    C. Siblings' influence on adolescent sex.
IV. Sex education & premarital sex.
    A. Delaying sex for teens.
    B. Clarifying values for teens.

Conclusion
V. What can reduce teenage sexual-activity level?
    A. Be careful of the friends you choose.
    B. Parent intervention helps.
    C. Sex education tends to reduce sexual activity.
    D. Abstinence makes the heart grow fonder.

A rough draft of a speech does not necessarily follow parallel form, nor is it as complete as the sentence outline, which often develops out of the rough draft. Mostly, the rough draft provides an overview so that you can see how the parts of the speech, the main and subpoints, fit together. When you are ready to finalize your outline, you have several options. The sentence outline and key-word outline are two possibilities.

The Sentence Outline

sentence outline

An outline consisting entirely of complete sentences.

The sentence outline does not have all of the words that will occur in the delivered speech, but it does provide a complete guide to the content. A **sentence outline** *consists entirely of complete sentences.* It shows in sentence form your order of presentation; what kinds of arguments, supporting material, and evidence you plan to use; and where you plan to place them. A look at your outline indicates strengths and weaknesses. You might note, for instance, that you have insufficient information on some main point or a surplus of information on another.

In addition to the sentence outline itself, you may want to make notes on the functions being served by each part of your outline. For example, where are you trying to gain and maintain attention? Where are you trying to back up a major argument with supporting materials such as statistics, testimony, or specific instances? A sentence outline, along with sidenotes indicating functions, is a blueprint for your speech. It can strengthen your speech performance by helping you present evidence or supporting materials that will make sense to audience members and will help you inform or persuade them.

The outline that follows is based on a student's speech (Smith, 1998). The immediate purpose of the speech is to recount the dangers of teenage intercourse, to consider the consequences. The long-term goal was to persuade the audience members to delay or cease having intercourse in order to reduce the number of young people taking risks with their health and their futures. Notice that the outline consists entirely of sentences:

Sexual Intercourse and Persuasion   **Functions**

Introduction of the Speech
I. Today more and more adolescents are having sex for the wrong reasons.
  A. Let me tell you the story of a girl who loses her virginity after drinking alcohol with her boyfriend.   **Attention-getting information**
  B. In the early 1970s 35 percent of young women and 55 percent of young men had intercourse by age 18.
  C. In this decade 56 percent of young women and 73 percent of young men have intercourse by age 18.   **Statistics to relate topic to audienc**
  D. My purpose is to encourage reduced sexual activity or abstinence for teenagers by using peer influence, parental influence, and sex education.   **Forecast and expectations**

Body of the Speech
II. Adolescents are encouraged to have intercourse by peer pressure.   **First main point**
  A. Adolescents with sexually active friends are more likely to be sexually active themselves.   **Supporting material**
  B. Learning theory says rewards such as the approval or acceptance of friends can encourage the early onset of intercourse.
  C. An interviewed student admitted that she had intercourse because she felt like "the last virgin on earth."
III. Family attitudes toward premarital sex can influence adolescent behavior.   **Second main point**
  A. Parents, who have legitimate power over teenagers, may not exercise that power against sexual behavior.   **Supporting material**
  B. Parents who talked with adolescent offspring about sex, pregnancy, and contraception were more likely to have teens who used birth control when sexually active.
  C. Older siblings make a difference: Research indicates that second-born adolescents "were more sexually active than firstborns at any age."   **Supporting quote**
IV. Sex education in the schools can, in cooperation with the community, churches, and families, discourage adolescent sex.   **Third main point**
  A. Several studies demonstrate that "sex education can help delay first intercourse for adolescents who are not sexually active."   **Supporting research**

B. Information on reproductive health can "enhance communication and negotiation skills, clarify their values, and change risky behaviors."

Conclusion of the Speech

V. To discourage the current trend of adolescents' becoming sexually active, I recommend peer pressure to discourage sexual activity, parental influence to reduce sexual activity, and sex education to persuade teenagers not to become sexually active so early in life.

   A. Peer pressure can discourage sexual activity, not just encourage it.

   B. Parental influence can reduce the number of early starters.

   C. Sex education seems to reduce sexual activity among teenagers.

   D. Absence may make the heart grow fonder, but abstinence certainly does.

Closure on topic

References

Barnett, Barbara. (1997, October 15). Education protects health, delays sex. **www.thi.org/to/tppubs/network/v17-3/nt1734.html.**

Barth, Richard, et al. (1992). Presenting adolescent pregnancy with social and cognitive skills. *Journal of Adolescent Research, 7,* 208–232.

Parrillo, A. V., Felts, W. M., & Mikow-Porto, V. (1997). Early initiation of sexual intercourse and its co-occurrence with other health-risk behaviors in high school students: The 1993 North Carolina youth risk behavior survey. *Journal of Health Education, 28,* 85–93.

Widmer, Eric D. (1997). Influence of older siblings on initiation of sexual intercourse. *Journal of Marriage and the Family, 59,* 928–938.

Sources of information

The Key-Word Outline

Using a manuscript for your entire speech sometimes invites you to become too dependent on the manuscript. It reduces your eye contact and minimizes your attention to audience responses. Nonetheless, you can become very proficient at reading from a manuscript on which you have highlighted the important words, phrases, and quotations. A complete sentence outline may be superior to a manuscript in that it forces you to extemporize, to maintain eye contact, and to respond to audience feedback. Key words and phrases can also be underlined or highlighted on a sentence outline. An alternative method is to simply use a **key-word outline,** *an outline consisting of important words or phrases to remind you of the content of the speech.*

key-word outline

An outline consisting of important words or phrases to remind the speaker of the content of the speech.

A key-word outline abstracts the ideas in a speech considerably more than does a sentence outline. A key-word outline ordinarily consists of important words and phrases, but it can also include statistics or quotations that are long or difficult to remember. The outline below came from a student speech. Notice how the key-word format reduces the content to the bare essentials.

Why Should You Go to College?

Introduction
I. What happens if you don't go and if you do?
  A. If you don't
    1. Fewer job opportunities
    2. Less income
    3. More job shifting
  B. If you do
    1. More job opportunities
    2. Higher income
    3. Fewer but better jobs
  C. Education more important, changing market, choices in college

Body
II. Simpson & Frost on need for more education
  A. Global economy/increased competition
  B. More skills and knowledge
III. Changing job market
  A. B.S. or B.A. required
  B. Semiskilled, only 10 percent by 2000
IV. Three college choices
  A. Major
  B. Global perspective
  C. Skills and knowledge

Conclusion
V. Go to college for income, opportunity, & stability
  A. Increased importance of education
  B. Changed job market
  C. College choices
  D. Go to college for a better future

A key-word outline fits easily on 3-by-5-inch or 4-by-6-inch notecards or on 8½-by-11-inch paper. If you choose notecards on which you write or type a key-word outline, the following suggestions may be helpful:

1. Write instructions to yourself on your notecards. For instance, if you are supposed to write the title of your speech and your name on the chalkboard before your speech begins, then you can write that instruction on the top of your first card.

2. Write on one side of the cards only. It is better to use more cards with your key-word outline on one side only than to write front and back, which is more likely to result in confusion.

Instant Recall

Complete the following statements:

1. An outline uses _____ , _____ , and _____ to reveal the order, importance, and substance of your speech.

2. An immediate purpose can be defined as _____ ; _____ while a long-range goal would be

   _____

3. Parallel form in outlining means _____

   _____

   _____

Answers: 1. symbols/margins/content   2. what you want to achieve on the day of your speech; what you expect to achieve over a period of time   3. repeating the same form throughout the outline by using complete sentences or phrases, not a combination of the two

3. Number your notecards on the top so that they will be unlikely to get out of order. If you drop them, you can quickly reassemble them.
4. Write out items that might be difficult to remember. Extended quotations, difficult names, unfamiliar terms, and statistics are items you may want to include on your notecards to reduce the chances of error.
5. Practice delivering your speech at least two times using your notecards. Effective delivery may be difficult to achieve if you have to fumble with unfamiliar cards.
6. Write clearly and legibly.

TRY◄►THIS

Name the two types of outlines, and list the advantages and disadvantages of each. Determine which is best for your topic.

Cultural Note

LINEAR OR CONFIGURAL ORGANIZATION: CULTURE AND COMMUNICATION

Outlining as taught in English composition and communication classes is almost entirely linear. In other words, the outline for a speech is based on a sequential development of ideas, moving from a beginning to a middle and finally to an end. It is hard to imagine an outline that is not sequential—for that matter, it's hard to imagine a speech that is not linear but is still organized and understandable. It's hard to imagine because we live in a linear culture.

What are some of the characteristics of our culture that could be termed "linear"? We like beginnings and endings, points and subpoints. We like text and words, evidence and proof. Sometimes we value objects over people or events—buildings are cooled to preserve the equipment, not the people, inside them. We tend to think directionally. Doing things in a timely fashion is essential to our sense of well-being.

Not all cultures are linear. *Configural* cultures are nonlinear—they tend to see how the arrangement of parts creates a whole object; thus contours or patterns are more important than the sequential development of an idea. Configural cultures tend to think in images. Relationships are valued over objects, and time is seen as flexible. In rural China the professor starts teaching when enough students have gathered; the gathering of the group, not a bell or specific time, determines when class begins.

Can you see how culture affects the way you create an outline for a speech? This chapter has introduced you to linear patterns of organization, but how might a person who thinks in configural patterns prepare a speech? See if you can develop arguments about the merits and limitations of our current instruction on organization in oral communication.

Organizational Patterns

The body of a speech can be outlined using a number of **organizational patterns,** *arrangements of the contents of the speech.* Exactly which pattern of organization is most appropriate for your speech depends in part on your

organizational patterns

Arrangements of the contents of a speech.

purpose and on the nature of your material. For instance, if your purpose is to present a solution to a problem, your purpose lends itself well to the problem/solution organizational pattern. If the nature of your material is something that occurred over a period of time, then your material might be most easily outlined within a time-sequence pattern.

In this section, we will examine five organizational patterns—the time-sequence pattern, the spatial/relations pattern, the cause/effect pattern, the problem/solution pattern, and the topical-sequence pattern. You should keep in mind that these five patterns of organization are prototypes from which a skilled speaker can construct many others. Also, a number of organizational patterns may appear in the same speech: An overall problem/solution organization may have within it a time-sequence pattern that explains the history of the problem.

The Time-Sequence Pattern

time-sequence pattern

A method of speech organization in which the speaker explains a sequence of events in chronological order.

The **time-sequence pattern** is *a method of speech organization in which the speaker explains a sequence of events in chronological order*. It is most commonly used in informative speeches. You can use this pattern in speeches that consider the past, present, and future of an idea, an issue, a plan, or a project. It is most useful on such topics as the following:

How the Salvation Army Began	The Future of Space Exploration
The "Today" Show: A Brief History	Building of the Hearst Castle
The Naming of a Stadium	The Development of Drugs for Treating AIDS

Any topic that requires attention to events, incidents, or steps that take place over time is appropriate for this pattern of organization. Following is a brief outline of a composition (Rogers & Hart, in press) organized in a time-sequence pattern:

History of Technology: The Pioneers

I. Vannevar Bush, an MIT engineering graduate and dean, invented a mechanical computer with rods and gears prior to World War II.
   A. Bush's "differential analyzer" did the math for radar-guided artillery shells in World War II.
   B. Bush had, by 1945, envisioned the "Memex," which he never built but which was remarkably like today's personal computers.
II. J. C. R. Licklider saw computers as a means of human communication, instead of simply computation, in the 1960s.
   A. Licklider challenged the "batch-processing" system in favor of computer time-sharing.
   B. Licklider proposed, for the first time, a concept like the current Internet.
III. Robert W. Taylor created ARPANET at the Pentagon to communicate among contractors.

The organizational pattern of your speech may depend on your speech purpose and the nature of your information.

A. Taylor brought in Dr. Larry Roberts to develop a wide-area network.
B. To allow communication among previously incompatible computers, they created the Interface Message Processor.

Notice that the emphasis in this brief outline is on the history of technology—something that occurred over a period of time. A simpler example of a time-sequence pattern of organization is a recipe that depends on the combining of ingredients in the correct order.

The Spatial/Relations Pattern

Another organizational pattern used mainly in informative speeches is called the **spatial/relations organization.** It is *a pattern that reveals how things relate to each other in space, position, and visual orientation.* Examples are a blueprint, a road map, or a diagram showing furniture arrangements in a room. In a speech, it is more likely to be an explanation of an audio board, how electricity gets from the power plant to your home, or how to best set up your stereo speakers. The following is a more detailed example, describing the parts of the human heart:

Immediate purpose: After listening to my speech, the audience will be able to describe the form and state the function of the human heart.

spatial/relations organization

A method of speech organization in which the speaker reveals how things relate to each other in space, position, and visual orientation.

The Human Heart: Form and Function

Introduction
  I. You should know about the organ that keeps you alive.
    A. The heart fails or falters in more than 1 million people each year.
    B. Learning the form and function of the heart can help you maintain it.
 II. First we will learn about the form and then the function of the heart.

Body
III. The form of the heart includes four chambers.
   A. The right atrium and the left atrium are located on the top of the heart, the top two humps on the valentine.
   B. The right and left ventricles are located on either side of the point at the bottom of a valentine.
IV. The function of the heart is to receive and to pump blood.
   A. The thin-walled atria are only one-third of the heart and act as receiving chambers for the blood.
   B. The thick-walled ventricles take up two-thirds of the heart and act as two pumping stations for the human heart.

Conclusion
V. The heart has four chambers with two receivers of blood called atria and two pumpers called ventricles.
   A. This simple organ pumps 18 million gallons of blood during a 70-year lifetime.
   B. Knowing how the heart works can help you understand how to care for it, because when it stops, so do you.

Because the informative speech about the heart shows how parts relate in space, it is called a spatial/relations organizational pattern.

The Cause/Effect Pattern

cause/effect pattern

A method of speech organization in which the speaker first explains the causes of an event, a problem, or an issue and then discusses its consequences, results, or effects.

In using a **cause/effect pattern,** the speaker *first explains the causes of an event, a problem, or an issue and then discusses its consequences, results, or effects.* The speech may be cause-effect, effect-cause, or even effect-effect. A speech on inflation that uses the causal-sequence pattern might review the causes of inflation, such as low productivity, and review the effects of inflation, such as high unemployment and high interest rates. The cause/effect pattern is often used in informative speeches that seek to explain an issue. It differs from the problem/solution pattern in that the cause/effect pattern does not necessarily reveal what to do about a problem; instead, it allows for full explanation of an issue. An example of the cause/effect pattern follows:

Immediate purpose: To inform the class that social drinking can lead to alcoholism

Alcoholism or Abstinence?
Introduction
I. Most people will never have a problem with alcohol, but for some individuals social drinking will lead to problem drinking and even acute alcoholism.
   A. Social drinking is a cause of alcoholism or chemical dependency on alcohol.
   B. Developmental effects move from social drinking to   **Cause** problem drinking to alcohol dependence.
II. Social drinking is a first step toward serious problems with alcohol.

A. People who drink alcohol at all risk chemical dependence on alcohol.

B. Nondrinking individuals cannot become alcoholic even if family history indicates a tendency toward alcoholism.

III. Problem drinking is just another step toward serious problems with alcohol.   **Effect**

A. A person who cannot seem to stop drinking is already a problem drinker.

B. A person who passes out or cannot remember what happened has a serious drinking problem.

C. A person who experiences failure in relationships with others has turned from people to alcohol.

IV. The problem drinker becomes an alcoholic.

A. The person who cannot stop drinking has become dependent on alcohol.

B. The person who is alcoholic can rarely stop without help or intervention.

Conclusion

V. Social drinking can be seen as a cause for problems with alcohol, including acute alcoholism.

A. Abstinence or complete avoidance of alcohol can avoid any cause for alcoholism.

B. Social drinking can lead to undesirable effects like problem drinking and acute alcoholism.

C. Knowing about the causes and effects of alcohol is important.

The cause/effect pattern of organization is a common pattern in fields as varied as medicine (tobacco causes cancer) and economics (inflation causes recession) and religion (lack of faith results in damnation).

The Problem/Solution Pattern

The fourth pattern of organization, used most often in persuasive speeches, is the **problem/solution pattern.** As the name suggests, *the speaker describes a problem and proposes a solution.* A speech based on this pattern can be divided into two distinct parts, with an optional third part in which the speaker meets any anticipated objections to the proposed solution.

The problem/solution pattern can have other patterns within it. For example, you might discuss the problem in time-sequence order, and you might discuss the solution using a topical-sequence pattern. Some examples of problem/solution topics follow:

◆ Reducing Fat in Your Diet

◆ A New Way to Stop Smoking

◆ Eliminating Nuclear Waste

problem/solution pattern

A method of speech organization in which the speaker describes a problem and proposes a solution to that problem.

- ◆ Breaking the "Glass Ceiling" for Women
- ◆ An Alternative to Welfare
- ◆ Helping the Homeless

Each example implies both a problem and a solution.

The problem/solution pattern of organization requires careful audience analysis because you have to decide how much time and effort to spend on each portion of the speech. Is the audience already familiar with the problem? If so, you might be able to discuss the problem briefly, with a few reminders to the audience of the problem's seriousness or importance. On the other hand, the problem may be so complex that both the problem and the solution cannot be covered in a single speech. In that case, you may have found a topic that requires a problem speech and a solution speech or speeches. Your audience analysis is an important first step in determining the ratio of time devoted to the problem and to the solution.

A problem/solution speech in outline form looks like this:

Immediate purpose: Persuade students to choose jogging as a relatively gentle introduction to physical fitness.

Physical Fitness for College Students

Introduction
 I. The fact that many college students are in dreadful physical condition is a problem, but a possible solution is to start jogging.
    A. Students should exercise their bodies as well as their minds.
    B. Jogging is one solution that almost anyone can adopt.

Body
 II. Many students are in poor physical condition.
    A. Americans, including American students, are among the fattest people on earth.
    B. Colleges and universities no longer require physical education.
 III. One solution is jogging, a sport that takes little talent, little expense, and limited effort.
    A. Joggers only have to place one foot in front of the other rapidly to qualify.
    B. Joggers need only jogging shoes and sweat clothes for equipment.
    C. Joggers can run as little or as much as they wish on a regular basis.

Conclusion
 IV. If lack of physical conditioning is a problem for students because they are fat and they are no longer required to take physical education, then jogging is one possible solution that demands no talent, little expense, and minimal effort.

The problem/solution pattern has many applications in speeches on contemporary problems and issues. It can be used to discuss price-fixing, poverty, welfare, housing costs, the quality of goods, the quality of services, or the problems of being a student.

The Topical-Sequence Pattern

The **topical-sequence pattern,** used in both informative and persuasive speeches, *emphasizes the major reasons the audience should accept a point of view by addressing the advantages, disadvantages, qualities, and types of persons, places, or things.* The topical-sequence pattern can be used to explain to audience members why you want them to adopt a certain point of view. It is appropriate when you have three to five points to make, such as three reasons people should buy used cars, four of the main benefits of studying speech, or five characteristics of a good football player. This pattern of organization is among the most versatile. Here is a portion of the topical-sequence outline for a speech informing audience members about tarantulas:

Immediate purpose: To inform the audience of the history and characteristics of the world's largest known spider

The Tarantula*

I. The name *tarantula* has an interesting history.
   A. The word *tarantula* is derived from the name of a small town in Italy.
      1. Taranto was a town in Italy where the people experienced a large number of spider bites.
      2. The people of Taranto were bitten so frequently they developed a dance to sweat the spider poison out of their blood.
   B. The name *tarantula* was applied originally to the European wolf spider, the one encountered in Taranto.
   C. The name was transferred to the tropical spider, which is now known as the tarantula.
II. The tarantula has five unusual characteristics.
   A. One unusual feature of the tarantula is its size.
      1. Tropical tarantulas are as large as 3 inches in body length and 10 inches in leg span.
      2. Species in the United States range from 1 to 3 inches in body length and up to 5 inches in leg span.
   B. A second unusual feature of the tarantula is that it is nocturnal; that is, it hunts at night.
   C. A third interesting feature of the tarantula is that it can see only a distance of 2 inches and relies on leg hairs to sense the presence of other things.
   D. A fourth characteristic of the tarantula is that the species is cannibalistic.
   E. A fifth characteristic of the tarantula is that it moults.
      1. Moulting decreases with age.
      2. Moulting can be accompanied by regeneration of lost parts, such as legs.

topical-sequence pattern

A method of speech organization that emphasizes the major reasons an audience should accept a point of view by addressing the advantages, disadvantages, qualities, and types of persons, places, or things.

---

*Based on an outline composed by Terry Hermiston, Iowa State University.

Instant Recall

13.3 PATTERNS OF ORGANIZATION

Match the correct letter from the choices below with each description:

- **A. Time-sequence pattern**
- **B. Spatial/relations pattern**
- **C. Cause-effect pattern**
- **D. Problem/solution pattern**

_____ 1. A speech on how the anchor and specialty stores should be arranged in the new Waterfront Harbor Project.

_____ 2. A speech which demonstrates that calcium, not sodium or salt, is the primary suspect for high blood pressure.

_____ 3. A speech in which you move from the terrorist attack to the horrible aftermath to the targeted response to the anti-American demonstrations to the retaliation by terrorists.

_____ 4. A speech in which you reveal why you are upset with the city's poor water quality and you unveil what the city should do to improve the water quality.

Answers:1. B   2. C   3. A or C   4. D

The outline could continue to develop main points on why tarantulas make interesting and economical pets and on the myths about their poison. However, the portion of the outline shown here illustrates the main advantage of the topical-sequence outline—it can be used to organize diverse ideas into a commonsense sequence that appeals to an audience.

TRY ◄►THIS

Select a topic and see if you can determine which of the organizational patterns would work best for that topic.

Transitions and Signposts

So far, we have examined the organization of a speech in its broadest sense. To look at the speech as a problem/solution or cause/effect pattern is like looking at a house's first floor and basement. It is important that we also look more closely at the design of the speech by examining the elements that connect the parts of a speech together—transitions and signposts.

A **transition** is *a bridge between sections of a speech that helps a speaker move smoothly from one idea to another.* It also relaxes the audience momentarily. A typical transition is a brief flashback and a brief forecast that tells your audience when you are moving from one main point to another.

The most important transitions are between the introduction and the body, between the main points of the body, and between the body and the conclusion of the speech. Other transitions can appear between the main heading and main points, between main points and subpoints, between subpoints and sub-subpoints, between examples, and between visual aids and the point being illustrated. Transitions can review, preview, or even be an internal summary, but they always explain the relationship between one idea and another. Transitions are the mortar between the building blocks of the speech. Without them, cracks appear, and the structure is less solid. Table 13.1 gives examples of transitions.

Signposts are *ways in which a speaker signals to an audience where the speech is going.* Signposts, as the name implies, are like road signs that tell a driver there is a curve, bump, or rough road ahead; they are a warning, a sign that the speaker is making a move. Whereas transitions are often several to many sentences in length, signposts are usually no longer than a sentence or a few words. Whereas transitions review, state a relationship, and forecast, signposts just point.

Beginning speakers often are admonished by their instructors for using signposts that are too blatant: "This is my introduction," "This is my third main point," or "This is my conclusion." More experienced speakers choose more subtle but equally clear means of signposting: "Let me begin by showing you . . . ," "A third reason for avoiding the sun is . . . ," or "The best inference you can draw from what I have told you is. . . ." Table 13.2 gives examples of signposts.

Transitions and signposts help speakers map a speech for the audience. Transitions explain the relationships in the speech by reflecting backward

transition

A bridge between sections of a speech that helps the speaker move smoothly from one idea to another.

signposts

Ways in which a speaker signals to an audience where the speech is going.

TABLE 13.1 TRANSITIONS

Transition from one main point to another: "Now that we have seen why computers are coming down in cost, let us look next at why software is so expensive."

Transition from a main point to a visual aid: "I have explained that higher education is becoming more and more expensive. This bar graph will show exactly how expensive it has become over the past 5 years."

Transition that includes a review, an internal summary, and a preview: "You have heard that suntanning ages the skin, and I have shown you the pictures of a Buddhist monk and a nighttime bartender who hardly ever exposed themselves to direct sunlight. Now I want to show you a picture of a 35-year-old woman who spent most of her life working in direct sunlight."

TABLE 13.2 SIGNPOSTS

"First, I will illustrate . . ."	"A second idea is . . ."
"Look at this bar graph . . ."	"Another reason for . . ."
"See what you think of this evidence . . ."	"Finally, we will . . ."
"Furthermore, you should consider . . ."	

and forward. Signposts point more briefly to what the speaker is going to do at the moment. Both transitions and signposts help bind the speech into a unified whole

> ### TRY ◀ ▶ THIS
>
> *Have a friend read over your speech to make sure it contains adequate signposts and transitions.*

The Conclusion

conclusion

The last part of the speech; a summary of the major ideas that is designed to induce mental or behavioral change in an audience.

The **conclusion** is *the summary review and challenging final words of a public speech.* Like the introduction, the conclusion fulfills functions. The four functions of a conclusion need not appear in the order shown here, but they are all normally fulfilled in the waning minutes of a public speech:

1. Forewarn the audience that you are about to end the speech
2. Remind the audience of your central idea and the main points of your speech
3. Specify what the audience should think or do in response to your speech
4. End the speech in a manner that makes audience members want to think and do as you recommend

Let us examine these functions of a conclusion in greater detail.

brakelight function

A forewarning to the audience that the end of the speech is near.

The first function, the **brakelight function,** *warns the audience that the end of the speech is near.* Can you tell when a song is about to end? Do you know when someone in a conversation is about to complete a story? Can you tell in a television drama the narrative is drawing to a close? The answer to these questions is usually yes because you get verbal and nonverbal signals that songs, stories, and dramas are about to end. How do you use the brakelight function in a speech? One student signaled the end of her speech by saying, "Five minutes is hardly time to consider all the complications of this issue. . . ." By stating that her time was up, she signaled her conclusion. Another said, "Thus, men have the potential for much greater role flexibility than our society encourages. . . ." The word *thus*, like *therefore*, signals the conclusion of a logical argument and indicates the argument is drawing to a close.

The second function of a conclusion—reminding the audience of your central idea or the main points in your message—can be fulfilled by restating the main points, summarizing them briefly, or selecting the most important point for special treatment. A woman who was delivering a pro-choice speech on abortion ended it by reminding her audience of her main point. Her method was to use two quotations:

> We need to protect ourselves from closed-minded opinions like that of Senator Jesse Helms, who proposed the following amendment: "The paramount right to life is vested in each human being from the moment of fertilization without regard to age, health, or condition of dependency." Instead, let's consider the words of Rhonda Copelon, a staff lawyer with the Center for Constitutional Rights: "To use the Bill of Rights—which also and not incidentally guarantees the separation of church and state—to establish laws as a religious belief on a matter of private moral conduct would be unprecedented. It would transform into a tool of oppression a document which guarantees rights by limiting the power of the state to invade people's lives."
>
> All I ask you to do is to look at the woman's side for a moment. Consider all the implications upon her life. The unborn is not the only one with a right to life. The woman has one too.

This was an insightful way to restate the main message and reiterate the conflicting viewpoints on the issue.

The third function of a conclusion is to specify what you expect audience members to do as a result of your speech. Do you want them to simply remember a few of your important points? Then tell them one last time the points you think are worth remembering. Do you want the audience members to write down the argument they found most convincing, sign a petition, talk to their friends? If so, you should state what you would regard as an appropriate response to your speech. One student who gave a speech on unions concluded with the slogan "Buy the union label." Her ending statement specified what she expected of the audience.

The fourth function of a conclusion is to end the speech in a manner that makes audience members want to think and do as you recommend. You can conclude with a rhetorical question: "Knowing what you know now, will you feel safe riding with a driver who has had a few drinks?"; a quotation: "As John F. Kennedy said, 'Forgive your enemies, but never forget their names' "; a literary passage: "We conclude with the words of Ralph Waldo Emerson, who said, 'It is one light which beams out a thousand stars; it is one soul which animates all men'"; or an action that demonstrates the point of the speech: The speaker quickly assembles an electric motor for the class and shows that it works, the speaker twirls and does the splits in one graceful motion, or an experiment is completed as the mixture of baking soda and vinegar boils and smokes.

Some cautions about conclusions: In concluding a speech, as in initiating one, you need to avoid being overly dramatic. At one large college in the Midwest, the communication classes were taught on the third floor of the building. In one room, a student was delivering a speech about insanity. As the speech progressed, the class became increasingly aware that the young man delivering the speech had a few problems. At first, it was difficult to understand what he was saying: Words were run together, parts of sentences were incoherent, pauses were too long. Near the end of the speech, the young man's eyes were rolling, and his jaw had fallen slack. At the very end of the speech, he looked wildly at the audience, ran over to the open window, and jumped. The class was aghast. The instructor and students rushed to the window, expecting to see his shattered remains. Far below, on the ground, were 20 fraternity brothers holding a large firefighter's net, with the speaker waving happily from the center. A better idea is to conclude your speech with an inspirational statement, words that make audience members glad they spent the time and energy listening to you. One student delivered a single line at the end of his speech on automobile accidents that summarized his speech and gave his audience a line to remember: "It is not who is right in a traffic accident that really counts," he said, "it is who is left." That conclusion was clever, provided a brief summary, and was an intelligent and safe way to end a speech.

TRY◄►THIS

List the four functions of a conclusion. In your speech, check your conclusion, making sure it performs these functions.

The Bibliography

bibliography

A list of sources used in a speech.

When you have completed your outline, you may be asked to provide a **bibliography,** *a list of the sources you used in your speech.* The main idea behind a bibliography is to inform others of what sources you used for your speech and to enable them to check those sources for themselves. Each entry in your bibliography should be written according to a uniform style. Several accepted style manuals can answer your questions about the correct format for a bibliography: *The Publication Manual of the American Psychological Association* (APA), *The MLA Style Sheet,* and *The Chicago Manual of Style.* Since some teachers prefer MLA and others prefer APA, you should ask your instructor for his or her preference. This textbook relies on the APA for its bibliography style; therefore, the examples below conform to APA guidelines.

Common sources of bibliographic material for student speeches are newspapers, magazines, journal articles, books, the Internet, and interviews. The correct forms for these sources are as follows:

Newspapers
Schwartz, J. (1998, August 3). Printing's future may be written in electronic ink. *The Washington Post,* p. A3.

Magazines
Paul, R. (1998, September). The great escape: Island hopping through the Florida keys. *Motor Trend, 50,* 87–88.

Journals
Lee, W. S. (1998). In the names of Chinese women. *Quarterly Journal of Speech, 84*(3), 283–302.

As you can see, the name of the author appears in reverse order so that the list can be easily alphabetized. Notice that the name of the author, the publication date, and the title of the article are followed by periods. Only the first words of the title and subtitle are capitalized. If a volume number is included in your entry, do not write "p." or "pp." before the page numbers. When there is no volume number, you should include "p." for a single page or "pp." for more than one page.

If there is no author, the bibliographic entry changes slightly. The title of the article should appear first and the date should follow the title. The entry can then be alphabetized according to the first significant word in the article title. For example:

On line. (1996, June 21). *The Chronicle of Higher Education,* p. A17.

Books
Pearson, J., West, R., & Turner, L. (1995). *Gender and communication* (3rd 3d.). Madison, WI: Brown & Benchmark.

Again, the authors' names are in reverse order for accurate alphabetization; the last author's name, date of publication, and book title are followed by periods. The place of publication is followed by a colon, and the name of the publisher is followed by a period. A bibliographic entry must specify the book pages if the entire book was not used.

For a book with two authors, use an ampersand (&) before the second surname. If a book has more than three authors, use commas to separate all the names and use an ampersand before the final surname.

Internet
Author, I. (date). Title of article. *Name of periodical* [on-line], *xx.* Available: Specify path

Bibliographic references to material taken from the Internet are fraught with difficulty because there are so many unknowns and possibly missing information. For instance, dates are often difficult to locate in on-line articles. If one is available, use the listed year of publication. Otherwise, you can use the date of the material's most recent update or, as a last resort, the precise date of your search.

The most important issue to keep in mind is that a reference is designed to enable someone else to locate the material you used in your speech.

Therefore, include as much information in your Internet reference as you can. If possible, conform the reference to the format above. Note that the italicized "xx" refers to a volume number when applicable. Also note that the reference does not end in a period because a period in the wrong place renders most Internet addresses unusable.

For more examples of Internet bibliographic entries, refer to the accompanying E-Note, which lists web sites dealing with this subject.

Interviews

Munshaw, J. (1999, January 5). Professor of communication at Southern Illinois University—Edwardsville, interviewed by author via e-mail.

Pamphlets, handbooks, and manuals may not have complete information about who wrote them, who published them, or when they were published. In that case, you are expected to provide as much information as possible so that others can verify the source.

If you run across sources you do not know how to place in bibliographic form, you can ask your bookstore or a librarian for *The Publication Manual of the American Psychological Association, The MLA Style Sheet,* or *The Chicago Manual of Style.* College composition texts also include the standard forms for footnote and bibliographic entries.

Summary

In this chapter, we discussed the three basic parts of a speech—the introduction, the body, and the conclusion—and their functions.

The five functions of an introduction are to (1) gain and maintain audience attention, (2) arouse audience interest in the topic, (3) state the purpose of the speech, (4) describe the speaker's qualifications, and (5) forecast the organization and development of the speech.

The body of a speech can be organized through outlining. The seven principles of outlining are (1) relating all items in an outline to the immediate purpose and the long-range goal, (2) limiting the outline to an abstract of the speech itself, (3) expressing ideas in single units of information, (4) indicating the importance of items with rank-ordered symbols, (5) indicating the importance of items with margins that increase with decreasing importance, (6) coordinating less important content with less important symbols and larger margins, and (7) stating items in parallel form. Useful outlines include the key-word outline and the sentence outline. Typical patterns of organization used in public speaking are time-sequence, topical-sequence, problem/solution, spatial/relations, and cause/effect organizational patterns.

Transitions are bridges from one idea to another. Signposts are a way of signaling to an audience where the speech is going. Both transitions and signposts bind the speech into a unified whole.

The functions of a speech conclusion are to (1) forewarn the audience the speech is about to end, (2) remind the audience of the central idea or the main points of your message, (3) specify the desired audience response, and (4) end the speech in a manner that encourages your audience to think and act as you recommend.

A completed outline should be accompanied by a bibliography that lists the sources used in your speech.

Issues in Communication

This Issues in Communication narrative is designed to provoke individual thought or discussion about concepts raised in the chapter.

Jim Davis' thirteen-year-old-son died several years ago when another junior high student opened fire in the school cafeteria. Since that time, Jim has poured his energy and time into researching the possible causes and prevention of violence in schools. He has become an authority on the subject and people frequently ask him to speak at different events. He recently accepted an invitation to speak on violence to a group of parents at a junior high school in a nearby town.

Violence is a broad topic so Jim knew he needed to narrow his focus to a topic that would be relevant to his audience. He chose to talk about violence in the media that can lead to more violence in our schools. His immediate goal was to help the parents understand the effect of media violence. His long-term goal was to challenge them to watch television with their children and then discuss the violent content of the programs and how it affects us in reality.

He prepared his speech carefully and spent several hours examining his final key-word outline to ensure that every point related to his overall goals and to the topic at hand. He decided to start his presentation by showing several clips from television shows and movies that cast violence in a humorous light. He knew he would end up using several different video cassettes throughout the speech, so he cued each cassette to begin exactly where he wanted them to, labeled them and then noted on his outline when he should start the video and what cassette he should use.

After he played the introductory clips, he decided to tell the story of his son's death to raise the question of the connection between fictional and real-life violence. He would then state his thesis: that television and movies find ways to make us laugh at violence and this leads to a more violent society. He would also explain that he would give them a few simple techniques to use with their own children that would help combat the effects of violence on television.

Throughout the body of his speech, he used short clips from popular television shows and quoted from well-known sources. He was always careful to use plenty of supporting evidence from respected sources since he couldn't rely only on his personal experience to persuade others. After working hard to organize and practice his speech, he felt confident that he would do a good job.

Right before the meeting where he was to give his presentation, Jim talked to the person who would be introducing him. Jim asked him to include a few specific notes about himself, including the articles he had written for several journals and his participation in research on violence at a state university.

His hard work paid off. The speech went smoothly, and as he made eye contact with different members of the audience, he could sense their concentration on what he was saying. When he explained the importance and effectiveness of talking with kids about what they see on TV, several parents nodded in agreement. In conclusion, he showed a last series of video clips and he didn't hear a single chuckle from anyone. He reviewed his main points and encouraged parents to talk with their kids to prevent losing more children to violence.

After the meeting, many parents stayed to talk with Jim and ask him questions. Several people asked if they could get together with him at a later date to continue their discussion. Jim went home that night feeling that he had fulfilled his goals with this speech and had made a difference in some people's lives.

Apply what you have learned about introducing, organizing and concluding a speech as you ponder and discuss the following questions:

Which functions of an introduction did Jim fulfill? How did he do it? How did he use the body of his speech to persuade and inform his audience? How did his choice of a key-word outline help during his presentation? What techniques did he use to hold his audience's attention and increase his own credibility in their eyes?

Additional Resources

American Psychological Association. (1994). *Publication manual of the American Psychological Association* (4th ed.). Washington, DC: Author.

Cooren, F., & Taylor, J. R. (1997). Organization as an effect of mediation: Redefining the link between organization and communication. *Communication Theory, 21*(2), 262–264.

Hager, P. J. (1997). *Designing and delivering scientific, technical, and managerial presentations.* New York: J. Wiley.

Ross, R. S. (1998). *The speechmaking process* (11th ed.). Boston: Allyn & Bacon.

References

Bell, T. H. (1984, January 6). State school official pleased by Ohio's grade. *Athens Messenger,* p. 13.

Bones found in Kenya may be from apes' progenitor. (1983, December). *Chronicle of Higher Education, 7,* 1.

Hacker, D. (1995). *A writer's reference* (3rd ed.). Boston: Bedford Books of St. Martin's Press.

Hentoff, N. (1998, December 26). The hecklers' veto. *The Washington Post,* p. A19.

Research notes. (1983, December). *Chronicle of Higher Education, 7,* 1–2.

Rogers, E., & Hart, W. (in press). New communication technology and the changing nature of conversation. In

Edie, W., & Nelson, P. E. (Eds.), *Conversation in America: Changing rules, hidden dimensions*. Newbury Park, CA: Sage. (The outline is based on the Rogers and Hart article.)

Smith, M. (1998). Sexual intercourse and persuasion. A speech presented in Spring Quarter, Interpersonal Communication 342, Communication and Persuasion, Ohio University, Athens.

Yardley, J. (1998, August 3). For heaven's sake, lawyers, haven't you ever heard of free speech? *The Washington Post*, p. D2.

When you have read and thought about this chapter, you will be able to:

1. Distinguish between normal and high communication apprehension.

2. Utilize some of the methods for reducing your fear of public speaking and, if you experience high communication anxiety, for managing symptoms.

3. State the advantages and disadvantages of each mode of delivery.

4. Name and explain each of the vocal aspects of delivery.

5. Name and explain each of the bodily aspects of delivery.

6. Understand when and why you should use visual aids in your speech.

7. Demonstrate the use of visual aids effectively and correctly in a speech.

Communication Apprehension, Delivery, and Visual Resources

"Courage is grace under pressure."

ERNEST HEMINGWAY

"Nothing great was ever achieved without enthusiasm."

RALPH WALDO EMERSON

This chapter explores communication apprehension, the delivery of your speech, and the various visual aids you may use in your speech. First, you'll learn about the differences between normal, healthy communication anxiety and high communication apprehension, as well as some strategies for overcoming both types. Next, you'll discover the four modes of delivery and the various vocal and bodily aspects of delivery. The final section of this chapter examines the various types of visual aids you can use in your speech—from chalkboards to electronic presentations—and explains how to use them.

"I call him eloquent who more wondrously and largely can enhance and adorn what he will, and hold in mind and memory all the sources of things that pertain to public speaking."

CICERO

Reggie Washington was a talented quarterback on the university's varsity football team and a tough competition on the field. But now, sitting in front of an audience of middle school football players and their parents, it was Reggie's turn to be afraid. Reggie's coach had asked him to come to an awards banquet and give a speech—flattered, he had agreed at once, but he quickly came to regret that decision. He thought about the impending speech constantly, and he hadn't slept well either. When it was finally his turn to talk, he fidgeted with his tie, kept his eyes glued to the speech he had written out word for word, heard himself saying "ummm" a lot, and felt his knees weakening. When he finished speaking and sat down, he realized he was out of breath from talking so fast.

Julia Gustaferro was an engineering student who loved technology. Unlike Reggie, who dreaded public speaking, she looked forward to giving her speech because she was already familiar with PowerPoint. She prepared her entire speech on her computer, using snappy graphics, fonts, and fading techniques. She delivered the speech in a dim room, her new super laser pointer piercing the semidarkness. The PowerPoint presentation unfolded without a hitch. Julia was surprised when she received a mediocre grade from her public-speaking teacher for being "overly dependent" on her visual aids, for letting PowerPoint do her speech for her, and for not showing her face during the presentation.

This chapter is dedicated to helping people like Reggie and Julia overcome fear of public speaking; learn effective vocal and bodily methods of delivery; and learn how to strike an appropriate balance between content and delivery and between personal presentation and visual resources.

What Is Communication Apprehension?

communication apprehension

The generalized fear of communication, regardless of context.

The fear of speaking in public goes by many names. Once called "stage fright," a fear most often seen in beginning actors, the concept is now called **communication apprehension** and includes *many kinds of communication fears in diverse situations:* fear of talking on the telephone, fear of face-to-face conversations, fear of talking to authority figures or high-status individuals, fear of speaking to another individual, fear of speaking in a small group, and fear of speaking to an audience.

TRY ◀▶ THIS

One of the reasons you probably took this class was to become more comfortable with public speaking. Can you determine ways to reduce your own fears? What are some methods you could try?

Why should you know about communication apprehension? Even the question is controversial. Some teachers of public speaking feel that discussing communication apprehension—even in a textbook—is questionable because students who read about the fear of public speaking may see themselves as more apprehensive than those students who do not know about apprension. However, as more teachers learn about communication apprehension, they want the subject discussed in texts.

You should know about communication apprehension for two reasons. The first is that you need to be able to see the difference between normal communication anxiety, which most people experience before they give a speech, and high communication apprehension, which is a more serious problem. The second reason is that if you are highly apprehensive about communication, you should receive treatment for your problem or you will spend a lifetime handicapped by your fear.

Since most people experience a normal, healthy anxiety when public speaking, normal communication apprehension will be discussed first, including the signs of normal fear and what you can do to make that fear work for you, rather than against you.

Normal Communication Apprehension

Most human beings feel fear when they speak in public. In fact, more people fear public speaking than fear death (Bruskin & Goldring, 1973). For instance, new teachers march into their first classes, armed with 12 hours' worth of material—just to be sure they will have plenty to say in their 1-hour class. Experienced speakers feel fear when they face audiences that are new to them. Nearly all the students in a public-speaking class feel anxiety when they think about giving their speeches and when they deliver them.

What are the classic symptoms of communication apprehension for the public speaker? The authors of this book have given hundreds of speeches but still cannot sleep well the night before an important speech—one sign of anxiety or fear. Another common symptom is worry: You can't seem to get the speech out of your mind. You keep thinking about giving the speech, and you keep feeling inadequate for the task. When you actually give the speech, the common symptoms of fear are shaking—usually the hands, knees, and voice; dryness of the mouth—often called cottonmouth; and sweating—usually on the palms of the hands. One wit noted that public speakers suffer so often from dryness of the mouth and wetness of the palms that they should stick their hands in their mouths. For the public speaker, however, fear is no laughing matter. Let us turn from what the normal speaker *feels* to how the normal speaker *behaves* when afraid.

The speaker who is afraid—even with normal fear—tends to avoid eye contact, speak softly, utter vocalized pauses ("Well," "You know," "Mmmmm"), speak too slowly or too quickly, fumble with hands or feet, stand as far away from the audience as possible, and place as many obstacles as possible between himself or herself and the audience (distance, lecterns, notes). The speaker who is overcoming fear looks at the audience; speaks so all can hear easily; avoids vocalized pauses; speaks at a normal rate; moves body, arms, and feet in ways that do not appear awkward; stands at the usual distance from the audience; and uses the lectern to hold notes instead of as a hiding place.

Research on audience responses to public speakers indicates the importance of overcoming fear for improved public-speaking effectiveness. For example, one study showed that speakers who look at their audience are judged as credible and are seen as more persuasive than those who do not (Hemsley & Doob, 1978). Another study showed that apprehensive speakers who use more vocalized pauses or hesitations are less persuasive (Lind & O'Barr, 1979). Finally, speakers who appear unusually slow or powerless are perceived as less knowledgeable about the topic and, therefore, as less credible (Miller et al., 1976).

Now that you understand the fear of public speaking and the way a speaker acts when afraid, you need to focus on the more positive topic of what to do about reducing normal apprehension.

Reducing the Fear of Public Speaking

If you expect to overcome your fear of public speaking, the first thing you need is a strong desire to do so. You need incentive, motivation, and determination. The Dale Carnegie organization has taught public-speaking skills to millions of adults who did not believe in the merits of public speaking until they got out of school. An executive from the organization once admitted that before he took the Dale Carnegie course, he was so afraid of public speaking and so outraged that his fear limited his life in so many ways that he decided to overcome his fear by sheer determination. Ironically, the man who was so afraid of public speaking devoted his life to teaching others how to become effective public speakers.

You can reduce your anxiety about public speaking if you have a strong desire to overcome the fear.

Fortunately, there are some other things besides sheer determination you can do to overcome normal fears of public speaking:

1. *Know your topic.* Know more than most of your audience about the topic, find information and interview others about the topic, and organize your speech into the time allowed.

2. *Know your audience.* Know who is in your audience, what your listeners are interested in, and how they are likely to respond to your topic.

3. *Know yourself.* If you feel good about yourself—your intelligence, talents, and competence—then you will be more secure and less afraid.

4. *Know your speech.* Practice your speech so that you know the ideas, the order in which they appear, and the main messages you want to communicate to the audience.

5. *Focus on the message, not on yourself.* If you have selected a topic important to you and your audience and you see your purpose as successfully communicating that message, then you will not be thinking about your hands, mouth, or knees—and neither will your audience.

6. *Recognize your value and uniqueness.* You are the only one who can share what you know with audience members—they cannot get exactly the same perspective anywhere else.

Your instructor may be able to suggest some additional ideas for reducing your anxiety about public speaking, and you may be able to think of some ideas yourself. When some students in a beginning public-speaking class were asked what they did to reduce their fears, they mentioned the following ideas:

1. Walk to the lectern calmly and confidently; acting confident and poised can make you feel confident and poised.

2. Do not start talking until you feel comfortable in front of your audience. Look at the people in your audience before you start talking to them, just as you would in a conversation.

3. Focus on the friendly faces in the audience—the people who nod affirmatively, smile, and look friendly and attentive—they will make you feel good about yourself and your speech.

4. Have your introduction, main points, and conclusion clear in your head and practiced. The examples and supporting materials will come to mind easily when you remember the important items.

Perhaps you will not find this information startling, but the best cure for normal fear of public speaking is exactly what you are doing: taking a course in which you are invited to deliver a number of supervised public speeches to an audience that is sympathetic because they have to speak too. In other words, the speech classroom is a laboratory in which you can work systematically to reduce your fears. Your instructor's comments and those of your classmates can help you discover your strengths and weaknesses. Repeated experiences in front of an audience tend to reduce fear and permit the learning of communication skills that have application both inside and outside the

COMMUNICATION CHALLENGE

Reducing Your Fear During Your Speech: A Checklist

Check each of the following items to ensure you have thought about them before your speech and to improve the chances you will do them during your speech:

_____ 1. I will look at the audience members during my speech.

_____ 2. I will speak loudly enough for people in the back row to hear me with ease.

_____ 3. I will have my thoughts ready to avoid hesitations.

_____ 4. I will avoid vocalized pauses.

_____ 5. I will try to move and gesture naturally.

_____ 6. I will not avoid my audience with distance or obstacles.

_____ 7. I will speak calmly at a conversational pace.

_____ 8. I will look my best to feel my best.

_____ 9. I will sleep and eat before I speak.

_____ 10. I will practice my speech in the actual setting if possible.

_____ 11. I will imagine facing my audience until public speaking worries me less.

_____ 12. Most important: I will reduce my fear by focusing on communicating my message to my audience.

classroom. In short, you are now in the process of reducing your normal fear of public speaking.

Fear of public speaking is a burden for those who suffer with it. For most of us, however, the fear can be reduced to levels at which it helps, rather than hinders. Ask anybody who has to deliver the same lecture three times a day. Often, the second lecture is the best because of the confidence borne of practice. The third lecture is usually the worst because reduced fear makes delivering the lecture a bit boring, even to the speaker.

You *can* learn to control and reduce your fear of public speaking. You can look your audience members in the eye, move and gesture with purpose, speak conversationally but with strength, and focus on the reason for your speech: to communicate your message to your audience.

TRY ◄►THIS

Several days before giving a speech, talk to a parent or friend about the speech and the anxiety that you feel.

High Communication Apprehension

High communication apprehension is more extreme than normal speech anxiety. About one of every five persons—20 percent of all college students—is communication-apprehensive. Fortunately, that statistic means that four of every five students, or 80 percent, are not apprehensive. Communication-apprehensive people may not appear apprehensive unless they are engaging in a particular type of communication. High communication apprehension seems unrelated to general anxiety and intelligence. You may show no overt signs of anxiety in such activities as playing football, studying, eating, watching television, or walking to class. However, a high communication apprehensive (HCA) person has such strong negative feelings about communicating with other people that he or she typically avoids communication or exhibits considerable fear when communicating. The scope of the communication-apprehension problem may not appear large, but millions of people suffer from it.

Characteristics

One symptom of communication apprehension is that an HCA person tries to avoid communication situations. Two researchers conducted a study to find out what would happen if HCA students had a choice of an interpersonal communication course or a public-speaking course. HCA students overwhelmingly chose the interpersonal communication course. The researchers suspected that the students perceived the public-speaking course as much more threatening than the interpersonal communication course (Pearson & Yoder, 1979). Similarly, in small-group communication, HCA students tend to be nonparticipants in the class or to repeatedly register for, and drop, the class. HCA students try to avoid participating in the kind of communication that arouses their fears.

What are some other characteristics of HCA people? They may choose rooms away from other people, such as at the ends of halls in dormitories, or housing away from busy streets and playgrounds in a housing development. HCA people may sit away from others or in places in which leadership is not expected (along the side of a table, far from the end). When HCA individuals do find themselves in a communication situation, they may talk less, show less interest in the topic, take fewer risks, and say less about themselves than their classmates do. HCA people may be difficult to get to know. Even when they are in a situation in which communication is unavoidable, they discourage talk with signs of disinterest and silence.

The effects of high communication apprehension can be serious. HCA people are rarely perceived as leaders. They are seen as less extroverted, less sociable, less popular, and less competent than their peers (Feingold, 1983). They are not perceived as desirable partners for courtship or marriage. They are viewed as less composed, less attractive socially, and less attractive as coworkers. Because they communicate reluctantly, and seem so uneasy when they do, HCA people are perceived negatively by others. Therefore, they tend to do poorly in interviews and tend not to get the same quality of jobs as non-apprehensive people do. However, they are not less intellectual, mentally healthy, or physically attractive (Feingold, 1983). The consequences of being HCA seem serious enough to encourage us to look next at solutions.

Solutions

One way to overcome high communication apprehension is to be aware of the malady and to understand that people with anxiety actually prepare differently, and less effectively, than do people without anxiety. Professor John Daly, of the University of Texas at Austin, and three doctoral students (1989) showed that anxious people are overly concerned with self and are negative in their assessments. They choose speech topics with which they are less familiar, and they have less sensitivity to public-speaking situations. A self-fulfilling prophecy is thus created. Anxious individuals are fearful, they prepare less effectively, and they perform worse, which reinforces their fear about the public-speaking situation. The cycle may be broken by more effective preparation, which is discussed later in this chapter.

A second way to resolve feelings of high apprehension is through relaxation. Two techniques are possible. First, you can practice muscle relaxation, which will assist you with the physical symptoms you may have. When you deliberately tense a muscle and then relax it, you experience physical relaxation. You can become less physically tense by consciously tensing and relaxing the muscles in the various parts of your body (see Table 14.1). You may wish to work systematically from head to toe or in another reasonable progression. You may want to sit in a comfortable position or lie down as you relax your muscles. The other side of relaxation is stopping thoughts that make you nervous. When you begin to have anxiety-producing thoughts, you may wish to consciously calm yourself. Textbook writers Teri and Michael Gamble (1999) described this technique:

> A variation on the "calm technique" is to precede the word *calm* with the word *stop.* In other words, when you begin to think upsetting thoughts, say to yourself, "Stop!" Then follow that command with, "Calm." For example:
> "I just can't get up in front of all those people. Look at their cold stares and mean smirks."
> "Stop!"
> "Calm."

These two techniques can calm your physical and mental fears and allow you to be more relaxed in a communication situation.

TRY ◄►THIS

To reduce nervousness before giving a speech, be sure to get plenty of sleep, take a warm shower or bath, and wear comfortable clothing.

TABLE 14.1   CALMING NORMAL COMMUNICATION APPREHENSION

To practice the relaxation techniques, do the following:

1. Sit in a comfortable chair or lie down in a comfortable place. As much as possible, rid the area of distracting noises. If possible, play relaxing music or a tape with the sounds of nature.
2. Begin with your face and neck and tense the muscles. Then relax them. Tense again and hold the tensed position for 10 seconds. Relax again.
3. Tense your hands by clenching your fists. Relax. Tense again and hold for 10 seconds. Relax.
4. Tense your arms above your hands and to your shoulders. Relax. Tense again and hold for 10 seconds. Relax.
5. Tense your chest and stomach. Relax. Tense again and hold for 10 seconds. Relax.
6. Tense your feet by pulling the toes under. Relax. Tense again and hold for 10 seconds. Relax.
7. Tense your legs above the feet and up to the hips. Relax. Tense again and hold for 10 seconds. Relax.
8. Tense your entire body and hold for 10 seconds. Relax and breathe slowly.
9. Repeat the word *calm* to yourself. This will help you relate the word to the relaxed feeling you are now experiencing. In the future, when you feel anxious, the word *calm* should help you arrest the apprehension you experience.

SOURCE: Adapted from two exercises from *Communication Works,* (2nd ed., pp. 401–402), by Teri Kwal Gamble and Michael Gamble, 1987, New York: Random House.

Another remedy for high communication apprehension is to get professional help. The negative feelings about communication in the HCA person have often been developing since childhood. They do not disappear easily. Many schools and colleges have psychologists and counselors who have had professional training in reducing students' fears about speaking in public. Treatments that include training in the control of anxiety appear to be particularly helpful (Worthington et al., 1984). If you think you are among the small minority of people who have unusually high fear in a public-speaking situation, then you may want to talk to your public-speaking teacher about any services available to you.

A final way of alleviating fear of public speaking is called systematic desensitization. **Systematic desensitization** is *the repeated exposure to small doses of whatever makes you apprehensive.* A public-speaking student might be asked over a number of weeks to think of what is frightening (e.g., going to the front of the room to speak) and then to immediately follow the frightening thought with thoughts that relax. This process repeated over time tends to diminish a person's anxiety about communicating.

systematic desensitization

The process of reducing apprehension through repeated exposure to small doses of whatever makes one apprehensive.

Learning to manage your fear of public speaking—whether it is a normal case of anxiety or extreme communication apprehension—is a

What Is Delivery?

Instant Recall

Write T *for true or* F *for false in each blank on the left:*

_____ 1. Approximately half the U.S. population suffers from high communication apprehension.

_____ 2. The fear that nearly everyone feels just before and early in a speech is high communication apprehension.

_____ 3. High communication apprehensives make their fears come true: Because they are fearful, they prepare less and perform poorly as expected.

_____ 4. Systematic desensitization works through repeated exposure to the fear followed by more pleasant thoughts that relax.

_____ 5. Speakers who are very determined to communicate their message are less anxious because they are not thinking about themselves.

Answers: 1. F   2. F   3. T   4. T   5. T

---

prerequisite to learning effective delivery skills. **Delivery** is *the presentation of a speech by using your voice and body to reinforce your message.*

People have contradictory ideas about the importance of speech delivery. Some people think, "It's not what you say but how you say it that really counts." Others think, "What you say is more important than how you say it." Actually, what you say and how you say it are both important, but some researchers suggest that the influence of delivery on audience comprehension is overrated (Petrie, 1963). Those who challenge the importance of delivery do not say that it is unimportant but that, in evaluating the relative importance of delivery and content, content is more important than delivery. That said, the effective public speaker cannot ignore the importance of delivery.

delivery

The presentation of a speech by using your voice and body to reinforce your message.

What Are the Four Modes of Speech Delivery?

The four modes of delivery—extemporaneous, impromptu, manuscript, and memorized—vary in the amount of preparation required and their degree of spontaneity. Although the four modes are all possible choices, students of public speaking are least likely to use the manuscript and memorized modes. They may be asked to try the impromptu mode at times, but most speech assignments require the extemporaneous mode.

The Extemporaneous Mode

A speech delivered in the **extemporaneous mode** is *carefully prepared and practiced, but it is delivered conversationally without heavy dependence on notes.* This mode is message- and audience-centered, with the speaker focused not on the notes but on the ideas being expressed. Considerable eye contact, freedom of movement and gesture, the language and voice of conversation, and the use of an outline or key words to keep the speaker from reading or paying undue attention to the written script characterize this mode.

The word *extemporaneous* literally means "on the spur of the moment" in Latin; however, as practiced in the classroom, this mode of delivery only appears to be spontaneous. The speaker may choose different words as the speech is practiced and as it is finally delivered, but the focus is on communicating the message to the audience.

You have seen this mode in the classroom, in some professors' lectures, sometimes in the pulpit, often in political and legal addresses, and usually in speeches by athletes, businesspeople, and community leaders who are experienced speakers. This mode is the one you will learn best in the classroom and the one that has the most utility outside the classroom.

The Impromptu Mode

In the **impromptu mode,** *you deliver a speech without notes, plans, or formal preparation and with spontaneity and informal language.* The word *impromptu* comes from Latin and French roots and means "in readiness."

You use the impromptu mode when you answer a question in class, when you say who you are, and when you give people directions on the street. You cannot say much in these situations unless you are "in readiness," unless you know the answers. Ordinarily, this mode requires no practice, no careful choice of language. The impromptu mode encourages you to "think on your feet" without research, preparation, or practice.

The Manuscript Mode

As the name implies, in the **manuscript mode,** *you deliver a speech from a script of the exact words to be used.* The advantage of this mode is that the speaker knows exactly what to say. The disadvantages of this mode are that the written message invites a speaker to pay more attention to the script than to the audience, discourages eye contact, and prevents response to audience feedback.

Politicians, especially those who are likely to be quoted, as well as clergy and professors, sometimes use this mode of delivery, but students are not often asked to use it, except in oral interpretation of literature.

extemporaneous mode

A carefully prepared and researched speech with a conversational delivery.

impromptu mode

Delivery of a speech without notes, plans, or preparation; characterized by spontaneity and informal language.

manuscript mode

Delivery of a speech from a script of the entire speech.

The Memorized Mode

memorized mode

Delivering a speech that has been committed to memory.

A speech delivered in the **memorized mode** is *committed to memory*. This mode requires considerable practice and allows ample eye contact, movement, and gestures. However, this mode discourages the speaker from responding to feedback, from adapting to the audience during the speech, and from choosing words that might be appropriate at the moment. In other words, memorization removes spontaneity and increases the danger of forgetting.

Practice your delivery on your own or in front of friends.

You have experienced this mode if you ever acted in a play and memorized your part. Politicians, athletes, and businesspeople who speak to the same kind of audience about the same subjects often end up memorizing their speeches. Even professors, when they teach a class for the third time that week, may memorize the lesson for the day.

As a student in the speech communication classroom, you need to avoid over-rehearsing your speech so much that you memorize the script. Most speech communication teachers and audiences respond negatively to speeches that sound memorized. As one person put it, "Any presentation that 'sounds memorized'—and most memorized presentations do—never lets the audience get beyond the impression that the speaker's words are not really his or her own, even if they are."

The mode you choose should be appropriate for the message, the audience, and the occasion. Students use the extemporaneous mode most often in learning public speaking because it teaches good preparation, adaptation to the audience, and focus on the message. Nonetheless, mode of delivery does not determine effectiveness. Comparing extemporaneous and memorized modes, two researchers concluded that the mode is not what makes the speaker effective. Instead, the speaker's ability is more important. Some speakers are more effective with extemporaneous speeches than with manuscripts, but some speakers use both modes with equal effectiveness (Hildebrandt & Stephens, 1963).

TRY ◀▶ THIS

List the four modes of delivery and the advantages and disadvantages of each. Determine which mode is best suited for your speech.

What Are the Vocal and Bodily Aspects of Speech Delivery?

As you have already observed, delivery is how your voice and body affect the meaning of your speech. They are important parts of the message you communicate to your audience.

Effective speech delivery has many advantages. Research indicates that effective delivery—the appropriate use of voice and body in public speaking—contributes to the credibility of the speaker (Bettinghaus, 1961). Indeed, student audiences characterize the poorest speakers by their voices and the physical aspects of delivery (Henrikson, 1994). Poor speakers are judged to be fidgety, nervous, and monotonous. They also maintain little eye contact and show little animation or facial expression (Gilkinson & Knower, 1941). Good delivery increases the audience's capacity for handling complex information (Vohs, 1964). Thus, public speakers' credibility—the audience's evaluation of them as good or poor speakers—and their ability to convey complex information may all be affected by the vocal and bodily aspects of delivery.

The Vocal Aspects of Speech Delivery

Studying the vocal aspects of speech delivery is like studying music. The words of a speech are like musical notes. As people speak, they create music. Just as different musicians can make the same notes sound quite different, public speakers can say words in different ways to get the audience to respond in various ways. The seven vocal aspects of delivery are pitch, rate, pauses, volume, enunciation, fluency, and vocal variety.

Pitch

Pitch is *the highness or lowness of a speaker's voice*—the voice's upward and downward movement, the melody produced by the voice. Pitch is what makes the difference between the "ohhh" you utter when you earn a poor grade in a class and the "ohhh" you utter when you see something or someone really attractive. The "ohhh" looks the same in print, but when the notes turn to music, the difference between the two expressions is vast. The pitch of your voice can make you sound either lively or listless. As a speaker, you learn to avoid the two extremes: You avoid the lack of change in pitch that results in a monotone, and you avoid repeated changes in pitch that result in a singsong delivery. The best public speakers use the full range of their normal pitch.

Control of pitch does more than make a speech sound pleasing. Changes in pitch can actually help an audience remember information (Woolbert, 1920). Voices perceived as "good" are characterized by a greater range of pitch, more upward inflections, more downward inflections, and more pitch shifts (Black, 1942). Certainly, one of the important features of pitch control is that it can alter the way an audience responds to the words. Many subtle changes in meaning are accomplished by changes in pitch. The speaker's

pitch

The highness or lowness of a speaker's voice; technically, the frequency of sound made by vocal cords.

pitch tells an audience whether the words are a statement or a question, whether the words mean what they say, and whether the speaker is expressing doubt, determination, or surprise.

Pitch control is learned only through regular practice. An actor who is learning to deliver a line has to practice it many times and in many ways before he or she can be sure that most people in the audience will understand the words as intended. The public speaker practices a speech before friends to discover whether the words are being understood as intended. You may sound angry when you do not intend to, opposed when you intend to sound doubtful, or frightened when you are only surprised. You are not always the best judge of how you sound to others, so you have to seek out and place some trust in other people's evaluations.

Rate

How fast should you speak when delivering a public speech? Teachers often caution students to "slow down" because talking fast is a sign of anxiety or nervousness. Debaters speak very rapidly, but usually their opponents understand their message. What is the best way for you to deliver your speech?

rate

The speed at which speech is delivered, normally between 125 and 190 words per minute.

Rate is *the speed of delivery,* or how fast you say your words. The normal rate for Americans is between 125 and 190 words per minute, but many variations occur. You need to remember that your rate of delivery depends on you—how fast you normally speak and on the situation—few people talk fast at a funeral. Rate also depends on the audience and the subject matter. For example, children listening to a story understand better at slower rates, and complex materials may require more patient timing and more repetition.

Pauses

pause

The absence of vocal sound used for dramatic effect, transition, or emphasis of ideas.

A third vocal characteristic of speech delivery is the **pause,** *an absence of vocal sound used for dramatic effect, transition, or emphasis of ideas.* Speeches are often a steady stream of words, without silences, yet pauses can be used for dramatic effect and to get an audience to consider content. The speaker may begin a speech with rhetorical questions: "Have you had a cigarette today? Have you had two or three? Ten or eleven? Do you know what your habit is costing you in a year? A decade? A lifetime?" After each rhetorical question, a pause allows each member of the audience to answer the question mentally.

vocalized pauses

Breaks in fluency; filling in silences with meaningless words or sounds that negatively affect an audience's perception of the speaker's competence and dynamism.

On the other hand, **vocalized pauses** are *breaks in fluency that negatively affect an audience's perception of the speaker's competence and dynamism.* The "ahhhs" and "mmhhs" of the beginning speaker are disturbing and distracting. Unfortunately, even some experienced speakers have the habit of filling silences with vocalized pauses. One group teaches public speaking to laypersons by having members of the audience drop a marble into a can every time a speaker uses a vocalized pause. The resulting punishment, the clanging of the cans, breaks the habit. A more humane method might be to rehearse your speech before a friend who signals you every time you vocalize a pause so that you vocalize less often when you deliver your speech to an audience. One speech instructor hit on the idea of rigging a light to the lectern so that every time a student speaker used a vocalized pause, the light went on for a moment. Try not to fear silence when you give your speech. Many audiences would prefer a little silence to vocalized pauses.

One way to learn how to use pauses effectively in public speaking is to listen to how your classmates use them. You should also listen to professional speakers. Watch a talk show host such as Jay Leno or David Letterman during his monologue, listen to radio personalities who do commentary and opinion, and watch and listen to people who give public lectures on campus for ideas on how to use pauses effectively.

TRY ◀▶ THIS

Next time you hear someone speak in class or on TV, notice vocalized pauses. Notice how it affects or distracts you and the audience.

Volume

Volume is *the relative loudness of your voice*, but it is more than just loudness. Variations in volume can convey emotion, importance, suspense, and changes in meaning. You can use a stage whisper in front of an audience, just as you would whisper a secret to a friend. You can speak loudly and strongly on important points and let your voice carry your conviction. Volume can change with the situation. For example, a pep rally may be filled with loud, virtually shouted speeches teeming with enthusiasm, whereas a eulogy may be delivered at a lower, respectful volume. An orchestra never plays so quietly that patrons cannot hear, but the musicians vary their volume. Similarly, a public speaker who considers the voice an instrument learns how to speak softly, loudly, and everywhere in between to convey meaning.

volume

The loudness or softness of a person's voice.

Enunciation

Enunciation, the fifth vocal aspect of speech delivery, is *the pronunciation and articulation of sounds and words.* Because people's reading vocabulary is larger than their speaking vocabulary, in speeches they may use words they have rarely or never heard before. It is risky to deliver unfamiliar words. One student in a speech class gave a speech about the human reproductive system. During the speech, he managed to mispronounce nearly half the words used to describe the female anatomy. The speaker sounded incompetent to his audience. Rehearsing in front of friends, roommates, or family is a safer way to try out your vocabulary and pronunciation on an audience. Your objective should be to practice unfamiliar words until they are easy for you to pronounce and you are comfortable with them. Also be alert to the names of

enunciation

The pronunciation and articulation of sounds and words.

people you quote, introduce, or cite in your speech. Audiences are impressed when a student speaker correctly pronounces such names as Goethe, Monet, and de Chardin.

pronunciation

The conformity of the speaker's production of words with agreed-upon rules about the sounds of vowels and consonants, and for syllabic emphasis.

Pronunciation is *the conformity of the speaker's production of words with agreed-upon rules about the sounds of vowels and consonants, and for syllabic emphasis.* The best way to avoid pronunciation errors is to look up unfamiliar words in a dictionary. Every dictionary has a pronunciation key. For instance, the entry for the word *belie* in the *Random House Dictionary of the English Language* looks like this:

be-lie (bi-līe′), v.t.,–lied, –ly-ing. 1. to show to be false; contradict: His trembling hands belied his calm voice . . .*

The entry indicates that the word *belie* has two syllables. The pronunciation key states that the first *e* should be pronounced like the *i* in *if*, the *u* in *busy*, or the *ee* in *been*. The *i*, according to the pronunciation key, should be pronounced like the *ye* in *lye*, the *i* in *ice*, or the *ais* in *aisle*. The accent mark (′) indicates which syllable should receive heavier emphasis. You should learn how to use the pronunciation key in a dictionary, but if you still have some misgivings about how to pronounce a word, you should ask your teacher for assistance.

Another way to improve your pronunciation is to learn how to prolong syllables. Prolonging the syllables can make even a simple statement dramatic. Prolonging vowel sounds, for instance, gives your voice a resonance attractive to audiences. Prolonging syllables can also make you easier to understand, especially if you are addressing a large audience, an audience assembled outside, or an audience in an auditorium without a microphone. The drawing out of syllables can be overdone, however. Some radio and television newspersons hang onto the final syllable so long the practice draws attention to itself.

articulation

The production of sounds; a component of enunciation.

Articulation is another important part of enunciation. Poor **articulation,** poor *production of sounds,* is so common that people tell articulation jokes. One adult remembers hearing a song about Willie the cross-eyed bear in Sunday school. The actual song title was "Willing the Cross I Bear." Some children have heard the Lord's Prayer mumbled so many times they think that one of the lines is either "hollow be thy name" or "Howard be thy name."

Articulation problems are less humorous when they occur in your own speech. They occur because we often articulate carelessly. Among the common articulation problems are the dropping of final consonants and "-ing" sounds ("goin'," "comin'," and "leavin'"), the substitution of "fer" for "for," and the substitution of "ta" for "to." An important objective in public speaking, as it should be in all communication, is to state words clearly for more accurate transmission.

---

*From *The Random House Dictionary of the English Language.* Reprinted by permission of Random House, Inc.

Fluency

The sixth vocal characteristic of speech delivery is **fluency**—*the smoothness of the delivery, the flow of the words, and the absence of vocalized pauses.* Fluency cannot be achieved by looking up words in a dictionary or by any other simple solution. Fluency is not even very noticeable. Listeners are more likely to notice errors than to notice the seemingly effortless flow of words in a well-delivered speech. Also, you can be too fluent. A speaker who seems too glib is sometimes considered dishonest. One study showed the importance of fluency: The audiences tended to perceive the speaker's fluency and smoothness of presentation as a main determinant of effectiveness (Hayworth, 1942).

To achieve fluency, public speakers must be confident about the content of their speeches. If the speakers know what they are going to say and have said it over and over in practice, then they reduce disruptive repetition and vocalized pauses. If speakers master what they are going to say and focus on the overall rhythm of the speech, their fluency improves. Speakers must pace, build, and time the various parts of the speech so they unify in a coherent whole.

fluency
The smoothness of delivery, the flow of words, and the absence of vocalized pauses.

Vocal Variety

The seventh vocal aspect of speech delivery—one that summarizes many of the others—is **vocal variety.** This term refers to *voice quality, intonation patterns, inflections of pitch, and syllabic duration.* Public speaking encourages vocal variety because studies show it improves effectiveness. One of the founders of the National Communication Association, Charles Woolbert, in a very early study of public reading, found that audiences retain more information when there are large variations in rate, force, pitch, and voice quality. More recently, researcher George Glasgow studied an audience's comprehension of prose and poetry and found that comprehension decreases 10 percent when the material is delivered in a monotone. Another study proved that audience members understand more when listening to skilled speakers than when listening to unskilled speakers. They also recall more information immediately after the speech and at a later date. The skilled speakers are more effective, whether or not the material is organized, disorganized, easy, or difficult. Good vocalization was also found to include fewer but longer pauses, greater ranges of pitch, and more upward and downward inflections (Beighley, 1952; Black, 1942; Glasgow, 1952; Woolbert, 1920).

vocal variety
Vocal quality, intonation patterns, inflections of pitch, and syllabic duration; a lack of repetitious patterns in vocal delivery.

Guidelines for Improving Vocal Aspects of Delivery

As you conclude this section on the vocal aspects of speech delivery, the nonverbal aspects of public speaking, you may wonder how you can improve in all these areas. One thing is certainly true: Reading about aspects of delivery does little or nothing to improve your performance. Delivery is not something you read about; it is something you do. Here are some specific suggestions for improving the vocal aspects of your speech:

1. *Choose one aspect of vocal delivery, and work on it until you are confident enough to move to another.* Do not think that you have to

Instant Recall

Write the correct letter(s) from the choices below in each blank on the left:

A.	Extemporaneous	B.	Impromptu	C.	Pitch
D.	Vocalized pause	E.	Projection	F.	Enunciation
G.	Pronunciation	H.	Articulation	I.	Fluency

_____ 1. The seven vocal aspects of delivery.

_____ 2. Two modes of delivery other than memorized and manuscript.

_____ 3. The term that comes closest to meaning "volume."

_____ 4. A brief speech delivered without formal preparation.

_____ 5. Saying "Aaaaa," "Mmmmmm," or "Uhhhh."

Answers: 1. I, H, G, F, E, C, D   2. A, B   3. E   4. B   5. D

improve in all areas at once. Most likely, you are already competent in some aspects of vocal delivery and need improvement only in a few areas. If you think—and others have told you—that you speak in a monotone, perhaps you ought to start working on that area. You decide what you need to improve and then move to the following step.

2. *Try practicing the skill in your everyday life.* You already use most of the vocal aspects of delivery in conversation: rate, volume, variety, etc. Often the person who speaks without vocal variety in a public speech talks that way to friends as well. To improve your skill in that area, you can consciously practice making your voice more expressive. Do not think you can work on improving your skills only when you are performing in the classroom. You can improve every time you talk to somebody. Unlike your chemistry, biology, or physics class, where much of what you practice must be done in the laboratory, your communication class has your world as its lab, and you can do your experiments any time you wish.

3. *Be doggedly determined about improvement.* You took many years to become the person you are today, and you will not change your behavior overnight. If you have always been a rapid-fire speaker, a soft-spoken whisperer, or a person who has never used an "-ing" ending, then you are going to have to be determined to achieve any change in your behavior. On the other hand, you should be confident in the knowledge that thousands of people like you learn how to improve their vocal delivery through persistent effort. You are not being asked

to do the impossible, but neither should you be deceived into thinking that changing your vocal aspects is easy to achieve.

Next you will move from the vocal aspects of delivery to another nonverbal area—the bodily aspects of delivery.

TRY◄►THIS

List the seven vocal aspects of delivery. Practice your speech for a friend and have that person evaluate these aspects of your delivery.

The Bodily Aspects of Speech Delivery

The four bodily aspects of speech delivery are gestures, facial expression, eye contact, and movement. These nonverbal indicators of meaning show how speakers relate to audiences, just as they show how individuals relate to each other. When you observe two persons busily engaged in conversation, you can judge their interest in the conversation without hearing their words. Similarly, in public speaking, the nonverbal bodily aspects of delivery reinforce what the speaker is saying. Research conducted years ago (Kramer & Lewis, 1931) showed that audience members who can see the speaker comprehend more of the speech than do audience members who cannot see the speaker. Apparently, the speaker's bodily movements convey enough meaning to improve the audience's understanding of the message.

Gestures

Gestures are *movements of the head, arms, and hands used to illustrate, emphasize, or signal ideas in a speech.* People rarely worry about gestures in a conversation, but when they give a speech in front of an audience, arms and hands seem to be bothersome. Perhaps people feel unnatural because public speaking is an unfamiliar situation. Do you remember the first time you drove a car, the first time you tried to swim or dive, or the first time you tried to kiss your date? The first time you give a speech, you might not feel any more natural than you did then. Nonetheless, physically or artistically skilled people make their actions look easy. A skilled golfer, a talented painter, and a graceful dancer all perform with seeming ease. The beginners are the ones who make a performance look difficult. Apparently, human beings have to work diligently to make physical or artistic feats look easy.

What can you do to help yourself gesture naturally when you deliver your speech? The answer lies in feelings and practice. When representatives from Mother's Against Drunk Drivers (MADD) deliver speeches protesting lax laws on driving while intoxicated, they frequently deliver speeches with sincerity and a lot of strong gestures. They also look very natural. The main reason for their natural delivery may be their feelings about the issue that they are

gestures

Movements of the head, arms, and hands to illustrate, emphasize, or signal ideas in the speech.

TABLE 14.2 SEVEN SUGGESTIONS FOR GESTURING EFFECTIVELY
1. Keep your hands out of your pockets and at your sides when not gesturing.
2. Do not lean on the lectern.
3. Gesture with the hand not holding your notes.
4. Make your gestures deliberate—big and broad enough so that they do not look accidental or timid.
5. Keep your gestures meaningful by using them sparingly and only when they reinforce something you are saying.
6. Practice your gestures just as you do the rest of your speech so that you become comfortable with the words and gestures.
7. Make your gestures appear natural and spontaneous.

SOURCE: Adapted from two exercises from *Communication Works,* (2nd ed., pp. 401–402), by Teri Kwal Gamble and Michael Gamble, 1987, New York: Random House.

discussing. They are upset, and they show their emotion in their words and movements. They are mainly concerned with getting their message across. You can also deliver a speech more naturally by concentrating on getting the message across. Self-conscious attention to your gestures is often self-defeating—the gestures look studied, rehearsed, or slightly out of rhythm with your message. Selecting a topic you find involving can have the unexpected benefit of improving your delivery, especially if you concentrate on your audience and your message.

Another way of learning to make appropriate gestures is to practice a speech in front of friends who are willing to make positive suggestions. Constructive criticism is also one of the benefits you can receive from your speech instructor and your classmates. Actors spend hours rehearsing lines and gestures so that they will look spontaneous and unrehearsed on stage. In time, and after many practice sessions, public speakers learn which arm, head, and hand movements seem to help and which seem to hinder their message. Through practice, you too can learn to gesture naturally, in a way that reinforces, rather than detracts from, your message (see Table 14.2).

Facial Expression

facial expression

Any nonverbal cue expressed by the speaker's face.

Another physical aspect of delivery is facial expression. Your face is the most expressive part of your body. **Facial expression** consists of *the nonverbal cues expressed by the speaker's face.* Eyebrows rise and fall; eyes twinkle, glare, and cry; lips pout or smile; cheeks can dimple or harden; and a chin can jut out in anger or recede in yielding. Some people's faces are a barometer of their feelings; others' faces seem to maintain the same appearance whether they are happy, sad, or in pain. Because you do not ordinarily see your own face when you are speaking, you may not be fully aware of how you appear when you give a speech. In general, speakers are trying to maintain a warm and positive relationship with the audience, and they signal that intent by smiling as they would in conversation with someone they like. However, the topic, the speaker's intent, the situation, and the audience all help determine the appropriate facial expressions in a public speech. You can discover the appropriateness of your facial expressions by having friends, relatives, or classmates tell you how you look when practicing your speech. You can also observe how famous people use facial expressions to communicate.

Eye Contact

Another physical aspect of delivery important to the public speaker is eye contact. **Eye contact** refers to *sustained and meaningful contact with the eyes with persons in the audience.* Too much eye contact, "staring down the audience," is too much of a good thing, but looking too much at notes—lack of eye contact—is poor delivery.

eye contact

The extent to which a speaker looks directly at the audience.

Audiences prefer maintenance of good eye contact (Cobin, 1962), and good eye contact improves source credibility (Beebe, 1974). Such conclusions are particularly important, since individuals in other cultures may view eye contact differently. A public speaker from another country may be viewed less positively by an American audience than she would be in her native country. Similarly, Americans need to recognize and appreciate cultural differences in eye contact as well as other nonverbal cues.

Eye contact is one of the ways people indicate to others how they feel about them. People are wary of others who do not look them in the eye during a conversation. Similarly, in public speaking, eye contact conveys your relationship with your audience. The public speaker who rarely or never looks at the audience may appear disinterested in the audience, and the audience may resent it. The public speaker who looks over the heads of audience members or scans audience members so quickly that eye contact is not established may appear to be afraid of the audience. The proper relationship between audience and speaker is one of purposeful communication. You signal that sense of purpose by treating audience members as individuals with whom you wish to communicate—by looking at them for responses to your message.

How can you learn to maintain eye contact with your audience? One way is to know your speech so well that you have to make only occasional glances at your notes. The speaker who does not know the speech well is manuscript-bound. Delivering an extemporaneous speech from key words or an outline is a way of encouraging yourself to keep an eye on the audience. One of the purposes of extemporaneous delivery is to enable you to adapt to your audience. That adaptation is not possible unless you are continually observing the audience's behavior to see if your listeners appear to understand your message.

Other ways of learning to use eye contact include scanning your entire audience and addressing various sections of the audience as you progress through your speech. Concentrating on the head nodders may also improve your eye contact. In almost every audience, some individuals overtly indicate whether your message is coming across. These individuals usually nod yes or no with their heads, thus the name *nodders*. Some speakers find that friendly faces and positive nodders improve their delivery.

Movement

bodily movement

What the speaker does with his or her entire body during a speech presentation.

A fourth physical aspect of delivery is **bodily movement**—*what the speaker does with his or her entire body during a speech presentation.* Sometimes the situation limits movement. The presence of a fixed microphone, a lectern, a pulpit, or any other physical feature of the environment may limit your activity. The length of the speech can also make a difference. A short speech without movement is less difficult for both speaker and audience than is a very long speech.

Good movement is appropriate and purposeful. The "caged lion" who paces back and forth to work off anxiety is moving inappropriately and purposelessly in relation to the content of the speech. You should move for a reason, such as walking a few steps when delivering a transition, thereby literally helping your audience to "follow you" to the next idea. Some speakers move forward on the points they regard as most important.

Because of the importance of eye contact, the speaker should always strive to face the audience, even when moving. Some other suggestions on movement relate to the use of visual aids. Speakers who write on the chalkboard during a speech have to turn their backs on the audience. Avoid turning your back either by writing information on the board between classes or by using a poster or an overhead projector.

You can learn through practice and observation. Watch your professors, teaching assistants, and fellow students when they deliver their speeches to determine what works for them. (They may provide positive or negative examples.) Similarly, you'll need to determine what works best for you when you practice your speech. The form in Table 14.3 can be used to evaluate nonverbal delivery.

TABLE 14.3   EVALUATION FORM FOR NONVERBAL ASPECTS OF DELIVERY

To summarize the material on vocal and bodily aspects of delivery, you should examine the sample evaluation form below. Use this scale to evaluate yourself and others on each of the following items: 1 = Excellent, 2 = Good, 3 = Average, 4 = Fair, 5 = Weak

VOCAL ASPECTS OF DELIVERY—THE VOICE

_____ Pitch: Upward and downward inflections
_____ Rate: Speed of delivery
_____ Pause: Appropriate use of silence
_____ Volume: Loudness of the voice
_____ Enunciation: Articulation and pronunciation
_____ Fluency: Smoothness of delivery
_____ Vocal variety: Overall effect of all of the above

BODILY ASPECTS OF DELIVERY

_____ Gestures: Use of arms and hands
_____ Facial expression: Use of the face
_____ Eye contact: Use of eyes
_____ Movement: Use of legs and feet

TRY◀▶THIS

Attend a speech and take notes on aspects of the speaker's delivery. Use these observations as a basis for developing your own style of delivery.

What Are Visual Aids?

Do you learn best when you read something, when you watch something, or when you do something? Certainly, some skills are best learned by doing. Reading about how to program a VCR or watching another person do it is no substitute for trying it yourself. However, not everything lends itself to doing. You cannot do economics in the same way you can change a tire. Because so much of public speaking deals with issues and topics that cannot be performed, you must know the most effective methods of communicating for a public speech.

To determine if people remember best through telling alone, through showing alone, or through both showing and telling, researchers measured retention 3 hours and 3 days after a communication attempt. The results follow (Zayas-Boya, 1977–78).

METHOD	RETENTION 3 HOURS LATER	RETENTION 3 DAYS LATER
Telling alone	70%	10%
Showing alone	72	20
Showing and telling	85	65

Apparently, people retain information longer when they receive the message both through their eyes *and* through their ears. Audiences that remember a message because the visual aids helped their comprehension are more persuaded by the presentation than are audiences that do not see visual aids.

Students sometimes think that public-speaking instructors like them to use visual aids, but they will not use visual aids for public speaking outside of the classroom. In fact, the use of visual aids is big business. Can you imagine an architect trying to explain to a board of directors how the new building will look without using models, drawings, and large-scale paintings? Can you envision a business presentation without PowerPoint? Can you sell most products without showing them? Apparently, the skillful use of visual aids is an expectation in the world of business and industry. The place to learn how to use visual aids is in the classroom.

What are **visual aids?** They are *any items that can be seen by an audience for the purpose of reinforcing a message,* from the way you dress, to words on the chalkboard, to items brought in to show what you are talking about. A student who wears a police uniform when talking about careers in law enforcement, one who provides a handout with an outline of her speech for the class, and yet another who brings in chemistry equipment are all using visual aids.

visual aids

Any items that can be seen by an audience for the purpose of reinforcing a message.

The Uses of Visual Aids

One of the main reasons for using visual aids has already been stated: People tend to learn and retain more when they both see and listen. The effective speaker knows when words alone will be insufficient to carry the message. Some messages are more effectively communicated through sight, touch, smell, and taste. Use visual aids when they reduce complexity for easier understanding (such as when you are explaining many or complex statistics or ideas) and when they support your message better than words (such as when you display a bar graph showing the increasing costs of home ownership). The use of visual aids demands that you become sensitive to what an audience will be unable to understand only through your words.

Visual aids are not appropriate for all speeches at all times. In fact, because they take preparation and planning, they may be impossible to use in many impromptu situations. Also, visual aids should not be used for their own sake. Having visual aids is no virtue unless they help the audience in understanding your message or unless they contribute in another way to your purpose.

Visual aids should be visible to the audience only when needed and should be out of sight during the rest of the speech. Otherwise, visual aids can become a distraction that steals the focus from you. See Table 14.4 for additional hints on the use of visual aids.

Visual aids, like the facts in your speech, may require documentation. You should either show on the visual aid itself or tell the audience directly where you got the visual aid or the information on it.

The Types of Visual Aids

What kinds of visual aids can you choose from? They are too numerous to catalog all of them here, but several of the primary sources used by public

---

TABLE 14.4 SOME HELPFUL HINTS FOR USING VISUAL AIDS

1. Do not talk to your visual aids. Keep your eyes on your audience.
2. Display visual aids only when you are using them. Before or after they are discussed, they usually become a needless distraction to the audience.
3. Make sure everyone in the room can see your visual aids. Check the visibility of your visual aid before your speech, during practice. If the classroom is 25 feet deep, have a friend or family member determine if the visual aid can be read from 25 feet away. Above all, make sure you are not standing in front of a visual aid.
4. Leave a visual aid in front of the audience long enough for complete assimilation. Few things are more irritating to an audience than to have a half-read visual aid whipped away by a speaker.
5. Use a pointer or your inside arm for pointing to a visual aid. The pointer keeps you from masking the visual, and using your inside arm helps you to avoid closing off your body from the audience.

speakers are chalkboards, posters, opaque or overhead projectors, films and slides, videotapes, photographs, drawings, models and physical objects, handouts, yourself or an assistant, and electronic presentations.

Chalkboards

Chalkboards are the most readily available visual aid. Any statistics, facts, or details difficult to convey orally can be written on the chalkboard. You can write your name and the title of your speech on the chalkboard. You can also write down important or unusual words you use in your speech. You can also use the chalkboard to list the items from your speech you want your audience to remember.

The following are some suggestions for using a chalkboard:

1. *Ask your instructor when writing on the chalkboard is appropriate.* Some instructors prefer that you write the information on the chalkboard before class, rather than between speeches.
2. *Practice writing on the chalkboard.* Writing legibly on a chalkboard actually takes some practice. You need to print legibly and large enough so that even people in the last row can read your words. Avoid that tooth-shattering squeal of the chalk on the chalkboard by using used chalk and writing with the chalk at an angle.
3. *Practice delivering your speech while talking about items written on the chalkboard.* Try to face your audience while you speak, and use a pointer or your hand to direct the audience's attention to the statements or illustrations on the chalkboard.

A skillful speaker knows when to place the information on the chalkboard, how to write the information on the chalkboard, and how to deliver the speech when using the chalkboard. The effective speaker also knows what kinds of information should be placed on the chalkboard and whether telling, showing, or doing both will help the audience the most. Effective speakers use the chalkboard for "point clinchers," as a way to indicate to the audience the most important points in the speech (Haas & Packer, 1955).

Posters

Posters are another way to present your ideas visually. They are handier than the chalkboard because they can be prepared ahead of time. The general directions for creating an effective poster are similar to those listed for the chalkboard: The information on the poster should be information that is difficult to convey or to understand through listening; the information should be drawn or written in large scale so that people in the back of the room are able to see every word or illustration; the speaker should face the audience while working with the information on the poster; and the visual message should highlight important points.

The message on a poster may be a written message showing the number of calories in hamburgers from fast-food restaurants, stating the three primary reasons tuition should be raised, or listing the advantages of co-op

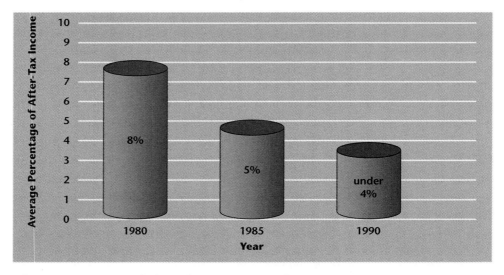

Figure 14.1 How much do millionaires give to charity?
SOURCE: Office of Tax Analysis, U.S. Department of Treasury.

bookstores. When using numbers, you should remember to round off the numbers for easier understanding.

Three means for illustrating information on posters are bar graphs, pie charts, and line graphs. A *bar graph* helps you show an audience how a number of different items compare. For example, the bar graph in Figure 14.1 compares the amount of aftertax contributions to charity by American millionaires. As the bar graph clearly indicates, millionaires gave less and less money to charity between 1980 and 1990.

The *pie chart* in Figure 14.2 shows what portion of the family budget goes for shelter, food, transportation, and entertainment. Although pie charts show proportions quite well, people are more likely to understand a bar graph than a pie chart. What percentage of the family income in the pie chart in Figure 14.2 is spent on entertainment? Naturally, the speaker could help by showing the percentages in each slice of the pie.

Figure 14.3 is an example of a *line graph,* showing the dramatic decline in the percentage of Americans who earn their living on a farm. The line graph helps the audience visualize the precipitous drop in numbers.

Some suggestions for using posters follow:

1. Keep the message simple. A common problem with visual aids is too much clutter. The audience should be able to grasp your point quickly.
2. Use bar graphs rather than pie charts whenever possible because people tend to underestimate the relative area of circles (MacDonald-Ross, 1977).
3. Use color and your artistic talents to make the poster attractive and to gain and maintain attention.

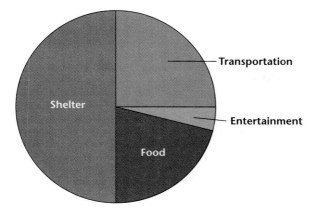

Figure 14.2 A pie chart.

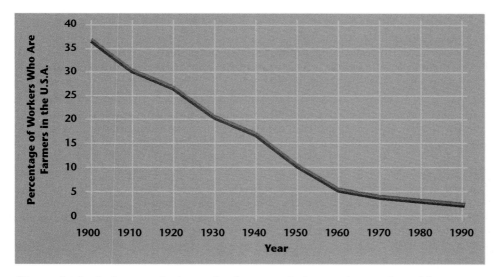

Figure 14.3 The line graph shows the dramatic decline in the number of farmers in the 20th century.

SOURCE: Data from U.S. Census Bureau and U.S. Dept. of Agriculture.

4. Be sure the poster is large enough for everyone to see.
5. Use ready-made posters or pictures, such as travel posters, or get hints for your own illustrations from those used on television commercials. Television advertisers tend to use outdoor, daytime shots, with one person but not crowds (Hebyallah & Maloney, 1977–1978).
6. Learn to use a flip chart—a series of posters. For special effects, uncover each item as you come to it.

Keep your poster in front of the audience as long as you are talking about the subject portrayed. In some cases, place the used poster on the chalk tray so that you can refer to it again in your conclusion as you review the content of your speech.

Opaque or Overhead Projectors

Opaque and overhead projectors demand special equipment and practice, but they, too, have advantages in a speech. An opaque projector or Elmo, a small object projector, can project a picture or print from a magazine or book or relatively small objects. Opaque projectors require dim lights and an empty wall or screen. An overhead projector can project transparencies or sheets of clear plastic on which the speaker can write with a special pencil or marker. Transparencies are best prepared ahead of time, but short messages can be printed on them as the speaker talks.

Films and Slides

Films and slides are good visual supplements to your speech as long as they do not become the speech. Both have the disadvantage of placing the audience and the speaker in the dark, where audience response is hidden. Even so, a 1-minute film showing violence on the basketball court or five or six slides showing alternative energy sources can add force to your speech. When you use slides and films, you should check the equipment and rehearse. An upside-down slide or a jittery film can ruin your speech. You should also arrange for a classmate to turn off the lights so that you do not have to interrupt your speech by asking someone to turn off the lights or by doing it yourself.

Videotapes

Videotapes of movies, homemade videos, and portions of cable and network television offer the speaker another opportunity to fortify a speech. The downside of videos is that the speaker must supply and set up equipment, prepare the video carefully before presentation, and ensure that the equipment works properly. Resist the temptation to show too much. You should not let the video become the speech; instead, the video is an attention getter or a form of support or evidence that should not overshadow your contributions to the presentation. The shorter the speech, the shorter the video should be.

Photographs

Another kind of visual aid is photographs. A student who is speaking about Spanish architecture can use photographs of homes and public buildings; a student who is talking about identifying types of trees can have pictures of each type; and a student who is discussing how to do something—such as assembling a bicycle—can have a series of photographs to illustrate and clarify the point. In Figure 14.4, the student speaker used a photograph of a computer "painting" to show the capability of a computer to compose pictures.

Figure 14.4 Generate graphics on your computer.

A word of warning about photographs: Ordinary-size photographs are too small to be seen easily by a classroom full of students. You should consider using enlarged, poster-size photographs for all to see. Passing around individual photographs is also a questionable practice because the audience will be distracted from your speech as they view the pictures individually. If you have a number of photos, the audience will still be looking at them when the next speaker gets up to speak.

Drawings

Drawings are another type of visual aid useful in public speaking. Most line drawings are simple and are used to clarify. When you draw a map to show your audience how to get to a specific place, when you draw the human foot and name the bones, or when you draw a cartoon character, you are using drawings as visual aids. Figure 14.5 shows a drawing used by a student speaker to illustrate a healthy lifestyle.

Models and Physical Objects

Living models and physical objects can also be used as visual aids. For a speech on fashion design, you can have people model the clothes. For a speech on exercise machines, you can have someone demonstrate the machine.

Physical objects might be the best visual aid if your speech is about something small enough or controllable enough to show but large enough to be seen by everyone without being passed around. Students have brought in model cars, chemistry sets, musical instruments, mountain climbing equipment, weights, and volcanic lava. Live pets, however, can

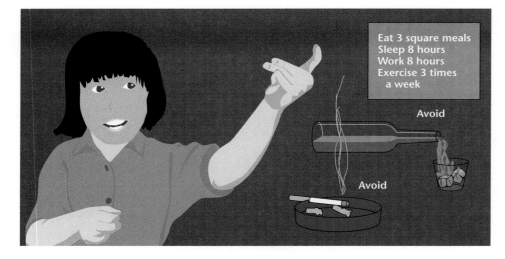

Figure 14.5 A drawing used as a visual aid.

pose special problems for the speaker. Snakes, dogs, cats, hamsters, and monkeys have a unique ability to make fools of their owners. They also are often highly distracting before and during the speech. Finally, some public-speaking teachers or college or university rules prohibit animals in the classroom.

Handouts

Handouts are an especially effective way to communicate messages difficult to convey orally. One student passed out the American Cancer Society's list of cancer danger signs. Another distributed a handout with the names and call numbers of all the country-and-western music stations because he knew the audience was unlikely to remember all the names and numbers. Still another student distributed the contract used when people will parts of their body to a medical center. Such handouts carry the impact of your speech beyond the classroom. They are usually kept, sometimes taken home where they are seen by others, and often discussed later by roommates and spouses.

Handouts have many advantages, but they also have some shortcomings. One shortcoming is that they can be very distracting to the audience and disturbing to the speaker. When distributed during your speech, the handout gets the focus of attention instead of you. The problem is not entirely solved when you distribute handouts at the end of your speech because then they steal the focus from the next speaker. A second disadvantage is that handouts sometimes carry too much of the content of the speech and may become a substitute for the speech. The audience does not have to listen to the speech because they already have the message in print.

Helpful Hints for Speech Delivery

1. Practice your speech so that you can deliver your message with only occasional glances at your notes.
2. Keep your eyes on your audience so that you can sense whether you are communicating your message.
3. Use facial expressions, gestures, and movements to help communicate your message.
4. Use your voice like a musical instrument to keep the sounds interesting and to affect the audience's response.
5. Speak loudly enough for audience members to hear, slowly enough so that they can listen with understanding, and smoothly enough so that they do not focus on your faults.
6. Use visual images to communicate material not easily understood through listening.
7. Make your writing on the chalkboard or on posters large enough for all to see and simple enough for all to understand.
8. Consider using photographs, drawings, live models, objects, slides, films, handouts, videotapes, and yourself to help communicate your message.
9. Sound conversational, look natural, and strive to communicate your message to your listeners.
10. Observe how your classmates, professors, and other speakers deliver their speeches so you can learn from them.

Yourself or an Assistant

Sometimes you or a friend or an acquaintance might be the best visual aid for your speech. You or your assistant can demonstrate karate, show some dance steps, or wear a lead apron. One of you can wear clothing appropriate for your speech: a suit when telling how to succeed in an interview for a white-collar job, a lab coat when demonstrating chemical reactions, or a uniform when telling why other students should join the ROTC program. One student wore an old flannel shirt, tattered jeans, and a rag tied around his head. He carried a lantern. His speech was about "steam tunneling," an unauthorized sport in which students explored the university's steam tunnels. He was faulted for encouraging his audience to participate in an activity strongly discouraged by the university administration, but he certainly was appropriately dressed for his speech.

Electronic Presentations

Finally, you may wish to use an electronic presentational software program as a visual aid. The use of such programs has become increasingly common in education and business. Many presentational software programs are available, but Microsoft's PowerPoint is one of the more popular ones. Most presentational software programs allow speakers to develop on-screen slide shows; use printed slides (including 35 millimeter); make black-and-white or color transparencies; produce slide shows with customized transitions; create charts and graphs using graphic files; and make speaker notes, audience handouts, and speech outlines. You can also insert clip art on a slide; use dissolves as transitions; create builds (a bulleted list that begins with the first bullet on the first slide, then adds the second bullet onto the second slide, and so on); or scan in pictures, text, or other visuals. Presentational software also allows you to customize your presentation for different audiences.

As with other visual aids, you must follow certain guidelines when using presentational software in your speech:

1. *Don't rely too heavily on an electronic presentational tool.* As with any visual aid, your electronic presentation should enhance your speech, not become the speech. Your instructor needs to assess your delivery skills, not just your technical prowess.

2. *Avoid cluttered screens by minimizing words and images.* Stick to only a few words per slide and only a few words per line; then elaborate as needed when you give your speech. Graphic images can enhance your presentation, but too many graphics can distract your audience from your speech.

3. *Use an appropriate font, and don't use too many different typefaces.* The font is the size of your letters, and the typeface is the style of the letters. Don't use a font smaller than 48 points in your presentation. In a large lecture, use 60 to 72 points for headings and no less than 48 points for subtopics or additional explanations. As far as typefaces are concerned, stick with one or two typefaces in the same presentation.

4. *Practice your speech using your electronic presentational aid.* If possible, practice in the classroom in which you will give the speech with the equipment that you will use during your actual speech.

5. *Make sure everything is arranged in advance.* Before your presentation, check to make sure a room with the proper equipment is available and reserved for your presentation.

6. *Be prepared to abandon your presentation.* In case of a power outage or faulty equipment, be prepared with handouts you can use instead.

Most presentational software packages are user-friendly, and often the software itself will lead you through the program. However, to learn about all the options that are available to you within a given software package, you may wish to take a short workshop, many of which are offered by college or university technology departments.

14.3 USING VISUAL AIDS

Fill in the blanks:

1. Clip art, dissolves, and builds are examples of _____ _____ visual aids.

2. A _____ is the most readily available visual aid.

3. Three means of illustrating information on posters are _____, _____, and _____.

4. _____ might be the best visual aid if your speech is about something small and controllable enough to show but large enough that it doesn't have to be passed around in order for your audience to see it.

*Answers: 1. Electronic presentation   2. Chalkboard   3. Bar graphs/pie charts/line graphs
4. Physical objects*

Summary

This chapter explored communication apprehension, the fear of communicating with others. The 20 percent of the population who suffer from high communication apprehension show their fear by avoiding communication with others. They tend to live away from other people, sit away from other people, and speak and disclose less than others. They also tend to be judged negatively by others. In the public-speaking situation, people suffering from high communication apprehension exhibit the signs of fear that make them seem ineffective as speakers: They look at the floor, hesitate, pause unexpectedly, and appear powerless and slow. Remedies for high communication apprehension include professional help and systematic desensitization.

Fortunately, most people have only normal anxiety about public speaking and can overcome their fear through self-determination; by knowing their topic, audience, speech, and themselves; by focusing on communication, not themselves; and by recognizing their value and uniqueness.

The four modes of speech delivery are the manuscript mode, the extemporaneous mode, the impromptu mode, and the memorized mode. Each mode has advantages and disadvantages and appropriate circumstances for its use.

An effective speech requires both vocal and bodily aspects of delivery. Vocal aspects of speech delivery include (1) pitch—the highness or lowness of the speaker's voice; (2) rate—the speed of delivery; (3) pauses—for dramatic effect and for an audience to consider content; (4) volume—the relative loudness of a speaker's voice; (5) enunciation—the pronunciation and articulation of words; (6) fluency—the smoothness of delivery; and (7) vocal variety—voice quality, intonation patterns, inflections of speech, and syllabic duration.

Bodily aspects of speech delivery include (1) gestures—movements of the head, arms, and hands; (2) eye contact—sustained and meaningful contact with the eyes and faces of audience members; (3) facial expression—the varieties of messages the face can convey; and (4) movement—what the speaker does with the entire body during a speech presentation.

Visual aids should be used in speeches when they contribute to or reinforce the message. You can use chalkboards, posters, opaque and overhead projectors, films and slides, videotapes, photographs, drawings, models and physical objects, handouts, yourself or an assistant, or electronic presentational software to help communicate your message. Visual aids should be used only when they clarify your message, not just for the sake of using them.

Issues in Communication

This Issues in Communication narrative is designed to provoke individual thought or discussion about concepts raised in the chapter.

Danny O'Neill was an assistant sales manager at a Buick dealership by day and a college student by night. He worked hard on his speech, "How to Buy a Used Car without Losing Your Shirt." With lots of personal knowledge and experience to draw on, he developed a carefully crafted, three-point outline with supporting materials under each point. He even found additional sources, more than were required for the assignment. Because he was so familiar with his topic, he practiced the speech only once.

But, as soon as Danny began speaking, he knew he was in trouble. To ease his nervousness, he read his notes and avoided eye contact when he looked up. He heard his own voice racing through the speech in a monotone. Remembering past speech evaluations, Danny slowed his pace and gripped the lectern tightly to keep from fidgeting.

Danny's instructor complimented him on the solid content and organization of the speech but noted his weak delivery skills, especially since this was his third speech in the class. The instructor gave Danny a C+. Danny felt this grade was unfair and decided to talk to the teacher about his performance and his grade.

Apply what you have learned about communication apprehension, delivery, and visual resources as you ponder and discuss the following questions: Does Danny appear to suffer from high communication apprehension or normal apprehension? What are some possible solutions for Danny's nerves? In what specific ways could Danny work to improve his vocal and bodily delivery skills? What visual resources would have been appropriate for this type of speech? Does Danny have a basis for requesting a higher grade? Which is more important in your mind, delivery or content?

Additional Resources

Daly, J. A., & McCrosky, J. C. (Eds.). (1984). *Avoiding communication: Shyness, reticence and communication apprehension.* Beverly Hills, CA: Sage.

Edwards, M. (1992). "Now presenting . . . (use of visual aids during sales presentations)," *Sales & Marketing Management, 14,* 23–24.

Feyereisen, P., & deLannoy, J.-D. (1991). *Gestures and speech: Psychological investigations.* London: Cambridge University Press.

Pierson, W. S. (1993). Talking through your eyes. *American Salesman, 10,* 21–24.

Pogatos, F. (Ed.). (1992). *Advance in nonverbal communication: Sociocultural,* *clinical, esthetic, and literary perspectives.* Philadelphia: Benjamins.

Rader, S. (1997). **www.nvgc.vt.edu/support/fall97.html**

Richmond, V. P. & McCrosky, J. C. (1992). *Communication: Apprehension, avoidance, and effectiveness* (3rd ed.). Scottsdale, AZ: Gorsuch Scarisbrick.

References

Beebe, S. A. (1974). Eye contact: A nonverbal determinant of speaker credibility. *Speech Teacher, 23,* 21–25.

Beighley, K. C. (1952). An experimental study of the effect of four speech variables on listener comprehension. *Speech Monographs, 19,* 249–258.

Bettinghaus, E. (1961). The operation of congruity in an oral communication situation. *Speech Monographs, 28,* 131–142.

Black, J. W. (1942). A study of voice merit. *Quarterly Journal of Speech, 28,* 67–74.

Bruskin, & Goldring, (1973). What are Americans afraid of? *Bruskin Report, 53.*

Cobin, M. (1962). Response to eye contact. *Quarterly Journal of Speech, 48,* 415–418.

Daly, J. A., Vangelisti, A. L., Neel, H. L., & Cavanaugh, P. D. (1989). Pre-performance concerns associated with public speaking anxiety. *Communication Quarterly, 37,* 39–53.

Feingold, A. (1983). Correlates of public speaking attitude. *Journal of Social Psychology, 120,* 285–286.

Gamble, T. K., & Gamble, M. (1999). *Communication works* (6th ed.). New York: McGraw-Hill.

Gilkinson, H., & Knower, F. H. (1941). Individual differences among students of speech as revealed by psychological test—I. *Journal of Educational Psychology, 32,* 161–175.

Glasgow, G. M. (1952). A semantic index of vocal pitch. *Speech Monographs, 19,* 64–68.

Haas, K. B., & Packer, H. Q. (1955). *Preparation and use of audiovisual aids.* New York: Prentice-Hall.

Hayworth, D. (1942). A search for facts on the teaching of public speaking. *Quarterly Journal of Speech, 28,* 247–254.

Hebyallah, I. M., & Maloney, W. P. (1977–1978). Content analysis of TV commercials. *International Journal of Instructional media, 5,* 9–16.

Hemsley, G. D., & Doob, A. M. (1978). The effect of looking behavior on perceptions of a communicator's credibility. *Journal of Applied Social Psychology, 8,* 136–144.

Henrikson, E. H. (1994). An analysis of the characteristics of some "good" and "poor" speakers. *Speech Monographs, 11,* 120–124.

Hildebrandt, H. W., & Stephens, W. (1963). Manuscript and extemporaneous delivery in communicating information. *Speech Monographs, 30,* 369–372.

Kramer, E. J. J., & Lewis, T. R. (1931). Comparison of visual and nonvisual listening. *Journal of Communication, 1,* 16–20.

Lind, E. A., & O'Barr, W. M. (1979). The social significance of speech in the classroom. In H. Giles & R. St. Clair (Eds.), *Language and social psychology.* Oxford, England: Blackwell.

MacDonald-Ross, M. (1977, Winter). How numbers are shown: A review of research on the presentation of quantitative data in texts. *AV*

Communication Review, 25, 359–409.

Miller, N., Maruyama, G., Beaber, R. J., & Valone, K. (1976). Speed of speech and persuasion. *Journal of Personality and Social Psychology, 34,* 615–625.

Pearson, J. C., & Yoder, D. D. (1979, May). *Public speaking or interpersonal communication: The perspective of the high communication apprehensive student.* East Lansing, MI: National Center for Research on Teacher Learning (ERIC Document Reproduction Service No. ED 173 870).

Petrie, C. R., Jr. (1963). Informative speaking: A summary and bibliography of related research. *Speech Monographs, 30,* 81.

Vohs, J. L. (1964). An empirical approach to the concept of attention. *Speech Monographs, 31,* 355–360.

Woolbert, C. (1920). The effects of various modes of public reading. *Journal of Applied Psychology, 4,* 162–185.

Worthington, E. L., Tipton, R. M., Comley, J. S., Richards, T., & Janke, R. H. (1984). Speech and coping skills training and paradox as treatment for college students anxious about public speaking. *Perceptual and Motor Skills, 59,* 394.

Zayas-Boya, E. P. (1977–1978). Instructional media in the total language picture. *International Journal of Instructional Media, 5,* 145–150.

When you have read and thought about this chapter, you will be able to:

1. Recognize the goals of informative speaking.

2. Identify topics appropriate for informative speaking.

3. Provide examples of immediate behavioral purposes for an informative speech.

4. Define concepts related to informative speaking, such as information hunger, information relevance, extrinsic motivation, informative content, and information overload.

5. Use the skills of defining, describing, explaining, and narrating in an informative speech.

15

The Informative Speech

> **"Nothing is so firmly believed as what we least know."**
>
> MICHEL DE MONTAIGNE

> **"Everything has been thought of before; the challenge is to think of it again."**
>
> J. W. GOETHE

> **"A word to the wise is not sufficient if it does not make sense."**
>
> JAMES THURBER

In this chapter you will learn that the goal of informative speaking is to increase or enhance an audience's knowledge and understanding of a topic. You will learn how to identify and choose topics for an informative speech and how to develop behavioral purposes for them. The chapter discusses techniques that will help you effectively present an informational speech to an audience and explains how to organize your speech. Effective informative speakers demonstrate certain skills that contribute to their effectiveness, so the chapter explains the four skills of defining, describing, explaining, and narrating. Finally, the chapter includes an example of an informative speech.

Anita Byers was the new literature teacher in a suburban middle school; her class included 33 highly energetic teenagers. Anita spent a lot of time preparing her lesson plan for the opening weeks of school. She knew she needed to teach the students how to write without making serious grammatical errors, and she wanted to instill positive attitudes toward literature. But her most immediate goal was to inspire her students to read and enjoy novels, short stories, and poetry. Once Anita had her basic lesson plan outlined, she spent hours brainstorming how she might make the class interesting and relevant. Whenever she could, Anita decided to use music or clips from popular movies to grab her students' interest and to illustrate the concepts she wanted them to understand. She hoped that her students would deepen their interest in reading and writing well and that they would develop a strong sense of how fundamental these skills are for their future success.

Samantha Kuhn was a Seventh Day Adventist. Often, when people at work or school heard of her faith, she ended up explaining—sometimes at great length—what she believes and how her religion works. When she was younger, Samantha found the repeated explanations to be tiresome, but as she matured, she discovered that both she and her conversational partner gained something in the exchange. The other person knew more than he or she did before about Seventh Day Adventists, and Samantha often learned a little more about the other person's system of belief as well. Most of the time the conversations were enjoyable and informative (she had spoken with a Muslim and a Buddhist so far this year), and she looked forward to such exchanges.

Anita and Samantha are involved in similar situations. They are both trying to find ways to effectively communicate information to others so that their respective audiences gain knowledge and understanding about the topic, which is exactly the goal of an informative speech—to increase what an audience knows and understands.

At some time in your life you will probably find yourself informing others through oral reports, instructions, and speeches. The primary vehicle for informing others is the informative speech—a speech intended to increase what an audience knows and understands.

How Do You Prepare an Informative Speech?

To prepare an informative speech, you should know (1) the intent and the goal of informative speaking, (2) the kinds of topics that best lend themselves to informative speaking, and (3) the kinds of immediate behavioral purposes of informative speaking and how to determine if you have fulfilled them.

The Goal of Informative Speaking

Understanding the goal or intent of informative speaking requires that you understand the "end product" you seek and how to reach that end in ways that enlighten the audience and clarify the topic. The end product of informative speaking is *to increase an audience's knowledge or understanding of a topic.* You accomplish that goal by clarifying your topic in ways that retain the interest of your audience. To *clarify* means "to make clear," from Latin, Middle English, and Old French roots. To clarify a concept for an audience, the speaker assumes the audience does not understand the topic clearly until the speaker has an opportunity to explain it. Typically, most audience members have insufficient knowledge or understanding to master or comprehend the informative speech topic. For example, the Irish have been fighting for 30 years, but how many college students understand who is a unionist, a republican, the Garda, the IRA, or the Real IRA (McGuire, 1998)? An informative speech defines, explains, and increases audience understanding.

Clarifying a topic for an audience is a primary goal of informative speaking, but a second concern is to make the topic of an informative speech interesting and significant to the audience. You arouse an audience's *interest* in a topic by showing how the subject can be of importance, by relating stories of your own experiences with the subject, and by demonstrating gaps in your listeners' knowledge that they will want to fill. In fact, if a bit of persuasion is likely to slip into an informative speech, the appropriate place is early in the speech, where you relate the topic to the audience. Here you may reveal why the audience should know more about Wagnerian opera, cross-country skiing, the federal debt, or hamster breeding. How to make a topic palatable to the audience is a continuing concern of the informative speaker.

Besides being interesting, the informative speech should meet the standard of significance. The *significance* of your message is its importance and meaningfulness to, or its consequences for, the audience. The audience, not the speaker, determines significance. For instance, a speech on fathers who illegally withhold child support is more likely to be both interesting and significant to a roomful of struggling single mothers than to a roomful of sophomore fraternity men. A speech on the history of matches might lack interest and significance, and a speech on tax support for emerging nations might be high in significance but low in audience interest.

TRY◄ ►THIS

Make a list of hobbies, interests, and historical and current events that might make a good topic for a demonstration or an informative speech.

Topics for Informative Speeches

Selecting a topic for an informative speech and narrowing the topic to the length restrictions of the speech are early concerns for the informative speaker. You need to know how to brainstorm for topics and how to conduct personal inventories of your reading and viewing habits to determine your interests. Even with that information, you may not know exactly what kinds of topics are most appropriate for informative speeches.

An informative speech should be predominantly informative; that is, most of the content of the speech should focus on increasing audience knowledge and clarifying concepts for greater understanding. Many informative speeches reveal how to do something, what something is, or how something happens—speeches of exposition, definition, and description, respectively. A list of topics for a number of student-delivered informative speeches is presented below.

The informative speaker must arouse the interest of the audience and show the significance of the topic.

Gun control	Electric cars
Youth gangs	Additions
Genetic cloning	Alcohol misuse
Exam anxiety	Earthquakes
Volcanoes	Bulimia
Osteoporosis	Holistic health
Youth suicide	Cancer
Inner-city living	Chemical warfare
TV violence	Plastic surgery
Career planning	Résumé writing
Caffeine	Total fitness
Dieting	Spirituality
Internet sites	Deer hunting
Fly-fishing	CPR
Used cars	Snowboarding
Tennis	Disaster relief
Backpacking	Horse grooming
Gift baskets	Investment strategies
Birth control	New software

Auto accidents

Active listening

Math literacy

Anorexia

Taxation

What is an engineer?

Greenhouse effect

Nutrition

Cover letters

Beauty pageants

Diabetes treatment

Mountain climbing

Mountain bikes

Self-defense

Refinishing furniture

Jump-starting a car

Vacation retreats

Mobile phones

Buddhist beliefs

Fat substitutes

Computer viruses

Telemarketing

Infrastructure

Adventures of a bartender

Depression and treatment

Athletic injuries

Types of music

Cosmetics

Farm subsidies

White-water rafting

Ski equipment

Career planning

Cooking with a hotpot

Loading a printer

Recycling

Pagers

Interviewing

Finance major

The homeless

Energy

Social Security

Cocaine/opiates

School prayer

Child care

Steroids

Gymnastics

Effective notes

Doing taxes

First aid

Blood pressure

Blood sugar

The topics, not necessarily the titles of the speeches, are listed. Therefore, many of the topics look broader than they would be if they were delivered as speeches. Nonetheless, this list of topics may give you some ideas for an informative speech topic.

Once you have selected and narrowed a topic in a manner appropriate for you, your audience, and the situation, you are ready to specify the behavioral purposes of your informative speech.

The Behavioral Purposes of Informative Speeches

Two important questions for the informative speakers are (1) What do I want my audience to know or do as a result of my speech? (2) How will I know if I am successful? A teacher can teach more effectively if the students know exactly what they are expected to learn. Similarly, an audience learns more from an informative speech if the speaker states expectations early in the speech. The effects of an informative speech, however, are unknown unless you make the effects behavioral; that is, your speech should result in observable behavioral change. A teacher discovers whether students learned from a lecture by giving a quiz or having the students answer questions in class. In the same way, the informative speaker seeks to discover whether or not a message was effectively communicated by seeking overt feedback from the audience. The overt feedback you seek concerns the **immediate behavioral**

immediate behavioral purposes

Actions a speaker seeks from an audience during and immediately after a speech.

408

purposes of your speech, *the actions expected from an audience during and immediately after the speech.*

The most common immediate behavioral purposes in an informative speech encourage audience members to do the following:

1. *Describe objects, persons, or issues.* For example, after hearing a speech, audience members can *describe* an English setter, a person with Down syndrome, or the Libertarian position on welfare.
2. *Distinguish between different things.* For example, after hearing a speech, audience members can *distinguish* between fool's gold and real gold, between a counterfeit dollar and a real dollar, or between a conservative position and a liberal position.
3. *Compare items.* For example, after hearing a speech, audience members can *compare* prices on automobiles with the same features and options, a poetic song and a sonnet, or diamonds for cut, clarity, and carats.
4. *Define words, objects, or concepts.* For example, after hearing a speech, audience members can *define* what kerogen is, describe an English Tudor house, or explain the concept of macroeconomics.
5. *State what they have learned.* After hearing a speech, audience members can tell you, or can write, the most important points of your speech or are able to tell others what you said.

The common behavioral purposes of an informative speech are to describe, distinguish, compare, define, and state. How does a speaker know whether or not these behavioral purposes were accomplished? One method of discovering whether audience members learned anything from your speech is to find out what they know both at the beginning and at the end of the speech. For instance, you could ask at the beginning of your speech, "How many of you have ever taken a personality test?" If you get a small but enthusiastic response, you know you will be informing them about something that is unfamiliar but interesting to them. After you explain the different types of tests and the discrepancies between them, you can ask certain students at the end of the speech to contrast the Thematic Apperception Test and the Myers-Briggs Type Indicator.

Similarly, you may ask your classmates to write down something that indicates whether or not they understood your message. If you explained how to administer CPR, you could ask your classmates to list the steps they would take if they encountered an unconscious man lying on the ground. Likewise, if your topic was to inform them about nutrition, you could ask them to list the foods with the highest or lowest fat content. In each case, the speaker states the purpose in such a way that he or she can determine whether or not the purpose was accomplished.

Once you have decided on specific behavioral purposes for addressing an audience, you must select strategies for achieving those purposes. In other words, you must decide how to adapt your behavioral purposes and the materials of your speech to your particular audience.

TRY ◀▶ THIS

Make a list of questions you can ask the audience to determine the immediate behavioral purposes of your speech.

How Do You Effectively Present Information to an Audience?

Audience analysis should help you determine how much audience members already know and how much you will have to tell them to engender understanding. Then you will have to decide how to generate information hunger, achieve information relevance, use extrinsic motivation, select content, and avoid information overload in your speech.

Information Hunger

information hunger

The audience's need for the information contained in the speech.

rhetorical questions

Questions asked for effect, with no answer expected.

An informative speech is more effective if the speaker can generate **information hunger** in the audience—that is, if the speaker can create *a need for information in the audience.* Information hunger is easiest to create when a speaker has analyzed the audience and believes hunger for the information can be aroused. Arousal of interest during the speech is related to how much the audience will comprehend (Petrie, 1963). The following **rhetorical questions,** *questions asked for effect, with no answer expected,* could be used to introduce an informative speech and to arouse audience interest: "Are you aware of the number of abused children in your hometown?" "Can you identify five warning signs of cancer?" "Do you know how to get the best college education for your money?" Depending on the audience, these rhetorical questions could be of interest.

Rhetorical questions are just one method of arousing information hunger. Another method is to arouse the audience's curiosity. For example, you might state, "I have discovered a way to add 10 years to my life," "The adoption of the following plan will ensure world peace," or "I have a secret for achieving marital success." In addition, a brief quiz on your topic early in the speech arouses interest in finding the answers. Unusual clothing is likely to arouse interest in why you are so attired, and an object you created will likely inspire the audience to wonder how you made it. These are just a few ways the public speaker can generate information hunger.

Information Relevance

information relevance

The importance, novelty, and usefulness of the topic and the information.

A second factor relating an informative speech to an audience is **information relevance,** *the importance, novelty, and usefulness of the information to the* *audience.* When selecting a topic for an informative speech, the speaker should carefully consider the relevance of the topic. Skin cancer might be a better topic in the summer, when students are sunbathing, than in the winter, when they are not. An audience might find a speech on tax laws dull. A speech on how present tax laws cost audience members more than they cost the rich might be more relevant, and a speech on three ways to reduce personal taxes might be even more relevant. However, if your audience happens to be composed of 18- to 21-year-olds who have never paid taxes, none of the three topics might be relevant. Similarly, a speech on raising racehorses, writing a textbook, or living on a pension might be informative but not relevant because of the financial status, occupation, or age of the listeners. The informative speaker, then, should exercise some care in selecting a topic that interests the audience (Cofer, 1961).

People expose themselves first to information that is supportive or that fits in with what they already believe or know, and they reject less supportive information first. Thus your intended listeners' predisposition toward a topic can determine whether they will come to hear your speech and then whether they will listen (Wheeless, 1974).

Extrinsic Motivation

A third factor in relating an informative speech to an audience is **extrinsic motivation,** *reasons outside the speech itself for listening to the content of the speech.* An audience is more likely to listen to, and comprehend, a speech if there are reasons outside the speech itself for concentrating on the content of the speech (Petrie & Carrel, 1976). A teacher who tells students to listen carefully because they will be tested at the end of the hour is using extrinsic motivation. A student can use extrinsic motivation at the beginning of a speech by telling an audience, "Attention to this speech will alert you to ways you can increase energy and creativity," or "After hearing this speech, you will never purchase a poor-quality used-car again."

Extrinsic motivation is related to the concept of information relevance. The audience member who would ordinarily be disinterested in the topic of fashion might find that topic more relevant when it is linked to job interviews and the kinds of clothing, jewelry, and shoes that employers seem to prefer. The audience member's interest in getting a job makes the interviewer's preferences an extrinsic motivation for listening carefully to the speech.

Any external reasons for listening need to be mentioned early in the speech, before the message you want them to remember. A statement such as "You will need this background material for the report due at the end of this week" provides extrinsic motivation for the managers who hear this message from their employer. Similarly, in an informative speech, you may be able to command more attention, comprehension, and action from audience members if they know some reasons outside the speech itself for attending to your message.

extrinsic motivation

A method of making information relevant by providing the audience with reasons outside the speech itself for listening to the content of the speech.

```
TRY ◄►THIS
```

List the reasons your audience should listen to your speech.
Determine how you could motivate your audience to listen.

Informative Content

informative
content

The main points and
subpoints,
illustrations, and
examples used to
clarify and inform.

A fourth factor in relating an informative speech to an audience is the selection of **informative content,** *the main points and subpoints, illustrations, and examples used to clarify and inform.* The following are principles of learning and research findings that can guide you in selecting your speech content:

1. Audiences tend to remember and comprehend generalizations and main ideas better than details and specific facts (Petrie, 1963). The usual advice to speakers—that content should be limited to a relatively small number of main points and generalizations—seems to be well grounded. Specifically, public speakers are well advised to limit themselves to two to five main points or contentions. Even if the speech is very long, audiences are unlikely to remember a larger number of main points.

2. Relatively simple words and concrete ideas are significantly easier to retain than more complex materials (Baird, 1974; Ernest, 1968). Long or unusual words may dazzle an audience into thinking you are intellectually gifted or verbally skilled, but they may also reduce audience understanding of the speech content. Keep the ideas and the words used to express those ideas at an appropriate level.

3. Humor can make a dull speech more interesting to an audience, but humor does not seem to increase information retention. The use of humor also improves the audience's perception of the character of the speaker, and it can increase a speaker's authoritativeness when a speech is dull, although not when the speech is interesting (Gruner, 1970).

4. Early remarks about how the speech will meet the audience's needs can create anticipation and increase the chances that the audience will listen and understand (Petrie, 1963). Whatever topic you select, you should tell audience members early in your speech how the topic is related to them. Unless you relate the topic to their needs, they may choose not to listen.

5. Calling for *overt audience response,* or actual behavior, increases comprehension more than repetition does. In a study of this subject, the overt responses invited were specific, "programmed" questions to which the appropriate overt responses were anticipated (Tucker, 1964). An informative speaker can ask for overt responses from audience members by having them perform the task being demonstrated (for example, two people dance after you explain the technique of the waltz); by having them stand, raise hands, or move chairs to indicate

affirmative understanding of the speaker's statements (for example, "Raise your hand if you are familiar with local building codes"); or by having them write answers that will indicate understanding of the informative speech (for example, "List four ways to lower your blood pressure"). Having an audience go through an overt motion provides feedback to the speaker and can be rewarding and reinforcing for both speaker and listener.

Information Overload

The informative speaker needs to be wary about the amount of information included in a speech. The danger is **information overload,** providing *much more information than the audience can absorb in amount, complexity, or both.*

Information overload comes in two forms. One is *quantity:* The speaker tells more than audience members ever wanted to know about a subject, even when they are interested in it. The speaker tries to cram as much information as possible into the time allowed. Unfortunately, this cramming of information makes it more difficult to understand. A second form of information overload is *complexity:* The speaker uses language or ideas that are beyond the capacity of the audience to understand. An engineer or a mathematician who unloads detailed formulas on the audience or a philosopher who soars into the ethereal heights of high ideas may leave the audience feeling frustrated and more confused than before the speech. The solution to information overload is to speak on a limited number of main points with only the best supporting materials and to keep the message at a level the audience can understand.

information overload

A situation that occurs when the quantity or difficulty of the information presented is greater than the audience can assimilate within the given time.

413

Instant Recall

Write the correct letter from the choices below in each blank on the left:

A. **Information hunger**   B. **Information relevance**
C. **Extrinsic motivation**   D. **Information content**
E. **Information overload**

_____ 1. Giving an informative speech about relational maintenance around Valentine's Day.

_____ 2. Telling audience members that you will ask them the three main points after your speech.

_____ 3. Giving an informative speech with three main points instead of a speech with eight main points.

_____ 4. Using rhetorical questions to introduce your informative speech.

_____ 5. Giving an informative speech on the history of taxation and its relationship to fiscal policy in the United States and Great Britain.

Answers: 1. B   2. C   3. D   4. A   5. E

Content Organization

The suggestions that follow are based on studies that reveal specific ways the informative speaker can help an audience understand the content of the speech. In general, the research supports the old saying that you should tell audience members what you are going to tell them, tell them, and then tell them what you told them.

Charles R. Petrie, Jr. (1963), in his studies of informative speaking, found that the use of transitions can increase an audience's comprehension. That finding underlines the importance of building transitions between your introduction and body and between your body and conclusion. You should also use transitions when you move from one main point to another and when you move into and out of the use of visual aids.

In organizing your informative speech, you should determine which ideas, points, or supporting materials are of greatest importance. Apparently, an audience understands the important points better if the speaker signals their importance by saying, "Now get this," or "This is very important." Some redundancy, or planned repetition, also can increase comprehension (Pence, 1954). Some of that planned repetition can be included in the previews and reviews in your informative speech (Baird, 1974). *Advance organizers,* or *previews* in written work, aid retention by providing the reader with key points prior to their presentation in a meaningful, but unfamiliar, passage (Ausubel, 1960). In speaking, as well as in writing, listeners can more easily grasp information when they are invited to anticipate and to review both the organization and the content of a speech.

When you have completed an outline that includes everything you plan to say, you should check your speech for information overload. Overload is a special problem in the informative speech because speakers have a tendency to inundate listeners with information. Just as some writers believe a longer paper is a better paper, some speakers think the sheer quantity of information improves a speech. The most effective public speakers know the quantity of material in a speech makes less difference than its quality. They also know listeners pay more attention to carefully selected material that is well adapted to their needs. In a 5- to 8-minute informative speech, the speaker has only 4 to 6 minutes to present supporting materials; the remainder of the time is spent introducing the subject, making transitions, and making internal and final summaries. Your organizational plan should show what material you intend to include in your speech and should be your final check on the quantity and quality of the information you intend to present.

Skills for Informative Speaking

Public speakers who are highly effective at informative speaking demonstrate certain skills that contribute to their effectiveness. One of these skills is *defining.* Much of what an informative speaker does is reveal to an audience what certain terms, words, and concepts mean. Another skill is *describing;* the informative speaker often tells an audience how something appears: what it looks, sounds, feels, and even smells like. A third skill is *explaining,* or trying to say what something is in words the audience can understand. A fourth skill is *narrating,* an oral interpretation of a story, an event, or a description.

Defining

A student who was a model gave a speech in which she talked about *parts modeling;* a student who made his own butter gave an informative speech in which he talked about the *dasher* and the *clabber, bilky* milk, and butter that *gathered;* an informative speech on aerobics included such terms as *arteriosclerosis, cardiovascular-pulmonary system,* and *cardiorespiratory endurance.* What were these students talking about? In each case, they were using words most persons in the audience did not understand. To use terms audience members do not understand is all right as long as you explain the terms in language they *can* understand. You clarify by defining your terms. Among the most useful methods of defining are the use of comparison, contrast, synonyms, antonyms, etymology, and operational definitions.

comparison

A means of defining by pointing out similarities between the known and the less known.

The student who told about making butter defined through **comparison,** *pointing out similarities between the known and the less known,* by explaining that "the dasher consists of a stick similar to a broom handle. A cross made of two slats, 4 inches long and 2 inches wide, is nailed to the end of the handle. The dasher is inserted into the churn, and the churn's opening is covered by a tightly fitted wooden lid with a hole in the middle for the dasher." The student defined a dasher by comparing it to the better-known broomstick and by revealing how it was constructed.

contrast

The comparison of unlike things.

Another means of definition is **contrast,** the *comparison of unlike things.* In an informative speech, you can contrast between hypochondriasis and psychotic disorders by contrasting the symptoms and effects of each.

synonym

A word that means approximately the same as another word.

A speaker also might define through a **synonym**—*a word that is close or similar in meaning to another word.* For example, in an informative speech, the speaker might say depressive psychosis is characterized by loss of interest, dejection, stupor, and silence—a series of words similar to behaviors exhibited by a depressive psychotic patient.

antonym

A word that means the opposite of another word.

An **antonym** is *a word that means the opposite of another word.* A hyperactive child is not quiet, immobile, silent, patient, or unexpressive.

etymology

The historical origin of a word.

Sometimes it is easier to explain a concept or term by revealing its **etymology,** *the historical origin of a word.* A desk dictionary may give a very brief statement on the origin of a word. You can locate more complete origins in such specialized dictionaries as the *Oxford English Dictionary* or the *Etymological Dictionary of Modern English.* A speaker talking about sexual variations might use the term *lesbianism* and could define the term by explaining that the Greek poet Sappho wrote poetry about sexual love between women about 600 years before Christ. Because Sappho lived on the island of Lesbos, "followers of Sappho," or female homosexuals, became known as lesbians. The story about the origin of the word provides a memorable way for the audience to relate to the word.

operational definition

A definition which states the process that results in the thing being defined.

Another means of defining is the **operational definition,** which *defines a term by revealing how it works, how it is made, or what it consists of.* The earlier description of a dasher was an operational definition revealing how a dasher is constructed. A student delivering an informative speech on rhinoplasty, or "a nose job," did so through the following operational definition:

> Modern rhinoplasty is done for both cosmetic and health reasons. It consists of several minioperations. First, if the septum separating the nostrils has become deviated as the result of an injury or some other means, it is straightened with surgical pliers. Then, if the nose is to be remodeled, small incisions are made within each nostril, and working entirely within the nose, the surgeon is able to remove, reshape, or redistribute the bone and cartilage lying underneath the skin. Finally, if the nose is crooked, a chisel is taken to the bones of the upper nose, and they are broken so that they may be straightened and centered.

An operational definition, then, defines by revealing the formula for the thing named: rhinoplasty is the surgery described in the previous sentences; a cake is its recipe; concrete is lime, cement, and water; a secretary is what a secretary does: word processing, filing, and answering phones.

Describing

A second skill of the informative speaker is distinguishing between abstract and concrete words and between general and specific words. One of the best ways to make an informative speech interesting is by using language forcefully and effectively. You can do that best if you recognize certain differences among words.

For instance, some words *refer generally to ideas, qualities, acts, or relationships:* these are called **abstract words.** Examples of abstract words are *freedom* (an idea), *mysterious* (a quality), *altruism* (an act), and *parent-child* (a relationship). Other words are more specific, or **concrete,** because they *refer to definite persons, places, objects, and acts,* such as Dr. Bettsey L. Barhorst, the Eiffel Tower, and your economics textbook. Abstract words are useful in theorizing, summarizing, and discussing and are commonly used by educated persons discussing ideas. Concrete words are most useful in relating your personal experiences, direct observations, and feelings or attitudes. The important point about abstract and concrete language is to use each where it is most appropriate. The most common error in informative speeches is the use of abstract terms where concrete words would be more forceful and clear. "I have really liked some courses of study here at Oklahoma University," says a student to her classmates and adds, "but others I have disliked." This abstract, general statement has minimal impact. If speaking in concrete terms, the same student might say, "I have most enjoyed English, speech, and political science courses, and I have disliked courses in chemistry, mathematics, and physics." Descriptions in informative speeches should be specific, accurate, and detailed, rather than general and ambiguous.

Informative speakers should also attempt to use colorful imagery that appeals to the senses. A speaker describing a place might say that "the sun sets in an orange sky against the purple mountain," a victim of shock "appears lifeless, pallid, and clammy," or a manufactured meat "tastes like top-grade sirloin."

A valuable exercise for the informative speaker is to carefully review the rough draft of the speech to discover abstract, general, ambiguous words that can be replaced by concrete details.

abstract words

Words or phrases that refer generally to ideas, qualities, acts, or relationships.

concrete words

Words that refer to definite persons, places, objects, and acts.

TRY ◄►THIS

Make a list of abstract words and another of concrete words that relate to your topic.

Explaining

A third skill for the informative speaker is explaining an idea in terms the audience can understand. An **explanation** is *a means of idea development that simplifies or clarifies an idea while arousing audience interest.*

explanation

A means of idea development that simplifies or clarifies an idea while arousing audience interest.

An important step in explaining is analyzing something or taking it apart so the audience can understand it. Unless you become skilled at dissecting a concept, your explanation may leave audience members more confused than they were before your speech. You have to determine what you can do to make the concept more palatable to the audience and increase audience understanding. For example, John Kenneth Galbraith, a retired professor of economics from Harvard University, wrote many books explaining economics to people who did not know very much about the subject. A close look at one of his explanations is instructive. Galbraith is trying to make the point that politicians and the public often take the voices of a few influential persons as a shift of opinion by the majority:

> On the need for tax relief, investment incentives, or a curb on welfare costs, the views of one articulate and affluent banker, businessman, lawyer, or acolyte economist are the equal of those of several thousand welfare mothers. In any recent year, the pleas by Walter Wriston of Citibank or David Rockefeller of Chase Manhattan for relief from oppressive taxation, regulation, or intrusive government have commanded at least as much attention as the expressions of discontent of all the deprived of the South Bronx. (Galbraith, 1981)*

Galbraith is analyzing a situation: Why do the persons of economic advantage have a bigger say in our economy than the millions who live with it? His language is concrete. He is expanding on an idea with descriptive language, and he is doing so by dissecting the concept so that you can understand its parts.

Narrating

narrating

The oral presentation and interpretation of a story, a description, or an event; includes dramatic reading of prose or poetry.

A fourth skill for informative speakers is **narrating,** *the oral presentation and interpretation of a story, a description, or an event.* In a speech, narration includes the dramatic reading of some lines from a play, a poem, or another piece of literature; the voice-over on a series of slides or a silent film to illustrate a point in a speech; and even the reading of such information as a letter, a quotation, or a selection from a newspaper or magazine. The person who does the play-by-play account of a ball game is narrating, and so is the speaker who explains what a weaver is doing in an informative speech on home crafts.

The person who uses narration in a speech moves just a little closer to oral interpretation of literature, or even acting, because the real cue to narrating is that the narration is highlighted by being more dramatic than the words around it. Sections of your speech that require this kind of special reading also require special practice. If you want a few lines of poetry in your speech to have the desired impact, you will need to rehearse them.

---

*Reprinted from an article in *The New York Review of Books.* Reprinted with permission.

15.2 RESEARCH RESULTS ON INFORMATIVE SPEAKING

Write T *for true or* F *for false in each blank on the left:*

_____ 1. You can increase your audience's comprehension or understanding through planned repetition.

_____ 2. The use of transitions increases audience comprehension.

_____ 3. Informative speakers should avoid abstract language.

_____ 4. Advance organizers *do* work in writing and *may* work in speaking.

_____ 5. *Etymology* is the study of insects.

Answers: 1. T   2. T   3. F   4. T   5. F

An Example of an Informative Speech

So far in this chapter, you have gained additional information on how to select a topic for your informative speech, how to determine behavioral purposes and goals for the informative speech, how to present information to an audience, how to organize the informative speech, and how to define, describe, explain, and narrate the concepts in your speech. Now let's look at the manuscript of an informative speech delivered by a student.

Notice how the speaker gains and maintains the audience's attention, relates the topic to himself and to the audience, and forecasts the organization and development of the topic. Notice also how the speaker attempts to clarify the topic with examples high in audience interest; translates the ideas into language the audience can understand; and defines, describes, and explains. The marginal notes will help identify how the speaker is fulfilling the important functions of the introduction, body, and conclusion of an informative speech.

Investing from Home

In the past, ordinary people did not invest in stocks; investing was reserved for the rich and elite. In the past, even the rich people had to invest through brokers, who took a commission for services rendered both when they bought stocks and when they sold them. In the past, only the savvy reader of *The Wall*

Topic is announced: Speaker arouses information hunger by talking about what "used to be."

419

Street Journal, Business Week, and *Money Magazine* had the foggiest notion of what stocks to buy, hold, or sell. What occurred in the past is no more: Ordinary people like you and me can invest, can avoid a large brokerage fee, and can access free information that was once reserved for the elite, the rich, and the bold. Even 6 months ago industry experts said, "The typical online investor was male, college educated, from 32 to 42 years old, with an annual salary of $75,000" (Segal, 1998). But as David Segal (1998) says in his article "Investors are trading brokers for computers": "These days the crowd has been joined by legions of home-makers, retirees, precocious teenagers and disgruntled employees dreaming of going pro" (p. H1). The craze has even been joined by me, a lowly finance major, who has earned little this year but learned much about investing, trading, and having fun in the market and on the net.

My informative speech will introduce you to the world of personal investing, to the idea of being your own broker, and to the possibility of having some fun with your money.

The first, and maybe most important, point of this speech is that any investing you might do because of what you learn today should not be money you might need for your mortgage, your impending marriage, or your mother's nursing home. In fact, James Glassman (1998), an expert on investing, says you should start with a "fun and games account," or FGA, which he calls "a pot of money for *playing* the market, as opposed to investing for a long-term goal such as retirement" (p. H1). So, remember, this speech is about playing with your money, not about buffetting your way to the country club set.

Some of you may already be feeling that this informative speech cannot be about you: "I've got no investments, I'm not knowledgeable about investing, and I have no reason to even want this information." Well, just to keep you interested, I will point out that 5 years ago you could not even do what I am suggesting today: Internet trading did not exist. But, according to David Segal (1998) in *The Washington Post,* "Today there are more than 3 million online accounts, and by 2002 that number is expected to rise to 14 million with nearly $700 billion in assets" (p. A1). Apparently, some people have a lot of FGM, fun and games money.

Topic is related to audience: Topic relevance is highlighted by "join-the-crowd" approach.

Topic is related to speaker: Speaker credibility is enhanced by her own involvement.

Forecast: Organization and development revealed: Forecast of contents.

Organization: First main point.

New term defined: FGA.

Appeal to audience's sense of adventure: Doing what could not be done before.

Appeal to join the party: Learn by knowing information.

You already know that I recommend you only do on-line investing with FGM. Next, you need to know what stocks cost, how much or how little you have to invest. You do have to open an account with some on-line brokerage firm because you have to buy your stock from somebody. But unlike what it "used to be" when traditional brokers had high minimums and trades cost over $100, now trades cost as little as $8, according to David Segal (1998). According to Segal, some firms like Fidelity Brokerage want $5,000 in cash or securities to open an account, and Brown & Co. opens at $15,000; but four firms, which I have included in my handout, have no minimum investment at all: SureTrade, Quick and Reilly, National Discount Brokers, and Jack White & Co. (Looking into, 1998). You will also find on the handout their cost per stock trade and other services rendered. The second point of my speech, then, is that you can start investing your FGM at very low cost to yourself compared to what "used to be."

Transition: Internal summary and forecast.

Cost-benefit analysis: Investing is inexpensive.

Refers to handout.

Second main point: Costs are lower than they were before.

Now you might be wondering, "How do I determine who to invest through?" Albert B. Crenshaw (1998), another expert on money and investing, says that so many financial and on-line service companies are on the World Wide Web today that you have many options for finding the most useful investment sources. You can see the web addresses listed on my PowerPoint slide, but I'd like to point out a few of the more common names: Quicken.com, Yahoo, and Microsoft are among the many companies that have created web sites to guide you to investment information (Crenshaw, 1998). Julio Gomez, consultant for online financial services, has a site **(www.score card.com)** that ranks more than 80 on-line brokers. He recommends starting "with an inexpensive online broker that has seedy Web site navigation and trade execution" (Burkstrand, 1998). At one web site investors conduct bulletin board discussions about the advantages and disadvantages of brokerage firms **(www.onlineinvestors.com).** Occasionally a competing firm plants misinformation on this bulletin board, and often the ones who do chat have complaints rather than compliments. Nonetheless, you should pay attention if the complaints about an on-line company are numerous (Burkstrand, 1998).

Third main point: Who to broker your account?

Presentational aid: Refer to web site addresses on the board.

Presentational aid: Provides World Wide Web addresses on PowerPoint slide.

To test an on-line broker before doing business, Beth Burkstrand (1998) recommends trying to contact the company's customer service representative by e-mail or telephone: See if and how quickly the firm responds. Also, see if the broker provides you with tax reports, an unlimited account history, and profit and loss for each individual stock. Does the on-line broker have a backup way to trade in case of server overload or Internet connection failure? And, finally, how much does the company charge per trade and any ancillary services? Some firms charge extra for providing stock quotes, for making large trades, and even for talking with a human being (Burkstrand, 1998).

So far you know that you should only invest with FGA, that you can invest small amounts, and that on-line brokers are ranked and discussed on the net. Now you need to know exactly how you do a stock transaction. For the uninitiated, a broker like Charles Schwab **(Schwab.com)** will train you in one of its many offices. On-line customers use **schwab.com** to make 66,000 orders per day, more than half of the company's daily trading volume (Knight, 1998). To actually execute a trade is simple. You fill out a form to buy or sell a certain security at a specific price, then click "send" (Burkstrand, 1998). Schwab is a discount broker that charges $39 minimum for conventional orders, $29.95 for an on-line stock trade, and a 20 percent discount for on-line trades of mutual funds. However, Datek Securities, a deeper discount broker, charges as low as $9.95 for transacting a trade (Knight, 1998). How do you find out how much your stock or mutual fund costs when you buy it? The company web sites provide real-time quotes, so you will know what price to pay.

My four main points are complete: Play with a fun and games account, invest modest amounts, find an on-line broker who provides the services you need, and learn how to transact a trade on your computer. Now I leave you with one warning: On-line investing can be so much fun that "the game" gets you in trouble. Many new investors find that seeking stocks, researching them, and buying and selling them gives them such a high that they become almost obsessive about buying and selling all the time. But there is good reason to think twice before you let the game consume you. Two University of California finance professors, Barber and Odean, looked at almost

Inside information on evaluating on-line brokers: Information on how to transact a buy or sell.

Transition: Second repetition of main points.

Conclusion: Summary and repetition of four main points.

Upbeat ending: Signals end of speech with one last piece of advice.

65,000 discount brokerage accounts and found that those that did the least trading earned 75 percent higher returns than those that traded the most (Glassman, 1998). That is good enough reason for me!

I hope you will keep my handout, which tells you how to set up an on-line account, and I hope you learned a lot today about on-line trading. Whether you ever choose to do it or not, I hope you found the topic an interesting one to learn about. The on-line trading craze is definitely sweeping the investment business.

Support materials: Finance professors provide credible fact and figures about investing.

Endnotes

Burkstrand, B. (1998, August 23). Taking the trading floor to the home front: Choosing the right broker on the Internet isn't always easy. *The Washington Post,* p. H1.

Crenshaw, A. (1998, August 23). Cash flow: Answers about money at a web site near you. *The Washington Post,* p. H1. [The web sites: **www.quicken.com, www. quote.yahoo.com,** and **www.Investor.msn.com.**]

Glassman, J. (1998, August 23). Internet is ideal for a "fun" account. *The Washington Post,* pp. H1, H15.

Knight, J. (1998, August 23). Schwab, clients save money online. *The Washington Post,* p. H4.

Looking into online trading. (1998, August 23). *The Washington Post,* p. H4.

Segal, D. (1998, August 23). Investors are trading brokers for computers: By going online, Wall Street is just a keystroke away. *The Washington Post,* pp. H1, H15.

The immediate purpose of this informative speech was to inform the audience about on-line investing. The long-term purpose of the speech was to enable the audience to know why people might choose to invest from home, how much or little to invest, how to select and evaluate an on-line broker, how to find a security in which to invest, and how to actually transact a buy or sell. The speaker introduced some new vocabulary: FGA, on-line accounts, Internet trading, minimum investment, and on-line broker. Finally, the speaker appealed to the audience to listen, and to learn about the information, by portraying home investing as a new, even amusing activity and, hopefully, a profitable one as well.

Summary

The primary vehicle for informing others is the informative speech. To prepare an informative speech, you should know (1) the intent and the goal of informative speaking, (2) the kinds of topics that lend themselves best to informative speaking, and (3) the kinds of immediate behavioral purposes of informative speaking and how to determine if you have fulfilled them.

In presenting information to an audience, you should strive to generate information hunger (an audience need for the information), achieve information relevance (providing information that is not simply informative), use extrinsic motivation (reasons outside the speech itself for concentrating on the content of the speech), select informative content (a limited number of main points, generalizations, relatively simple words and concrete ideas, humor, and statements about how the speech will meet audience needs), and avoid information overload (too much information in a speech or information beyond the capacity of the audience to understand).

Issues in Communication

This Issues in Communication narrative is designed to provoke individual thought or discussion about concepts raised in the chapter.

Huan Yi works for a company that sells financial software to small- and medium-size businesses; his job is to show customers how to use the new software. He spends 2 weeks with each client demonstrating the features and functions of the software most applicable to the client's needs. The first few months on the job were difficult—he often left a client feeling that even after 2 weeks he hadn't been able to show the employees everything they needed to know. It's not that they weren't interested—they obviously appreciated his instruction and showed a desire to learn. Huan couldn't figure out if the software was difficult for them to understand or if he was not doing a good job of teaching.

During the next few months, Huan started to see some patterns. He would get to a new client site and spend the first week going over the software with the employees—what it could do, how it worked, and what they needed to learn. He usually did this in shifts, with different groups of employees listening to him lecture. He had developed one handout, but he mostly relied on the company's manual to determine what topics to cover. He always reached his goal of going over the manual from cover to cover with each group of employees. Then he would spend the next week installing the program and helping individuals troubleshoot.

Huan realized that during the week of troubleshooting and answering questions, he ended up addressing the same issues over and over, especially about technical terms and functions. He was frustrated because he felt that these topics had been covered very well during the first week. He was also annoyed because most of the individuals with whom he worked seemed to have retained very little information from the first week. They asked very basic questions and often needed prompting from beginning to end. At first he wondered if these people were just a little slow, but then he began to get the distinct feeling that some of the problem might be his style of presenting the information.

Apply what you have learned about the informative speech as you ponder and discuss the following questions: What was Huan's immediate behavioral goal? Was he successful in reaching this goal? In what specific ways would an understanding of information hunger and relevance, extrinsic motivation, informative content, and information overload give Huan insight into what is going wrong? What skills could Huan use to become a more effective informative speaker?

Additional Resources

www.yearbooknews.com
A site for finding experts, especially in the United States.
www.facsnet.org/ sources_online/ facs_source/main. html Foundation for American

Communications (FACS) site (FACSNet) for experts in economics, science, public policy, and law.
ps.superb.net/FAQ
A good site for beginning your

research on an informational speech because it contains both questions and answers in its FAQ Finder. (*FAQ* is an acronym for "frequently asked questions.")

References

Ausubel, D. (1960). The use of advance organizers in the learning and retention of meaningful material. *Journal of Educational Psychology, 51,* 267–272.

Baird, J. A. (1974). The effects of speech summaries upon audience comprehension of expository speeches of varying quality and complexity. *Central States Speech Journal, 25,* 119–127.

Cofer, N. C. (1961). *Verbal learning and verbal behavior.* New York: McGraw-Hill.

Ernest, C. (1968). Listening comprehension as a function of type of material and rate of presentation. *Speech Monographs, 35,* 154–158.

Galbraith, J. K. (1981, January 4). The three

attacks on social and economic consensus. *The Des Moines Sunday Register.*

Gruner, C. R. (1970). The effect of humor in dull and interesting informative speeches. *Central States Speech Journal, 21,* 160–166.

McGuire, S. (1998, August 24). More blood for Ireland: Will the peace survive a brutal bombing? *Newsweek,* p. 31.

McGuire, M., Stillbourne, L., McAdams, M., & Hyatt, L. (1997). *Internet handbook for writers, researchers, and journalists.* New York: Guilford.

Pence, O. L. (1954). Emotionally loaded argument: Its effectiveness in stimulating recall. *Quarterly Journal of Speech, 40,* 272–276.

Petrie, C. R., Jr. (1963). Informative speaking: A summary and bibliography of related research. *Speech Monographs, 30,* 79–91.

Petrie, C. R., Jr., & Carrel, S. D. (1976). The relationship of motivation, listening, capability, initial information, and verbal organizational ability to lecture comprehension and retention. *Speech Monographs, 43,* 187–194.

Tucker, C. D. (1964). An application of programmed learning to informative speech. *Speech Monographs, 31,* 142–152.

Wheeless, L. R. (1974). The effects of attitude, credibility, and homophily on selective exposure to information. *Speech Monographs, 41,* 329–338.

When you have read and thought about this chapter, you will be able to:

1. Identify four action goals of persuasive speaking.

2. Distinguish between immediate behavioral purposes and ultimate goals.

3. Describe and utilize persuasive-speaking strategies.

4. Recall four ethical guidelines for persuasive speaking.

5. State and utilize some persuasive-speaking skills.

6. Understand the difference between public speaking and presentational speaking.

7. Reveal some strategies for resisting persuasive appeals.

16

Persuasive and Presentational Speaking

This chapter explores persuasive and presentational speaking. First, you learn how to prepare a persuasive speech, examine some methods of persuasion, and review some skills useful to the persuader. Ethical considerations are followed by strategies for resisting persuasive appeals. In the final section you will learn about the presentational speech and see how it differs from public speeches. An example of a presentational speech is provided.

E dward was chosen by his coworkers to give the final presentation to Compu-Work's board of directors. He and a team of three other consultants had been hired by CompuWork to do a thorough evaluation of its business and make recommendations about how to streamline the company and improve its bottom line. Edward graduated with his MBA only a year before, so he was worried that the board of directors would not take his recommendations seriously—all the directors were men and women with successful career tracks. His coworkers didn't seem to think their status would be a problem.

Georgia grew up in a tough, inner-city neighborhood, and her family didn't have any money to help her go to college, but she was determined to get a good education. In high school she studied hard, worked to save as much money as she could, and volunteered to help younger children learn to read. During Georgia's senior year in high school, her chemistry teacher helped her apply for different scholarships that ultimately allowed her to get a bachelor's degree. After graduation, Georgia became an advocate for the university's scholarship program, volunteering to speak to groups of alumni to encourage them to give generously so that others like her would be able to go to school. At first she relied solely on her personal experience when talking to people, but she soon learned that she needed more than this approach to persuade people to give to the scholarship fund.

Like Edward and Georgia, most of us will need to give persuasive or presentational speeches during our lifetimes. The goal of this chapter is to prepare you for such situations.

What Is Persuasion and What Are the Goals of Persuasive Speaking?

persuasion

An ongoing process in which verbal and nonverbal messages shape, reinforce, and change people's responses.

Many people have a mistaken view of how persuasion works. For instance, some people think persuasion is the skillful manipulation of images to get people to do something they would not otherwise do. To them, persuasion is seduction, getting their way with people by influencing them against their will. Others see persuasion not as seduction or manipulation but as a more noble pursuit of the best ideas and most workable solutions and of greater support for an idea through effective speaking. The best speakers know how to assemble an effective persuasive message through their knowledge of critical thinking, and they use the same tools to analyze what others are saying.

Persuasion is *an ongoing process in which verbal and nonverbal messages shape, reinforce, and change people's responses* (Miller, 1980). Rarely do people change greatly as a result of a one-shot persuasive effort. If they change at all, they change because of ongoing exposure to messages from speakers, newspapers, magazines, broadcasts, friends, and relatives.

These multiple messages *shape* our responses by pushing us to act or think in a certain way (Miller, 1980). In the past, you might have disliked dancing, but because your closest friend loves to dance, you changed your behavior over time until you now enjoy dancing. A single persuasive speech can *start* to push an audience in a direction desired by the speaker.

Persuasive messages can also *reinforce* past behavior or beliefs—that is, reward a person for persisting in a certain response or for avoiding a certain response. In persuasive speaking, the general goal of reinforcing consists of two action goals: continuance and deterrence. **Continuance** means that *you encourage the audience to continue its present behavior or beliefs,* such as using seat belts, going to synagogue, or eating low-fat foods. **Deterrence** means that *you encourage the audience to avoid an activity or a belief,* such as using drugs, smoking, or joining a gang.

Persuasive messages can also *change* people's actions or thoughts. Under this general goal of changing an audience's responses are the action goals of adoption and discontinuance. **Adoption** is *inducing the audience to accept a new idea, attitude, behavior, belief, or product,* such as starting a daily exercise program. **Discontinuance** means that *the audience is encouraged to stop doing or believing something,* such as voting Republican, eating junk foods, or drinking alcoholic beverages (Fotheringham, 1966). Think of shaping, reinforcing, and changing as very broad general goals of persuasion, and the action goals—continuance, deterrence, adoption, and discontinuance—as the "acting out" of those goals.

You can improve your chances of persuading an audience if you write out the ultimate goal of your speech and your action goals, or immediate behavioral purposes. **Ultimate goals** are *purposes that you wish to fulfill with additional messages and more time—perhaps days, months, or years.* **Immediate goals** are *purposes that you wish to accomplish during the speech or within minutes or hours.* (Figure 16.1 illustrates the relationships among the various persuasive goals.) For example, a student delivering a persuasive speech against jogging might write down the following as an ultimate goal:

> The ultimate goal of my persuasive speech is to convince people who jog that they should quit [discontinuance] and to convince people who do not jog that they should never start [deterrence].

continuance

Persuading an audience to continue present behavior or beliefs.

deterrence

Persuading an audience to avoid an activity or a belief.

adoption

Inducing an audience to accept a new idea, attitude, behavior, belief, or product and to demonstrate that acceptance through behavioral change.

discontinuance

Inducing an audience to stop doing something or thinking in a certain way.

ultimate goals

Purposes that a speaker wishes to fulfill with additional messages and more time.

General Goals	Action Goals	Expected Behavior	Immediate Goals	Ultimate Goals
To shape	To move toward action goals	To move toward expected behavior	To move toward immediate goals	To move toward ultimate goals
To reinforce	Continuance	Keep doing it	Continue now	Continue later
	Deterrence	Don't do it	Avoid now	Avoid later
To change	Adoption	Start doing it	Start now	Start later
	Discontinuance	Stop doing it	Stop now	Stop later

Figure 16.1 The relationship among persuasive goals.

Instant Recall

For each statement, identify which action goal of persuasion is indicated by writing the correct letter from the choices below in the blank on the left:

A. Continuance   **C. Discontinuance**
B. Deterrence   **D. Adoption**

_____ 1. "My purpose in talking to uninsured college students is to encourage them to purchase relatively inexpensive 'term insurance' instead of relatively expensive 'whole-life' insurance."

_____ 2. "My immediate purpose in talking to an audience of drug offenders from juvenile court is to persuade them to quit using illegal drugs."

_____ 3. "My ultimate goal is to persuade the people in my morning aerobics class to stay with the program."

_____ 4. "My goal in speaking to second-grade students who have never seen a real gun is to persuade them to avoid touching a gun of any kind because of the danger."

_____ 5. "In talking to people who have never purchased Girl Scout cookies before, I am trying to convince them to buy their first box of Girl Scout cookies from my daughter."

Answers: 1. D   2. C   3. A   4. B   5. D

immediate goals

Purposes that a speaker wishes to accomplish during the speech or shortly after it.

The same speaker might state her immediate behavioral purposes as:

One of my immediate behavioral purposes is to have the audience write down at the conclusion of my speech the three harmful effects of jogging on the body: shin splints, bone bruises, and knee problems. A second immediate behavioral purpose of my speech is to have the joggers in the audience start reducing their workout times to avoid problems encouraged by fatigue.

The persuasive speaker need not reveal the ultimate goal of the speech itself but, ordinarily, should reveal the immediate behavioral purposes of the speech.

COMMUNICATION CHALLENGE

Persuasive Speech Document

Put the title of your persuasive speech and your name at the top of a sheet of paper. State your action goal and your immediate behavioral purposes. Then compose a manuscript of your persuasive speech, with marginal notes to indicate what functions you are fulfilling in the introduction and conclusion, what your main points and subpoints are, and what kinds of evidence you are using. Include endnotes or footnotes and a bibliography in proper form.

Audience members are more likely to write down the harmful effects of jogging if they are told early in the speech of that expectation. They may resist the persuasive speaker, however, if they know the ultimate goal of the speech.

Many speech communication professors will want you to use the general goals of shaping and changing and the action goals of adoption and discontinuance. They may even discourage speeches with the general goal of reinforcing and the action goals of deterrence and continuance. One of the reasons for encouraging you to give persuasive speeches with adoption and discontinuance action goals is that you and the teacher will be better able to observe change in the audience. With deterrence and continuance action goals, the audience's behavior may remain the same, but to attribute that lack of change to your speech would be risky.

TRY◀▶THIS

Make a list of some things you enjoy doing. Examine the list and notice how many things were introduced to you by another person. That person played a part in persuading you to do something you had never tried before.

What Are Some Persuasive Speech Topics?

The previous chapter mentioned that the perception of a topic as informative or persuasive depends not only on the topic but also on the speaker and the audience. A topic like "equal pay for women" could be presented as informative by including pay scales and percentages of pay differences in your speech. "Equal pay for women" also could be persuasive by including arguments for challenging and changing the current system. Even if a speaker's intent is to inform, a female giving an informative speech on equal pay for women might be perceived by her audience as advocating a position. The main point to remember is that in a persuasive speech you are trying to change an audience's attitudes, beliefs, or values about some issue; changing audience attitudes assumes that the audience members have a position on the issue and that they are not neutral or completely unknowledgeable about the topic.

Chapter 11, Topic Selection and Audience Analysis, provided a detailed account of how to use brainstorming and inventories to find topics. Approaches that may serve as shortcuts to finding a topic are to look through newspapers and magazines, listen to talk radio, watch TV news and talk shows, and search the Internet for issues that interest you. Another shortcut is to look through topics that students have already used for their persuasive speeches to see if any of them give you some ideas. Following are some possibilities:

Build more prisons	Against child support
Learn a language	Against premarital sex
Improving day care	Stop sexual assaults
Volunteer your time	Help the homeless
Become a vegetarian	Lower your cholesterol
Join aerobics	Rebuild the inner city
Against fast foods	Avoid pesticides
Stop immigration	Fighting video violence
Favor divorce	Avoid anorexia
Favor celibacy	Yes to surrogate mothers
Favor cohabitation	Against animal experimentation
Stop smoking	No negotiation with terrorists
Favor gay adoption	Improve Social Security
Improve race relations	Favor higher drinking age
Adopt a child	Wean yourself from television
Better parenting	Appreciate modern art
Restructure juvenile justice	Against gun control
Against assisted suicide	Against managed care
Support the cancer drive	Stop dieting
Support the humane society	Stop drinking
Restructure taxation	Stop abortion

SEARCHING ELECTRONIC DATABASES

Some databases cannot be reached from your home because they require a subscription, but college and university libraries often pay for these self-service databases and students use them for no charge. See if your library has these sources:

SOCIOFILE: Includes communication, speech, sociology, criminal justice, political science, demography, etc.

LEXIS/NEXIS: Includes law, medicine, business, accounting, and government.

PSYCLIT: Includes information from over 1,400 journals in psychology, and education.

INFOTRAC: An index of more than 1,000 newspapers and journals on communication, religion, science, social science, humanities, and other subjects.

MEDLINE: Includes 3,600 journals in medicine, biomedicine, and health sciences.

Find out if your library is a subscriber and if students can have a PID (personal identification) code to gain access from anywhere.

SOURCE: McGuire, Stilbourne, McAdams, and Hyatt, 1997.

How Do You Persuade an Audience?

You can persuade an audience in a variety of ways. Researchers Marvin Karlins and Herbert I. Abelson (1970) observed, "Information by itself almost never changes attitudes." In addition to offering information in support of your persuasive message, you can attempt to persuade an audience by using motivational appeals, your source credibility to your advantage, and logical or emotional appeals; by organizing your materials effectively; and by observing ethical guidelines for persuasion.

Motivational Appeals

The word *motivation* is based on a Latin term that means "to move," which is how the term is used in everyday conversations: "What was his motivation in buying that expensive car?" "She had plenty of motivation for getting a job"; or "His motive was to act just like the other firefighters." If you boil down motivation to its essential ingredients, you can see that three forces move people to behave in one way or another (McConnell, 1977).

One motivating force is *what our bodies tell us to do*. This physical basis of motivation explains our need for air, water, and food. You can get along without air for less than 3 minutes, without water for only a couple of days, and without food for only about a week. Having unpolluted air to breathe, clean water to drink, and desirable food to eat takes much human energy, but our basic bodily needs motivate us to do what is necessary to preserve these resources.

The second motivating force is *what our minds tell us to do*. This psychological motivation is based on our sense of rationality, as well as on our emotions, feelings, and perceptions. You are moved to do some things because you think it is reasonable to do so. You may do other things because you feel good about doing them. You may avoid still other activities because they make you feel bad about yourself. The human mind motivates us to act in ways that comfort and preserve it.

TRY ◄►THIS

Think about the actions you are motivated to do and why. For example, why do you date certain people? Why do you enjoy a certain type of food?

The third motivating force is *what other people want us to do*. This third force is a powerful social motivator that encourages us to conform to roles and norms. You may act like a student because your fellow students reinforce you when you do and punish you when you do not. You may attend classes because that is what students are to do. You might find yourself doing any number of things because family, friends, and coworkers expect and reward such behavior.

Human behavior is very complicated. No explanation of why human beings behave the way they do is entirely satisfactory. Simply knowing the three kinds of motivational forces will not permit you to manipulate an audience to elicit the behavior you seek. Nonetheless, the most effective persuasive speakers—advertisers, politicians, and lawyers—have learned how to analyze their audiences—consumers, voters, and juries—so that they are more often successful than unsuccessful in reaching their objectives.

Emotional Appeals

Emotional appeals are *attempts to persuade audience members to change an attitude or a behavior through an appeal—usually in a narrative form—to their* *emotions.* Although logical and emotional appeals are often seen as diametrically opposed concepts, most of our behavior and beliefs are based on a mixture of emotional and rational "reasons." A speaker may persuade an audience to accept his or her immediate behavioral purposes for emotional, rather than logical, reasons. A story about one person's bad experience with the campus bookstore may inspire many persons in the audience to take their business to another store. The experience may have been a one-in-a-thousand situation, it may have been as much the customer's fault as the manager's, or it had never happened before. Such is the power of our emotions that they can persuade us to defy the law, fight another nation, or ignore evidence. As one writer put it,

> The creature man is best persuaded
> When heart, not mind, is inundated:
> Affect is what drives the will:
> Rationality keeps it still.*

The appeal that has received the most attention from researchers is the *fear appeal.* Janis and Feshbach (1953) examined three levels of fear appeals in communication on maintaining dental hygiene and found that a weak threat works better than a moderate threat, which works better than a strong threat. On the other hand, Powell (1965) used strong and weak fear appeals in a civil defense message that threatened loved ones and found more opinion change when the fear appeal was strong. These results are contradictory, but the research on reassurance with fear appeals is not. Your fear appeals are likely to work better if you reveal how the audience can avoid the fearsome consequences of a behavior or belief. For example, you could say, "Not brushing your teeth can lead to gum disease and tooth loss, so listen to my tips on dental hygiene." Omitting reassurance does not influence the audience's ability to recall facts from the speech, but a speech with reassurance results in greater shifts of opinion than one without reassurance. Also, a speaker who includes reassurance is regarded by the audience as a better speaker than one who does not (Cope & Richardson, 1972).

Fear appeals are just one kind of emotional appeal commonly found in speeches. Other examples of possible emotional appeals are testimonials at funerals about the virtues of the deceased, appeals to loyalty and dedication at retirement ceremonies, appeals to patriotism in political season and times of war, and appeals to justice in times of legal strife.

emotional appeals

Attempts to persuade audience members to change an attitude or a behavior through an appeal—usually in a narrative form—to their emotions.

Logical Appeals

Motivational appeals and speaker credibility are just two tools for persuading an audience; a third important method is the use of reasoning or logic to

---

*Reprinted from Marvin Karlins and Herbert I. Abelson, *Persuasion: How Opinions and Attitudes Are Changed,* (2d ed). Copyright © 1970 by Springer Publishing Company, Inc., New York. Used by permission.

logical appeals

Propositions and evidence used to persuade an audience.

convince an audience. The main ingredients of **logical appeals** are *propositions and evidence.*

A *proposition* is a statement that asserts or proposes something: "The United States should have uniform regulations for child support"; "The city should reduce the fines for traffic offenses"; or "The college should change its definition of 'a student in good standing.'" Notice that a proposition always recommends a change in the status quo, the way things are right now. The primary method of persuading an audience that a current policy should be changed and another policy should be adopted is through the use of evidence.

evidence

Any material that supports a proposition.

Evidence, *any material that supports a proposition,* is central to the persuasive process (Reinhard, 1988). The persuasive speaker can use a wide array of evidence to demonstrate the wisdom of retaining present practices or changing current policies, such as quotations from authoritative persons, conclusions from studies and reports, or experiences of individuals injured or helped by current policies. The underlying principle in logical appeals is that the audience should accept the side that presents the most convincing or the "best" evidence to support itself. In other words, our behavior or changes in behavior should be based on the best evidence; it should be consistent with the persuasive speaker who provides the most effective evidence.

Logical appeals can also be refuted; that is, they can be attacked. Another persuasive speaker can analyze the situation suggested in a proposition and find it faulty. The opposing persuasive speaker may find that the authorities who were quoted were biased, that the reports and studies were flawed, or that better evidence would invite a different conclusion.

Finally, to recognize that the world does not run by logic or evidence alone is important; sometimes beliefs and behaviors are irrational or not based on evidence. A persuasive speaker might present considerable evidence on why you should eat legumes and cheese instead of meat without changing audience behavior or beliefs on that subject. The persuasive speaker is always faced with the disconcerting fact that even the best evidence in support of a persuasive proposition might not alter audience beliefs or behavior.

Organizational Considerations

The organizational patterns used most often in persuasive speaking are problem/solution, cause/effect, and topical-sequence. In the first two patterns, you have to gauge carefully how much time to spend on the problem or cause and how much time to spend on the solution or effect. The key to deciding is how much the audience needs to know and which part contains your most important persuasive effort. The topical-sequence pattern is highly versatile and, for example, is used in providing three reasons you should use fishing scents, five characteristics of quality clothing, and evidence for using fetal tissue to help victims of Parkinson's disease.

Besides choosing a basic pattern of organization, you need to consider how much to say in your introduction. In informative speaking, you usually say exactly what you want your audience to learn from your speech. In persuasive speaking, you may not want to say your ultimate goal, because the audience is unlikely to accept your point of view until you have presented your **arguments,** *your propositions, justifications, and evidence.* You might, therefore, omit your ultimate goal until the audience is more prepared.

Other organizational considerations in persuasive speaking concern placing your arguments, presenting one or more sides of the issue, deciding whether to include counterarguments, and using familiar or novel arguments in your speech:

1. *Should my best arguments come first, in the middle, or last in my persuasive speech?* Arguments presented first or early in the body of the speech seem to have more impact in speeches on controversial issues, on topics with which the audience is uninvolved, on topics the audience perceives as interesting, and on topics highly familiar to the audience. On the other hand, arguments seem to have more impact on an audience later in a persuasive speech when audience members are involved in the issue, when the topic is likely to be less interesting, and when the issue is moderately unfamiliar to the audience (Janis & Feshbach, 1953). No research to date indicates that the most important arguments should be presented in the middle of the speech. The middle is the place where audience attention is likely to wane, so the effective speaker usually builds in human interest stories and interesting supporting materials to maintain audience attention.

2. *Should I present one side of the issue, both, or many?* A persuasive speaker should present one side of an issue when the audience is friendly, when the speaker's position is the only one the audience is likely to hear, and when the speaker is seeking immediate, but temporary, change of opinion. A persuasive speaker should present both sides or many sides of an issue when the audience initially disagrees with the speaker, or when it is likely the audience will hear other sides from other people (Powell, 1965). Presenting both sides or multiple sides to a hostile audience may make the speaker seem more open-minded or less rigid to the audience. Also, presenting the other sides of the issue reduces the impact of **counterarguments,** or *rebuttals to your arguments.*

3. *Should I refute counterarguments?* The best advice based on current research is to refute counterarguments before proceeding to your own position on the issue, especially when the audience is likely to know the counterarguments already (Karlins & Abelson, 1970). If you favor freedom of choice on the abortion issue and your audience is familiar with the pro-life side, then you should refute the known counterarguments—point out their relative weaknesses or flaws—before you reveal your own position on the issue.

4. *Should I use familiar or novel arguments in my persuasive speech?* On most topics, you will have to acknowledge familiar arguments, and possibly refute them. However, research indicates that *novel*

arguments

Propositions, justifications, and evidence used to persuade.

counterarguments

Rebuttals to an argument.

arguments, or arguments the audience has not heard before, have more impact than familiar ones (Sears & Freedman, 1965). A student who delivered a persuasive speech in favor of gun control pointed out that a common counterargument from anticontrol forces was that gun registration would provide national enemies with a ready-made list of gun owners. The student who favored gun control pointed out that the membership list of the National Rifle Association already provided an extensive list of gun owners that could be used by national enemies. The argument was novel and served to nullify the claim made by the anticontrol side on the issue. You, too, should seek novel arguments in support of your own case and against the positions of others. Old, familiar arguments may be somewhat useful in your persuasive speech, but arguments the audience has not heard before have greater impact.

Monroe motivated sequence

A problem-solving format that encourages an audience to become concerned about an issue; especially appropriate for a persuasive speech.

The **Monroe motivated sequence** is *a problem-solving format that encourages an audience to become concerned about an issue.* Widely acclaimed for its usefulness in organizing speeches (Ehninger, 1970), the sequence has five steps:

1. *Attention.* You must gain and maintain audience attention, and you must determine a way to focus audience attention on the content of your speech.
2. *Need.* Once you have the audience's attention, you must show audience members how the speech is relevant to them. You must arouse a need for the change you suggest in your persuasive speech.
3. *Satisfaction.* Your speech either presents the information the audience needs or is a solution to their needs. You satisfy the audience by meeting their needs with your plan.
4. *Visualization.* You reinforce your idea in the audience's minds by getting audience members to *see* how your information or ideas will help them.
5. *Action.* Once the audience has visualized your idea, you plead for action. The audience might remember your main points in an informative speech and state them to others, or the audience may go out and do what you ask in a persuasive speech.

The Monroe motivated sequence is an appropriate organizational pattern for persuasive speeches, especially when the audience is reluctant to change or to accept a proposed action.

Speaker Credibility

source credibility

The audience's perception of your effectiveness as a speaker.

In Chapter 12 you learned that **source credibility** is *the audience's perception of your effectiveness as a speaker* and that the concept has four dimensions: expertise, trustworthiness, dynamism, and co-orientation. Recall also that a speaker does not have to exhibit all four dimensions; sometimes one dimension, such as the speaker's trustworthiness, is the sole source of credibility.

This speaker's police uniform signals source credibility on certain subjects for these children.

You would probably favor expertise over dynamism in a mechanic, trustworthiness over expertise in a spiritual leader, and expertise over co-orientation in a physician.

Who and what you are can make a powerful difference in your effectiveness as a persuasive speaker. A highly credible speaker has more impact on an audience than a speaker with low credibility. Also, a persuasive speaker who is seen as similar to the audience is more likely to be effective than one who is perceived as dissimilar. Sometimes a highly credible speaker can attain more attitude change when he or she simply asks for more change (Hovland & Pritzker, 1957).

All speakers need to avoid asking for too much change, however, lest they get a **boomerang effect,** *an unintended situation in which the speaker and the message induce an audience response that is the opposite of what the speaker intended.* For instance, the speaker wants the audience members to vote Republican, but they find him and his message so repugnant that they are less likely than before to vote Republican.

You can signal the origins of your credibility to your audience by describing how you earned the right to speak on the topic. Perhaps your major will help: A nuclear engineer has the authority to speak on nuclear energy; a business major is a credible source on buying stocks and bonds; a physical education major can speak with authority on exercise programs. Maybe your experience is the key to your credibility: Your years in the military may have given you some insights into military waste; your years as a mother and homemakers may have given you the authority to speak on managing time effectively, raising children, or relating to a spouse; or your part-time job at a fast-food establishment may permit you to speak with some authority on the minimum wage.

boomerang effect

An unintended situation in which the speaker and the message induce an audience response that is the opposite of what the speaker intended.

SOURCE: Hamilton, 1998.

Whatever the origins of your credibility, remember to reveal them early in the speech. Your authority may very well provide a reason for the audience to listen. If you reveal your credibility late in the speech, audience members may have paid little attention because they did not know you spoke with authority on the topic.

Another caution is in order: Although you must demonstrate your credibility to the audience, you can go too far in self-disclosing. Psychologists Burger and Vartabedian (1985) showed that as a speaker's prestige increases, the appropriateness of self-disclosure, as determined by the audience, decreases. Thus, people who are high in prestige, such as those in Congress, are well advised to avoid high levels of personal revelation. Some personal information can be offered by anyone, but perhaps no speaker should "tell all" in attempting to establish credibility.

Ethical Considerations

Ethics are written and unwritten rules of conduct. Many of our standards for ethical behavior are codified into law: not slandering or libeling someone who is an ordinary citizen; not starting a panic that can endanger the lives of others; not advocating the overthrow of our form of government.

Many principles of ethics are not matters of law, but violations of these unwritten or uncodified rules do have consequences. There is no law against pointing out acne sufferers in the audience during your speech on dermatology, or having your audience unknowingly eat cooked rat meat is not illegal, but audience members may find your methods so distasteful that they reject you and your persuasive message.

The following are some of the generally accepted ethical standards that govern the preparation and delivery of persuasive speeches:

1. *Accurately cite sources.* When you are preparing and delivering your speech, you should be very careful to gather and state your information accurately. Specifically, you should reveal from whom you received information if it was not your own idea. Making up quota-

Instant Recall

16.2 WHAT BEST PERSUADES?

Write T *for true or* F *for false in each blank on the left:*

_____ 1. By presenting more than one side of an issue, you can reduce the impact of counterarguments or rebuttals.

_____ 2. If your audience is likely to later hear arguments against the position you propose, you should present more than one side of the issue.

_____ 3. When the audience is uninvolved in the issue, interested in the topic, and familiar with the issue, arguments presented late in the speech have greater impact.

_____ 4. When the audience initially disagrees with the speaker, the speaker should present only his or her side of the issue.

_____ 5. Considerable research supports the idea that your best argument should be nestled in the middle of your speech.

Answers: 1. T   2. T   3. F   4. F   5. F

tions, attributing an idea to someone who never said it, omitting important qualifiers, quoting out of context, and distorting information from others are all examples of ethical violations.

2. *Respect sources of information.* Have you ever gone to the library to do research for a paper or speech only to find that an inconsiderate individual had already cut out the information you seek? Removing or defacing information meant for everyone is a serious violation of ethics punishable in most colleges and universities. Unfortunately, few of the offenders are caught, but the idea of "doing unto others as you would have them do unto you" is in operation here. Unless all students respect public sources of information, everyone suffers. This rule extends to respect for persons you interview. These people are willing to share information with you, so it behooves you to treat them and their information with respect in person and in your speech.

3. *Respect your audience.* Persuasion is a process that works most effectively with mutual respect between speaker and audience. Attempts to trick the audience into believing something, lying to the audience, distorting the views of your opposition, or exaggerating claims for your own position are all ethically questionable acts. A speaker

443

Jurors can turn on an attorney who seems unethical or unfair even when her arguments meet legal requirements.

should speak truthfully and accurately; the best persuasive speakers can accurately portray the opposing arguments and still win with their own arguments and evidence. Audiences can be very hostile to a person who has tricked them or who has lied, distorted, or exaggerated information simply to meet an immediate behavioral purpose or an ultimate goal.

4. *Respect your opponent.* Persuasive speeches invite rebuttal. Nearly always someone inside or outside your audience thinks your ideas or positions are wrong. A good rule of thumb is to respect your opponent, not only because he or she may be right but also because an effective persuasive speaker can take the best the opposition has to offer and still convince the audience he or she should be believed. The idea that you should respect your opponent means you should not indulge in name calling or in bringing up past behaviors that are irrelevant to the issue. You should attack the other person's evidence, sources, or logic—not the person. Practical reasons for observing this rule of ethics are that few of the issues about which people persuade are ever settled, that you may find in time that your opponent's position is better in many respects than your own, and that you will have to live with many issues not resolved in the manner you most desire.

You may get the impression from these four ethical guidelines that every persuasive speaker must be part angel. Not quite. The ethical rules for persuasive speaking allow for considerable verbal combat, for devastating the arguments of others with better or more persuasive evidence, for finding new supporting materials your opposition has not found, and for majority acceptance of your ideas. Persuasive speaking is not for the fainthearted, but verbal combat is much cleaner if you obey the ethical guidelines that call for the accurate citation of sources, respect for sources of information, respect for your audience, and respect for your opponent.

Persuasive speeches can occur in a variety of settings, including in the workplace. When they do, they are called presentational speeches. You will learn more about presentational speaking later in the chapter.

Just as an informative speaker must learn skills in defining, describing, explaining, and narrating, a persuasive speaker must learn skills in arguing and providing evidence.

What Are Some Persuasive Speaking Skills?

Remember that an argument consists of propositions, justifications, and evidence. In persuasive speaking, a proposition embodies what you want the audience to believe or do—for example, to believe that communication classes should be required, physicians' fees should be competitive, or welfare payments should be increased. The speaker presents evidence to get the audience to accept the proposition (Ehninger, Gronbeck, & Monroe, 1984). To be persuasive, evidence must meet the tests of evidence and believability.

Your evidence must meet the **tests of evidence,** *questions you can use to test the validity of the evidence* in your speeches or in the speeches of others:

tests of evidence

Questions that can be used to test the validity of evidence.

1. *Is the evidence consistent with other known facts?* For instance, did the speaker look at a relatively large number of student co-ops to determine that student co-ops are successful? Have any student co-op stores failed?
2. *Would another observer draw the same conclusions?* Has anyone other than the speaker determined that other student co-ops are successful? What does the speaker mean by "success"?
3. *Does the evidence come from unbiased sources?* Does the vice-president for student affairs have anything to gain by favoring student co-op bookstores? Who made the claim that students will get better value for their used books? Who said other schools have established successful student co-ops?
4. *Is the source of the information qualified by education and/or experience to make a statement about the issue?* The vice-president may be well educated, but what does she know about co-op bookstores? What about the qualifications of the sources of the information on used books or successful co-ops?
5. *If the evidence is based on personal experience, how typical is that personal experience?* Personal experience that is typical, generalizable, realistic, and relevant can be good evidence.
6. *If statistics are used as evidence, are they from a reliable source, comparable with other known information, current, applicable, and interpreted so that the audience can understand them?*
7. *If studies and surveys are used, are they authoritative, valid, reliable, objective, and generalizable?* A study done by persons who favor student co-op bookstores, for instance, would be questionable because the source of the study is biased.
8. *Are the speaker's inferences appropriate according to the data presented?* Does the speaker go too far beyond the evidence in concluding that students should establish their own co-op bookstore?

9. *Is important counterevidence overlooked?* Often, in our haste to make a positive case, we ignore or omit counterevidence. What evidence against student co-ops is left out?

10. *What is the speaker's credibility on the topic?* Has the speaker earned the right to speak on the topic through research, interviews, and a thorough examination of the issue? Has the speaker had experience related to the issue?

The answers to these 10 questions are important. Evidence that meets these tests has met the first requirement of good evidence.

believability

A criterion of good evidence—the audience must trust and accept the evidence.

The second requirement of good evidence is **believability**—*the audience believes the evidence, trusts it, and accepts it.* Finding evidence that meets the tests of evidence is difficult enough, but at least the speaker has some guidelines. Believability is more mysterious; however, audience analysis can help a speaker determine which kinds of evidence will be most believable to a particular group of listeners. For instance, a speaker addressing a group of fundamentalist Christians may know that evidence from scripture will fall on friendly ears and be accepted as proof; that same evidence may not be believed by groups who do not accept the authority of the Bible. The effective persuasive speaker knows all the major arguments for and against a persuasive proposition. He or she chooses the evidence to be used in the speech both because the evidence meets the tests of evidence and because the speaker's audience analysis indicates that this evidence is most likely to be believed.

How Do You Resist Persuasion?

Listed below are some measures you can take to resist persuasion, not only in public speaking but also on the telephone, from salespeople, and in advertising:

1. *Your best form of resistance is avoidance.* You do not have to watch or read advertising, go into stores where you do not intend to buy, listen to telemarketers, or watch half-hour television "infomercials."

2. *You should exercise healthy skepticism about all messages.* Persuaders who are seeking easy prey look for the uneducated, the desperate, the angry, and the unsuspecting. They avoid people who are educated, articulate, cautious, and careful. You should use your knowledge of argumentation, evidence, and proof to analyze claims.

3. *On serious matters, you should check claims with other, unbiased sources.* A good rule is to verify any persuasive claims with at least two other sources of information. A politician tells you that lower taxes will be good for you. What do the editorials, the political commentators, and the opposition say about that plan? Consumer magazines, especially those that take no advertising, are less likely to be biased, as are news sources that embrace objectivity.

4. *You should check out the credibility of the source.* Be suspicious if a salesperson will not reveal the phone numbers of satisfied customers, if a business is new or changes location often, and if a speaker has a questionable reputation for truth or reliability. Credible sources have people, institutions, and satisfied audiences who can vouch for them. Con artists typically do not.

5. *You should not be in a hurry to accept a persuasive appeal.* Most states have laws that allow even a signed contract to be rejected by the customer in the first 24 to 48 hours—in case you have second thoughts. Accepting claims on impulse is a dangerous practice that you can avoid by never making an important decision in the context of a sales pitch. Have you ever heard of a businessperson who refused to take the money the next day?

6. *You should question the ethical basis of proposed actions.* Angry people are easy to turn to violence, desperate people willingly consider desperate measures, and frustrated people can be easily convinced to undermine. You need to ask if the proposed action is self-serving, if it is based on pitting one group against another, and if it is going to be good for you when viewed in retrospect.

7. *You should use your knowledge and experience to analyze persuasive claims.* If a claim sounds too good to be true, it probably is. If you have a "gut feeling" that a claim seems wrong, you should find out why. You should use all you know about logic, evidence, and proof to see if the persuader is drawing a sound conclusion or making an inferential leap that is justified by the evidence. Finally, all evidence should be open to scrutiny. Check it out.

8. *You should use your own values as a check against fraudulent claims.* If someone is trying to get you to do something that runs counter to what you learned in your religion, in your home, about the law, or from your friends, you should be wary. Sales always enrich the seller but rarely the buyer. You can choose to sacrifice, but you should not sacrifice unwittingly. Your values are good protection against those who would cheat you. You should ask the question, What would my parents, my friends, my neighbors, my professor, or the church think of this decision?

9. *Check what persuaders say against what they do.* You might add: Judge them more by what they do than by what they say. Talk may not be cheap, but it costs less than deeds, and the proof of what a person says is in his or her behavior. Many an "education governor" has cut the budget for education. You learn to trust people who do what they say; you learn to distrust those who say one thing and do another.

10. *Use your freedom of expression and freedom of choice as protection against unethical persuaders.* In the United States, you can hear competing ideas and the choice is yours. You can educate yourself about issues and ideas by reading, watching, and listening. Education and learning are powerful protection against persuaders who would take advantage of you. Use your freedoms to help defend yourself.

Instant Recall

Fill in the blanks:

1. The best form of resistance to persuasion is _____.

2. A good rule is to verify any persuasive claims with at least two _____ _____.

3. Most states have laws that allow even a signed contract to be rejected by the customer in the first _____ to _____ hours.

4. Check what persuaders say against what they _____.

5. Use your own _____ as a check against fraudulent claims.

Answers: 1. avoidance   2. other sources   3. 24/48   4. do   5. values

Now that you know 10 suggestions for resisting persuasion, you can practice the strategies for keeping others from manipulating your mind and your pocketbook.

TRY ◄►THIS

Think about ways that you have avoided being persuaded. Did you have sound reason to avoid being persuaded? List the reasons and decide if they were founded or not.

What Is Presentational Speaking?

Presentational speaking is another context for communication. Just as interpersonal communication occurs in different contexts—in the family, in dyads, and in small groups—public speaking can occur in different contexts as well, such as in a business or professional setting. **Presentational speaking** is *informative, persuasive, or special-occasion speaking that occurs in a business or professional context.* An example of an informative presentational speech is one given by a quality control specialist to a group of line

448

managers about a new piece of equipment guaranteed to reduce error and improve quality. A persuasive presentational speech might be given by a regional manager to sales representatives about the benefits of using a new computer system for tracking clients. And a special-occasion presentational speech might be given by a CEO in honor of retiring middle managers, warmly and gratefully recounting their years of dedicated service to the company.

The similarities and differences between a public speech and a presentation lie in source credibility, the audience, and the setting. Let's examine each of them individually.

Source Credibility

Earlier in this chapter we discussed source credibility—the audience's perception of your effectiveness as a speaker. In Chapter 11 you learned that a speaker's credibility partly depends on the topic of the speech, the situation, and the audience. People giving a presentational speech may be deemed credible before they even speak due to the nature of their positions. A person may be known within the organization for his or her title, such as payroll manager; responsibilities, such as managing the company payroll; or reputation, such as being conscientious and dedicated. In some cases, the public speaker is already well known by the audience and perceived as credible. In other cases, particularly in a public-speaking class, the speaker's reputation is unknown; thus, source credibility is more difficult to establish.

Sometimes a person in a higher-status position gives a presentational speech—upper management speaks to middle management, or management to labor—but other times the speaker and the audience are perceived more as equals. In the latter case, the speaker, who may have simply been chosen to be the spokesperson for a given project, may be no more of an expert than his or her audience and may find it difficult to establish source credibility. This situation is also true when a speaker is giving a presentation to an **external audience,** which is *composed of people outside the company.* For example, when an advertising team presents their ideas for promoting the latest new cereal on the market, they may have to work quite hard to establish their credibility.

The Audience

Public-speaking audiences are typically more diverse than are audiences of presentational speakers. A public-speaking audience is usually **heterogeneous,** which you may recall from Chapter 11 means *characterized by many differences among individuals.* In contrast, the audience of a presentational speaker, especially when it is composed of people within the company, tends to be **homogeneous,** *characterized by individuals who are more like one another.* Of course, even at a presentational speech, an external audience may

presentational speaking

Informative, persuasive, or special-occasion speaking that occurs in a business or professional context.

external audience

An audience composed of people outside the speaker's company or organization.

heterogeneous

Characterized by many differences among individuals in an audience.

homogeneous

Characterized by audience members that are more like one another.

cross-disciplinary address

A presentation in which professionals in one field train, inform, or persuade individuals in another field.

captive audience

An audience that has not chosen to hear a particular speaker or speech.

voluntary audience

An audience that has chosen to listen to a particular speaker or speech.

sales presentation

A presentation intended to persuade a potential buyer to purchase a service or product.

technical report

A presentation that includes detailed information about a procedure or device so that the audience can decide whether or not to adopt it or purchase it.

staff report

A presentation that informs managers and other employees of developments that might affect them and their work.

not be so homogeneous. An example is the potential client's representatives who are listening to the presentation of the advertising team mentioned above. Another is the audience at a **cross-disciplinary address,** in which *professionals from one department in the company train, inform, or persuade individuals from another department.* For example, someone from a company's legal department may advise a room full of managers about the legal requirements of the Americans with Disabilities Act.

Another difference between the audiences of public speakers and those of presentational speakers is that the audience of a presentational speaker is usually a **captive audience,** *one whose members have not chosen to hear a particular speaker or speech.* They may be expected to hear the same presenter several times during the course of a project or a series of meetings. On the other hand, a public-speaking audience is usually a **voluntary audience,** *one whose members have chosen to listen to a particular speaker or speech,* and who typically expect to attend a one-time event.

The Setting

The setting of a presentational speech is often more sophisticated than that of a public speech. A public speech can be delivered just about anywhere, but a presentational speech usually requires a location that is convenient for the audience and can accommodate any special equipment that must be set up in advance.

Types of Presentations

According to Lesikar, Pettit, and Flatley (1993), the five most common types of business and professional presentations are sales presentations, technical reports, progress reports, staff reports, and investigative reports. The purpose of a **sales presentation** is to *persuade a potential buyer to purchase a service or product described by the speaker.* Most of us will be audience members at a sales presentation at some time in our lives. A **technical report** is *a presentation that includes detailed information about a procedure or device so that the audience can decide whether or not to adopt or purchase it.* For example, a work team at the XYZ Company might be looking at the options for new software that would better facilitate the tracking of client data. One team member is then chosen to present to management the top three options and how they work. **Staff reports** *inform managers and other employees of developments that might affect them and their work.* For example, the president of the XYZ Company tells employees about the work team's mission, saying, "The work team is looking for software that will help you to know who our clients are and what products they're using." A **progress report** can be defined as *an accounting of the developments in an ongoing project.* A progress report is similar to a staff report but involves people outside

This manager provides a staff report to other managers.

progress report

A presentation that reports developments in an ongoing project.

investigative report

A presentation that gives an accounting of a problem, includes recommendations and is usually conducted by someone outside the company.

the company as well as within. The XYZ work team might have 3 months to investigate and test all their options, but every month they have to report to management what they have uncovered thus far. An **investigative report** is *an accounting of a problem that includes recommendations and is usually conducted by someone outside the company.* For example, when companies believe they are not operating as efficiently as possible but can't pinpoint why, they may bring in an outside evaluator. The evaluator observes employees at work and conducts interviews with them (they usually remain anonymous in the evaluator's final report) before reporting his or her findings and providing suggestions for changes.

A Presentational Speech Example

The speech below is an example of a presentational speech with a persuasive purpose; the speech could also be considered an *investigative report.* The audience is 55 academic staff and faculty of the English department at a midwestern college. The speaker is an outside consultant, who is also a professor from a state university. He was hired by the dean to evaluate the department and then report his findings. Apparently, the faculty members have grown so caustic toward each other in the last few years that to recruit professors from other colleges to the department has been difficult; English master's students have been complaining that finding a committee of five professors who aren't combative toward each other is nearly impossible; and currently no one chairs the department because the four internal candidates quit in despair.

Shape Up!

As you know, I have recently completed my evaluation of the English department at this university. Although I've spent two decades conducting evaluations of businesses and colleges, I've never seen a group so close to terminally ill as this one. Terminal illness in an academic department can be measured in these ways: The faculty no longer respects each other, and their utter disrespect for each other has had an impact on people outside the department, including the students they were hired to serve. Such a department may be fired up inside, but to outsiders its pulse is hardly perceivable.

The good news is that I am in front of you today only because your dean thinks you are so valuable that you must be given one more opportunity to thrive. Keep in mind, I have no control over any of you and cannot make you do anything. I can only suggest some ways that you can heal yourselves and repair this department. My mission is to give you some ideas about how you can accomplish this goal by following three rules.

First, I advise you not to disparage your colleagues. Not only do I want you to avoid any negative reference to another person in your department, but I want you to stop anyone who violates this rule. You must hush anyone who starts to say anything negative about a colleague just as you would if the person were starting to tell an obviously sexist or racist joke. This department has to create an atmosphere in which negative regard is actively resisted, openly admonished, and faithfully countered.

A second rule of conduct is not to let any graduate or undergraduate student know of any animosities between faculty members. In other words, keep students out of departmental politics. I presume you do not realize the degree to which your internal warfare has poisoned the atmosphere around here for your students. Contrary to what you may be thinking, I am not suggesting that you are to have absolutely no disagreements with your colleagues. You are to avoid interpersonal, not ideological, conflict.

The first and second rules are necessary, but they are not enough to undo all the damage that's been done over the years. Therefore, the third rule is to say or do at least one positive thing each week to or for a member of

Source credibility reminder: an experienced evaluator who has helped other departments.

Fear appeal: Department is described as "terminally ill."

Discontinuance of past behavior.

Organizational signpost and a logical and emotional appeal for order.

Organizational signpost with both a discontinuance goal on negative collaboration with students and an adoption goal for a policy of not involving students in faculty issues.

Organizational signpost for third rule and adoption goal with specific application.

the department faculty or staff. Try starting with the department secretary. Treat her with the respect she deserves, help her out by giving her plenty of lead time with the items you need copied, and maybe even say something positive to her. All it takes is something as simple as, "I really appreciate your getting this done so quickly for me." I'm not suggesting that you all start gushing over each other tomorrow, but I do expect you to seize the opportunity to congratulate a colleague for something praiseworthy, no matter how minor. If a student mentions that Dr. Wu prepared her well for your class, send an e-mail to Dr. Wu passing along the good word.

Adopting new policy with possible script.

Let me reiterate my three points: First, do not disparage a colleague; second, do not let any student be aware of your animosities; and third, do or say something positive for or to someone on the faculty or staff each week. You may be surprised how quickly the atmosphere changes around here and how much more enjoyable the workplace can be.

Adoption goal of new attitude and positive toward colleagues.

Summary review of contents.

I'll end my presentation today with a surprise. During my visit here I learned that many of you feel your animosities stem from limited exposure to each other. That is, you know one another only as colleagues. Therefore, as another gesture of his faith in your ability to change the atmosphere in this department, your dean has agreed to pay for renovating the storage room on the second floor so that it can be used as an informal gathering space. The dean has also agreed to pay for a coffee machine and supplies for the first semester, as you gradually get used to relating positively to each other again. For my part, after 4 months I will ask your acting chair and five faculty members selected at random for a report on how you have been doing in implementing positive change in the department. I am hoping that since none of you know who will be asked for a progress report, all of you will try to make this plan work. Your future depends on it.

Signpost signals ending logical proof with evidence.

Nonrational appeal.

Action goal: Progress reports.

I thank you for the opportunity to meet all of you. I want you to know I have considerable confidence in your ability to break the cycle of negativity and to start a new way of relating to each other. If you follow the rules, then, hopefully, next year at this time the negativity surrounding this department will have been replaced by talk about the dramatic change in the department. Thank you again, and best of luck on what will be a challenge for one and all.

Vision of positive change.

Summary

Preparing a persuasive speech requires that you classify your ultimate purpose in behavioral terms, stating your action goals of adoption, discontinuance, deterrence, or continuance; that you write an ultimate goal and immediate behavioral purposes; and that you find an appropriate topic.

You can persuade audience members through motivational appeals (physical, psychological, and social), speaker credibility, logical appeals, and emotional appeals. Concerns about the organization of a persuasive speech include the placement of arguments and evidence, the number of sides presented to different kinds of audiences, the use of refutation, and the use of familiar or novel arguments.

You can learn to use persuasion, and to resist it, by being skeptical, cautious, ethical, analytical, and intelligent. You should take advantage of your freedom to speak, listen, and learn so that no one can take advantage of you through persuasion.

Presentational speaking is informative, persuasive, or special-occasion speaking that occurs in a business or professional context. The similarities and the differences between public speeches lie in source credibility, the audience, and the setting. The five different kinds of presentational speeches are sales presentations, technical reports, staff reports, progress reports, and investigative reports.

Issues in Communication

This Issues in Communication narrative is designed to provoke individual thought or discussion about concepts raised in the chapter.

Jody Hubbard is a dietician and nutritionist who travels around the state to speak at middle, junior high, and high schools. She primarily speaks to students in health classes, but sometimes the school will arrange for her to speak to several different groups of girls. Her biggest concern is the emphasis our culture places on thinness and the negative ways this affects girls today. Jody has a Ph.D. in nutrition, but, more important, she has personal experience—her mother taught her to diet when she was only 8 years old.

Jody has created several different presentations which she gives to different types of audiences, and she tries to establish an emotional connection with the students so that they will feel comfortable asking questions or talking to her privately. She shows them pictures and images from popular culture of beautiful women and explains how computers are used to make the women look even more thin and "beautiful" than they are in real life. She describes how the definition of *beauty* has changed over the years and even from culture to culture. She then talks about health issues and the physical damage that can occur as a result of dieting. Finally, she addresses self-esteem and the notion that a person's sense of beauty must include more than how much a person weighs.

Sometimes, Jody feels that she succeeds in persuading some students to stop dieting; other times, she feels that she fails.

Apply what you have learned about persuasive and presentational speaking as you ponder and discuss the following questions: What were Jody's action goals? What types of appeals did she make to persuade her audience? How did she seek to gain credibility in students' eyes? What ethical considerations would Jody need to be especially careful about? Would you categorize her speech as persuasive or presentational—or both? Why?

Additional Resources

Brody, M. (1998). *Speaking your way to the top: Making powerful business presentations.* Needham Heights, MA: Allyn and Bacon.

Fitch, S., & Mandziuk, R. (1997). *Sojourner Truth as orator.* Westport, CT: Greenwood.

Gass, R. H., & Seiter, J. S. (1999). *Persuasion, social influence, and compliance gaining.* Needham Heights, MA: Allyn and Bacon.

Kearney, P., & Plax, T. (1999). *Public speaking in a diverse society* (2nd ed.). Mountain View, CA: Mayfield.

References

Burger, J. M., & Vartabedian, R. A. (1985). Public self-disclosure and speaker persuasiveness. *Journal of Applied Social Psychology, 15,* 153–165.

Cope, F., & Richardson, D. (1972). The effects of measuring recommendations in a fear-arousing speech. *Speech Monographs, 39,* 148–150.

Ehninger, D., (1970). Argument as method: its nature, its limitations, and its uses. *Speech Monographs, 37,* 101–110.

Ehninger, D., Gronbeck, B. E., & Monroe, A. H. (1984). *Principles of speech communication* (9th brief ed.). Glenview, IL: Scott, Foresman.

Fotheringham, W. (1966). *Perspectives on persuasion.* Boston: Allyn and Bacon.

Hamilton, G. (1998). *Public speaking for college and career* (5th ed.). New York: McGraw-Hill.

Hovland, C., & Pritzker, H. (1957). Extent of opinion change as a function of amount of change advocated. *Journal of Abnormal and Social Psychology, 54,* 257–261.

Janis, I. S., & Feshbach, S. (1953). Effects of fear-arousing communications. *Journal of Abnormal and Social Psychology, 48,* 78–92.

Karlins, M., & Abelson, H. I. (1970). *Persuasion: How opinions and attitudes are changed* (2nd ed.). New York: Springer.

Lesikar, R. V., Pettit, J. D., & Flatley, M. (1993). *Basic business communication* (6th ed.). Boston: Irwin.

McConnell, J. V. (1977). *Understanding human behavior: An introduction to psychology.* New York: Holt, Rinehart and Winston.

McGuire, M., Stillbourne, L., McAdams, M., & Hyatt, L. (1997). *Internet handbook for writers, researchers, and journalists.* New York: Guilford.

Miller, G. R. (1980). On being persuaded: Some basic distinctions. In M. E. Roloff & G. R. Miller, *Persuasion: New directions in theory and research.* Beverly Hills, CA: Sage.

Powell, F. A. (1965). The effects of anxiety-arousing messages when related to personal, familial, and impersonal referents. *Speech Monographs, 32,* 102–106.

Reinhard, J. C. (1988). The empirical study of the persuasive effects of evidence: The status after 50 years of research. *Human Communication Research, 15,* 3–59.

Sears, D., & Freedman, J. (1965). Effects of expected familiarity with arguments upon opinion change and selective exposure. *Journal of Personality and Social Psychology, 2,* 420–426.

When you have read and thought about this appendix, you will be able to:

1. Distinguish an interview from other communication contexts.

2. State how relationship dimensions affect an interview.

3. Recognize the approaches to interviews and know when it is appropriate to use them.

4. Distinguish between job-seeking and information-seeking interviews.

5. Identify the different types of questions used in interviews.

6. Prepare appropriately for job- and information-seeking interviews.

Interviewing for Information and Employment

WITH MARGARET KING

> **"I keep six honest serving men They taught me all I know. Their names are What and Why and When And How and Where and Who."**
>
> RUDYARD KIPLING

> **"Chance favors only the mind that is prepared."**
>
> LOUIS PASTEUR

> **"What you are stands over you the while, and thunders so that I cannot hear what you say to the contrary."**
>
> RALPH WALDO EMERSON

I n this appendix, you will learn about interviewing, a form of interpersonal communication that focuses on information seeking. You will be introduced to the interview context and to the principles of asking and answering questions in interviews. You will learn about information-seeking interviews in general and job-seeking interviews in particular, and you will learn how to be a more effective participant in both.

Cathy Hunter was starting her first week on the job as a social worker. Part of her training included shadowing her supervisor, John. Since she would be dealing almost exclusively with new clients, she was especially attentive when John was screening and interviewing new referrals.

John obviously exerted control over each new interview—he asked rapid-fire questions and never made small talk. He even cut people off when he had gotten all the information he wanted. At first, Cathy took a lot of notes on what questions John asked and how he asked them since his methods elicited a lot of information in a short amount of time. But once Cathy observed the atmosphere in the room, she realized that the clients often exhibited a high level of tension and distrust toward John.

When Cathy began working on her own, she decided that one of her goals in interviewing new clients would be to establish trust and rapport. She wasn't sure how to do this, so she stopped at the library to see if she could find a book on the topic.

Under John's supervision, Cathy learned about information-seeking interviews—she realized that both the interviewer and the interviewee can affect the final outcome. This principle is true in job-seeking interviews as well. This appendix is designed to develop your skills in both information-seeking and job-seeking interviews. You will learn how the approach, structure, and types of questions affect the interview process and how to prepare for future job interviews.

What Is Interviewing?

Interviewing is a form of oral communication that involves the sending and receiving of messages. According to *Webster's Dictionary* (1983), the word *interview* derives from the French *entrevue, entrevior* ("to see one another," "to meet"). Culturally, we have come to understand an **interview** as *a dyadic communication context with a purpose or goal.* That is, in an interview, two persons or parties communicate in a preplanned situation, primarily by asking and answering questions.

interview

A dyadic communication context with a purpose or goal.

The interview context most often, but not always, involves a face-to-face encounter that is relational in character, because there is personal interaction and an interpersonal connection between the two parties. Conceptually, if the parties agree to meet for an interview, the implication is that the context will be dynamic: The participants will be influenced and changed by the interaction process itself. The information elicited through questioning and the verbal and nonverbal feedback that regulate the interaction contribute to the dynamics, and the roles of the interviewer and respondent interchange frequently (Stewart & Cash, 1994).

Our subjective perceptions emanate from our background and experience. An interview is influenced by the perceptions that each party in the interview has about self, about the other party, and about the situation. Failure to account for differing perceptions may result in a less than effective interview.

Although most of us share some understandings, experiences, and expectations, significant differences in how we organize these factors are likely to influence an interview. Regardless of the sender's intent, the message received is subject to the interpretation of the receiver. You need to anticipate the possibility of differences, adapt to the situation, and attempt to find areas of common understanding. You will want to speak the language of the other person, when possible. Anticipating the likely relationship between you and the other party is our next area of consideration.

What Are the Relationship Dimensions of an Interview?

Many communication researchers have emphasized three underlying dimensions that affect human relationships (Schutz, 1976). These dimensions—control, inclusion, and affection—have the potential to enhance or diminish your effectiveness in an interview.

Control of a situation relates to power. *Status, prestige, and custom dictate who will exert the most influence in an interview situation.* Interview participants should anticipate that, at least initially, hierarchical status and prestige will enhance the level of control available (Stewart & Cash, 1994). Participants in the interview should analyze carefully the degree to which they can influence both the nature and the outcome of the interview and then plan a strategy to manage the role assigned to them (Burgoon & Hale, 1984; Phillips & Wood, 1983). That strategy should include becoming aware that although the interviewer may control the structure of the interview and the questions asked, the respondent can control the content of the answers. In other words, some degree of control resides in how and what is said, regardless of who asks the questions.

Inclusion refers to *how much each party wants to participate in an interview and how much each party wants to include others in the interview* (Stewart & Cash, 1994). Willing participation by cooperative parties creates a situation conducive to establishing a relationship of mutual trust. Trust becomes the basis upon which communication thrives in an interview (Stewart & Cash, 1994).

Friendship and a warm demeanor are preferable in an interview setting, but often goals and perceptions conflict, and an atmosphere of **affection** simply is not possible. For various reasons, people send out signals that warn others to be cautious when approaching them, and that affects the context. The level of affection is less than ideal but can be managed.

Knowing the significance of control, inclusion, and affection is essential to participating in an effective interview. The first step in managing a potential interview relationship is analysis. Assess the degree of control, inclusion, and affection that each party is likely to have.

control

The most influence or power in an interview situation.

inclusion

How much each party wants to participate in an interview and how much each party wants to include others in the interview.

affection

Friendship and warm demeanor, which is preferred in an interview setting.

Encourage mutual enthusiasm, be willing to include the other party, and establish common ground. Often relationships evolve throughout the interview with the use of rapport-building techniques that seek areas of common interest and concern. Similarly, if your analysis of the degree of affection at first leads you to anticipate that an atmosphere of respect and warmth may not be possible, consider ways to improve that situation. Attempt to find out why the other party is distant, or make an effort to present yourself in a nonthreatening way. Although the circumstances under which interviews are arranged vary, the principles of adaptation remain the same. *Anticipate, analyze,* and *adapt* to the situation, and your chances of being an effective interview participant will increase (Stewart & Cash, 1994). Basic approaches to interviews and their uses will be introduced next.

What Are Interview Approaches?

direct approach

An approach in which the interviewer determines the purpose of the interview and exerts control over the types of questions and the pace of the interview.

indirect approach

An approach in which the interviewer shares control of the pace, content, and focus of the interview with the respondent.

combination approach

A mixture of indirect and direct approaches when freedom of expression is called for but pertinent facts and information are needed.

The choice of an interview approach depends on the desired goal of the interviewer. Available approaches proceed along a continuum from highly controlling to merely suggestive, but the most frequently used approaches in interviews are the direct approach and the indirect approach (Stewart & Cash, 1994). In the **direct approach,** *the interviewer determines the purpose of the interview and exerts control over the types of questions and the pace of the interview.* Typically, this approach is used when time is brief, standardized responses are required, and when the answers could be problematic. The direct interview approach requires less skill from the interviewer than do other methods because the interviewer controls the questions and responses. When using an **indirect approach,** *the interviewer shares control of the interview's pace, content, and focus with the respondent.* Great skill is required with this approach, along with larger time blocks.

At times a combination approach is most appropriate in an interview (Stewart & Cash, 1994). The decision to use both the direct and the indirect interview approaches in a single interview depends on the purpose and circumstances of the situation. Most often an interviewer uses a **combination approach** *when freedom of expression is called for but pertinent facts and information are needed.* Salespeople, recruiters, counselors, journalists, and social service and medical personnel often combine interview approaches, depending on the purpose of the interview and the information needed (Benjamin, 1987; Gordon, 1987; Kreps & Thornton, 1988).

The following interview exchanges illustrate the direct and indirect approaches:

Direct Approach

Interviewer: How long have you lived at your present address?

Respondent: Eight years.

Interviewer: Do you own your home?

Respondent: Yes, I do.

Interviewer: Are you currently employed, and where?

Respondent: Yes, I work at the local college.

Interviewer: What is your job title?

Respondent: I guess I'm a stationary engineer.

Indirect Approach

Interviewer: Give me an overview of your current job responsibilities.

Respondent: Well, I work in the maintenance department at the local college. I've been there for about 10 years and have moved around to various locations, depending on where I'm needed at the time. You just never know what is going to come up in a job like mine, but I guess I must like it, or I would have quit long ago.

What Are the Types of Interviews?

Interviews are classified according to their use (Goyer et al., 1968). This functional perspective describes (1) information giving, (2) information seeking, and (3) persuasion as the primary types of interviews, as illustrated in Figure A.1.

The primary function of information-giving interviews is to inform, whereas information-seeking interviews are intended to elicit facts, attitudes, and feelings. In a persuasive interview, the interviewer attempts to influence the perception of the other party and to induce some sort of change. Obviously, some elements of information giving, information seeking, and persuasion are present in all interviews, but often a primary function predominates.

The focus of this chapter is on the information-seeking interview, the strategies and tactics that are essential for effective interviewing, and the preparation

1. *Information giving*

   Teaching, coaching   Instructing patients, clients
   Orientation, training   Employment briefing
   Counseling   Appraisal, discipline

2. *Information seeking*

   Employment   Diagnosis
   Research   Problem solving
   Surveys, polls   Grievances, complaints
   Investigative journalism

3. *Persuasion*

   Recruiting   Fundraising
   Selling   Advocacy

Figure A.1 Types of interviews.

for and participation in job-seeking interviews. Before moving to a discussion of these aspects, however, let us look at the basic structure of an interview.

What Is the Structure of an Interview?

Like effective written communication, an interview is structured logically, with (1) an opening, (2) a body, and (3) a closing organized in such a way as to establish the overall message and to make sense of the interaction (Goyer et al., 1968).

The Opening

The primary function of the opening of an interview is to motivate participation, so what you say and how you say it at the beginning set the tone for the interaction. Interviewers should introduce themselves properly, establish some rapport with the respondent, and provide an orientation to the interview. This process reduces what is known as **relational uncertainty** (Knapp, 1978), *a state of suspicion or doubt.* If respondents know what to expect during an interview, they will be more trusting and will be more apt to relax and concentrate on the process of answering questions. An incomplete interview opening can create an atmosphere of distrust that may prevail throughout the entire interview. Furthermore, the interviewer will want to establish the purpose of the interview at the outset, as illustrated in these sample openings:

> "Mary, I'm John Smythe from the Citizens' Action Coalition, and I would like 10 minutes of your time to get your input on the proposed utility rate hike."

relational uncertainty

A state of suspicion or doubt.

First impressions occur the instant an interview begins.

"Good evening. I'm John Smythe from the Citizens' Action Coalition. Your next-door neighbor suggested you might be willing to participate in a brief interview about the proposed utility rate hike that is coming up. We could really use your help."

What you state as the purpose for the interview should reflect the appropriate appeal to the particular respondent; otherwise, cooperation may not result. For example, if John Smythe was an executive with the utility, the "rate hike" topic would have no appeal for him.

The Body

The best method for organizing the body of an interview is to develop *an outline of topics and subtopics to be covered.* This article then becomes your **interview guide.** You will want to arrange your interview guide in a logical fashion that permits you to investigate all critical areas. You can pattern your guide by (1) topic, (2) time, (3) space, (4) cause-effect, or (5) problem-solution, depending on the issue involved. You could also use a journalism format and ask who, what, why, when, where, and how (Stewart & Cash, 1994).

An interview guide is usually sufficient for your interview preparation. However, when you want to be more prepared and confident, you should develop the outline into a more elaborate document, an interview schedule. An **interview schedule** *contains major questions and follow up questions; it is a useful tool in keeping the interview focused on the topic or issue of concern* (Stewart & Cash, 1994). The schedule is usually a list of questions which can be developed into a manuscript that allows the interviewer to write out arguments or instructions to be used in the interview. Each interviewer needs to decide what format is necessary and sufficient for each interview.

interview guide

An outline of topics and subtopics used in an interview.

interview schedule

An elaborate outline of primary questions and secondary questions that helps keep focus on the topic.

The Closing

The closing of an interview involves both verbal and nonverbal communication. You are probably familiar with some of the more subtle signals that a meeting is concluding. For instance, when someone ways, "Well . . . ," you may be about to be dismissed. Similarly, if one party looks at a clock on the wall, the other can anticipate that "time is up." Standing up, straightening in your seat, leaning forward, moving away from the other party, breaking eye contact, and offering to shake hands are clearly nonverbal cues that the interaction is coming to a close. Expressing appreciation, summarizing the interview, and planning for another meeting are verbal indications that a participant intends to close the interview (Knapp et al., 1973). In an ideal interview closing, both parties understand the signals and respond appropriately. In the worst-case scenario, one participant feels rushed or offended, and the closing negates any positive, productive results achieved so far. Thus, be aware of the importance of closing an interview effectively.

What Are the Types of Interview Questions?

Asking and answering questions make up an integral part of an interview. Questions are the instruments that drive the interview process; they help govern the flow of information exchange. The efficiency of that process depends in large measure on the types of questions used in the interview.

Although question types are described differently by various teachers and trainers, an examination of the research on interview questions leads to the conclusion that a question can be typed by its traits. Basically, questions are (1) open or closed, (2) primary or secondary, and (3) neutral or leading (Payne, 1951).

open questions

Questions designed to permit freedom in the length and nature of the response.

closed questions

Questions that restrict the response, often asking for specific information or supplying optional answers for the respondent.

bipolar question

A question that limits the answer options to two choices.

Open and Closed Questions

Open questions *permit freedom in the length and nature of the response,* whereas **closed questions** *restrict the response, often asking for specific information or supplying answer options from which the respondent chooses.* A subcategory of the closed question is a **bipolar question,** which is *a question that limits answer options to two choices.* The following examples illustrate how differently you can word questions about a single topic:

Open question: "What do you know about our company?"

Closed question: "In your opinion, what word best describes our company?"

Bipolar question: "Do you know anything about our company?" (Invites a "yes" or "no" response.)

Asking and answering questions is the primary mode of communication in interviews.

Primary and Secondary Questions

The second characteristic of a question is whether it is primary or secondary. **Primary questions** are used to *introduce areas of inquiry and are coherent in themselves,* whereas **secondary questions** are used to *pursue the trail of information discovered in the response to a previous primary question.* Think of a secondary question as a device to probe for further information or to clarify what has been said. The value of a secondary question is that, by using follow-up questions, the interviewer is less likely to form false conclusions about a topic and is more apt to find useful, accurate information. The types of secondary questions that can assist an interviewer are the (1) clearinghouse question, (2) nudging question, (3) reflective question, and (4) informational question. The **clearinghouse question** is used to *assure an interviewer that all essential information is provided.* The **nudging question** is used to *motivate further interaction.* The **reflective question** is used to *verify information* when accuracy is a concern, and the **informational question** is used to *clarify an answer that appears to be vague or superficial.* Table A.1 illustrates these four types of secondary questions.

Some additional tactics that can assist an interviewer in getting information are to rephrase the question in slightly different words, to restate the question, and to use what is known as a silent probe. To use a **silent probe** simply means *to refrain from saying anything for a brief time, letting the respondent fill in the silence.* These tactics, along with the four types of secondary questions, should prove useful to interviewers in many interview contexts.

Neutral and Leading Questions

Neutral questions *permit respondents to provide an answer consistent with their position on an issue, with their beliefs, with their attitudes and values, or with the facts as they know them.* **Leading questions** often are used to *elicit a particular response from an interviewee.* The wording of a question usually suggests the direction of the answer. Obviously, a leading question can be intentional or unintentional, but interviewers and respondents should know that the content of the question has the potential for

---

TABLE A.1   EXAMPLES OF SECONDARY QUESTIONS

Clearinghouse question	What else do you want me to know?
Nudging question	And then what did you do?
Reflective question	So, you think you'll go to the party after all?
Informational question	Tell me a little about that. . . .

---

primary questions

Questions that are used to introduce areas of inquiry and are coherent in themselves.

secondary questions

Questions that probe further or clarify.

clearinghouse question

A question used to assure an interviewer that all essential information has been provided.

nudging question

A question used to motivate further interaction.

reflective question

A question used to verify information.

informational question

A question used to clarify an answer that appears to be vague or superficial.

silent probe

Silence held for a brief time to let the respondent fill in the silence.

neutral questions

Questions that invite the respondent to provide an answer consistent with his or her position on an issue.

leading questions

Questions used to elicit a particular response from an interviewee.

TABLE A.2 NEUTRAL VS. LEADING QUESTIONS	
NEUTRAL QUESTIONS	LEADING QUESTIONS
What do you think about the new federal budget?	Don't you think senior citizens will be harmed by the new federal budget?
What is your attitude toward the situation in Bosnia?	Don't you think the situation in Bosnia is uncivil?
How does this product compare with what you normally purchase?	Surely you would agree that this product is superior to any other, wouldn't you?

bias. The examples in Table A.2 indicate how differences in phrasing can influence the quality of a response.

How Can You Be an Effective Participant in Information-Seeking Interviews?

♦ A representative from an environmental action coalition wants to solicit funds for a recycling program and recruit new members to the organization. He goes from door to door, searching for the opportunity to talk with interested people about environmental issues.

♦ A college student gathers information for a class project about the selection criteria used by human resource practitioners. To enhance her research, she calls local and regional organizations and arranges to meet with several company representatives.

♦ A physician, meeting patients for the first time, takes a detailed medical history of the patients. He asks standard questions but often follows the clues given and asks about other significant factors that will help him make a diagnosis.

information-seeking interview

An interview conducted to find out about an issue, a person, or a situation in a timely fashion.

tools of journalism

The basic question format used by journalists: what, why, when, how, where, and who.

These situations are examples of information-seeking interviews—the most common interview type (Stewart & Cash, 1994). The purpose of an **information-seeking interview** is to *find out about an issue, a person, or a situation in a timely fashion.* How good you are at doing that task depends largely on how curious you are. A curious participant in an interview seeks more than the superficial facts, much like an investigative journalist intent on knowing as many aspects of a given circumstance as possible. Rarely are the indifferent as successful as the inquisitive. Careful preparation and research on the topic will also help interviewers achieve success.

The most successful interviewers in information-seeking interviews rely on the **tools of journalism** known as the *six-question format.* A successful investigative journalist asks the *what, why, when, how, where,* and *who* of the

Instant Recall

IDENTIFYING QUESTIONS

Test your knowledge by analyzing the following questions. Classify each question by writing the correct letter from each group of choices below in the corresponding blank on the left:

I. a) Open   **II. a) Primary**   **III. a) Neutral**   **IV. a) Clearinghouse**
   b) Closed   **b) Secondary**   **b) Leading**   **b) Nudging**
   c) Bipolar   **c) Reflective**
                                                                    d) Informational

I.	II.	III.	IV.	
____	____	____	____	1. Why do you say that?
____	____	____	____	2. How do you feel about the ridiculous campus parking rules?
____	____	____	____	3. You think, then, that your skills meet our requirements?
____	____	____	____	4. Tell me about your supervisory experience.
____	____	____	____	5. What else do we need to discuss?

Answers:	I.	II.	III.	IV.
1.	a	b	a	a
2.	a	a	b	—
3.	b	b	a	d
4.	a	a	a	—
5.	a	b	a	b

situation. A successful information-seeking interviewer must do the same. Although experienced interviewers may need only a five-question format as an interview guide, most others will need to prepare a much more elaborate interview schedule that includes open-ended primary questions and some follow-up or secondary questions written out in advance. A schedule of questions will keep the interviewer focused on the topic and will provide a "safety net" when interruptions occur or when the interview gets off track.

Research interviews, surveys, and polls often are structured differently than are other kinds of information-seeking interviews. The question schedule in research interviews is designed so that all questions are alike and all respondents participate in the identical interview. Since decisions and conclusions about behavior, attitudes, beliefs, and product development often are predicated on the results of these types of interviews, interviewers must be concerned that they can quantify the answers given and that they have not introduced bias into the interview process. Consequently, the opening of a research interview is written out and recited word-for-word, all questions are phrased carefully to avoid influencing the responses, and the closing is consistent, polite, and brief.

In other information-seeking interviews, the interviewer can plan a comprehensive opening so that both parties understand the purpose of the interaction and what the interviewer will do with the information. An introduction and orientation, and a brief reference to the amount of time that will be needed, help establish a congenial atmosphere. Typically, when the interview has reached the intended goal, the interviewer should conclude the interaction. To close the interview in a positive way and to thank the respondent for the information and the time commitment involved are always good.

If you are contacted to be interviewed about a topic or an issue, you should immediately ask why. The answer to that initial question will disclose the purpose and motivation behind the request and will help you decide if you want to commit to the interview. If you are satisfied that you can be a willing participant, you will then want to know (1) who will interview you, (2) where the interview will take place and when, (3) who will be there, and (4) what the interviewer will do with the information.

Once you have agreed to the interview, prepare yourself as much as possible by investigating the background of the interviewer and the organization and by familiarizing yourself with their style and tone. Know your topic well and be able to relate your responses in a coherent manner. Once in the interview, listen to the questions asked and think over your answers. If you do not like a question or the answer options available to you, say so. Remember, you do not have to answer a question just because it has been asked. You may politely, but firmly, refuse to do so.

Should you be caught off-guard with a request for an interview, you can always ask if you can think it over and call back. This delay will give you time to coordinate your thoughts and information before you say something that is "quotable" and to your disadvantage. This advice is particularly important if you represent an organization or have a position that gives you an official voice for an institution or a group. Furthermore, you may want to discover if a policy is in place that requires a coordinated and approved message for members and spokespersons. Respondents should ask pertinent questions prior to an interview and choose their answers carefully when they participate in an information-seeking interview.

How Can You Be an Effective Participant in Job-Seeking Interviews?

As you move into this discussion about job-seeking interviews, remember the issues and concerns surrounding interviews mentioned earlier in this chapter. Perception, relationship dimensions, the types and uses of questions, and the approaches to interviews are relevant in the job-seeking context. The underlying principles of information seeking in interviews apply to employment interviews as well. The distinction that makes a difference lies in the degree of preinterview preparation required for job seeking, as you will see next.

A Prescription for Success in Job-Seeking Interviews

Students spend years pursuing a formal education and developing special skills that will enable them to function in their chosen careers. Unfortunately, they often believe that proof of that education and skill is all that is required to get the "ideal job." In fact, getting a job can be a job in itself. Some self-knowledge and the ability to express what you believe to be true about yourself are essential in an interview. Background information about the company or organization for which you would like to work and the position for which you are applying is also a factor to consider before the interview. You should have a clear understanding of the career field in which you plan to spend your productive years, as well as some insight into the effect that current social and economic conditions may have on that field (Stewart & Cash, 1994).

Assess Yourself

What do you really know about yourself? When was the last time you took inventory of your assets and liabilities? Could you express these qualities intelligently? Answers to these questions are essential when you are preparing for a job-seeking interview. One way of approaching this difficult task is to ask yourself what your friends, family, and coworkers would say about you. What words would they use to describe you, and why? What successes and failures would they attribute to you? Why do you need to know this just to get a job? The answer is simply that you cannot talk cogently about the product you hope to promote—yourself—if you don't know very much about it.

In an employment interview, no one speaks for you but you. No one knows your best features better than you do, and no one will benefit from your description of those assets more than you will. As painful and tedious as it may be, you must begin your preparation for a job search with a thorough assessment of your (1) skills, (2) interests, (3) attributes, and (4) achievements. Although not exclusive of other possible areas to explore, consider tallying the following:

1. Your work and educational experiences.
2. Your motivations and goals.
3. Your strengths and weaknesses.
4. Your likes and dislikes.
5. Your skills.
6. Roles you played in campus extracurricular activities.
7. What, if any, professional experience you have had (including co-op programs and internships).

8. Your interests and hobbies.
9. Your talents, aptitudes, and achievements.
10. What is important to you in a position, in an organization.

Be thorough in your analysis so that when you get ready to participate in a job-seeking interview, you will be able to define and describe yourself in terms of the benefits you can bring to an organization. Ideally, you should then be able to summarize what you know about yourself in a single, lengthy answer to the most commonly used first question in an employment interview: "Tell me about yourself."

Research the Organization and the Job

You should have a comprehensive understanding of the organization to which you are applying. You should be familiar with the current information on company officers, products or services that are offered, geographical locations, and potential mergers, acquisitions, and expansion plans. You should have a realistic concept of the duties and responsibilities associated with the position for which you are applying and be able to discuss how your training, experience, and skills are compatible with the requirements for the position. Often you can find this background information in annual reports or recruitment literature. If neither is available to you, make use of the library resources in your community or on your university campus or check their web site.

Research the Career Field

To present yourself as a mature candidate for employment, you will want to know about your chosen field—how current social and economic conditions may influence it and the trends that are occurring in the field. This information is available in newspapers and periodicals. You will want to keep current on all aspects of the career field. Employers will view you more positively if you are conversant on these issues.

The best way for applicants to understand their role in job-seeking interviews is to know what employers look for in applicants and how employers elicit pertinent information. A few specific suggestions are shown in Tables A.3 and A.4.

TABLE A.3 SUGGESTIONS

1. If the issue of salary comes up, mention a range rather than an exact amount.
2. Try to discover what specific traits or skills are being sought, and then find a way to discuss how you have those traits and skills.
3. Show how enthusiastic and motivated you are through your examples and your manner of talking.
4. Ask the interviewer what separates this organization from all others.

TABLE A.4   NEVER DO THAT

1. Don't ask about benefits in an employment interview. (You haven't been hired yet.)
2. Don't tell the interviewer your goal is to have his or her job.
3. Don't ask what you stand to gain from this job. To say what you can do for the organization is better.
4. Avoid asking if you will "have to" work any overtime. (Assume that you will.)

Employer Preparation for Job-Seeking Interviews

Legally, employers must approach the hiring process with reference to the laws that govern employment. These laws are known as *equal employment opportunity (EEO) laws;* they are written and enacted by Congress and by individual state legislatures (Bergeson, 1991). The purpose of such laws is to assure that individuals are selected for employment without bias.

Employers should (1) describe the qualities and skills needed for the position they hope to fill, (2) construct questions that relate to those attributes, and (3) ask the same question of all candidates for the position. These questions are known as *bona fide occupational qualification (BFOQ) questions.* BFOQ questions should be about skills, training, education, work experience, physical attributes, and personality traits. With rare exceptions, questions should not be about age, gender, race, religion, physical appearance, disabilities, ethnic group, or citizenship.

Employers review applications and résumés and check pertinent references, looking for the qualities needed to meet the requirements for the position. They may even require that applicants take some prescreening tests, such as aptitude tests, honesty tests, or personality tests, in order to determine their overall suitability for the position. Aptitude tests may be basic math and grammar measures or more elaborate and job-specific tests. Honesty tests may be overt questionnaires about honesty or may be questions hidden in attitude and personality-trait assessments. The employer then has comprehensive information about the applicant to bring to the interview.

The Types and Uses of Job-Seeking Interviews

Throughout this Appendix, you have read that the primary focus for employers in job-seeking interviews is to gather information about applicants. Applicants must be prepared to present themselves as capable, self-aware candidates who have researched their career field, the company, and the position for which they are applying. The opportunity to make a personal connection between employers and applicants comes during the screening stage in the selection process. The **screening interview** is *an initial interview*

screening interview

An initial interview used to reduce the pool of applicants in the employment selection process.

used to reduce the pool of applicants in the employment selection process. It combines with the prescreening written information provided to employers to create a sense of who the applicants are and what they can bring to the organization. Organizations hire because they have a need or problem, and they are looking for solutions in those candidates.

Once employers decide that certain applicants meet their criteria for further consideration, those applicants are asked to participate further in the interviewing process. The second part of the process is known as the **determinate-interview phase,** *at which time applicants are either (1) hired, (2) interviewed further, or (3) dropped from consideration.* The determinate interview is often referred to as a *plant trip, site trip,* or *second interview.* Current employees of a company or an organization may participate in a reinterview process similar to a determinate interview when they are considering transferring within their organization. Applicants and current employees should recognize and anticipate that the tactics discussed below may be used in the determinate-interview phase.

Stress Tactics

Many organizations use atypical interview tactics and contexts. **Stress tactics** are *deliberate attempts to create anxiety for applicants in order to observe and assess their ability to handle difficult situations.* Some examples of stress tactics are (1) insults or affronts, (2) long periods of staring, (3) change from a cordial attitude to a hostile attitude, (4) unexplained silence, and (5) abrupt and unexplained departure from the interview location by the interviewer.

Stressful interview contexts, such as board interviews, group interviews, and teleconferences, present unique problems and opportunities for applicants. **Board interviews** are *interviews in which one person is interviewed by a panel;* **group interviews** are *those in which one person interviews a large group of applicants at one time.* **Teleconferences** are becoming more commonplace, because *a number of people can ask questions of an applicant by phone,* thereby saving time and money for the potential employing agency.

The stress involved in the board interview emerges because an applicant must answer questions and deal with numerous personalities at one time. The group interview generates stress for applicants because they must find a positive vehicle for being acknowledged within the large group of candidates. In teleconferences, the obvious lack of face-to-face interaction eliminates nearly all nonverbal clues for applicants.

During determinate interviews, employers may create stress for applicants by asking them to make technical presentations to members of the organization, or employers may use job simulations and involve applicants in actual job tasks. Hypothetical situations or role-play situations may be described, and the applicants may be required to decide how to handle the circumstances, thereby putting applicants in unfamiliar territory. However, the best way for students to prepare for stress-filled interviews is to anticipate that they may occur and then to adapt to the situation. Being cooperative and

determinate-interview phase

The point at which the interviewee is either hired, interviewed further, or dropped from consideration; often referred to as the *second interview, plant trip,* or *site trip.*

stress tactics

Deliberate attempts to create anxiety for applicants to see if they can handle difficult situations.

board interviews

Interviews conducted with a panel of interviewers and one interviewee.

group interviews

Interviews with one interviewer and many applicants.

teleconferences

Interview situations in which a number of interviewers speak to the respondent by telephone.

calm and taking the opportunity to discuss your ideas, abilities, and experiences will reduce the stress considerably.

The Selection Interview

Typically, a job-seeking interview lasts between 20 and 30 minutes. As stated earlier in the chapter, the opening of the interview sets the tone for the interview and establishes the guidelines for applicants. Interviewers begin with an appropriately friendly greeting and handshake and follow up with some small talk to build rapport with the candidates. An orientation to the **selection interview** is generally provided for applicants at this juncture, and applicants are informed that *the interviewer will (1) ask questions, (2) provide information about the company and the position, and (3) answer applicant questions.* When this initial information is provided, the interviewer will make a smooth transition to the question-and-answer phase of the interview, which may take as much as 75 percent of the time allotted for the interview.

The body of the interview involves questions about education, experience, goals, and personal characteristics. Open-ended to gradually closed questions, followed by more open-ended questions, allow for both voluntary information and brief but pertinent responses from applicants. When this phase of the interview is completed, the interviewer should tell the applicant about the company and the position and then permit the applicant to ask questions. Examples of interviewer and applicant questions are presented in Figure A.2.

The closing of the interview is strategic to the success of the interview for all parties. If the interviewer has the positional power to hire or decline applicants, that decision may occur at the end of the question-and-answer period. If further interviews are necessary before a decision can be made, applicants will be told what to expect. They will find out who will contact them, when they will be contacted, and how they will be contacted. This information eliminates any doubt about the next step in the process. If this information is not provided, applicants will need to ask for it politely and clarify any aspects of the directions that remain unclear. The closing of the interview is also a good time for applicants to make a link between the requirements of the job and their abilities and experience, as well as to indicate an interest in being considered for the position. A genuine expression of thanks from both parties then concludes the interview.

selection interview

An interview in which a job applicant is asked questions, provided with information about the potential employer, and given an opportunity to ask questions.

Interviewer Questions

How would you describe yourself?
Why did you select your college or university?
What led you to choose your career field and major?
What courses did you like best? Why?
What courses did you like least? Why?
Do you plan to pursue an advanced degree?
Describe your most rewarding college experience.
What accomplishments are you most proud of? Why?
Do you think your grades reflect your ability?
What are your long-range goals? Short-range goals?
What do you consider your greatest strengths? Weaknesses?
What motivates you?
What work environment do you prefer?
Describe your ideal job.
What major problem or obstacle have you encountered and how did you handle it?
What have you learned from the experience?
Why did you decide to interview with our organization?
Describe your work experience.
How does your work experience relate to our organization and this position?

Applicant Questions

Describe a typical day for an employee in this position.
How is performance evaluated?
How is success in this position measured and rewarded?
Are most assignments completed in teams or individually?
What is a typical career path for someone with my experience?
Does this position offer growth and advancement?
What professional education is encouraged?
What is the greatest challenge to people in this position?
Does the company promote on merit and promote within?
What is the company policy on relocation?

Figure A.2 Examples of interview questions.

Summary

In this Appendix, you learned about the investigative context of interviewing, and how it differs from other types of interpersonal communication. Unlike some interpersonal communication contexts, interviews involve a preplanned and serious purpose. Interviews are dynamic interactions that are influenced by the relationship dimensions of control, inclusion, and affection and each participant's perception of self, of the other party, and of the situation. Analyzing the situation, anticipating the relationship, and adapting to the overall circumstances are necessary.

The Appendix introduced the approaches to interviews and their uses. The direct approach is used by less skilled interviewers or by interviewers who need to control the content and direction of the interview. The indirect interview approach requires more skill and time and permits the respondent more freedom of expression. Interviewers often combine the direct and indirect approaches when the situation demands more flexibility.

The functional approach to interviewing classifies interviews as information-giving, information-seeking, and persuasive. The Appendix focused on the information-seeking interview and, specifically, on the job-seeking interview. The job-seeking interview requires considerable interviewee preparation. Hiring rules are a significant factor for the interviewer who must conduct interviews in a nonbiased manner. Moreover, applicants must analyze themselves and research the organization, position, and career field before an interview. Failure to do so will diminish the effectiveness of the applicant and reduce the chances of employment.

Additional Resources

Adams, B. (1993). *The complete résumé and job search book for students*. Hollbrock, MA: Adams.

Lester, M. C. (1998). *Real life guide to life after college*. Chapel Hill, NC: Pipeline Press/Associated Publishers Group.

Lester, M. C. (1998). *Real life guide to starting your career: How to get the right job now!* Chapel Hill, NC: Pipeline Press/Associated Publishers Group.

Wilson, G. L., & Goodall, H. L. (1992). *Interviewing in context*. New York: McGraw-Hill.

References

Benjamin, A. (1987). *The helping interview*. Boston: Houghton Mifflin.

Bergeson, P. T. (1991). *The Americans with Disabilities Act (ADA): Practical considerations for employers*. Chicago: Pope, Ballard, Shepard & Fowle.

Burgoon, J. K., & Hale, J. L. (1984). The fundamental topoi of relational communication. *Communication Monographs, 51*, 193–214.

Gordon, R. L. (1987). *Interviewing: Strategy, techniques, and tactics*. Belmont, CA: Wadsworth.

Goyer, R. S., Redding, W. C., & Rickey, J. T. (1968). *Interviewing principles and techniques: A project text*. Dubuque, IA: William C. Brown.

Knapp, M. L. (1978). *Social intercourse: From greeting to goodbye*. Boston: Allyn and Bacon.

Knapp, M. L., Hart, R. P., Friedrich, G. W., and Shulman, G. M. (1973). The rhetoric of goodbyes: Verbal and nonverbal correlates of human leave-taking. *Speech Monographs, 40,* 182–198.

Kreps, G., & Thornton, B. (1988). *Health communication: Theory and practice.* Prospect Heights, IL: Waveland.

Payne, S. L. (1951). *The art of asking questions.* Princeton, NJ: Princeton University Press.

Phillips, G. M., & Wood, J. T. (1983). *Communication and human relationships: A study of interpersonal communication.* New York: Macmillan.

Schutz, W. C. (1976). *The interpersonal underworld.* Palo Alto, CA: Science and Behavior Books.

Stewart, C. J., & Cash, W. B., Jr. (1994). *Interviewing principles and practices.* Madison, WI: Brown & Benchmark.

Webster's Ninth New Collegiate Dictionary. (1983). Springfield, MA.

glossary

glossary

A

absolute criteria   249
Criteria that *must* be met; the group has no leeway.

abstract words   417
Words or phrases that refer generally to ideas, qualities, acts, or relationships.

abstractions   55
Simplifications of what words stand for.

accuracy   114
In evaluating a deductive argument, the truth or verifiability of the major and minor premises.

action model   14
A depiction of communication as one person sending a message and another person or group of persons receiving it.

active listening   107
Involved listening with a purpose.

active perception   27
Perception in which our minds select, organize, and interpret that which we sense.

adoption   431
Inducing an audience to accept a new idea, attitude, behavior, belief, or product and to demonstrate that acceptance through behavioral change; an action goal of the persuasive speech.

affection   152, 461
(1) The emotion of caring for others and/or being cared for by them. (2) Friendship and warm demeanor, which is preferred in an interview setting.

affective conflict   253
Conflict that stems from personal dislikes and power struggles.

agenda setting   134
The process of selecting what topics an audience will read about and hear about.

aggressiveness   165
Standing up for one's rights at the expense of others.

analogy   310
A comparison of things that are basically unalike.

androgynous   169
A term used in reference to persons who possess stereotypical female and male characteristics.

antonym   416
A word that means the opposite of another word.

appeal to authority   116
A fallacy that occurs when a person offers information that is outside his or her area of expertise.

appeal to the people   116
A fallacy that invites you to join the group and do something because "everyone is doing it"; also known as the *bandwagon effect*.

area of freedom   246
The limitations placed on a group as part of the group's charge.

argot   190
The specialized language of disreputable underground co-cultures.

argument against the person   116
A fallacy in which the person, rather than the issue at hand, becomes the focus.

arguments   439
Propositions, justifications, and evidence used to persuade.

articulation   380
The production of sounds; a component of enunciation.

artifacts   87
Ornaments or adornments we display that hold communicative potential.

assertiveness   164
The ability to communicate feelings and ideas directly and honestly.

attitude   278
A predisposition to respond favorably or unfavorably to a person, an object, an idea, or an event.

audience analysis   274
The collection and interpretation of data on the demographics, attitudes, values, and beliefs of the audience obtained by observation, inferences, questionnaires, or interviews.

audience interest   277
The relevance and importance of the topic to an audience; sometimes related to the uniqueness of the topic.

audience knowledge   277
The amount of information the audience already has about the topic.

autocratic leaders   240
Leaders who maintain strict control over group members.

avoiding   157
In Knapp's relational development model, the stage characterized by partners' reluctance to interact, active avoidance, and hostility.

B

bargaining   153
The process in which two or more parties attempt to reach an agreement on what each should give and receive in a relationship.

begging the question   117
A fallacy that occurs when you use a conclusion that is also your premise; also called a *circular argument*.

behavioral flexibility   169
The ability to alter behavior to adapt to new situations and to relate in new ways when necessary.

belief   278
A conviction; often thought to be more enduring than an attitude and less enduring than a value.

believability   446
A criterion of good evidence—the audience must trust and accept the evidence.

bibliography   356
A list of sources used in a speech.

bipolar question   466
A question that limits the answer options to two choices.

blended family   174
A type of family that consists of two adults and step-, adoptive, or foster children; sometimes called a *reconstituted family*, a *step family*, or a *remarried family*.

board interviews   474
Interviews conducted with a panel of interviewers and one interviewee.

bodily movement   386
What the speaker does with his or her entire body during a speech presentation.

body   333
The largest part of the speech, which contains the arguments, evidence, and main content.

bonding   156
In Knapp's relational development model, the stage in which partners commit to each other.

bookmark   302
A feature of most web browsers by which important links can be saved in a file without having to look up the URL.

boomerang effect   441
An unintended situation in which the speaker and the message induce an audience response that is the opposite of what the speaker intended.

brainstorming   251, 268
(1) A technique to help groups increase the number of creative options available by suspending judgment or evaluation. (2) Listening to or naming as many ideas as a group or an individual can within a limited period of time.

brakelight function   354
A forewarning to the audience that the end of the speech is near.

C

cant   190
The specialized language of nonprofessional, usually noncriminal, groups.

captive audience   274, 450
An audience that has not chosen to hear a particular speaker or speech.

card catalog   297
A source of information about materials in a library.

cause/effect pattern   348
A method of speech organization in which the speaker first explains the causes of an event, a problem, or an issue and then discusses its consequences, results, or effects.

celebrity testimony   309
Statements made by a public figure that support a point of view.

channel   11
The means by which a message moves from the source to the receiver of the message.

channels   131
The means by which a message is sent; in mass communication, the channels are technological devices.

charge   246
The group's assignment.

charisma   238
An extreme type of referent power that inspires strong loyalty and devotion from others.

circumscribing   157
In Knapp's relational development model, the stage marked by a decrease in partners' interaction, time spent together, and depth of sharing.

clearinghouse question   467
A question used to assure an interviewer that all essential information has been provided.

cliché   59
An expression that has lost originality and force through overuse.

closed questions   466
Questions that restrict the response, often asking for specific information or supplying optional answers for the respondent.

closure   34
The tendency to fill in missing information in order to complete an otherwise incomplete figure or statement.

co-culture   30, 189
A group whose beliefs or behaviors distinguish it from the larger culture of which it is a part and with which it shares numerous similarities.

co-languages   190
Specialized languages used by co-cultures to facilitate effective communication and to distinguish group members from nonmembers.

co-orientation   316
Also known as common ground, it is the degree to which the speaker's values, beliefs, attitudes, and interests are shared with the audience; an aspect of credibility.

code   12
A systematic arrangement of symbols used to create meanings in the mind of another person or persons.

code sensitivity   198
The ability to use the verbal and nonverbal language appropriate to the cultural or co-cultural norms of the individual with whom you are communicating.

coercion   238
A form of punishment that attempts to force compliance with hostile tactics.

cohabiting-couple household   174
A type of family that includes two unrelated adults who share living quarters, with or without children.

cohesiveness   226
The attachment members feel toward each other and the group.

collectivist cultures   194
Cultures that value the group over the individual.

colloquialisms   58
Words and phrases that are used informally.

combination approach   462
A mixture of indirect and direct approaches when freedom of expression is called for but pertinent facts and information are needed.

committees   211
Task-oriented small groups that have been given an assignment by a person or an organization.

communication   6
The process of understanding and sharing meaning.

communication apprehension   366
The generalized fear of communication, regardless of context.

communication network   222
The pattern of message flow, or who talks to whom.

communicative competencies approach   242
An approach to leadership that focuses on how leaders exert influence by using specific communication skills and behaviors.

comparison   416
A means of defining by pointing out similarities between the known and the less known.

competence   314
The degree to which the speaker is perceived as skilled, reliable, experienced, qualified, authoritative, and informed; an aspect of credibility.

complementarity   167
The idea that we sometimes bond with people whose strengths are our weaknesses.

complementary relationships   152
Relationships in which each person supplies something the other person or persons lack.

computer catalog   297
An electronic source of information about materials in a library.

conclusion   354
The last part of the speech; a summary of the major ideas that is designed to induce mental or behavioral change in an audience.

concrete language   65
Words and statements that are specific rather than abstract or vague.

concrete words   417
Words that refer to definite persons, places, objects, and acts.

confirmation   42
Feedback in which others treat us in a manner consistent with whom we believe we are.

conflict   252
Expressed disagreement between people who are interdependent.

conjunctive tasks   245
Tasks for which no one group member has all the necessary information but each member has some information to contribute.

connotative meaning   54
An individualized or personalized meaning of a word, which may be emotionally laden.

constructivist model   15
A theory of communication which posits that receivers create their own reality in their minds.

context   17
A set of circumstances or a situation.

contingency approaches   241
Approaches to studying leadership that assume that different leadership situations require different leadership behaviors.

continuance   431
Persuading an audience to continue present behavior or beliefs; an action goal of the persuasive speech.

contrast   416
The comparison of unlike things.

control 152, 254, 461
(1) The ability to influence others, our environment, and ourselves. (2) A highly aggressive conflict management style in which one person tries to win at all costs. (3) The most influence or power in an interview situation.

cost-benefit theory 153
A theory of interpersonal relationships which suggests that individuals will maintain a relationship only as long as the benefits of the relationship outweigh the costs.

counterarguments 439
Rebuttals to an argument.

couples with no children 173
A family type that includes two adults and no children.

criteria 248
Standards against which a group's solution or decision is evaluated.

critical listening 103
A type of active listening that challenges the speaker's message by evaluating its accuracy, meaningfulness, and utility.

critical thinking 110
Analyzing and judging the accuracy of messages.

cross-disciplinary address 450
A presentation in which professionals in one field train, inform, or persuade individuals in another field.

cultural relativism 191
The belief that another culture should be judged by its context rather than measured against your own culture.

culture 29, 132, 189
(1) A system of shared beliefs, values, customs, behaviors, and artifacts that the members of a society use to cope with one another and with their world. (2) A set of beliefs and understandings a society has about the world, its place in it, and the various activities used to celebrate and reinforce those beliefs.

D

dating 65
Specifying when you made an observation, since everything changes over time.

decision making 246
Choosing among alternatives.

decode 53
The process of assigning meaning to others' words in order to translate them into thoughts of your own.

decoding 12
Assigning meaning to the idea or thought in a code.

deductive argument 114
An argument that progresses from a general proposition to a specific instance.

defensive climate 227
An atmosphere of tension in which members feel they have to defend themselves from verbal or psychological attacks.

defensiveness 105, 162
(1) An impediment to listening that occurs when individuals act threatened, as if they must defend what they have said or done. (2) The tendency to protect and support our ideas and attitudes against attack by others.

definitions 311
Determinations of meaning through description, simplification, examples, analysis, comparison, explanation, or illustration.

delivery 374
The presentation of a speech by using your voice and body to reinforce your message.

democratic leaders 240
Leaders who encourage members to participate fully in group decisions.

demographic analysis 276
The collection and interpretation of data about the characteristics of people, excluding their attitudes, values, and beliefs.

denotative meaning 54
The agreed-upon meaning or dictionary meaning of a word.

descriptiveness   64
The practice of describing observed behavior or phenomena instead of offering personal reactions or judgments.

designated leader   237
Someone who has been appointed or elected to an official position of leadership.

determinate-interview phase   474
The point at which the interviewee is either hired, interviewed further, or dropped from consideration; often referred to as the *second interview, plant trip,* or *site trip.*

deterrence   431
Persuading an audience to avoid an activity or a belief; an action goal of the persuasive speech.

differentiating   157
In Knapp's relational development model, the stage in which partners emphasize their individual differences rather than their similarities.

direct approach   462
An approach in which the interviewer determines the purpose of the interview and exerts control over the types of questions and the pace of the interview.

disconfirmation   42
Feedback in which others fail to respond to our notion of self by responding neutrally.

discontinuance   431
Inducing an audience to stop doing something or thinking in a certain way; an action goal of the persuasive speech.

disjunctive tasks   245
Tasks with low coordination requirements that can be completed effectively by one member working alone.

distributed leadership   244
A leadership approach that expects each member, not just the leader, to take responsibility for the group by exerting appropriate influence.

doublespeak   60
Language used to mask a reality by portraying something ugly as neutral or positive.

dual-worker families   174
Families that include two working adults.

dyadic communication   18
Two-person communication.

dynamism   315
The extent to which the speaker is perceived as bold, active, energetic, strong, empathic, and assertive; an aspect of credibility.

E

egocentrism   104
Excessive self-focus, which interferes with listening.

emergent leader   237
Someone who becomes an informal leader by exerting influence in a group but does not hold the official position or title of leader.

emotional appeals   436
Attempts to persuade audience members to change an attitude or a behavior through an appeal—usually in a narrative form—to their emotions.

emotional proof   113
Evidence based on feelings or emotions.

empathic listening   108
A type of active listening in which you listen with a purpose and attempt to understand the other person.

empathy   108
The ability to perceive another person's world view as if it were your own.

encode   53
The process of translating your thoughts into words.

encoding   12
Converting an idea or thought into a code.

enthymemes   115
Parts of a deductive argument, such as a premise or a conclusion.

enunciation   379
The pronunciation and articulation of sounds and words.

ethics 228
Rules or standards for right conduct or practice.

ethnocentrism 191
The belief that your own group or culture is superior to other groups or cultures.

etymology 416
The historical origin of a word.

euphemism 59
A polite, more pleasant expression used instead of a socially unacceptable form.

evidence 312, 438
(1) Data or information from which you can draw a conclusion, make a judgment, or establish the probability of something occurring. (2) Any material that supports a proposition.

examples 307
Illustrations drawn from specific instances.

experiential superiority 105
An impediment to listening that occurs when you look down on others because their experience is less extensive than yours.

experimenting 155
In Knapp's relational development model, the stage in which partners attempt to discover information about each other.

expert power 238
power derived from knowledge or expertise valued by the group.

expert testimony 309
Statements made by someone who has special knowledge or expertise that support a point of view.

explanation 311, 417
(1) A means of clarification by simplifying, amplifying, or restating. (2) A means of idea development that simplifies or clarifies an idea while making it interesting to the audience.

explicit-rule culture 195
A culture in which information and cultural rules are explicit, procedures are explained, and expectations are discussed.

extemporaneous mode 375
A carefully prepared and researched speech with a conversational delivery.

extended families 174
Families in which not only parents and children are part of the family unit but also grandparents, aunts, uncles, cousins, and others.

external audience 449
An audience composed of people outside the speaker's company or organization.

extrinsic motivation 411
A method of making information relevant by providing the audience with reasons outside the speech itself for listening to the content of the speech.

eye contact 385
The extent to which a speaker looks directly at the audience.

F

facial expression 384
Any nonverbal cue expressed by the speaker's face.

factual distractions 102
A source of internal interference that occurs when you focus so intently on the details that you miss the main point.

fallacies of ambiguity 116
Arguments that are flawed because they contain a word or words with two or more meanings.

fallacies of relevance 116
Arguments that are flawed because the conclusion is based on irrelevant premises.

fallacy 115
An argument that is flawed, does not follow rules of logic, and therefore is not to be believed.

fallacy of division 118
A fallacy in which you argue that what is true of the parts must be true of the whole or that what is true of the whole must be true of the parts.

fallacy of equivocation 117
A fallacy that occurs when you purposefully use the ambiguous qualities of language to your advantage or when you use two different meanings of the same word within a single context.

false alternatives   117
A fallacy which suggests that only two alternatives are possible and that one of the two is disastrous or to be avoided.

false cause   117
The fallacy of attributing the cause of something to whatever happened before it.

family   172
An organized, naturally occurring relational, transactional group, usually occupying a common living space over an extended time period and possessing a confluence of interpersonal images that evolve through the exchange of meaning over time.

family rituals   176
The forms of symbolic communication that are systematically repeated and that contribute to family satisfaction.

fantasy   223
The creative and imaginative shared interpretation of events that fulfills a group's need to make sense of their experience and to anticipate their future.

fantasy chain   223
A line of fantasies to which all (or most) group members contribute to create a kind of group storytelling.

fantasy theme   224
The content, obvious or hidden, of a fantasy.

feedback   11, 107, 131
(1) The receiver's verbal and nonverbal response to the source's message. (2) The listener's verbal and nonverbal responses to the speaker and the speaker's message. (3) A response that allows the source to determine if the message was correctly understood.

figure   34
The focal point of a person's attention.

first-person observation   112
Your description of what you sensed.

fluency   381
The smoothness of delivery, the flow of words, and the absence of vocalized pauses.

formal role   218
An assigned role based on a member's position or title within a group.

framing   134
Taking a particular perspective on a story.

functions approach   241
An approach to studying leadership that assumes groups have certain task and interpersonal functions that must be performed, but they may be performed by any member, not just the designated leader.

G

gatekeeping   133
The process of determining what news, information, or entertainment will reach an audience.

gender   214
Characteristics of femininity and masculinity that are learned.

gender constancy   43
The tendency to see oneself consistently as male or female.

gestures   383
Movements of the head, arms, and hands to illustrate, emphasize, or signal ideas in the speech.

grammar   12
The rules of function in language.

ground   34
The background against which a person's focused attention occurs.

group climate   225
The emotional tone or atmosphere that exists within a group.

group interviews   474
Interviews with one interviewer and many applicants.

groupthink   252
The failure of a group to evaluate its options thoroughly and critically because members fail to express their disagreement.

H

hasty generalization   116
A fallacy in which an inference is drawn from insufficient observation; also called a *premature generalization*.

hearing   98
The physiological act of receiving sound.

heterogeneous   274, 449
(1) Characterized by many differences among individuals. (2) Characterized by many differences among individuals in an audience.

hidden agendas   225
Secret motives that place individual needs and wants ahead of the group.

home page   301
The first page on a web site, to which supporting materials are linked.

homogeneous   275, 449
(1) Characterized by similarities among individuals. (2) Characterized by audience members that are more like one another.

hyperlink   300
A link in a web document that leads to another web site or to another place within the same document.

I

immediate behavioral purposes   408
Actions a speaker seeks from an audience during and immediately after a speech.

immediate goals   432
Purposes that a speaker wishes to accomplish during the speech or shortly after it.

immediate purpose   334
What you expect to achieve on the day of your speech.

implicit-rule culture   195
A culture in which information and cultural rules are implied and already known to the participants.

important criteria   249
Criteria that *should* be met if at all possible, but the group has some flexibility.

impromptu mode   375
Delivery of a speech without notes, plans, or preparation; characterized by spontaneity and informal language.

inclusion   152, 461
(1) The state of being involved with others. (2) How much each party wants to participate in an interview and how much each party wants to include others in the interview.

indexing   67
Identifying the uniqueness of objects, events, and people.

indirect approach   462
An approach in which the interviewer shares control of the pace, content, and focus of the interview with the respondent.

individualistic cultures   193
Cultures that value individual freedom, choice, uniqueness, and independence.

inductive arguments   113
An argument that progresses from specific instances to general conclusions.

inference   282
A tentative conclusion based on some evidence.

inferences   67, 112
(1) Conclusions drawn from observations. (2) Conclusions from or about information you have received through your senses.

informal role   219
A role that is developed spontaneously within a group.

information hunger   410
The audience's need for the information contained in the speech.

information overload   413
A situation that occurs when the quantity or difficulty of the information presented is greater than the audience can assimilate within the given time.

information relevance   410
The importance, novelty, and usefulness of the topic and the information.

information-seeking interview 468
An interview conducted to find out about an issue, a person, or a situation in a timely fashion.

informational question 467
A question used to clarify an answer that appears to be vague or superficial.

informative content 412
The main points and subpoints, illustrations, and examples used to clarify and inform.

initiating 155
In Knapp's stages of relational development, the short beginning period of a relationship.

integrating 155
In Knapp's relational development model, the stage in which partners start mirroring each other's behavior.

intensifying 155
In Knapp's relational development model, the stage in which partners become more aware of each other and actively participate in the relationship.

intentionality 75
The purposefulness of nonverbal codes.

interaction model 14
A depiction of communication as one person sending a message and a second person receiving the message and then responding with a return message.

intercultural communication 188
The exchange of information between individuals who are unalike culturally.

Internet 140, 299
A global network of interconnected computer networks.

interpersonal communication 18
The personal process of coordinating meaning between at least two people in a situation that allows mutual opportunities for both speaking and listening.

interpersonal relationship 148
The association of two or more people who are interdependent, who use some consistent patterns of communication and who have interacted for a period of time.

interpretation 37
The process of assigning meaning to stimuli.

interpretive perception 37
Perception that involves a blend of internal states and external stimuli.

interview 460
A dyadic communication context with a purpose or goal.

interview guide 465
An outline of topics and subtopics used in an interview.

interview schedule 465
An elaborate outline of primary questions and secondary questions that helps keep focus on the topic.

intrapersonal communication 17
The process of understanding and sharing meaning within the self.

introduction 326
The first part of the speech; its function is to arouse the audience and to lead into the main ideas presented in the body.

investigative report 451
A presentation that gives an accounting of a problem, includes recommendations, and is usually conducted by someone outside the company.

involvement 269
The importance of the topic to the speaker; determined by the strength of the feelings the speaker has about the topic and the time and energy the speaker devotes to that topic.

irrelevant conclusion 117
A fallacy that occurs when evidence supports one conclusion but you draw another one.

J

jargon 60, 190
The technical language of a particular trade, profession, or group.

justification 113
As part of an argument, all the evidence you have gathered that supports the proposition.

K

key-word outline 342
An outline consisting of important words or phrases to remind the speaker of the content of the speech.

kinesics 76
The study of bodily movements, including posture, gestures, and facial expressions.

L

laissez-faire leaders 240
Nonleaders who take little or no initiative for structuring a group discussion.

language 52
A code consisting of symbols, letters, or words with arbitrary meanings that are arranged according to the rules of syntax.

lay testimony 309
Statements made by an ordinary person that substantiate or support a point of view.

leader 236
A person who influences the behavior and attitudes of others through communication.

leadership 236
The process of using communication to influence the behaviors and attitudes of others to meet group goals.

leading questions 468
Questions used to elicit a particular response from an interviewee.

legitimate power 238
Power by virtue of having a particular position or title.

listening 99
The process of receiving and interpreting aural stimuli.

logical appeals 438
Propositions and evidence used to persuade an audience.

logical proof 113
Evidence based on reasoning.

long-range goal 334
What you expect to achieve over a time period longer than the day of your speech.

M

main points 335
The most important points in a speech; indicated by Roman numerals in an outline.

maintenance functions 221
Behaviors in a group that focus on the interpersonal relationships among members.

manuscript mode 375
Delivery of a speech from a script of the entire speech.

mass communication 20, 130
(1) Communication mediated, via a transmission system, between a source and a large number of unseen receivers. (2) The process in which professional communicators using technological devices share messages over great distances to influence large audiences.

meaning 7
The shared understanding of the message constructed in the minds of the communicators.

memorized mode 376
Delivering a speech that has been committed to memory.

mental distraction 102
An internal source of interference: the wandering of the mind when it is supposed to be focused on something.

message 11, 131
(1) The verbal or nonverbal form of the idea, thought, or feeling that one person (the source) wishes to communicate to another person or group of people (the receivers). (2) Whatever the source attempts to share with another person.

message analysis 111
A step in critical thinking and listening that includes evaluating the process by which information or knowledge was discovered and evaluating the message itself.

metatalk 58
Talk in which meaning is not literal.

mindfulness   109
The state of being fully engaged in the moment.

Monroe motivated sequence   440
A problem-solving format that encourages an audience to become concerned about an issue; especially appropriate for a persuasive speech.

N

narrating   418
The oral presentation and interpretation of a story, a description, or an event; includes dramatic reading of prose or poetry.

negative feedback   107
Verbal and nonverbal responses intended to disconfirm the speaker and the speaker's message.

neutral questions   467
Questions that invite the respondent to provide an answer consistent with his or her position on an issue.

noise   13, 101
(1) Any interference in the encoding and decoding processes that reduces message clarity. (2) Interference in the communication process from external and internal sources.

nonconfrontation   254
The passive conflict management style in which the individual gives in or avoids disagreement.

nonverbal codes   12, 75
(1) All symbols that are not words, including bodily movements, use of space and time, clothing and adornments, and sounds other than words. (2) Codes consisting of symbols that are not words, including nonword vocalizations.

norms   216
Informal rules for interaction.

nuclear families   174
Families that have a breadwinning father, a homemaking mother, and resident children.

nudging question   467
A question used to motivate further interaction.

O

objectics   86
The study of the human use of clothing and other artifacts as nonverbal codes; object language.

observation   280
Seeing and sensing the behavior and characteristics of an audience.

observations   67, 112
(1) Descriptions of what is sensed. (2) Descriptions based on phenomena that can be sensed—seen, heard, smelled, or felt.

open questions   466
Questions designed to permit freedom in terms of the length and nature of the response.

operational definition   416
A definition which states the process that results in the thing being defined.

operational definitions   64
Definitions that identify something by revealing how it works, how it is made, or what it consists of.

oral footnote   298
An abbreviated manuscript footnote that tells the audience where you found your information.

organization   33
The grouping of stimuli into meaningful units or wholes.

organizational patterns   345
Arrangements of the contents of a speech.

outline   333
A written plan that uses symbols, margins, and content to reveal the order, importance, and substance of a speech.

P

P-MOPS   250
An acronym for Procedural Model of Problem Solving, a structured, flexible procedure groups can use to ensure that no important step needed for effective problem solving is missed.

paralinguistic features   84
The nonword sounds and nonword characteristics of language, such as pitch, volume, rate, and quality.

parallel form   337
The consistent use of complete sentences, clauses, phrases, or words in an outline.

paraphrasing   64
Restating another person's message by rephrasing the content or intent of the message.

passive perception   27
Perception in which people are simply recorders of stimuli.

pause   378
The absence of vocal sound used for dramatic effect, transition, or emphasis of ideas.

perception   26
The process of becoming aware of objects and events from the senses.

perceptual constancy   29
The idea that our past experiences lead us to see the world in a way that is difficult to change; that is, our initial perceptions persist.

personal experience   294
Your own life as a source of information for your speech.

personal inventories   269
A speaker's surveys of his or her reading and viewing habits and behavior to discover what topics are of personal interest.

personal proof   113
Evidence based on the authority and knowledge of a credible source.

persuasion   430
An ongoing process in which verbal and nonverbal messages shape, reinforce, and change people's responses.

physical distractions   102
All the stimuli in the environment that keep you from focusing on the speaker and the message.

pitch   377
The highness or lowness of a speaker's voice; technically, the frequency of sound made by vocal cords.

plagiarism   299
The use of someone else's ideas or words without credit.

positive feedback   107
Verbal and nonverbal responses intended to affirm the speaker and the speaker's message.

power   237
The ability to influence others.

presentational speaking   449
Informative, persuasive, or special-occasion speaking that occurs in a business or professional context.

primary groups   211
Groups whose main purpose is to meet our needs for inclusion and affection (e.g., a family).

primary questions   467
Questions that are used to introduce areas of inquiry and are coherent in themselves.

problem questions   247
Group discussion questions that focus on the problem and imply that many solutions are possible.

problem solving   245
The process of moving from an undesirable present situation to a desirable goal by overcoming obstacles to that goal.

problem/solution pattern   349
A method of speech organization in which the speaker describes a problem and proposes a solution to that problem.

process   6
An activity, exchange, or set of behaviors that occur over time.

profanity   60
Language that is disrespectful of things sacred, commonly known as "swearing."

progress report   451
A presentation that gives an accounting of the developments in an ongoing project.

pronunciation   380
The conformity of the speaker's production of words with agreed-upon rules about the sounds of vowels and consonants, and for syllabic emphasis.

proof   312
Evidence that is sufficient to convince an audience of the truth of a claim.

proposition   113
As part of an argument, a statement of what you believe.

proxemics   79
The study of the human use of space and distance.

proximity   35, 165
(1) The principle that objects which are physically close to each other will be perceived as a unit or group. (2) Term referring to location, distance, range between persons and things.

public communication   20
The process of generating meanings in a situation where a single source transmits a message to a number of receivers who give nonverbal and, sometimes, question-and-answer feedback.

punishment power   238
Power derived from the ability to withhold what others want and need.

Q

quality control circle   212
A small group of employees that meets on company time to recommend improvements in products and work procedures.

questionnaire   283
A set of written questions developed to obtain demographic and attitudinal information.

R

racist language   61
Language that insults a group because of its color or ethnicity.

rapport talk   161
Tannen's term for women's view of conversation as a way to develop relationships, strengthen ties, and share experiences.

rate   378
The speed at which speech is delivered, normally between 125 and 190 words per minute.

receiver   11
A message target.

receivers   131
The people who are the intended recipients of the message.

referent power   238
Power based on others' admiration and respect.

reflective question   467
A question used to verify information.

reflective thinking model   250
A problem-solving model developed by philosopher John Dewey that is based on his assessment of how individuals solve problems.

regionalisms   61
Words and phrases that are specific to a particular region or part of the country.

rejection   42
Feedback in which others treat us in a manner that is inconsistent with our self-definition.

relational deterioration   157
In Knapp's model, the process by which relationships disintegrate.

relational development   155
In Knapp's model, the process by which relationships grow.

relational maintenance   156
In Knapp's model, the process of keeping a relationship together.

relational uncertainty   464
A state of suspicion or doubt.

report talk   160
Tannen's term for men's view of conversation as instrumental or as a way to demonstrate knowledge and reveal information.

responsiveness   166
The idea that we tend to select our friends from people who demonstrate positive interest in us.

reward power   238
Power derived from the ability to give others tangible or intangible things they want and need.

rhetorical questions   410
Questions asked for effect, with no answer expected.

role   29, 218
(1) The part an individual plays in a group; an individual's function or expected behavior. (2) A position in a group that is part of an interlocking structure of other parts.

rough draft   339
The preliminary organization of the outline of a speech.

S

Sapir-Whorf hypothesis   56
A theory which holds that our perception of reality is determined by our thought processes and our thought processes are limited by our language and, therefore, that language shapes our reality.

sales presentation   450
A presentation intended to persuade a potential buyer to purchase a service or product.

screening interview   473
An initial interview used to reduce the pool of applicants in the employment selection process.

search engine   301
A program on the Internet that allows users to search for information.

second-person account   112
Your (or some else's) report of what another person observed.

secondary groups   211
Groups whose main purpose is completing a task (e.g., a committee).

secondary questions   467
Questions that probe further or clarify.

selection   32
The process of neglecting some stimuli in the environment to focus on other stimuli.

selection interview   475
An interview in which a job applicant is asked questions, provided with information about the potential employer, and given an opportunity to ask questions.

selective attention   32
The tendency, when we expose ourselves to

information and ideas, to focus on certain cues and ignore others.

selective exposure   32
The tendency to expose ourselves to information that reinforces rather than contradicts our beliefs or opinions.

selective perception   32
The tendency to see, hear, and believe only what we want to see, hear, and believe.

selective retention   32
The tendency to remember better the things that reinforce our beliefs than those that oppose them.

self-actualization   41
According to Maslow, the fulfillment of one's potential as a person.

self-awareness   39
An understanding of and insight into one's self, including one's attitudes, values, beliefs, strengths, and weaknesses.

self-centered functions   221
Behaviors that serve the individual's needs at the expense of the group.

self-concept   41
An individual's evaluation of himself or herself, that is, an individual's self-appraisal.

self-disclosure   158
The process of making intentional revelations about oneself that others would be unlikely to know.

self-esteem   43
The feeling an individual has about his or her self-concept, that is, how well the individual likes and values himself or herself.

self-fulfilling prophecy   40
The idea that we behave and see ourselves in ways that are consistent with how others see us.

self-image   42
The picture an individual has of himself or herself; the sort of person an individual believes he or she is.

self-managed work teams   212
Groups of workers who have freedom to manage their own work, including deciding which member will perform which job in what order.

self-monitoring   239
The degree to which individuals pay attention to social cues and adjust their behavior to fit.

semantic distractions   103
A source of internal interference that occurs when you overrespond to an emotion-laden word or concept.

semantics   53
The branch of language study that is concerned with meaning.

sentence outline   340
An outline consisting entirely of complete sentences.

sex   214
Biological characteristics with which people are born.

sexist language   61
Language that excludes individuals on the basis of gender.

sharing   7
An interaction between people in order to exchange meaning.

sights and sounds   104
What you see and hear that affects listening.

signposts   353
Ways in which a speaker signals to an audience where the speech is going.

silent probe   467
Silence held for a brief time to let the respondent fill in the silence.

similarity   36, 166
(1) The principle that elements are grouped together because they share attributes such as size, color, or belief. (2) The idea that our friends are usually people who like or dislike the same things we do.

single-parent family   174
A family that comprises one adult and adopted, natural, step-, or foster children.

situational models   242
Models of leadership that encourage leaders to focus on specific factors within the group situation to determine the most appropriate leadership behaviors.

slang   60, 190
(1) A specialized language of a group of people who share a common interest or belong to a similar co-culture. (2) Language derived from cant and argot that consists of terms widely known to the dominant culture but not acceptable for use in formal writing and speaking.

sleeper effect   317
A change of audience opinion caused by the separation of the message content from its source over a period of time.

small-group communication   18, 207
The interaction of a group of people, small enough to be perceptually aware of each other, to achieve an interdependent goal.

social attractiveness   165
A concept that includes physical attractiveness, how desirable a person is to work with, and how much "social value" the person has for others.

social class   149
A group whose members share the same economic or social status.

social comparison   150
Evaluation of the self by comparing oneself to others.

social penetration theory   154
A theory that explains how relationships develop and deteriorate through the exchange of intimate information.

solution orientation   254
A cooperative and assertive conflict management style that encourages conflicting parties to search jointly for a mutually acceptable solution.

solution questions   247
Group discussion questions that bias discussion because they focus the group's attention on a particular solution instead of the problem.

source   11, 131
(1) A message initiator. (2) Someone who shares information, ideas, or attitudes with someone else; in mass communication the source is professional communicators.

source credibility   111, 313, 440
(1) The speaker's competence to make a claim, as perceived by the listeners. (2) The audience's perception of a speaker's effectiveness.

spatial/relations organization   347
A method of speech organization in which the speaker reveals how things relate to each other in space, position, and visual orientation.

special others   150
People who take a special interest in you, mentor you, or encourage you to be something more than you would have been otherwise.

staff report   450
A presentation that informs managers and other employees of developments that might affect them and their work.

stagnating   157
In Knapp's relational development model, the stage of deterioration marked by the partner's lack of activity, especially together.

statistics   310
Numbers that summarize numerical information or compare quantities.

status   103
A person's social standing, rank, title, or value; can affect listening.

stereotype   192
A generalization about some group of people that oversimplifies their culture.

stereotypes   61
Beliefs, based on previously formed opinions and attitudes, that all members of a group are more or less alike.

strategic choices   288
What you choose to do in your speech, from the words to the arguments.

street language   61
Language that consists of highly informal words or phrases, often specific to one area, that are used to demonstrate unity.

stress tactics   474
Deliberate attempts to create anxiety for applicants to see if they can handle difficult situations.

structuration   208
The communicative process of forming and maintaining a small group through verbal and nonverbal communication that establishes the group's norms and rules.

style approaches   240
Approaches to studying leadership that focus on the leader's pattern of behavior.

subjective perception   27
Your uniquely constructed meaning attributed to sensed stimuli.

subpoints   335
The points in a speech that support the main points; indicated by capital letters in an outline.

substantive conflict   253
Conflict over ideas, meanings, issues, and other matters pertinent to the group's task.

supporting materials   307
Any information used to support an argument or idea.

supportive climate   227
An atmosphere of openness created by members' mutual respect and caring.

surveys   308
Studies in which a limited number of questions are answered by a sample of the population to discover opinions on issues.

syllogism   114
An argument with a major premise, a minor premise, and a conclusion.

symbolic interactionism   39
The process in which the self develops through the messages and feedback received from others.

symmetrical relationships   152
Relationships between people who mirror each other or who are highly similar.

synonym   416
A word that means approximately the same as another word.

syntax   12, 53
A set of rules about language that determines how words are arranged to form phrases and sentences.

systematic desensitization   373
The process of reducing apprehension through repeated exposure to small doses of whatever makes one apprehensive in a situation designed to reduce or eradicate the fear.

T

tactile communication   82
The use of touch in communication.

task functions   221
Behaviors in a group that are directly relevant to helping the group complete its assignment.

technical report   450
A presentation that includes detailed information about a procedure or device so that the audience can decide whether or not to adopt it or purchase it.

teleconferences   474
Interview situations in which a number of interviewers speak to the respondent by telephone.

terminating   157
In Knapp's relational development model, the stage of deterioration in which the partners are no longer seen as a pair by themselves or others.

testimonial evidence   309
Written or oral statements of other people's experience used by the speaker to substantiate or clarify points.

tests of evidence   445
Questions that can be used to test the validity of evidence.

time-sequence pattern   346
A method of speech organization in which the speaker explains a sequence of events in chronological order.

tolerating ambiguity   198
Being open-minded about differences.

tools of journalism   468
The basic question format used by journalists: what, why, when, how, where, and who.

topical-sequence pattern   351
A method of speech organization that emphasizes the major reasons an audience should accept a point of view by addressing the advantages, disadvantages, qualities, and types of persons, places, or things.

trait approaches   239
Approaches to studying leadership that focus on the leader's personal characteristics; they assume that leaders are born, not made.

transaction model   14
A depiction of communication as communicators simultaneously sending and receiving messages.

transition   353
A bridge between sections of a speech that helps the speaker move smoothly from one idea to another.

trustworthiness   315
The degree to which the speaker is perceived as honest, fair, sincere, honorable, friendly, and kind; an aspect of credibility.

U

ultimate goals   432
Purposes that a speaker wishes to fulfill with additional messages and more time.

uncertainty principle   151
The principle which suggests that when we initially meet others and thus know little about them, we eliminate the uncertainty by drawing inferences from the information presented to us.

uncertainty-accepting cultures   194
Cultures that tolerate ambiguity, uncertainty, and diversity.

uncertainty-rejecting cultures   194
Cultures that have difficulty with ambiguity, uncertainty, and diversity.

understanding   7
Perceiving, interpreting, and comprehending the meaning of the verbal and nonverbal behavior of others.

URL   299
Uniform resource locator; the address of a web site.

V

valid   114
In evaluating a deductive argument, the ability to logically derive a conclusion from its propositions.

value   278
A deeply rooted belief that governs our attitude about something.

verbal codes   12
Symbols and their grammatical arrangement, such as languages.

visual aids   387
Any items that can be seen by an audience for the purpose of reinforcing a message.

vocal cues   84
All the oral aspects of sound except words themselves; part of paralinguistic features.

vocal variety   381
Vocal quality, intonation patterns, inflections of pitch, and syllabic duration; a lack of repetitious patterns in vocal delivery.

vocalized pauses   378
Breaks in fluency; the use of meaningless words or sounds to fill in silences that negatively affect an audience's perception of the speaker's competence and dynamism.

volume   379
The loudness or softness of a person's voice.

voluntary audience   275, 450
A collection of people who choose to listen to a particular speaker or speech.

W

Web browser   300
A tool for viewing pages on the Web; e.g., Netscape, Mosaic, and Internet Explorer.

World Wide Web (WWW)   299
The part of the Internet that links together all the individual Web sites, hence the term *Web*.

written and visual resources   295
Books, newspapers, magazines, broadcasts, and documentaries consulted for information, arguments, and evidence for a speech.

credits

credits

Chapter 1

PHOTOS: p. 2, Chuck Savage/ Stock Market; p. 6, Jeff Greenberg/ PhotoEdit; p. 16, Esbin-Anderson/ Image Works

Chapter 2

PHOTOS: p. 24, Rhoda Sidney Stock Boston; p. 30, Aliza Averbach/Photo Researchers; p. 31, E. Crews/Image Works. *TEXT:* p. 40 "A View from Mount Ritter" by Joseph T. O'Conner. From *Newsweek*, May 25, 1998. © 1998 Newsweek, Inc. All rights reserved. Reprinted with permission.

Chapter 3

PHOTOS: p. 50, Tony Freeman/ PhotoEdit; p. 58, Michael Newman/PhotoEdit; p. 61, Charles Gupton/Stock Boston

Chapter 4

PHOTOS: p. 72, Mary K. Denny/ PhotoEdit; p. 82, B. Daemmrich/ Image Works; p. 87, B. Daemmrich/Image Works; p. 111, Vincent Dewitt/Stock Boston

Chapter 5

PHOTOS: p. 96, Tom Stewart/The Stock Market; p. 102, Michael Newman/PhotoEdit; p. 106, B. Daemmrich/Image Works; p. 111, Vincent SeWitt/Stock Boston

Chapter 6

PHOTOS: p. 128, E. Zuckerman/ Photo Edit; p. 131, David Young-Wolff/PhotoEdit; p. 133, Michael Newman/PhotoEdit; p. 139, Mark Richards/Photo Edit

Chapter 7

PHOTOS: p. 146, Rob Lewine/ Stock Market; p. 149, B. Seitz/ Photo Researchers; p. 168, Charles Gupton/Stock Boston; p. 177

Chapter 8

PHOTOS: p. 186, Christopher Bissel/Tony Stone Images; p. 189, Bob Daemmrich/Stock Boston; p. 191, Jose Palaez/Stock Market; p. 198,

Chapter 9

PHOTOS: p. 202, Rob Lewins/ Stock Market; p. 205, B. Seitz/ Photo Researchers; p. 212, Charles Gupton/Stock Boston

Chapter 10

PHOTOS: p. 234, Billy Barnes/PhotoEdit; p. 237, Mark Richards/PhotoEdit; p.243, Jon Feingersh/Stock Market

Chapter 11

PHOTOS: p. 266, Chuck Savage/Stock Market; p. 270, Bob Daemmrich/Image Works; p. 275, Loren Santow/Tony Stone Images; p. 281, Bob Daemmrich / Image Works

Chapter 12

PHOTOS: p. 292, Jose L. Pelaez/ Stock Market; p. 300, B. Daemmrich/Image Works; p. 306, K. Preuss/Image Works *TEXT:* p. 302, Text and artwork copyright © 1999 by YAHOO! Inc. All rights reserved. YAHOO! and the YAHOO! logo are trademarks of YAHOO! Inc.; p. 303, Text and artwork copyright © 1999 by YAHOO! Inc. All rights reserved. YAHOO! and the YAHOO! logo are trademarks of YAHOO! Inc.

Chapter 13

PHOTOS: p. 324, David Young-Wolff/PhotoEdit; p. 327, Matthew Borkoski/Stock Boston; p. 334, David Young-Wolff/PhotoEdit; p. 347, Ron Sherman/Stock Boston

Chapter 14

PHOTOS: p. 364, Richard Hutchings/PhotoEdit; p. 368, Bruce Ayres/Tony Stone Images; p. 376, Michael Newman/ PhotoEdit; p. 393, Richard Paisley/Stock Boston

index